The Native Mind and the Cultural Construction of Nature

Life and Mind: Philosophical Issues in Biology and Psychology
Kim Sterelny and Robert A. Wilson, editors

The Native Mind and the Cultural Construction of Nature

Scott Atran and Douglas Medin

A Bradford Book

The MIT Press
Cambridge, Massachusetts
London, England

For information about special quantity discounts, please e-mail special_sales@ mitpress.mit.edu

This book was set in Times New Roman and Syntax on 3B2 by Asco Typesetters, Hong Kong.
Printed on recycled paper and bound in the United States of America.

Library of Congress Cataloging-in-Publication Data

Atran, Scott, 1952–
The native mind and the cultural construction of nature / Scott Atran and Douglas Medin.
    p.   cm.—(Life and mind)
Includes bibliographical references and index.
ISBN 978-0-262-13489-7 (hardcover : alk. paper)
1. Cognition and culture. I. Medin, Douglas L. II. Title.

BF311.A755   2008
306.4′2—dc22   2007013988

10 9 8 7 6 5 4 3 2 1

Contents

Preface

The research described in this book began when we found ourselves sitting next to each other at a workshop dinner at the University of Michigan more than two decades ago. We talked. The patterning of shared and distinctive perspectives made the prospect of research collaboration exciting. When graduate students, postdoctoral fellows, and faculty colleagues were added to the mix, a community of scholars evolved to address what we think are fundamental theoretical, empirical, and methodological issues at the interface of anthropology and psychology.

The research was and is intense. In the field, hot days of interviewing were followed by heavy nights of analysis, spiked and lightened occasionally with rotgut rum (not charged to our grants). We worked through discussions that ranged from competing definitions of culture and nuances of cultural modeling to speculating about how soon the first Jet Skis would be seen on Lake Peten Itza in the Guatemalan rain forest. We vividly recall one night of analyses when the power went out (a not infrequent occurrence). We continued in the dark, going from three to two to one computer as battery power played out. Finally, we called it quits for the night when we could no longer distinguish between the cursor and the insects landing on the computer screen.

Not everything was fun. This sort of research is expensive, and we spent an inordinate amount of time writing grant proposals. In a classroom, if you flub an experiment, you can go to the next class. In the field, you may have to wait for the next season—if you're lucky—to get people from several countries, universities, academic disciplines, and different forest activities to coordinate schedules again. It also was not a thrill to discover that the first set of soil samples we collected was useless because the critical identifying information was put down on paper in pencil, only to become some unidentifiable fungus after being enclosed in the humid sample containers. Finally, we collected so much data that sometimes we spent a lot of time tracking down where the original data were and in what stage of analysis.

These examples are exceptions. There's a lot to be thankful for. Our informants often found our tasks to be meaningful and engaging, but also sometimes from Mars or the Evening or Morning Star (they originally took our computers for some kind of *sastun*, a sorceress stone akin to a crystal ball). They argued with us about why you can't just think and therefore be, but had to think about *something*, or why soldiers marched with their arms swaying in lockstep—not because they were big-brained robots but because that's a fine way for a group to fan itself on a hot day. And they laughed and laughed, and made us laugh, whenever we stumbled with words or on a forest hike, and they always picked us up. Sometimes they became partners in the research enterprise by pointing to problems with our procedures and suggesting other avenues to pursue. Our community of scholars constantly demonstrated the excitement and value of interdisciplinary research. And as for the data—well, we couldn't have made up results that were as intriguing as those we obtained. We are happy to share them with the reader (as they stand in 2007).

Acknowledgments

This research was supported by grants from NSF (SBR 931978, SBR 9422587, SBR 9707761, SBR 9983260, BCS 0216762, SBR 0424629, BCS-0132469, REC-0529650), NSF/EPA (SES-9981762), NIH (MH55079), the Russell Sage Foundation (87-99-02), and CNRS (contract no. 92 C 0758, MRT). This work is the summary of a combined effort by a number of long-term research collaborators: Norbert Ross, Sandra Waxman, Elizabeth Lynch, Edilberto Ucan Ek', Valentina Vapnarsky, John Coley, and Ximena Lois. Other important contributors and collaborators include: Jeremy Bailenson, Michael Baran, Serge Blok, Russell Burnett, Doug Cox, Paul Estin, Brett Hayes, Alejandro Lœpez, Brad Love, Bobbi Low, Richard Nisbett, Connie Pankratz, Elizabeth Proffitt, A. Kimball Romney, Hillarie Schwartz, Michael Shum, Brian Smith, Edward Smith, Paolo Sousa, Gert Storms, Christopher Timura, Sara Unsworth, Dan Bartels, and Phil Wolff. Dan Sperber, Lawrence Hirschfeld, Michael Cole, Lance Rips, Susan Gelman, Ed Hutchins and William Batchelder provided constructive comments on earlier drafts of the manuscript. Jennie Woodring was instrumental in the copyediting and detail tracking part of the production process. We are deeply grateful to our research partners and participants in Guatemala, Mexico, Brazil, Wisconsin, Illinois, and Michigan, and especially to the Maya and Menominee communities that took us in. Last but foremost, we are thankful for our loved ones who support our scholarly passions.

1 Introduction

It is the best of times; it is the worst of times. Recent years have seen stunning advances in understanding the basis of life, ranging from unraveling the human genome to discovering extraterrestrial sources of generation and extinction. Although some would argue that macrobiology has been neglected in favor of microbiology and biotechnology, there has been undeniable progress in understanding complex systems, including ecosystems. From remote sensing to environmental chemistry, scientists are delivering insights into how to protect the environment. And awareness and concern about life on our planet is widespread. A recent survey found overwhelming endorsement of the statement that we "have a moral duty to leave the Earth in as good or better shape than we found it" (Kempton, Boster, and Hartley 1995, 257). No part of the earth is untouched by advances in both the science of nature and commitments to support it.

But it is also the worst of times. There is an increasing sense of diminished human contact with nature, a phenomenon some refer to as the "extinction of experience" (Nabhan and St. Antoine 1993) and others as a "Nature-deficit disorder" (Louv, 2006). Respondents in the same survey above agreed that "the majority of people are completely cut off from nature. They spend their time indoors and when they're outdoors, nature is just an inconvenience to them."

Under such circumstances, commonsense knowledge of nature is poor, sometimes surprisingly so. As we write this, buckeyes and horse chestnuts are flowering in northern Illinois, but fewer than half of Northwestern University students surveyed say they have even heard of horse chestnut or buckeye. Below is part of an interview with a Northwestern Honors student who expressed surprise that 3- and 4-year olds were asked to give examples of plants. She was then asked to generate examples herself:

I: Tell me all the kinds of trees you know.
S: Oak, pine, spruce, ... cherry ... (giggle) evergreen, ... Christmas tree, is that
a kind of tree?... God, what's the average here?... So what do kids say, big tree,
small tree?
E: Tell me some plants.
S: I can't think of any plants that aren't trees ... I know a lot about angio-
sperms, gymnosperms, gametophytes, sporophytes ... but this is biology. It's not
really about plants and trees....

It would be hard to find such relative lack of knowledge about salient
local species, even—as we will see—among 4-year-old Mexican Maya.
Nevertheless, this extinction of experience is not confined to technologically advanced societies. Researchers studying small-scale societies report
diminishing knowledge about nature; they note that with greater formal
education comes lesser knowledge (Diamond and Bishop 1999; Wester
and Yongvanit 1995). A central theme of this book is tracing the cognitive consequences of this loss of knowledge.

1.1   Overview

It does not take a genius to figure out that we live in a fragile world. We
are told not to eat fish more than once a week and pregnant women are
advised to avoid fish altogether because of mercury contamination.
Recent droughts have left Lake Powell at half its former size and the
Western region of the United States faces serious water shortages. Global
warming seems almost minor by comparison. And it is not just what we
are doing to the earth. We live under the shadow of terrorism that
threatens to escalate into nuclear, chemical, or biological warfare.
Even "business as usual" involves frequent cultural clashes over natural
resources, such as access to salmon, preserving spotted owls, or rights to
land. This book is about both of these dimensions: first, the relationship
between how people think about the natural world and how they act on
it, and second, cultural differences in these understandings and how
they contribute to intergroup conflict or cooperation. Our enterprise is
grounded in the cognitive sciences, and relevant ascriptions include resource dilemmas, mental models, culture and cognition, folkbiology, categorization and reasoning, protected or sacred values, and environmental
decision making. Each of these topics is central to our efforts. An important overarching theme is that they can best be addressed by bringing psychology and anthropology together.
    Claims about the nature of human nature, with their associated policy
implications, require the very best analyses that an interdisciplinary cog-

nitive science has to offer. People's behavior toward the natural world is surely conditioned in part by their ways of knowing and modeling it. What are these modes of knowledge and understanding? How are they affected by goals, theories, and intimacy of contact with the biological world? What is universal, what is not, and what are the implications of such observations for insights into the development of biological cognition? How does cognitive and cultural development lead some people to protect their environment and others to destroy it? These questions shape the present book.

1.2   Why Focus on Biological Cognition?

Much of human history has been spent (and is being spent) in intimate contact with plants and animals, and it is difficult to imagine that human cognition would not be molded by that fact. In subsistence cultures, survival depends on a detailed appreciation of the habits, affordances, and interactions linked to the biological world. In technologically advanced cultures, which are increasingly faced with environmental degradation and nonsustainable use of natural resources, no less may be at stake.

There are a series of mutually reinforcing reasons for studying people's understanding of the biological world. First, biology represents a natural unit of analysis and appears to be a core component of human cognition. To get along in the world, people need to be able to understand and predict the general properties and behaviors of physical objects and substances (physics), the more specific properties of plants and animals (biology), and the particular properties of their fellow human beings (psychology). We will argue that biology represents a distinct module of mind that is associated with universal patterns of categorization and reasoning. Some of these principles are robustly universal and some depend on having more than modest contact with nature. Yet others are highly dependent on particulars of cultural models and associated values. Each of these three classes of findings has important theoretical and practical implications.

A second reason for a focus on biology is that biological kinds provide a natural metric for cultural comparisons. Although the specific animals and plants vary considerably across the world, scientific taxonomy constitutes a structure for comparing kinds at corresponding levels of specificity (e.g., bird and fish versus duck and trout). Ethnobiologists often begin their research in some area by conducting a survey of local plants and animals. These surveys constitute important background information for a variety of questions that one can ask in any cultural context. For example, one might ask about which species are important enough to be given distinct names and in general how folktaxonomies map onto scientific taxonomy.

Third, biological cognition may be a central factor in science education. Children do not enter the classroom free of knowledge and beliefs about nature, and these conceptions and conceptual frameworks may facilitate or interfere with classroom learning, depending on the relationship between the two spheres and the skill of the educational system in building on and otherwise taking advantage of this experience. A challenge and complication is that science education is not "culturally neutral" and, as we will see, one obstacle to success in science learning is the mismatch between the culture of science and the epistemological frameworks and worldviews associated with different cultural groups.

A fourth, closely related reason for an interest in biological cognition is that advancing technology and urbanization may be associated with a distancing of humans from nature. We are interested in the cognitive consequences of diminished contact with the natural world and, to anticipate, they are considerable and have serious implications.

A fifth motivation for research on biological cognition is its relevance for understanding environmental decision making. Knowledge, values, beliefs, and actions are often intricately interwoven in ways that render simple utilitarian models of decision making irrelevant. We will see that different cultural groups living in the same area and engaged in more or less the same activities may have strikingly different mental models of nature. These differences are associated with dramatic consequences for environmental decision making in general and sustainability of practices in particular. In many cases, they also may be at the heart of intergroup conflict over natural resources.

1.3 The Case for Interdisciplinary Approaches: Why Anthropology and Psychology Need Each Other

Critique of Cognitive Psychology

In many respects anthropology and psychology are perfect foils for each other because of their complementary strengths (and weaknesses). Initially, we focus on limitations of cognitive psychology in order to set up a contrast with anthropology.

Universality   One of our psychology colleagues is fond of saying that he is only interested in studying what is "universal." Of course, universality seems transparently desirable; it represents the ideal on the dimension of "findings of broad applicability." For the moment let's not quibble; let's adopt the view that the quest for universality is good for science. Nonetheless, it must be said that if cognitive psychology thinks that universals are desirable, it has a peculiar way of going about its quest for them. Research in cognitive psychology almost exclusively targets a single, select subset of a single culture and population: college freshmen and sophomores; and not freshmen and sophomores in general, but rather those at major research universities taking introductory psychology. Only with considerable effort could one come up with a more select, narrow population to study.

To be sure, there are exceptions to this narrowness. Some cognitive psychologists do research where they try to isolate distinct subsets of participants to explore possible (subgroup) differences. For example, one might study the performance of students who score high or low on some scale of interest (e.g., need for cognition) on some other task. Surprisingly, selecting within an already select population often does yield differences. To outsiders, however, this may seem like planning two vacations to be as different as possible subject only to the constraint that one travel no more than a kilometer from home.

The other prominent exception is research on cognitive development. Even in this case, however, populations are sampled with convenience and little else in mind (witness the frequency with which the population studied is children attending a university-sponsored grade school). In short, it would not be much of a caricature to suggest that cognitive psychology does not search for universality but rather assumes it. If cognitive psychology has laws or generalizations to offer about how the mind works, it has so far shown little interest in putting them to the test of whether they fit humanity at large.

Sampling of Stimulus Materials   One of the strengths of cognitive psychology is its focus on systematic, controlled comparisons. Historically, this concern was so strong that psychologists studying learning made use of nonsense syllables to limit any influence of prior experience or knowledge. Although this particular habit has been discarded in favor of using meaningful materials, experimentalists have concentrated on finding materials with particular desirable properties (in terms of controlling for extraneous factors), with little concern for the relation between such materials and the range of stimuli over which one might wish to generalize. The idea of systematic sampling is somewhat alien, perhaps because it is not always clear how to answer the question, "systematic with respect to what?" For example, if a psychologist wants to compare reasoning involving living kinds versus human artifacts as stimuli, he or she typically would generate examples, subject only to the constraint that undergraduates be familiar with them. Rarely, if ever, would it occur to the psychologist to ask what kinds of artifacts or what kinds of living kinds there are and how one might go about selecting a representative sample.

Reference A related limitation of research in cognitive psychology is that conceptual behavior is often studied with little concern about reference. For studies involving adults, the stimuli are often words and seldom does the researcher establish any relation between these words and what their referents are. For living kinds other than mammals, college students often have little idea about reference beyond a very general level (e.g., "such-and-such is a tree"). For developmental studies concerned with living kinds, the stimuli are typically toys, which are at best representations of living kinds. Again reference is rarely established. Of course, for some questions of interest, reference may not matter, but our impression is that, as in the case of populations and stimuli, convenience and control tend to dominate a systematic analysis of the domain of interest.

Anthropology as a Contrast

The above limitations of research in cognitive psychology would strike many cultural anthropologists and ethnobiologists as odd. Consider how an ethnobiologist would undertake the study of folkbiology in some new culture. The project could hardly get underway without asking what living kinds are found in that culture, what terms exist in the language referring to living kinds, and what the relation is between those terms and what is there (the issue of reference). How does one describe what living kinds exist in some cultural context? A reasonable starting point is to use scientific taxonomy as a reference or standard. For example, one might ask whether every kind that science recognizes as a distinct species has a distinct name (Diamond and Bishop 1999). On finding that many kinds do not have distinct names it is natural to ask what principles determine whether a species has a distinct name (Berlin 1992). For instance, naming could be driven by relevance to humans (utility), perceptual discontinuities, or even size (Hunn 1999).

Scientific taxonomies are, of course, hierarchical taxonomies and, as such, provide both a set of standards and a heuristic for asking other questions about universal aspects of folktaxonomies. There are two important analytic points involved here. One is that although the particular kinds of plants and animals to be found may vary across cultures, the abstract structure in terms of species, genus, family, order, class, division, and kingdom will be represented. Consequently, scientific taxonomy provides something of a conceptual grid for cross-cultural comparisons. The second, related point is that using a scientific taxonomy allows one to establish corresponding ranks such that it becomes meaningful to state that oak is at the same level or rank as is trout. This does not mean that they are psychologically at the same rank, but it does provide a basis for asking questions such as whether some culture differentiates mammals more than fish. As it turns out, ethnobiologists have found that folk ranks and folktaxonomies only loosely approximate scientific taxonomies but formal taxonomy has served as an effective standard for cross-cultural comparisons (Hunn 1975).

Note that the practices that are most natural for an ethnobiologist address each of the limitations that we have attributed to cognitive psychology. Folktaxonomic analyses provide a framework in which one can propose and evaluate hypotheses about cognitive universals (Berlin, Breedlove, and Raven 1973). The main criticism we can offer for the issues in question is that ethnobiologists have tended to focus first on small-scale subsistence cultures to the neglect of larger, more industrialized cultures, and second on culturally competent adults rather than children (Hirschfeld 2003). In sum, so far pretty good for anthropology.

Critique of Anthropology

We turn now to limitations of anthropological approaches to folk biology as seen through psychologists' eyes.

Where (and what) are the data? Again at the risk of caricature one might argue that ethnobiological observations often fall short of the minimum needed for scientific progress. In many cases ethnobiological facts and observations are presented in summary form with no clear indication of their source. Are the informants a representative sample or a few local wise people or experts? In some instances no mention is made at all of the informants as if the "facts" were free-floating entities in the culture. Without more precise identification of the data one cannot begin to assess basic requirements for science such as replicability. Only in the last couple of decades have some ethnobiologists started to question the summary notion of an "omniscient informant" in favor of an analysis of variation within human populations (Boster 1986b).

Commensurable Units of Analysis in Data and Theory   Philosophical argument to the contrary, cognitive psychologists bask in the belief that mental representations (and meanings) reside in the heads of individuals. To be sure, they might be sensitive to a social contribution in the construction of meaning, but they know where mental representations hang out. Not so in anthropology. Ethnobiologists seem as uncomfortable as behaviorists in talking about mental representations, whereas most psychologists do not know what to make of anthropology's talk of "cultural representations." Are cultural representations just the mental representations of some ideal informant, or are they differentially shared by the minds of several or all informants? If the latter, there are psychologically intriguing issues concerning the causal structure of such distributed knowledge (Hutchins 1995) and whether such knowledge might have emergent properties that cannot be reduced to the mental life of any single individual (Sperber 1996).

Different questions surely require different levels and units of analysis; however, there must be a measure of commensurability between psychological and anthropological analyses if there is to be cooperation and cumulative progress in understanding. To be blunt, ethnobiologists cannot make claims about how individuals perceive, organize, and act on the natural world without worrying about what is in the heads of individuals and how such mental representations are causally linked to one another and to individual actions.

An analogy may serve to make the point. Economists study systems at different levels of analysis and historically they have tended to assume that aggregate behavior derives from optimal behavior on the part of individuals. One important contribution of psychological studies of decision making and choice behavior has been to destroy the illusion of optimality and replace it with a systematic, theoretical, and empirical analysis of decision and choice (see Tversky and Kahneman 1986; Fischhoff 1997; Markman and Medin 2004). In exactly the same way, we think that ethnobiology needs to include individuals as units of analysis for claims about individuals. Anthropology cannot simply assume that culture (including language) is assimilated in something of the same way a body warms to the sun. (See Strauss and Quinn 1992 for a critique of this view from within anthropology.)

If anything we may be guilty of downplaying this issue. At times within anthropology, the methodological point that anthropological observations are socially constructed has been elevated to a form of self-immolation that threatens to destroy the science part of anthropology as a social science and move it squarely into literature. As one of our anthropological colleagues is fond of saying, fieldwork should focus on research that is liable to "awe" our own, often complacent culture with the diversity of collective human imagination and action. We readily grant the importance of demonstrating the rich variation in human thought and experience, but we think that more rigorous science could better help to make the case.

Role of Models and Theories   One tricky thing about knowledge is that there are no free peeks at mental representations. This is true both for the scientist and the informant. At one point researchers interested in developing computers as expert systems hoped that knowledge could be transferred from human expert to machine simply by asking the expert to report what he or she knew. This effort was largely unsuccessful because experts cannot, by an act of will, simply make their knowledge accessible. Artificial intelligence "knowledge engineers" and psychologists have learned to use indirect measures of knowledge and to draw inferences from patterns of behavior. This is an important operating procedure in cognitive science—that is, developing and testing methods and models that foster inferences about knowledge representation and use. Quantitatively based models and theories are not complete strangers to anthropology, but neither are they intimate friends.

Cognitive Psychology as a Contrast
The stock-in-trade of cognitive psychology is theoretical models of human cognition and a well-honed set of methodological tools for drawing inferences from behavior to internal processes. Also involved are tons of data (often from narrow, overly controlled, decontextualized settings, but data nonetheless); if anything, cognitive psychology suffers from rigor mortis.

We are convinced that a cognitive science of folkbiology that combines and integrates the strengths of its constituent subfields holds great promise for progress in understanding how people cognize the natural world.

The challenge of understanding biological cognition is daunting. Consider the presumably simpler task of understanding temperature regulation, a problem that has its own evolutionary history. Here it has been found that temperature regulation in human beings involves the integration of multiple parallel systems (e.g., shivering, sweating, putting on clothes) that vary in their refinement and redundancy (e.g., Satinoff 1983). We should not expect anything less for something as intricate as people's understanding of the natural world.

1.4   Theoretical Issues in the Cognitive Science of Folkbiology

Fortunately, progress can come in small steps. Folkbiology is a field blessed with many intriguing and important issues that lend themselves to an analysis in terms of culture and cognition. Let us turn to a sample of three of them before returning to the central themes of this book.

1. *Are folkbiological categories recognized or constructed?*   A basic issue within ethnobiology concerns whether categories are recognized versus constructed (see Malt 1995; Brown 1995). One view—known within ethnobiology as the "intellectualist" view—is that the structure of kinds in nature is comprised of "chunks" that more or less impose themselves on minds (at least minds with a perceptual system like ours). This position is reinforced by the finding that folk categories often correspond to scientific species or genera and by cross-cultural agreement in folktaxonomic systems (e.g., Atran 1990; Berlin 1992). (However, Atran interprets agreement in terms of universal properties of mind rather than the structure of nature alone.) The alternative, or "utilitarian," view is that folktaxonomic systems are influenced by goals, theories, and belief systems and may be culture-dependent constructions (Hunn 1982; Ellen 1993). Other intermediate positions hold that the intellectualist and utilitarian views are not necessarily mutually exclusive. For example, their relative influence may depend on factors such as rank in the hierarchy (Bulmer 1970): cultures may differ more in the structure and use of categories such as tree or bird (corresponding roughly to class in an evolutionary scientific taxonomy) than they do for oak or robin (corresponding roughly to the generic or species level).

2. *Is reasoning from folkbiological categories similarity-based or theory-based?*   Especially within cognitive psychology, folkbiology is an appealing domain from the contending standpoints of both similarity-based and theory-based views of categorization and category-based reasoning. On

the one hand, our perceptual system is surely an adaptation to the natural world, and if similarity-based models are going to succeed anywhere, it should be here. On the other hand, the biological world is apparently a world of fairly stable clusters of complex features whose remarkable endurance in the face of constant change can presumably be explained in terms of naturally occurring causal patterns. Understanding causal patterns in the world is a primary goal of theory-driven knowledge in science, and the history of science is coterminous with trying to understand biological causality in particular. If theory-based knowledge were to develop anywhere outside of science—in other cultures or in everyday thinking—it should be here.

From the perspective of similarity, there are evident patterns of covariation for biologically related attributes: toothless two-legged beings generally have wings, feathers, and fly; leaves, flowers, and fruits generally go together with stems and roots; and so on. Perhaps most people in the world are aware of these covariations without necessarily understanding their causal origins or interrelations, such as the role of feathers in flight or of leaves in stem development. In other words, there could be quite a bit of biologically relevant data that is stored but not theoretically assimilated.

Nevertheless, people in different cultures acknowledge, and often try to better understand, at least some of the causal interrelations among covariant biological attributes. These include irreversible patterns of biological growth (maturation); the apparent constancy of covariant morphological, anatomical, and behavioral patterns across generations (reproduction and inheritance); the success of mutually constraining actions of interrelated attributes in maintaining life (bodily functioning); and the breakdown of interrelated bodily functions (illness and death). Moreover, these "naive" attempts at causal explanation are themselves interrelated, often with the sort of resultant explanatory bootstrapping and integration of the database that could help to kick off the development of science.

Suppose, as ethnobiologists generally agree, people everywhere witness certain covariant biological patterns (roughly corresponding to perceptually salient species or genera), but interpret the causal relationships underlying these patterns in different ways. This might suggest that similarity-based reasoning is prior to theoretically based reasoning, at least in the biological domain. This was a message of developmental studies in the 1980s (Carey 1985; Inagaki and Sugiyama 1988; Keil 1989). More recent studies have lowered the age at which children are thought to reason causally about biological kinds. But the origins of causal reasoning in folkbiology remain a matter of controversy.

A closely related question concerns which factors shape the acquisition of biological knowledge and the extent to which their influence extends to adult (more or less steady-state) knowledge. Researchers in the area of cognitive development have been actively studying the role of language in conceptual development (see Waxman 1999, 2004) and are increasingly turning to an analysis of the role of input conditions (Hatano and Inagaki 2003; Gelman et al. 1998), at least at intermediate stages of development.

3. *Is folk biology a "naive" form of scientific biology?* To some extent, the fact that most psychologists prefer the label "naive biology" or "intuitive biology" over the ethnobiologist's "folkbiology" implies somewhat different understandings and uses of scientific biology as a standard of comparison. For those interested in the structure and development of biological causality in our own culture, folkbiological concepts often appear to contain "rudimentary" or "inchoate" elements and clusters of more sophisticated scientific concepts. Although there has been little systematic study of the input conditions and processes by which scientific concepts are assimilated into lay thinking, there is hardly any doubt that science is pervasively involved in how people in our culture come to think about the biological world. The influence of science may be especially pronounced among the university subpopulations psychologists prefer to study, but most of the general population is heavily exposed to scientific concepts in one form another through schooling, nature programs on television, popular books, the press, and so forth.

The elaborate folkbiological inventories that ethnobiologists have shown time and again for many small-scale subsistence societies often match and occasionally even surpass in intricacy and accuracy the knowledge of field biologists working in the same locales as those societies (e.g., Bartlett 1936; Simpson 1961; Bulmer and Tyler 1968). Moreover, few ethnobiologists would consider it enlightening—but rather misleading—to characterize the significant differences between folk knowledge in other cultures versus science in terms of relative degrees of intuition or naïveté. Admittedly, ethnobiologists might well agree with psychologists about referring to lay biology in our culture as "naive" in comparison to the relative sophistication of science as well as folkbiological knowledge in other cultures.

A key issue is whether basic folk concepts, such as folk species or generics, are different in kind from contemporary scientific concepts,

such as the idea of a species as a logical individual (i.e., a lineage of connected parts) rather than a logical class (i.e., a meaningful collection of
individuals) (Ghiselin 1999). If they are not really different in kind, but
only in degree of sophistication, then there may be no reason for holding
on to the lay concept at all, except perhaps as an optional psychological
convenience for navigating the everyday world (see also Kripke 1972;
Putnam 1975). If, however, folk and scientific concepts are different in
kind, then perhaps they have separate but equal—or at least different—
roles to play in the attainment of knowledge (Dupre 1999; see also
Braisby et al. 1996). Folk concepts would be useful for accommodating
to the everyday world and scientific concepts for exploring the cosmos at
large (including extended thoughts about evolutionary dimensions of
space and time that would be largely irrelevant to ordinary understanding
and action).

Finally, one might accept that folk and scientific concepts may be different in kind, or that folk concepts are in some sense psychologically
more convenient in a given culture or at a given stage of history or development, but argue that folk concepts ought to be replaced by scientific
concepts (Hull 1999; cf. Russell 1948). For example, if it is true that people ordinarily believe that living kinds (including humans) have underlying essences (see Hirschfeld and Gelman 1994), then it is also likely that
people will treat natural variation as deviance. If so, then the essentialist
folk concept should be discarded along with other outworn "commonsense" myths, such as belief in witches or races, no matter how hard it is
to unlearn them. Even if this should be case, however, understanding how
people do in fact think about biological kinds (and other biologically related phenomena discussed in this book, such as diseases) may help us all
to better cope with them.

Summary   What is at stake in the interdisciplinary study of people's understanding of biology? A lot. Can human beings make the transition
from locally sustainable adaptation to (technologically driven) global
economies without irreparably damaging our environment or destroying
local cultures? To address such issues researchers may need to integrate
questions about the structure of biological cognition with systematic analyses of how knowledge is linked to action in diverse ecological and cultural contexts (Atran and Medin 1997; Atran, Medin, and Ross 2005).
We hope that this book provides new intellectual tools for understanding
how humans come to know nature.

1.5   Themes

In this book, we describe historical, cross-cultural, and developmental research on how people conceptualize nature (naive or folkbiology) and how they act on it (folkecology). This represents the results to date of an ongoing multidisciplinary, multinational project begun in 1991. Here we concentrate on cognitive, cultural, and historical processes in the devolution of knowledge and the consequences of devolution for environmental management. Our approach integrates three disciplinary perspectives:

• For cognitive psychology, we examine how results gathered from "standard populations" in industrialized societies often fail to generalize to humanity at large. This leads us to an account of several fundamental human processes of categorization and reasoning that differ substantially from current accounts. An important factor motivating our experiments, and our interpretation of them, is how plausible the results appear in light of evolutionary biology and psychology.
• For developmental research, we find that usual study populations represent instances of impoverished experience with nature. This has serious implications for science education in our own society. Perhaps even more vital, this may help to reverse today's dismal prospects of integrating science and folk knowledge in other societies in ways that do not denigrate or destroy valuable and often irreplaceable local understandings of nature.
• For cultural and environmental studies, we show that even groups living in the same habitat can manifest strikingly distinct behaviors, cognitions, and social relations relative to it. Understanding why some people work in a way that degrades the environment while others manage to preserve and even enhance ecological diversity and resilience has critical implications for environmental and political decision making. It bears directly on how our species might deal with increasingly dire problems of sustaining our common environment as globalization advances. This line of research suggests a novel way of studying culture and culture processes and it points to a perspective on decision making that emphasizes values and meanings over probabilities and utilities.

We argue that cultural transmission and formation does not consist only, or even primarily, in the inheritance of shared codes of thought and behavior, but in complex distributions of causally connected representations across minds. Instead of viewing culture as a "top-down" structure that imposes itself on individual minds, we focus on modeling microprocesses at the level of individual cognitions, decisions, and actions. This allows us to trace how macrostructural cultural norms and other social regularities emerge from decentralized local interactions between people. This enables us to avoid essentializing culture, treating it as an independent variable, or using it as a circular source of explanation for differences between groups. This approach also contrasts markedly with "influence models" that are common to economics and political science. Such models seek to "explain" sociocultural macrophenomena (e.g., political conditions, religious ideology) in terms of the "influences" of other sociocultural macrophenomena (e.g., economic conditions, material mode of production), where the causal nature of these influences remains materially unanalyzed and inscrutable.

1.6 Book Summary

In this book we argue that the combination of cross-cultural research with conceptualizing biological cognition as a privileged, domain-specific competence provides a new perspective on a range of fundamental issues in cognition. This perspective includes

· A need to revise current models of categorization and reasoning, which have been developed on a narrow empirical base, culturally speaking
· An analysis of the relative contributions of universal versus culturally specific processes to people's conceptions of biological kinds
· A shift in the appraisal of the role of so-called standard populations from constituting a norm to seeing them as reflecting the cognitive consequences of diminished contact with nature
· An appreciation of the role of values and meanings in decision making and environmental management

Our civilization is currently in the midst of a conceptual, technological, and moral revolution with regard to biological knowledge and its uses. World political and scientific leaders have called for a concerted effort to improve public understanding of what likely will be one of the most important domains of human inquiry and endeavor in the coming century, if not millennium. This book is about that "public understanding" viewed from a cultural perspective.

The remainder of the book is organized as follows. The next chapter provides a further introduction by examining folktaxonomies in detail, describing their relation to scientific taxonomy from a historical perspective, and providing an analysis of devolution in cultural support for learning about the natural world. The introductory material concludes with chapter 3, which takes up methodological issues.

Chapter 4 presents a summary of our work on the role of culture and expertise in biological cognition and links these findings to theories of categorization and reasoning. Chapter 5 continues in this vein, focusing on developmental studies and corresponding implications for theories of cognitive development.

In chapter 6 we take up different approaches to the study of culture, and we argue for a cultural epidemiological approach to it. Chapters 7 through 9 illustrate our approach by presenting two intensive case studies, one focused on agroforestry among three cultural groups living in the lowland rainforest of Guatemala and the other focused on resource conflict between Native American and European-American fishermen in north-central Wisconsin. The final chapter summarizes conclusions and implications growing out of our work and points to some new and somewhat surprising directions in which our research is now headed.

2 Universals and Devolution: General Claims

For more than a decade we have been investigating the cognitive consequences of reduced contact with nature—what Nabhan and St. Antoine (1993) refer to as "extinction of experience" and what we call "devolution." This chapter provides background for our research program in the domain of naive or folkbiology. It bears not only on knowledge loss or devolution but also on universal aspects of biological cognition. We begin with a brief summary of candidate principles for evolved universals and associated historical developments in scientific taxonomy. Then we turn to evidence demonstrating that cultural support for attention to nature has been diminishing since the onset of the industrial revolution.

2.1 Evolved Universals in Cognition and Culture

We begin with aspects of folkbiology that appear to be universal as a backdrop for characterizing the consequences of diminished contact with nature. Humans everywhere classify animals and plants into specieslike groupings that are as obvious to a modern scientist as to a Maya Indian (Simpson 1961; Diamond and Bishop 1999). Such groupings are primary loci for thinking about biological causes and relations (Mayr 1969). In addition, "From the most remote period in the history of the world organic beings have been found to resemble each other in descending degrees, so that they can be classed into groups under groups. This classification is not arbitrary like the grouping of stars in constellations" (Darwin 1859, 431). This taxonomic array provides a natural framework for inference, and an inductive compendium of information, about organic categories and properties (Atran 1990). It is not as conventional or arbitrary in structure and content, nor as variable across cultures, as the assembly of entities into cosmologies, materials, or social groups.

Comparisons between folkbiological systems are sometimes based on analyses of a specious level of folktaxonomy called "terminal contrast." Terminal contrast occurs between named groupings that include no additional named groupings. For example, among folk in Michigan the class of terminal contrast includes BAT, SQUIRREL, WEASEL, BEAVER, BEAGLE (dog), POODLE (dog), CALICO (cat), SHORT-HAIRED TABBY (cat), LONG-HAIRED TABBY (cat), and so on. There is little systematic relation between terminal folktaxa and corresponding scientific taxa. Thus, BAT includes a variety of different scientific families, genera, and species in the order Chiroptera, many of which are locally represented in Michigan. SQUIRREL includes different local genera and species of the family Sciuridae. WEASEL encompasses two local species of the genus *Mustela*. BEAVER corresponds to the single local species *Castor canadensis*. BEAGLE and POODLE denote two "varieties" of the species *Canis familiaris*. CALICO refers to a "variety" of *Felis cattus*, whereas SHORT-HAIRED TABBY and LONG-HAIRED TABBY are (mongrelized) "races" of the species.

Using terminal contrast as the focus of comparison between folkbiology and scientific systematics thus reveals, at best, a modest relationship. In fact, several studies in psychology and anthropology that purport to compare the "taxonomic structure" of folk and scientific biology use terminal contrast as the basis of analysis (Conklin 1962; Lévi-Strauss 1966; Rosch 1975). This is unfortunate, because terminal contrast is a purely (ethno)linguistic feature that has little direct significance for the structure of living-kind taxonomies. As a result, deeper similarities between Linnaean and folkbiological taxonomies have often been ignored.

When people are asked to sort biological kinds into groups they show strong within- and across-culture agreement that also corresponds fairly well with classical evolutionary taxonomy, which we call "scientific taxonomy" for short.[1] For example, as we will see in our studies with a variety of populations, average correlations between folktaxonomies and scientific taxonomies of the local fauna and flora usually are quite high (e.g., +.75). Much of the remaining variability is due to greater folk than scientific attention to size (Hunn 1999), obvious perceptual properties, and local ecological concerns. Contrary to received notions about the history and cross-cultural basis for folkbiological classification, mere utility does *not* drive general-purpose folktaxonomy (Berlin, Breedlove, and Raven 1973; Atran 1990).

Folkbiological taxonomy also supports indefinitely many graded inferences regarding the distribution of biologically related properties among species. On finding out that red oaks are susceptible to some new disease, informants are likely to infer that other oaks may also be susceptible to this disease. As we will see, the detailed character of the induction varies with experience and cultural background.

There is also growing cross-cultural evidence of a commonsense assumption that each folkspecies—what we will refer to as "generic species" for reasons discussed below—has an underlying causal nature, or essence, uniquely responsible for the typical appearance, behavior, and ecological preferences of the kind. On evolutionary grounds one would expect that innate potential is vested at the generic-species level: for the most part, generic species are genetically, geographically, and reproductively isolated (Mayr 1982 calls these "nondimensional species"). Hence, we would expect presumptions of essence to be at the generic-species level, where innate potential is.

There are thus strong constraints—plausibly naturally selected—on how people organize local knowledge of biological kinds. Universal appreciation of generic species may be one such functional adaptation. Pigeonholing generic species into a hierarchy of mutually exclusive taxa allows incorporation of new species and biological properties into an inductively coherent system that can be extended to any habitat, facilitating adaptation to many habitats (a hallmark of *Homo sapiens*). In the chapters that follow, we will provide additional evidence that folkbiology is a constrained domain of development and that its core aspects are either innate or universally acquired under some minimal, adequate input conditions.

2.2 Universal Aspects of Folkbiology

In every society people think about plants and animals in the same special ways (Berlin 1992). The science of biology also treats plants and animals as special kinds of objects, but applies this treatment to humans as well. Folkbiology, which is present in all cultures, and the science of biology, whose origins are particular to the Western cultural tradition, have corresponding notions of living kinds. Consider four corresponding ways in which ordinary folk and biologists think of plants and animals as special (Atran 1998).

Four Points of General Correspondence between Folkbiological Taxonomy and Scientific Systematics

1. People in all cultures classify plants and animals into specieslike groups that biologists generally recognize as populations of interbreeding

individuals adapted to an ecological niche. We call such groups—like REDWOOD, RYE, RACCOON, or ROBIN—*generic species*. Generic species often correspond to scientific genera (e.g., oak) or species (e.g., dog), at least for the most phenomenally salient organisms, such as larger vertebrates and flowering plants. Ethnobiologists, historians of systematics, and field biologists mostly agree that "species come to be tolerably well defined objects... in any one region and at any one time" (Darwin [1872] 1883, 137) and that such local species recognized by ordinary people are the heart of any natural system of biological classification (Diamond and Bishop 1999). The term *generic species* is used here, rather than *folk genera/folk generic* (Berlin 1972) or *folk species/folk specieme* (Bulmer 1970), for three reasons.[2]

First, a principled distinction between biological genus and species is not pertinent to local folk around the world. The most phenomenally salient species for humans, including most species of large vertebrates, trees, and phylogenetically isolated groups such as palms and cacti, belong to monospecific genera in any given locale. In other words, generic species often correspond to scientific species (dog, apple tree); however, for a majority of perceptually salient organisms, a scientific genus frequently has only one locally occurring species (bear, cedar). Closely related species of a polytypic genus are often hard to distinguish locally, and no readily perceptible morphological or ecological "gap" can be discerned between them (Diver 1940).

Second, *generic species* reflects a more accurate sense of the correspondence between psychologically privileged folkbiological groups and historically privileged scientific groups (Stevens 1994). A distinction between genus and species did not appear until the influx of newly discovered species from the world over compelled European naturalists to mnemonically manage them within a worldwide system of genera built around (mainly European) species types (Atran 1987).

Third, the term *generic species* reflects a dual ontological character. As privileged mnemonic groups, they are akin to genera in being those groups most readily apparent to the naked eye (Cain 1956). As privileged causal groups, they are akin to species in being the principal loci of evolutionary processes responsible for the appearance of biological diversity (Mayr 1969).

Generic species are usually as obvious to a modern scientist as to local folk. Historically, the generic-species concept provided a pretheoretical basis for scientific explanation of the organic world in that different theories—including evolutionary theory—have sought to account for the apparent constancy of "common species" and the organic processes that center on them (Wallace [1889] 1901, 1).

2. There is a commonsense assumption that each generic species has an underlying causal nature, or essence, which is uniquely responsible for the typical appearance, behavior, and ecological preferences of the kind (Atran et al. 1997, 2001; Atran 1998; Gelman and Wellman 1991; Gelman 2003; Sousa, Atran, and Medin 2002). We speculate that this notion of biological essence may be universal. People in diverse cultures consider it responsible for the organism's identity as a complex entity governed by dynamic internal processes that are lawful even when hidden. This essence maintains the organism's integrity from birth even as it causes the organism to grow, change form, and transmit the same causal cycle across generations. Thus, a tadpole and frog are conceptualized as the same animal although they look and behave very differently, and live in different places. For these reasons, teleological essentialism, which applies uniquely to living kinds, is more specialized than mere sortal essentialism, which may apply to all nominalized objects (e.g., armchair, platinum) and intrinsic qualities (e.g., purple, liquid) (Rips 1995; Atran 1998).

Western philosophers, like Aristotle and Locke, attempted to translate this commonsense notion of essence into some sort of metaphysical reality, but evolutionary biologists reject the notion of essence as such (e.g., Mayr 1982). Nevertheless, biologists have traditionally interpreted this conservation of identity under change as due to the fact that organisms have genotypes separate from phenotypes.

Although science does not abide metaphysical essentialism, there is a wide variety of evidence supporting the notion of psychological essentialism (Ahn et al. 2001). That is, even when people do not have specific ideas about essences, they may nonetheless have a commitment to the idea that there is an underlying nature (i.e., they may have an "essence placeholder"; Medin and Ortony 1989). This hidden, causal essence is presumably responsible for the emerging and manifest properties of the kind. The fact that biological science can overturn psychological essentialism in theory construction in no way implies that psychological essentialism can be dismissed from everyday thought, any more than physical science's rejection of constant intervals of space and time implies alterations in our ordinary use of absolute space and time.

The idea of an essence placeholder allows that people may come up with different mechanisms for conveying or modifying causal essence. Some mechanisms may be more plausible choices than others. For example, beating of the heart and circulation of blood give prima facie mechanical evidence for causal activity. In addition, loss of blood and stopping of the heart are often signs of loss of life. Thus, heart and blood may be privileged candidates for the locus of essence, as they have been throughout the history of European societies (Atran 1990). Even contemporary Americans who undergo heart transplants show evidence of believing that at least some aspects of essence have been transmitted from the donor to the recipient (Sylvia and Novak 1997). In different cultural settings, other plausible candidates (e.g., milk as conveyer of essence through nursing) may have priority (Stoler 1995). Willingness to allow transformations of essential kindhood (e.g., through blood transfusions, organ transplants) also may depend on cultural context (Walker 1992; Mahalingam 1998; Waxman, Medin, and Ross 2007). Even in cultures where the adult discourse is antiessentialist, it appears that both children and adults essentialize animals (Astuti 2002; Astuti, Carey, and Solomon 2004). Indeed, essence-related notions of nonintentional and nonmechanical causal processes, continue to agitate science.

Vitalism is the folk belief that biological kinds—and their maintaining parts, properties, and processes—are teleological, and hence not reducible to the contingent relations that govern inert matter. Its cultural expression varies (cf. Hatano and Inagaki 1994). Within any given culture people may have varying interpretations and degrees of attachment to this belief: some who are religiously inclined may think that a "spiritual" essence determines biological causality; others of a more scientific orientation might hold that systems of laws that suffice for physics and chemistry do not necessarily suffice for biology. Many, if not most, working biologists (and cognitive scientists) implicitly retain at least a minimal commitment to vitalism: they acknowledge that physicochemical laws should suffice for biology, but suppose that such laws are not adequate in their current form, and must be enriched by further laws whose predicates are different from those of inert physics and chemistry.

It is not evident how complete elimination of teleological expressions (concepts defined functionally) from biological theory can be pursued without forsaking a powerful and fruitful conceptual scheme for physiology, morphology, disease, and evolution. In cognitive science, a belief that biological systems, such as the mind/brain, are not wholly reducible to electronic circuitry, like computers, is a pervasive attitude that implicitly drives considerable polemic, but also much creative theorizing. Even if this sort of vitalism represents a lingering folk belief that science may ultimately seek to discard, it remains an important and perhaps indispensable cognitive heuristic for regulating scientific inquiry.

3. In addition to the spontaneous division of local flora and fauna into essence-based species, such groups, as Darwin (1859, 431) noted, have "from the remotest period in ... history ... been classed in groups under groups." The structure of these hierarchically included groups, such as WHITE OAK/OAK/TREE or MOUNTAIN ROBIN/ROBIN/BIRD, is referred to as "folkbiological taxonomy." Especially in the case of animals, these non-overlapping taxonomic structures can often be scientifically interpreted in terms of speciation (related species descended from a common ancestor by splitting off from a lineage).

In all societies that have been studied in depth, folkbiological groups, or taxa, are organized into hierarchically organized ranks. Most folkbiological systems have between three and six ranks (Berlin 1992). Taxa of the same rank are mutually exclusive and tend to display similar linguistic, biological, and psychological characteristics. Ranks and taxa, whether in folkbiological or scientific classification, are of different logical orders, and confounding them is a category mistake. Biological ranks are second-order classes of groups (e.g., species, family, kingdom) whose elements are first-order groups (e.g., lion, feline, animal). Folkbiological ranks vary little across cultures as a function of theories or belief systems (Malt 1995). Ranks are intended to represent fundamentally different levels of reality, not convenience.

Generalizations across taxa of the same rank thus differ in logical type from generalizations that apply to this or that taxon. TERMITE, PIG, and LEMON TREE are not related to one another by a simple class inclusion under a common hierarchical node, but by dint of their common rank—in this case the level of generic species. A system of rank is not simply a hierarchy. Hierarchies—that is, structures of inclusive classes—are common to many cognitive domains, including the domain of artifacts. For example, CHAIR often falls under FURNITURE but not VEHICLE, and CAR falls under VEHICLE but not FURNITURE. But there is no ranked system of artifacts: no inferential link, or inductive framework, spans both CHAIR and CAR, or FURNITURE and VEHICLE, by dint of a common rank, such as the artifact *species* or the artifact family (see Coley et al. 2004 for experimental evidence that artifacts are treated differently from natural kinds).

Modern systematics—the branch of biology that concerns scientific taxonomy—is currently in the process of divesting itself of ranks in favor of unranked phylogenetic lineages (clades), although the process is far from complete. Ever since Darwin, biology no longer recognizes a principled ontological distinction between species and variety, genus and species, family and genus, and so forth. Nevertheless, contemporary systematists and other biologists continue to make use of ranked taxonomic hierarchies as a research heuristic. By tabulating the ranges of extant and extinct genera, families, classes, and so on, systematists can provide a usable compendium of changing diversity throughout the history of life. For example, by looking at just numbers of families, it is possible to ascertain that insects form a more diverse group than tetrapods (i.e., terrestrial vertebrates, including amphibians, birds, mammals, and reptiles). By calculating whether the taxonomic diversity in one group varies over time as a function of the taxonomic diversity in another group, evidence can be garnered for or against the evolutionary interdependence of the two groups. Some comparisons of the relative numbers of families of insects and flowering plants, reveal the surprising fact that insects were just as taxonomically diverse before the emergence of flowering plants as after. Consequently, evolutionary effects of plant evolution on the adaptive radiation of insects are probably less profound than previously thought (Labandeira and Sepkoski 1993). The heuristic value of (scientifically elaborated) folk-based strategies for inquiry is compelling, despite evolutionary theorists being well aware that no "true" distinctions exist between various taxonomic levels.

4. Biological taxonomies not only organize and summarize biological information, they also provide a powerful inductive framework for making systematic inferences about the likely distribution of organic and ecological properties among organisms. In modern systematics, this strategy receives its strongest expression in the "fundamental principle of systematic induction" (Warburton 1967; Bock 1973). On this principle, given a property found among members of any two species, the best initial hypothesis is that the property is also present among all species that are included in the smallest higher-order taxon containing the original pair of species. For example, finding that the bacteria *Escherichia coli* share a hitherto unknown property with robins, a biologist would be justified in testing the hypothesis that all organisms share the property. This is because *E. coli* link up with robins only at the highest level of taxonomy, which includes all organisms. This or any general-purpose system of taxonomic inference for biological kinds is grounded in a universal belief that the world naturally divides into the limited causal varieties we commonly know as (generic) species.

These four principles provide the backbone and background for studying the role of culture and experience in cognizing nature. That is, they suggest candidates for universals as well as variations that may derive from limited contact with plants and animals or from different cultural lenses for perceiving biological kinds. In the next section we will see how these principles have influenced the development of scientific taxonomy.

2.3 Historical Developments

To further illustrate how skeletal principles shape conceptions of nature we turn to a brief review of historical developments in biology. Understanding how scientific concepts in industrialized societies developed out of folk understanding is important for several reasons. First, it helps show where and how scientific understanding converges with and diverges from folk understanding. Second, the historical record can inform our knowledge of the conceptual difficulties and possibilities for children and ordinary folk in comprehending scientific concepts. This has obvious implications not only for science education, but more generally for public policy with regard to science. Third, tracking developments in industrialized society's understanding can help peoples from other cultural heritages avoid or take advantage of industrialized society's lessons. In developing countries, nearly all governments endeavor to impose "modernized" science education programs on their peoples, although there may be little attempt to explore compatibilities and incompatibilities between "our" science and other peoples' awareness of nature.

As in any native folkbiological inventory, ancient Greek and Roman naturalists contended with only 500 or 600 local species (Raven, Berlin, and Breedlove 1971). Because biological genus and species are often extensionally equivalent in any given locale, there was no conceptual basis for systematically distinguishing them. For Aristotle and Theophrastus, as for Dioscorides and Pliny, the term *atomon eidos*, or "species," referred to generic species (e.g., eagle, dog, oak, wheat), whereas the term *megiston genos*, or "genus," referred to superordinate life forms (e.g., bird, quadruped, tree, grass).

Europe's "Age of Exploration" introduced a multitude of new species. The French naturalist Joseph Tournefort (1694) originated the genus concept as the ranked class immediately superordinate to that of the species. This allowed the reduction of species by an order of magnitude to equivalence classes that the mind could easily manage again (from roughly

6,000 known species to 600 genera). The place of a new species in the natural order of genera would be initially determined in either of two ways:
(1) by empirical intuition, that is, readily visible morphological agreement
with a European representative or some other preferred type species of
the genus, or (2) by intellectual intuition, that is, analytic agreement with
the generic fructification (fruit and flower) according to the number, topo-
logical disposition, geometrical configuration, and magnitude of its constituent elements. Within this Cartesian framework, the one criterion
would be ultimately commensurate with the other, allowing a mathematical reduction of the new species to its associated type by reason of their
common fructification. In this way, the customary native knowledge of
the folk naturalist would be rationally extended to a worldwide scale.
Such was the aim of Carolus Linnaeus's (1735) "natural system."

Under John Locke's influence, the English naturalist John Ray (1703)
questioned whether fructification characters encoded the essential order
of plant life. Analytic convenience might justify reliance on readily visible
parts of the fruit and flower as a classificatory strategy, but there was no
guarantee such analytic characters could be arranged into a preset combi-
natory system. In the case of animals, reduction of visible parts to com-
putable characters proved unwarranted.

The geometrical rate of exploration and discovery further undermined
the taxonomic priority of the genus. As awareness of new forms increased
another order of magnitude, the family concept became the new basis for
taxonomy. The family was itself rooted in local groupings that native folk
implicitly recognize but seldom name, such as felines, equids, legumes,
and umbellifers. The ancients called these *eide anonyma* or *genera innomi-
nata*. The local series of such groupings does not fully partition a local
environment, but is riddled with gaps. A strategy emerged for closing the
gaps: looking to other environments to complete local gaps, naturalists
sought to discern a worldwide series that would cover the lacunae in any
and all environments. This would reduce the ever-increasing number of
species and genera to a mnemonically manageable set of basic, family
plans that were still perceptually distinguishable. Linnaeus (1751) dubbed
this strategy the *natural method* for completing "family fragments."

French Enlightenment naturalists elaborated the natural method,
favoring empiricism over rationalism. Michel Adanson (1763) introduced
the idea of classification by "family resemblances" (*air de famille*) for
completing a worldwide family series. Antoine-Laurent Jussieu (1789)
reduced the thousands of genera proposed since Tournefort to exactly
100 families, but acknowledged this number reflected convenience rather

than necessity. Jussieu's families became the standards of modern plant taxonomy. Extending the *méthode naturelle* to animals, including humans, Georges-Louis Buffon (1749–1767) first identified family plans as lineages of temporally related species. This idea became crucial to the evolutionary thinking of Jean-Baptiste Lamarck and Charles Darwin. Although Enlightenment taxonomy kept biological science tied to the readily visible world of species, genera, and families, it provided a cognitively expedient morphological framework for initial exploration of the causal relations and history of species.

Since the days of Ray and Linnaeus, folkbotanical life forms, like TREE or VINE, have not been considered scientifically valid concepts, because they have no anatomical or genealogical unity (e.g., legumes are variously trees, vines, bushes, and so on). The same may be true of many long-standing zoological taxa. Phylogenetic theorists question the "reality" of zoological life forms, such as BIRD and REPTILE, and the whole taxonomic framework that made biology conceivable in the first place. Thus, if birds descended from dinosaurs, and if crocodiles but not turtles are also directly related to dinosaurs, then crocodiles and birds form a group that excludes turtles; or crocodiles, birds, and turtles form separate groups; or all form one group. In any event, the traditional separation of BIRD and REPTILE is no longer tenable.

Still, even in the midst of their own radical restructuring of taxonomy, Linnaeus and Darwin would continue to rely on popular life forms like TREE and BIRD to collect and understand local species arrangements, as do botanists and zoologists today. As for ordinary people, and especially those who live intimately with nature, they can ignore such ecologically salient kinds only at their peril. That is why science cannot simply subvert common sense.

From Linnaeus to the present day, biological systematics has used explicit principles and organizing criteria that traditional folk might consider secondary or might not consider at all (e.g., the geometrical composition of a plant's flower and fruit structure, or the numerical breakdown of an animal's blood chemistry). Nevertheless, as with Linnaeus, the modern systematist initially depends implicitly, and crucially, on a traditional folk appreciation. As Bartlett (1936, 5) noted with specific reference to the Maya region of Petén (see Diamond 1966 for zoology),

A botanist working in a new tropical area is … confronted with a multitude of species which are not only new to him, but which flower and fruit only at some other season than that of his visit, or perhaps so sporadically that he can hardly hope to find them fertile. Furthermore, just such plants are likely to be character

plants of [ecological] associations. . . . Confronted with such a situation, the botanist will find that his difficulties vanish as if by magic if he undertakes to learn the
flora as the natives know it, using their plant names, their criteria for identification (which frequently neglect the fruiting parts entirely), and their terms for habitats and types of land.

As Linnaeus needed the life-form TREE and its commons species to actually do his work, so did Darwin ([1872] 1883, 353–354) need the life-form
BIRD and its common species:

[In the Galápagos Islands] There are twenty-six land birds; of these twenty-one
or perhaps twenty-three are ranked a distinct species, and would commonly be
assumed to have been here created; yet the close [family] affinity of most of these
birds to American species is manifest in every character, in their habits, gestures,
and tones of voice. So it is with other animals, and with a large proportion of
plants. . . . Facts such as these, admit of no sort of explanation on the ordinary
view of creation.

From a strictly cosmic viewpoint, the title of his great work, *On the
Origins of Species*, is ironic and misleading—much as if Copernicus had
titled his attack on the geocentric universe, *On the Origins of Sunrise*. Of
course, in order to attain that cosmic understanding, Darwin could no
more dispense with thinking about "common species" than Copernicus
could avoid thinking about the sunrise (Wallace [1889] 1901, 1–2). In
fact, not just species, but all levels of universal folktaxonomy served as
indispensable landmarks for Darwin's awareness of the evolving pathways of diversity: from the folkspecifics and varietals whose variation
humans had learned to manipulate, to intermediate-level families, and
life-form classes, such as bird, within which the godlier processes of natural selection might be discerned.

So far we have been discussing folktaxonomy at a fairly abstract level.
We now turn to a specific example that we examine in considerable detail,
taxonomy among the Itza' Maya of Guatemala.

2.4   Itza' Maya Folktaxonomy

In what follows, we outline a small but crucial part of the folkbiological
system of a people unschooled in Western notions of theories or science:
the folkbiological taxonomy of the Itza' Maya. Such taxonomies are crucial to understanding folkbiology for two reasons: biological taxonomies
seem to be culturally universal; and they are structured enough to impose
constraints on possible theories, thereby rendering biological theories possible, including evolutionary theory (at least historically). Western biolog-

ical theories emerged by decontextualizing nature: by tearing out water lilies from water so that they could be dried, measured, printed, and compared with other living forms detached from local ecology and most of the senses. For Itza', folkbiological taxonomy appears to hearken to a somewhat different calling in human life and cognition, one that is more embedded in the local environment.

Itza' Maya folkbiology provides evidence for generalizations about the specific taxonomic structure that delimits the universal domain of folkbiology, but also for the influence of local ecology and culture. The Itza' are the last Maya Indians native to the Petén tropical forest of northern Guatemala, once an epicenter of Classic Maya civilization. The Spanish conquest of the Itza' in 1697 put a brutal end to the last independent Maya confederacy (Atran 1999a). Although the Itza' cosmological system was destroyed, Itza' folkbiological knowledge—including taxonomic competence as well as practical application—has survived (Atran 1993; Atran, Lois, and Ucan Ek' 2004). Presently, however, Itza' forest culture verges on extinction: the language, banned for decades by government authorities with threats of fines and punishment, is dying among the young and the forest is being razed at an awesome rate by loggers, immigrant farmers, and cattle ranchers.

Kingdoms and Life Forms

The most general rank in any folkbiological taxonomy is the folk kingdom,[3] that is, plant or animal. Such taxa are not always explicitly named, and represent the most fundamental divisions of the (nonhuman) biological world. These divisions correspond to the notion of "ontological category" in philosophy (Donnellan 1971) and psychology (Keil 1979). From an early age, it appears, humans cannot help but conceive of any object they see in the world as either being or not being an animal, and there is evidence for an early distinction between plants and nonliving things (Gelman and Wellman 1991; Keil 1995; Hickling and Gelman 1995; Hatano and Inagaki 1996). Conceiving of an object as a plant or animal seems to carry with it certain presumptions that are not applied to objects thought of as belonging to other ontological categories, like the categories of person, substance, or artifact.[4]

The next rank down is that of life form.[5] The majority of taxa of lesser rank fall under one or another life form. Most life-form taxa are named by lexically unanalyzable names (primary lexemes), and have further named subdivisions, such as tree and bird. Biologically, members of a single life form are diverse. Psychologically, members of a life form share a small number of perceptual diagnostics, such as stem habit, skin covering, and so forth (Brown 1984). Life-form taxa may represent general adaptations to broad sets of ecological conditions, such as the competition of single-stem plants for sunlight and tetrapod adaptation to life in the air (Hunn 1982; Atran 1990). Classification by life form may occur relatively early in childhood. For example, familiar kinds of quadruped (e.g., dog and horse) are classed apart from sea-versus-air animals (Mandler, Bauer, and McDonough 1991; Dougherty 1979 for American plants).

Itza' kingdoms and life forms provide evidence for this universal cognitive structure in a Maya idiom. There is no common lexical entry for the plant kingdom; however, the numeral classifier *teek* is used with all and only plants. Plants generally fall under one of four mutually exclusive life forms: *che'* (trees), *pok~che'* (herbs, shrubs = undergrowth), *ak'* (vines), and *su'uk* (grasses). Each life form conforms to a distinct stem habit. Some introduced and cultivated plants are unaffiliated with any of these life forms, and are simply denoted *jun-teek* (lit. "one plant," e.g., *jun-teek ixi'im* = a maize plant). This is also true of many of the phylogenetically isolated plants, such as the cacti.

All informants agree that mushrooms (*xikin~che'*, lit. "tree-ear") have no *puksik'al* and are not plants, but take life away from the trees that host them. Lichens and bryophytes (mosses and liverworts) are not considered to be plants, to have an essence, or to live.

In Itza', the term for animals (*b'a'al~che'* = "forest-thing") polysemously refers to: (1) the whole animal kingdom (including invertebrates, birds, and fish); (2) a more restrictive grouping of quadrupeds (i.e., *b'a'al~che'+k-u-siit'* = "jumping animals" or amphibians; *b'a'al~che'+ k-u-jil-t-ik-u-b'aj* = "slithering animals" or reptiles; *b'a'al~che'+k-u-xi'- mal* = "walking animals" or mammals); (3) typically the mammals alone. Birds (*ch'iich'* including *sotz'* = bats) and fish (*käy*) exhibit patterns of internal structure that parallel those of the "unnamed" mammal and herpetofauna life forms.[6] Like the named life form, *ch'iich'*, the mammal group forms an inferentially self-contained category over which inductive generalizations can be made about biologically related properties. Snakes (*kan*) also form an inferentially self-contained group (Atran 1994); however, snakes are also consistently and exclusively sorted with the lizards at one (intermediate) level, and with the rest of the herpetofauna at the next (life-form) level.[7]

Like the life form of invertebrates (*mejen+b'a'al~che'* = "small animal"), herpetofauna seem to form a "residual" life-form category that does not have a conceptually distinctive role in the "economy of nature."

This contrasts with the other plant and life-form categories, which seem to have mutually defined ecological roles (see Atran 1990; Berlin 1992): birds and trees in the air (*ik'*) and upper forest tier; mammals and herbs on the ground (*lu'um*) in the forest understory; vines in the connecting "middle" (*tan-chumuk*) tiers; grasses in the open lands (*chäk'an*); fish in the water (*ja'*). To be sure, the boundaries between these "adaptive zones" are permeable by members of each life form; however, each life forms has its respective habitat, or "home" (*otoch*). Accordingly, because the chicken (*aj-kax*) has its home exclusively on the ground, and cannot live in the air like other birds, it is not a bird, nor is it included under any of the other life forms (although for Tzeltal Maya the chicken is the prototypical bird; Hunn 1977).

For the *mejen+b'a'al~che'*, whose morphologies and ecological proclivities are very distant from humans and other vertebrates, correspondence of folk to modern systematics blurs as one descends the ranks of the scientific ladder, and violations of scientific taxonomy tend to be more pronounced. Still, in this respect as in others, Itza' taxonomy differs little from that of any other folkbiological system, such as that which initially gave rise to systematics, including evolutionary systematics. For Linnaeus (1751, sec. 153), a natural system is rooted in "a natural instinct [that] teaches us to know first objects closest to us, and at length the smallest ones: for example, Man, Quadrupeds, Birds, Fish, Insects, Mites, or first the large Plants, last the smallest mosses."

Generic Species

As we noted before, the core of any folk taxonomy is rank of generic species, which contains by far the most numerous taxa in any folkbiological system. Most cultures have a set of life forms, but all cultures have a set of generic species. Ethnobiologists who otherwise differ in their views of folktaxonomy tend to agree that this level best captures discontinuities in nature and provides the fundamental constituents in all systems of folkbiological categorization, reasoning, and use (Bulmer 1974; Hunn 1982; Morris 1996; Descola 1996; Ellen 1999).

People in all societies studied—and thus likely in all cultures—spontaneously partition the ontological categories animal and plant into generic species in a virtually exhaustive manner. "Virtually exhaustive" means that when an organism is encountered that is not readily identifiable as belonging to a named generic species, it is still *expected* to belong to one. The organism is assimilated to one of the named taxa it resembles (Berlin 1999). This partitioning of ontological categories seems to be part and parcel of the categories themselves: no plant or animal can fail to uniquely belong to a generic species.

Taxa of the generic-species rank generally fall under some life form, but there may be outliers that are unaffiliated with any major life-form taxon.[8] This is often so for plants and animals of particular cultural interest, such as cassowaries for the Kalam of New Guinea (Bulmer 1970) and maize (*ixi'im*) for Itza' and other Maya (see Berlin, Breedlove, and Raven 1974; Barrera Marín, Barrera Vásquez, and López Franco 1976). Like life-form taxa, generic-species taxa are usually named by primary lexemes. Examples are oak and robin in English, or *oop* (custard-apple tree) and *pek'* (dog) in Itza'. Sometimes, generic species are labeled as binomial compounds, such as hummingbird or *k'u'~che'* ("god's tree" = tropical cedar). On other occasions, they may be optionally labeled as binomial composites, such as oak tree (as opposed to poison oak) or *ix-k'o'och(+che')* = the *k'o'och* tree (*Cecropia peltata*, as opposed to the *k'o'och* herb = *Ricinus communis*). In both cases the binomial makes the hierarchical relation apparent between the generic species and the life form.

The correspondence of the generic species to scientific species or genera is not isomorphic, and varies according to patterns of species distribution within biological families and other factors. For less perceptible organisms, whose morphologies and ecological proclivities are distant from humans (insects, bryophytes), violations of scientific taxonomy tend to be more pronounced, with a single generic species sometimes encompassing biological families, orders, and occasionally whole phyla. For Itza', the generic-species terms for many invertebrates, such as that for worm (*ix-nok'ol*), can encompass different orders and even phyla.

Moreover, generic species may on occasion correspond to locally represented families, orders, or higher scientific ranks. For example, the Itza' generic-species term for vulture (*ch'om*) refers to several genera of the family Cathardidae; the term for bat (*sotz'*) denotes several families of the order Chiroptera. Nevertheless, generic species usually encompass single biological species and usually do not extend beyond biological genera for the larger vertebrates and flowering plants—that is, for those organisms that are phenomenally most salient for human beings. For example, in a comparative study we found that about 80 percent of tree genera in both the Chicago area—40 of 48—and a sample portion of the Itza' area of Petén—158 of 229—are monospecific (AHG/APESA 1992; Medin et al. 1997). Moreover, 365 generic species of Petén trees and other plants, which Itza' have thus far identified to us as useful to them, correspond to some 438 biological species (Atran, Lois, and Ucan Ek' 2004).

A comparative study of mammal classification among Itza' and undergraduates from rural Michigan reveals a similar pattern. The great majority of mammal taxa in both cultures correspond to scientific species, and most also correspond to monospecific genera: 30 of 40 (75 percent) basic Michigan mammal terms denote biological species, of which 21 (70 percent, or 53 percent of the total) are monospecific genera; 36 of 42 (86 percent) basic Itza' mammal terms denote biological species, of which 25 (69 percent, or 60 percent of the total) are monospecific genera (López et al. 1997).

The rank of generic species is the level at which morphological, behavioral, and ecological relationships between organisms maximally covary. The majority of Itza' folkbiological taxa belong to this level. This is the level that Itza' privilege when they see and talk about biological discontinuities. Generic species represent cuts in nature that Itza' children first name and form an image of (for Highland Maya, see Stross 1973), and that Itza' adults most frequently use in speech, most easily recall in memory, and most readily communicate to others (for Highland Maya, see Berlin, Breedlove, and Raven 1974; Hunn 1977). It is the rank at which Itza', like other folk around the world, are most likely to attribute biological properties: including characteristic patterns of inheritance, growth, and physiological function as well as more "hidden" properties, such as hitherto unknown organic processes, organs, and diseases.

Folkspecifics and Varietals

Generic species may be further divided into folkspecifics. In general, whether a generic species is further differentiated depends on cultural importance. Itza' subdivide 257 useful plant generic species into 279 subordinate taxa. But even useful generic species are more likely to be monotypic than polytypic: Itza' have no subdivisions for two-thirds of useful trees (95 of 138) and other useful plants (79 of 119); however, Itza' subdivide the remaining one-third into 217 folkspecifics, 58 varietals, and 4 subvarietals (Atran, Lois, and Ucan Ek' 2004).

Folkspecific taxa are usually labeled binomially, with secondary lexemes. Such compound names make transparent the hierarchical relation between generic species and subordinate folkspecifics, like white oak and mountain robin. However, folkspecifics that belong to generic species with a long tradition of high cultural salience may be labeled with primary lexemes, like winesap (a kind of apple tree) and tabby (a kind of cat). Foreign organisms suddenly introduced into a local environment are often initially assimilated to generic species as folk specifics. For example, the Lowland Maya originally labeled the Spanish pig "village peccary," just as they termed wheat "Castillian maize." Similarly, the Spanish referred to the indigenous pacas and agoutis as "bastard hares," just as they denoted the Maya breadnut tree "Indian fig" (Beltrán [1742] 1859). Over time, as introduced species acquire their own distinctive role in the local environment, they tend to assume generic-species status and, as with most other generic species, are labeled by a single lexeme (e.g., "corn" in American English now refers exclusively to maize). Thus, the original Lowland Maya word for the peccary, $k'ek'en$, now refers exclusivey to the introduced pig, whereas the native peccary is obligatorily marked in the composite expression $k'ek'en(+)che'$ = forest $k'ek'en$."

The subordinate ranks of folkspecific and varietal correspond to ranges of perceptible natural variation that humans are most apt to appropriate and manipulate as a function of their cultural interests. Partitioning into subordinate taxa usually occurs as a set of two or more taxa that lexically contrast along some readily perceptible dimension (color, size, and so on); however, such contrast sets often involve cultural distinctions that language and perception alone do not suffice to explain (Hunn 1982). An example is the Itza' Maya contrast between red mahogany ($chäk[+]chäk-al{\sim}te'$) and white mahogany ($säk[+]chäk-al{\sim}te'$). Red mahogany actually appears to be no redder than white mahogany. Rather, red mahogany is preferred for its beauty because it has a deeper, darker woodgrain than white mahogany. But why "red" as opposed to "white," rather than simply "dark" as opposed to "light"?

A majority of Itza' folkspecifics reflect color contrasts, and the most habitual contrast is between chäk and säk (Atran et al. 2004), despite the fact that distinctions involving "green," "yellow," or "black" may be no less obvious to the naked eye. One interpretation is that use of contrasting color specifics, which almost invariably involve just the five primary colors, is related to the overriding importance of these colors in Maya cosmology (for Lacandón [Lakantun] see Bruce 1968; for Yukatek see Barrera Marín, Barrera Vásquez, and López Franco 1976). In this ancient cosmology, the red east is the true direction of rain and the good life, whereas the white north is the false direction of cold and deception. This is not to deny that color contrasts generally signal perceptible distinctions among folkspecifics. It merely suggests that color perception alone may underdetermine whether, say, "red" versus "white" is really more apparent for a given case than "black" versus "yellow."

Occasionally, an important folkspecific will be further subdivided into contrasting varietal taxa, such as short-haired tabby (cat) versus long-haired tabby (cat), or *ix-chäk[[+]]tzäma'[+](b'u'ul)* = "red *tzäm'a* (bean)" versus *ix-säk[[+]]tzäma'(b'u'ul)* = "white *tzäma'* (bean)." Varietals are usually labeled trinomially, with tertiary lexemes that make transparent their taxonomic relationship with superordinate folkspecifics and generic species. An example is northern red oak versus southern red oak, or *ix-kän[[+]]put-il[+]kaj* = "yellow village papaya" versus *ix-säk[[+]]put-il[+]kaj* = "white village papaya."

Intermediate Taxa

Intermediate levels also exist between the generic-species and life-form levels. Taxa at these levels usually have no explicit name (e.g., rats + mice but no other rodents), although they sometimes do (e.g., felines, palms). Such taxa—especially unnamed "covert" ones—tend not to be as clearly delimited as generic species or life forms, nor does any one intermediate level always constitute a fixed taxonomic rank that partitions the local fauna and flora into a mutually exclusive and virtually exhaustive set of broadly equivalent taxa. Still, there is an evident preference for forming intermediate taxa at a level roughly between the scientific family (e.g., canine, weaver bird) and order (e.g., carnivore, passerine) (Atran 1983; Berlin 1992).

Like folk around the world, Itza' also have a number of relatively stable intermediate categories, both named and unnamed. Such categories may be nested one within the other. For example, the named category of snakes is embedded in the larger unnamed category of squamates (snakes and lizards). In turn, the squamates are embedded in the (unnamed) life form that includes all herpetofauna. Other examples of named intermediate categories include *ch'uuy* (diurnal raptors), *aak* (turtles), *kab'* (bees), *sinik* (ants). A number of intermediates are also polysemously named after protoytpical species: *b'alum* (jaguars in particular, and large felines in general), *juj* (iguanas in particular, and lizards in general), *ya'* (chicle tree in particular and resinous Sapotaceae trees in general), *xa'an* (guano palm and palms in general). In such cases, the intermediate can generally be disambiguated from its prototypical generic species as *uy-et'~ok X* ("companions of *X*") or *u-ch'ib'-al X* ("lineage of *X*"), where *X* is the name of the generic species. Like the named intermediates, unnamed intermediates are usually restricted to locally occurring fragments of biological orders, families, or genera. Examples include Araneida (tarantulas and other spiders), Anura (frogs and toads), Psittacidae (parrots and macaws), Dasypractidae (agoutis and pacas), Meliaceae (mahogany and tropical cedars), and *Annona* (custard apples).

Insofar as they reflect a cognitively biased, phenomenal appreciation of the surrounding environment, taxonomies help to set the constraints on life that make a culture possible. It is little wonder, then, that folkbiological taxonomies tend to be among the most stable, widely distributed, and conservative cognitive structures in any culture. Once set into place, such a structure would likely survive even catastrophic historical upheaval to a clearly recognizable degree. Ancient and contemporary Maya societies would be no exception. Even with the social order and cosmological system sundered, the folkbiological structure would persist as a cognitive basis for cultural survival under three conditions. First, there must be significant biological continuity in the ecological distribution of species. Second, there must be significant linguistic continuity with the dialect that first encoded the knowledge. Third, there must be a sustained interaction between people and living kinds where knowledge of the various species matters.

As we will see, Itza' folkbiology (and that of many other indigenous small-scale societies) fulfills all three conditions, whereas the folkbiology of majority-culture Americans (and that of many other urbanized societies) fails to meet the third condition. The consequences of this failure for knowledge of the biological world and action toward it (environmental management) are dramatic. Let's take a look at some historical evidence on loss of knowledge or at least loss of cultural support for learning about nature.

2.5 Loss of Knowledge and Familiarity with Nature

Despite Western science's historical take-off from universal principles of folkbiology found across cultures, in globally mobile, technologically oriented societies there is a marked deterioration in commonsense understanding of the everyday living world. This impairment affects people's practical ability to sustainably interact with the environment: a person who cannot distinguish one kind of bird or tree from another cannot respond appropriately to changes in the ecological balance among these living kinds. Many recent immigrants to Phoenix, Arizona, cannot identify the pruned eucalyptus trees in their landscaped plots, much less surmise that the nonnative eucalyptus is not conducive to maintaining biodiversity in the face of competition for scarce water. Likewise, few residents of Chicago are able to identify a buckthorn, much less comprehend that a fire can selectively weed out invasive buckthorns without affecting bur oaks and other native prairie tree species.

It is hard to escape the impression that, on an individual and cultural level, knowledge about living kinds is diminishing. As we mentioned earlier, anthropologists studying traditional societies often note with concern the loss of indigenous language and a lessening of knowledge about the natural world (e.g., Diamond and Bishop 1999; Nabhan and St. Antoine 1993; Wester and Yongvanit 1995). In technologically oriented cultures, contact with biological kinds may be so minimal that researchers can demonstrate significant differences in children's biological reasoning as a function of whether they do or do not have goldfish as pets (Inagaki 1990; Hatano and Inagaki 1987).

A survey we conducted at Northwestern University provides some index of what undergraduates know about one domain of biology, namely trees. We provided the names of eighty trees and asked the students to circle the trees they had *heard of* before, regardless of whether they knew anything about them. More than 90 percent said they had heard of birch, cedar, chestnut, fig, hickory, maple, oak, pine, and spruce. But fewer than half indicated any familiarity with alder, buckeye, catalpa, hackberry, hawthorn, honey locust, horse chestnut, larch, linden, mountain ash, sweet gum, and tulip tree—all of which are common to the Evanston area where Northwestern University is located. Of course, these observations by themselves do not implicate a loss of knowledge. It may be that Northwestern undergraduates from a hundred years ago would have proved equally unfamiliar with biological kinds. Nevertheless, such low levels of knowledge are consistent with the possibility that knowledge about trees is declining.

The Devolution Hypothesis

With modernization, it may be that knowledge about living kinds has decreased, or as we will say, *devolved*. We will refer to this possibility as the *devolution hypothesis*. Devolution might result from two kinds of historical change. For one, the shift from rural to urban settings may result in a significant decrease in people's contact with the natural world. This reduced contact could lead to declines in knowledge, but not necessarily: the effects of reduced exposure may be offset by sufficient amounts of indirect experience with the natural world, through a culture's media, talk, and values. We will refer to this kind of exposure as *cultural support*. The idea of cultural support has to do with the degree to which a society promotes a particular area of knowledge. It does not, then, have to do with whether there are specialists who know or care about particular kinds. Rather, it has to do with the extent to which people focus on a domain of knowledge in their everyday interactions. For example, to what extent do parents call children's attention to plants and animals, and when they do so, is their reference to robins, trout, and maples or to birds, fish, and trees? Declines in cultural support, like declines in exposure to the natural world, could lead to devolution.

In the remainder of this section, we summarize our work on the devolution hypothesis with respect to the life-form trees (Wolff, Medin, and Pankratz 1999). Trees are of special interest because they could represent a particularly strong test of the devolution hypothesis. In terms of contact with the natural world, we may not expect devolution with respect to trees at all. While people in urban environments may have only limited exposure to all but a few mammals (e.g., cats, dogs, squirrels), they are likely to have seen many different kinds of trees. And trees, because of their size, are not likely to be ignored. As argued by Hunn (1999), size is a key factor in determining which natural kinds in a culture attract attention and get named. If the prerequisites for conceptual organization consist solely of an inherent curiosity about living kinds and a perceptual system tuned to discontinuities in nature (Berlin 1992), then even urbanized cultures should show an appreciation for different kinds of trees. On the other hand, it is possible, despite continued direct exposure to trees, that knowledge about them has devolved because cultural support for trees has declined.

Measuring Cultural Support

Cultural support may take a variety of forms, many of which may be difficult to measure, especially across time. Nevertheless, we are likely to have a pretty good measure of cultural support in terms of what people write about. Are people writing about plants and animals as much as they used to? When they do so are they writing at the life-form level (e.g., bird, tree) or the folk-generic level (sparrow, oak)? Not only are written records available, but these records are accessible in online databases that permit automated search. To the extent that there have been historical changes in the amount and specificity of discussion of biological kinds across a representative sample of sources, we have evidence for the changes in the cultural support for learning about the natural world. Note that this measure of cultural support is likely to be a conservative measure of what people may know. An author might write about noticing cottonwoods along a riverbank without being able to pick a cottonwood out of a biological lineup. The use of writing as a measure of what people know is therefore likely to overestimate the knowledge of an average citizen, hence underestimate devolution. By the same token, if changes are found, they are most likely to be historically significant.

Oxford English Dictionary (OED)   Because our interest is in a longer time span than U.S. written history affords (in terms of databases we might access), we selected a database from England for study: the OED, a historical dictionary. We chose the OED for a variety of reasons. The OED seeks to capture the evolution of all words in the English language except those that became obsolete before 1150 or are intelligible to only the specialist. The first edition was published in 1933 after nearly seven decades of work. The second edition, the OED2, was published in 1989. It combines the original edition, four supplemental volumes published after 1933, and results from a fourth major reading program.

The dictionary contains approximately 616,500 word forms (Berg 1993; Murray 1989). Definitions for these words are illustrated with quotations from each century of use, with extra quotations provided for significant changes in meaning. The quotations were drawn from a wide range of books, with special emphasis on great literary and scientific works, but also among other things, books of foreign travel, letters of foreign correspondents, magazines, and diaries. The total number of quotations in the OED2, roughly 2.5 million, was drawn from a sample of between 5 and 6 million quotations. Given the breadth of the inquiry, we have no reason to expect that the quotations represent a biased sample with respect to the questions we aim to address. The sample may well be biased in terms of reflecting interests, values, and accessibility, but these sorts of biases are more or less orthogonal to our focus.

Recently, the entire twelve-volume set was retyped into a special computer database format allowing for online searching of all definitions and quotations. The OED online corpus may be searched for any key words (e.g., *tree*, *maple tree*, *maple*, and so on) and search codes may be written such that the date, source, and full quotation context will be returned.

General Predictions   Evidence for devolution may be found with two kinds of measures: (1) the number of quotations referring to trees (including kinds of trees) relative to the total number of quotations associated with a given historical period (we used 100-year blocks for our analyses), and (2) the number of sources (kinds of publications from which the quotes are drawn) relative to the total number of sources associated with a given period. Our first analysis examines the general prediction that if knowledge of trees is devolving, there should be an overall drop in the number of quotes and number of sources across time. A second major analysis examines more specific hypotheses concerning the relative usage of tree terms at different levels of taxonomic organization.

Of course, there may be historical periods of time where cultural support for biological knowledge is increasing (evolution rather than devolution). The predictions here would be more or less reversed. As we will see, our analyses suggest both periods of evolution and devolution. Before turning to specific procedures, we first state our assumptions about levels of specificity and identify potential problems that may arise with analyses such as ours.

Methodological Issues

Threats to Validity   There are five general concerns associated with using texts to assess change across time. One problem involves changes in spelling and in naming. For example, our search revealed twenty different spellings of *oak* and twenty-five different spellings of *tree*. Spelling consistency only became fairly uniform in the nineteenth century. Obviously, one needs to search the corpus for each of the alternative spellings. Likewise, some trees have multiple common names—for instance, in England another name for linden is whitewood. The same prescription holds here.

A second concern is that the results may be affected by the particular meaning of the term being invoked in a quotation. For example, the term *pine* can be used to refer not only to a particular kind of tree, but also a particular kind of wood (e.g., pine floor), location (e.g., pine grove), activity (e.g., pine away), or proper name (e.g., the cleaning product, Pine Sol). In the following analyses, only direct references to particular kinds of trees (the first use) were included because it is for these uses that the devolution hypothesis makes the clearest predictions.

A third concern is that the sources for quotes may change across time in a systematically biased manner. For instance, during the age of exploration and colonization, new publications appeared (e.g., the *Australian Journal*) devoted not to life in England, but rather to life in the British colonies. These often include descriptions of the (novel) flora and fauna.

The rise of science also led to technical publications. We decided to omit technical and foreign quotations and focus on what we term *folk quotations*.

A fourth concern is that changes between levels of specificity might be affected by the introduction of new tree terms into the language. Descriptions involving new trees may elicit more attention and favor more specific descriptions. We addressed this and some related problems by selecting a subset of twenty-two tree folk generics that were common from the fifteenth century in English to the present day. Differences between levels of specificity cannot, then, be attributed to the introduction of novel kinds.

A final concern involves possible biases in our sampling of quotations due to the inherent nature of the dictionary, which seeks to include all but the most specialized terms. This means that even low-frequency terms may have entries with a certain number of quotations; thus, the number of quotations within a term's entry may not reflect its actual frequency of usage. For instance, the number of quotations for low-frequency tree terms might be significantly inflated compared to their actual frequency in everyday speech. In practice, however, the OED does not generally include entries for tree terms at the specific level or lower (e.g., pin oak). Nevertheless, to eliminate any chance of quotation inflation, all quotations found in the entry of any tree term were eliminated from the analyses. In other words, all quotations used in these analyses came from entries for other terms.

Other Issues   The use of the OED constrains our focus to England and its associated history of wars, colonialism, and increasing globalization of interests. Our task would have been more straightforward were we able to pick a more insular culture (though insularity of more traditional cultures may be more a myth than a reality). This factor, however, cuts both ways. It is precisely because of England's technological and global orientation that evolution or devolution of folkbiology in that cultural context is of interest. Given the importance often attached to science education, it is only reasonable to ask about the cultural supports for learning about the natural world in a scientifically oriented society.

Analysis 1: Examining the Overall Use of Tree Terms over Time
The purpose of this first analysis was to test the main prediction of the devolution hypothesis: If knowledge about trees is declining, there should be an overall drop in the use of tree terms.

Method   The process of preparing the quotes for analysis had three main phases: (1) abstracting the entries containing quotations, (2) coding the entries, and (3) correcting for uneven sampling in the OED. These three phases are discussed in turn.

Abstracting Entries   In the first phase, quotations containing tree terms were drawn from the OED using Open Text Corporation's PAT search engine. In searching for the word *tree* all alternative spellings were considered (including *trau, traw, tre, tren, treo, treu, treuwum, triu, troue, trow*, as well as, fifteen other spellings). Alternative spellings were obtained through a word's OED entry. In addition to searching for the word *tree* we searched for 22 folk-generic-level tree terms (including all associated 138 alternative spellings). The folk-generic-level tree terms included alder, ash, aspen, bay, beech, birch, cypress, elm, fir, hawthorn, hazel, juniper, laurel, maple, mulberry, myrtle, oak, pine, poplar, sycamore, walnut, and willow. All of these folk-generic tree terms have been in use since the fifteenth century or earlier. The search was limited to singular forms of these terms to avoid the problem of changes in pluralization conventions over time.

Coding Entries   The second phase of preparing quotations for analysis involved coding each entry's source, quotation, and time period. The source of the entry was coded as folk or nonfolk. An entry was considered folk if its source was neither technical (e.g., fruit trees, *Nature*, elementary botany, *Science News*, British plants, *Dictionary of Gardening*) nor foreign (e.g., Jamaica, *New York Times*, Barbados, *Journal of Upper India*, Central America, *Pennsylvania Archives*, African Hunting). Each quotation was coded as either direct or indirect. Only quotes making direct references to trees were included in the analyses.

Correcting for Uneven Sampling   The preface to the OED notes that prior to the 1400s, dialectal differences in the English language were quite pronounced. Hence, words and forms that occurred after 1500 and were dialectal were excluded from the dictionary. These factors led us to choose the late 1400s as a cutoff point for our analyses. Because the most recent quotations in the OED were entered in 1987, we rounded this date down slightly to look at quotations from 1975 back to 1475 in 100-year intervals. In the following analyses, the five resulting time periods are labeled by their median dates of 1525, 1625, 1725, 1825, and 1925.

Results   Our search for tree terms generated a total of 22,319 quotations. An automatic coding of each quotation's source was performed using a

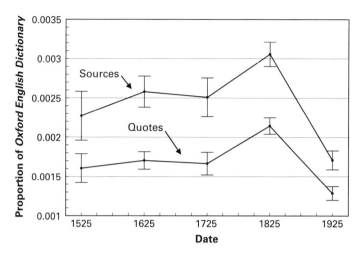

Figure 2.1
Proportion of quotations and sources in the OED referring to trees along with
associated 95 percent confidence intervals.

program that checked lists of 134 foreign and 45 technical sources. The
resulting 15,146 quotations with sources not present on these lists were
roughly equivalent to 900 pages of text and were further analyzed by
hand according to the criteria described in the method section. The resulting 6,548 quotations that both made direct reference to trees and
came from folk sources were roughly 29 percent of the original set of
quotations.

The findings provided strong support for the main prediction of the devolution hypothesis: Cultural support for trees, as measured by the relative number of quotations and sources in the OED, declined markedly in
the last century. As described above, tree counts were analyzed relative to
the estimated number of folk quotations and sources in the OED in order
to eliminate differences due to sampling. Figure 2.1 shows the resulting
proportions for each period of time. The confidence intervals in figure
2.1 represent ranges having a 95 percent probability of covering the true
population values, assuming a binomial distribution.

An examination of figure 2.1 shows that the proportions for quotations
and sources were fairly constant through the sixteenth, seventeenth, and
eighteenth centuries. In the nineteenth century, the relative number of
quotations and sources increased, suggesting that knowledge of tree terms
evolved during this period. However, the gains of the nineteenth century
were completely lost in the twentieth century, which witnessed a striking

decline in both quotations and sources using tree terms. Note that the start of the decline corresponds closely with the start of the industrial revolution. The confidence intervals indicate that the evolution occurring in the nineteenth century and the devolution occurring in the twentieth century are significant. The confidence intervals also indicate that the twentieth-century decline was so great that writing about trees is less extensive now than in any other time in the history of the English language.

The only difference between the two measures seems to occur between the sixteenth and seventeenth centuries: sources indicate evolution while quotations do not. This difference does not change the important conclusion that we can be confident that the observed changes in quotations are not due to an overrepresentation from a particular kind or set of sources. In sum, the findings are perfectly consistent with the idea that there have been periods of evolution and, more recently, devolution in knowledge about trees.

Analysis 2: Examining Tree Terms at Different Levels of Specificity
The same set of quotations used in Analysis 1 was used for an analysis of the specificity or level of quotes. One of the main goals in this analysis was to better understand the observed decline in tree terms in the twentieth century. However, a closer examination of the quotations could also be used to provide further insight into the apparent lack of change existing between the sixteenth and eighteenth centuries and the observed evolution of tree terms in the nineteenth century.

Method   Three levels of organization were coded (figure 2.2). The life-form level ("Life form") was indicated by use of the word *tree*, or one of its twenty-four other spellings. The folk-generic level ("Generic") was indicated by quotations containing one of the twenty-two prechosen tree terms listed in Analysis 1. Quotations demonstrating the folkspecific level contained one or another of the twenty-two prechosen folk-generic tree terms.

Results and Discussion   The findings from this second analysis provide further support for the devolution hypothesis: Cultural support for trees in the twentieth century, as measured by the relative number of quotations in the OED, declined over time for all levels of organization. As in Analysis 1, tree counts were analyzed relative to the estimated number of folk quotations and sources in the OED. Figure 2.2 shows the resulting

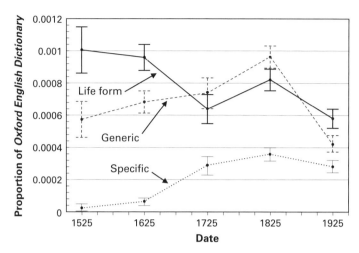

Figure 2.2
Proportion of quotations in the OED for different levels of specificity along with associated 95 percent confidence intervals (after Wolff et al. 1999). Note that before about 1700 folk "generic" terms (e.g. *oak*, *bear*) referred mostly to mono-generic European species, whereas after about 1700 generic terms often referred to polytypic species built around a European type.

proportions for level of specificity in each period of time along with 95 percent confidence intervals. Due to the fact that the proportions for sources and quotations did not differ in their overall patterning, only the proportions for quotations are displayed. The patterns of change shown in figure 2.2 indicate both periods of evolution and devolution. Periods of evolution are indicated by the steady rise in frequency counts between the sixteenth and nineteenth centuries for both the folkgeneric and folk-specific levels and a rise in frequency counts between the eighteenth and nineteenth centuries for the life-form level. As noted in Analysis 1, change seemed to be absent in the period between the sixteenth and eighteenth centuries. In fact, this apparent absence belied significant shifts in the use of different levels of specificity (figure 2.2). The nineteenth century seems to represent the evolutionary climax for knowledge of trees. Talk about trees was both more frequent and at a level of greater specificity than in any other time in the history of English. All this changed in the twentieth century.

Note the interaction between genus and life form in the nineteenth and twentieth centuries. This indicates that the use of genus terms is declining more rapidly than the use of the life-form term, *tree*. In a further analysis we found that the pattern shown in figure 2.2 holds whether the tree term was the topic of the quotation or was incidental to it.

The pattern of frequency counts during the twentieth century is most consistent with devolution. Crucially, the twentieth century is the only century where frequency counts for all levels of organization declined. Thus, in contrast to the shift-in-knowledge hypothesis, an overall drop in tree terms cannot be explained as a drop in the life-form level alone, which masked increases at more specific levels of organization.

Statistical Properties of the OED One potential challenge to the devolution hypothesis is that the observed decline in tree terms in the twentieth century may be a statistical artifact of the OED. Assuming the twentieth century experienced an enormous explosion in new categories, it is certainly possible that talk about any one category may have been diluted. Thus, the apparent decline in the twentieth century may not be due to devolution, but rather to decreased talk about any one thing because there were more things to talk about. This possibility is relatively easy to check. If the twentieth-century decline is due to dilution, similar rates of decline should be observed for categories other than tree categories. If, however, the decline is due to changes in knowledge, rates of decline are likely to vary widely between the categories. To test this possibility, life-form-level terms (or their equivalent) from three other domains were analyzed using the same criteria as used in Analyses 1 and 2. The specific categories analyzed were fish, weapon, and bird. The findings provide further support for the devolution hypothesis. In contrast to the dilution hypothesis, not all the categories declined during the twentieth century. Specifically, quotations referring to the category fish steadily increased from the sixteenth century until the present. This may partially be a function of the fact that *fish* also appears in food contexts. Quotations containing the category weapon slowly declined during the sixteenth to nineteenth centuries and then asymptote during the twentieth century. Changes in the category bird mirrored those of the category tree, but not as dramatically. In sum, because declines in the twentieth century are not inevitable, we can be more confident that the observed declines in tree terms are due to changes in knowledge and not dilution.

Implications The results from this research support the claim that knowledge about trees evolved during the sixteenth to nineteenth centuries and devolved during the twentieth century. We showed that the twentieth century was marked not only by a major decline in frequency in tree terms overall (Analysis 1), but at all levels of specificity (Analysis 2). These twentieth-century declines cannot be explained as simply due to an explosion of categories diluting talk about any particular kind of category. Diluting would predict that all categories should decline, but as indicated by the categories fish and weapon, decline is not inevitable.

What Happens When a Domain Dies?   When a domain devolves, does it reverse the order of its evolution? The answer to this question appears to be a cautious no. When a domain evolves, knowledge of the domain motivates the creation of ever more precise category labels. When a domain dies, it may be that the knowledge of the associated concepts declines faster than knowledge of specific terms. Thus, the language may preserve certain distinctions beyond the time these distinctions are still understood. It is as if knowledge builds up a terminological structure in the language, but when knowledge declines, the structure, like an abandoned building, may remain for a while. In chapter 4 we will describe evidence consistent with this suggestion.

2.6   Conclusions

We have given a great deal of background and perhaps tested your patience. This chapter has provided an introduction to folk and scientific taxonomies, elaborating in detail on the Itza' Maya taxonomic system. The historical review reveals parallel developments—folk conceptions find their way into science because there are certain ways to think and organize nature that are natural. Finally, cultural support for interest in biological kinds appears to be eroding in technologically oriented cultures. This observation sets the stage for many of our findings in chapter 4. But before turning to these findings, we outline our methodology in the next chapter.

3 Study Populations, Methods, and Models

Our choice and interpretation of methods and models is informed by well over a decade of intense ethnographic, ethnolinguistic, and ethnobiological fieldwork by an international team of anthropologists, psychologists, linguists, and biologists. A further goal of this book to provide anthropologists with an example of how experimental methods and quantitative models can be applied to issues of environmental cognition and management that are central to cultural survival. Without quantifiable replicability, dialogue with the larger scientific community—as with most governments and many nongovernmental organizations—is hampered and anthropological information risks becoming marginalized. This book also aims to provide psychology with a demonstration that replicable cross-cultural analyses involving small-scale societies are not only possible but necessary to discovering what is and what is not universal in human cognition.

To set the stage for our discussion, in the next several paragraphs we will briefly describe the main study populations in our research. Consider them as down payments on a more extensive description that will be needed later on.

3.1 Mesoamerican Populations

A key focus of our work concerns three cultural groups in the same municipality in Guatemala's Department of El Petén: native Itza' Maya, Spanish-speaking immigrant Ladinos, and immigrant Q'eqchi' Maya. Itza' and Q'eqchi' were each circumscribed by entirely overlapping and perfectly redundant criteria of proximity of residence, ethnic self-identification, and a multigenerational history of pervasive family interconnections. The Q'eqchi' were also identified by their mother tongue. The Ladino population was initially circumscribed by proximity of residence, language (Spanish), ethnic self-identification, and lack of a communitywide history of family interconnections. In addition, members of each community readily and distinctly identified the group affiliation of members of the other communities. This initial circumscription of cultural groups obviously relied on commonsense conceptions of cultural differences, but our analyses and subsequent findings were not bound by these initial selection criteria (see observations on circularity in cultural research in section 8.4).

In all three groups, men are primarily occupied with practicing agriculture and horticulture, hunting game and fish, and extracting timber and nontimber forest products for sale. Women mainly attend to household gardening and maintenance. One notable difference in childrearing, however, is that there are no orphans to speak of among the Itza' as households in the community invariably adopt parentless children, whether relatives or not. The climate is semitropical, with quasi-rainforest predominating (tropical, dry forest or hot, subtropical, humid forest). Topographic and microclimatic variation allow for a dramatic range of vegetation types over relatively small areas, and sustaining both this diversity and people's livelihood over the last two millennia has required correspondingly flexible agroforestry regimes (Atran, Lois, and Ucan Ek' 2004; Sabloff and Henderson 1993).

Native Itza' Maya

The Itza', who ruled the last independent Maya polity, were reduced to corvée labor after their conquest in 1697 (Atran, Lois, and Ucan Ek' 2004). San José was founded as one of a handful of "reductions" for concentrating remnants of the native Itza' population (and fragments of related groups). In 1960, the military government opened Petén (which includes 35,000 km², about one-third of Guatemala's territory) to immigration and colonization. In the following years, about half the forest cover of Petén was cleared. Supported by a debt-for-nature swap, Guatemala's government set aside remaining forests north of 17° 10' latitude as a Maya Biosphere Reserve in 1990. The San José municipality now lies within the Reserve's official "buffer zone" between that latitude and Lake Petén Itza' to the south. Today San José has some 1,800 habitants, about half of whom identify themselves as Itza', although only older adults speak the native tongue (a Lowland Mayan language related to Yukatek, Mopan, and Lakantun).

Immigrant Ladinos

The neighboring settlement of La Nueva San José was established in 1978 under jurisdiction of the Municipality of San José. The vast majority of households (about 600 people) are Ladinos (native Spanish speakers, mainly of mixed European and Amerindian descent), most of whom were born outside of Petén. The majority migrated to the area in the 1970s as nuclear families stemming from various towns in southern Guatemala.

Q'eqchi' Maya Immigrants

The hamlet of Corozal, also within the Municipality of San José, was settled at the same time by Q'eqchi' speakers, a Highland Maya group from the Department of Alta Verapaz, just south of Petén. Q'eqchi' filtered in as nuclear families, migrating in two waves that transplanted partial Highland communities to Corozal: (1) directly from towns in the vicinity of Cobán (the capital of Alta Verapaz), and (2) indirectly from Alta Verapaz via the southern Petén town of San Luis (home to a mixed community of Q'eqchi' and Mopan Maya). Q'eqchi' immigration into Petén began as early as the eighteenth century, though massive population displacement into Petén is recent. Although many of the nearly 400 Q'eqchi' of Corozal understand Spanish, few willingly converse in it. Q'eqchi' is not mutually intelligible with Itza'. To help understand results with Lowland Q'eqchi' immigrants, we also studied a native Highland Q'eqchi' group.

Native Highland Q'eqchi'

Studies with Highland Q'eqchi' from Aldea Paapa in the Cobán region of Alta Verapaz, Guatemala, focused on the issue of whether Q'eqchi' immigrants arrive in Petén with a cognitive model that is already impoverished with respect to knowledge of species relationships, or whether they are simply unable to use richer Highland models because these are inappropriate to Lowland ecology.

Native Lacandon (Lakantun) Maya

Studies with the Lacandon Maya, whose agroforestry practices closely resemble those of the Itza', were mainly concerned with intergenerational change among adult generations living in the community of Mensäbäk in Chiapas, Mexico.

Yukatek Maya Children

Yukatek Maya were chosen as subjects because of their close linguistic and cultural connection with our well-studied Itza' population, and because there are thousands of Yukatek-speaking children but no more children who speak Itza' as their first language. Most 4- or 5-year-olds are monolingual (Maya). Older children have begun learning Spanish in Mexican schools. Most adults have acquired Spanish as a second language. Our work was conducted among rural farming families in south-central Quintana Roo (particularly in the village of Xk'opchen) and central Yucatán (particular the village of Pixoy).

3.2   North American Populations

It has also been helpful to collect data from a number of U.S. populations. When we began to study folkbiology with the standard undergraduate populations it soon became clear that the typical college student knows very little about plants and animals. Consequently we sought out a variety of other U.S. populations. There is also evidence that urban and suburban children may have relatively impoverished experience with nature (compare Stross 1973 on Maya children's knowledge and naming of plants with Dougherty 1978 on Berkeley children) and, therefore, our developmental studies also involved several different groups.

Undergraduates
This sample consists of students taking introduction to psychology at major research universities in the Midwest. They come from all over the United States.

Biology "Experts"
This category includes diverse groups with distinct kinds of expertise: bird watchers, fishing experts, parks maintenance workers, landscape architects, and professional taxonomists. They typically had at least twenty years experience in their occupation or avocation.

Native American Menominee

Adults   The Menominee ("Wild Rice People") are the oldest continuous residents of Wisconsin. There are 4,000 to 5,000 Menominee living on tribal lands in and around three small communities. As in the past, the reservation is heavily forested. Hunting and fishing are important activities for most adult males and for many females. Education is an important value and there are two tribal colleges on the reservation.

Children   The Menominee children attend either a county elementary school in Keshena, Wisconsin, or a BIA-funded (but tribally managed) tribal school in Neopit, Wisconsin. Keshena and Neopit are the two largest towns on the Menominee reservation; Menominee Tribal Enterprises—responsible for managing the forest—is in Neopit and the main tribal offices are in Keshena. Although Menominee children tend to know some Menominee words, especially those for clan animals, they are basically monolingual English speakers (though there are vigorous efforts underway to restore the language, and the tribal school includes classes in the Menominee language).

Rural Majority Culture

Adults   Adjacent to the Menominee reservation is Shawano County, which consists of farmland, small forest plots (typically 40–80 acres), and numerous lakes and rivers. Hunting, fishing, water recreation in the summer, and snowmobiling in the winter are popular activities. Our adult participants came from in and around the community of Shawano, Wisconsin.

Children   The majority-culture children attended an elementary school in Shawano. About 20 percent of the children live on farms. As in the case of the Menominee children, it is not uncommon for preschool children to be introduced to fishing.

Urban Children

The urban children came either from Boston or Chicago. The Boston, Massachusetts, school is located in East Boston and serves a middle-class community. The Chicago school is a magnet school and serves a diverse population, most of whom are middle-class. For some comparisons we interviewed parents of these children.

3.3   Logic of Cross-Cultural Comparison

Our claims concerning folkbiology rely heavily on comparative research, typically within and across cultures. But one cannot begin to conduct this type of research without making a series of methodological and conceptual commitments.

   One reason comparative research has not been popular is that it is not always clear how to do it successfully. When one compares two groups and finds clear differences, interpretative problems quickly emerge. Which of the many ways in which the two groups differ are crucial? For example, in a study we will later go into in some detail, López et al. (1997) found that U.S. undergraduates and Itza′ Maya of Guatemala showed different patterns of responding on a reasoning task involving mammals.

Although this finding undermines the universality of the particular reasoning phenomenon, the two groups differ in myriad ways (e.g., age, education, literacy, livelihood, language, cosmology, and so on). Which of these differences matter? Practically speaking, it may be impossible to disentangle these various factors. Suppose we could control for age, education, literacy, and the like in comparing Itza′ Maya and undergraduates. How do we decide which variables represent "culture" and therefore should not be controlled, and which variables do not and must be controlled? The Itza′ Maya practice agroforestry and also hunt and collect plants in the forest. Should these factors be controlled or are they part of Maya culture?

Now suppose we control for every variable we can think of and still find differences. In this case, it seems that one is more or less forced to reify or essentialize culture. That is, the only explanation of the cultural difference would involve appealing to some abstract notion of "culture." In short, it seems we may be caught between two equally undesirable possibilities: one is to end up with a notion of culture that solely has recourse to circular explanations of differences ("the Itza′ are different because they are Itza′"). The other is to conclude that cultural comparisons just represent confounded experiments and that the notion of culture is not needed once proper experimental control is achieved.

Another problem associated with comparative research is the issue of sampling. If we want to know how the Itza′ categorize and reason, it seems that we had better take a random sample of Itza′, or else our results may not generalize to the Itza′ population as a whole. But the sample used by López et al. (1997) consisted of Itza′ Maya elders who speak Itza′ Maya. That fact alone makes the sample unusual and unrepresentative because Itza′ Maya is a dying language; the "typical" Itza′ speaks mainly Spanish. How can one justify nonrandom sampling? In what follows, we describe our methodological strategy for cultural comparisons.

3.4   Triangulation as a Research Strategy

There is no theoretically neutral way to define culture. We have just suggested that the idea that culture is whatever is left when all potentially confounding variables are controlled is self-defeating. Granted, it is useful to control for variables that are clearly irrelevant to culture, but one must bear in mind that decisions about what is irrelevant are necessarily theory-based and commit one to a particular notion of culture.

The general idea of triangulation is to use observations from a third group to get at least modest leverage for understanding initial-group differences. The third group should resemble the first group in some potentially important ways and the second group in other ways. If the third group performs like one of the groups and different from the other group, then the variables shared by the third group and the group it mimics become candidates for critical variables. Not to get ahead of our story, but in the case of the Itza'-undergraduate comparison we found a third group that was similar to the U.S. undergraduates in many ways and to the Itza' in just a few, and on the same task the third group performed just like the Itza'. This immediately rules out factors like income, age, and language as responsible for the difference.

At first glance, it might appear that the triangulation strategy is just a 2×2 design with one cell missing. But a 2×2 design presumes what the triangulation strategy is intended to discover, namely, which factors are crucial to group differences. The logic of triangulation implies compression of any number of possible 2×2 designs that together entail a host of possible explanations for group differences. Instead of 2^N controlled designs, each of which allows inference to a single factor, a carefully chosen third group deliberately confounds a number of variables. By carefully choosing a third group, C, that resembles the first group, A, in a number of ways and the second group, B, in a number of other ways, one can assess the relative importance of the set of culturally confounded variables by which C differs from A versus those by which C differs from B.

Purposive (Nonrandom) Sampling

Cultural values, beliefs, and behaviors are not static but relentlessly develop, dissolve, merge, and mutate. Nonetheless, it seems sensible to look for sharp contrasts by means of selecting subpopulations that have retained more traditional knowledge. These considerations lead one to employ sampling techniques most likely to reveal cultural differences rather than focusing on estimating population parameters. Consider again the López et al. studies with the Itza' Maya. Younger Itza' might have notions of biology that differ from those of Itza' elders, differences that reflect assimilation to "Western culture." Thus a random sample may tend to hide rather than reveal cultural differences. Instead of randomly selecting participants, López et al. restricted their sample to Itza'-speaking Maya as the best representatives of Itza' culture. It is not that there was some pure Itza' culture in the past that nowadays is being degraded—cultural change is a constant. Itza' cultural life is a rich blend of ideas and habits stemming from different inputs, including a great deal of Spanish influence. A random sample is only appropriate when one wants to make claims about population parameters, something that we believe is rarely relevant in cultural comparisons.

Cross-Cultural but Culturally Sensitive Methodogy

The streets of unfortunate cross-cultural comparisons are strewn with studies that began with methodologies developed in the United States and then rigidly applied to other populations of interest. It is very important to be sensitive to the potential for cultural misunderstandings arising from task instructions and interpretation. This threat can be substantially reduced through careful pretesting informed by ethnographic, ethnohistorical, ethnobotanical, and ethnolinguistic preparation.

For example, broad cross-cultural agreement in biological categorization should not conceal the fact that different elicitation procedures may yield different patterns of taxonomic or ecological sorting. Thus, in pretests with Itza', we asked them to sort things most "similar" (*b'ay*) or "alike" (*je-b'ix*) to replicate as closely as possible instructions given to American subjects (e.g., Boster and Johnson 1989). Initial results were discouraging: consensus across participants was low, and informants seemed to justify sorts by often idiosyncratic and conflicting notions of use (e.g., horses and cows are more similar to one another than to tapirs because tapirs do not carry loads; tapirs and cows are more similar to one another than to horses because horses are not eaten at festivals).

But ethnohistory indicates that the expression of a deeper taxonomic reasoning endures over time (Trager 1939; Bartlett 1940). Thus, sixteenth-century Itza' taxonomically assimilated the horse (a perissodactyl) by identifying it as a kind of tapir (the only native perissodactyl) (Landa 1985 [1566]). Itza' still attach the same name to the horse (*tzimin*) and tapir (*tzimin∼che'* = forest *tzimin*), although they are maximally distant by functional criteria: the former is terrestrial, domestic, and inedible; the latter is aquatic, wild, and edible. Interviews reveal that Itza' consider the tapir and horse to be "companions by nature" (*et'∼ok*, "go together"). This proved the key to asking Itza' to sort items that "go together by nature," which yielded taxonomies resembling those found in cultures the world over (López et al. 1997). By contrast, there was no significant difference in the performance of American students asked to sort items that "go together by nature" or as being "most similar."

Similar sorts of analyses and pretesting accompanied preparation of all of our instructions. One advantage of tailoring instructions to a variety of nonstandard populations is that they can be further applied to other populations with greater ease and confidence than if they had been simply translated from instructions given to undergraduates or other groups affiliated with large research universities and urban environments in the United States. Moreover, we have found that the instructions so pretested usually can be successfully reapplied to standard populations. We turn now to an important methodological tool, the cultural consensus model.

3.5   The Cultural Consensus Model

It obviously will not do to just assume that everyone in a given cultural group thinks exactly the same way. We need to be sensitive to the presence of multiple understandings within a group (and across groups). To provide a methodological grounding for our comparisons, we have relied extensively on the cultural consensus model (CCM) of Romney, Batchelder, and Weller (1986). The CCM is an important tool for analyzing commonalities and differences within and across cultural groups and has been used as an effective tool by cognitive anthropologists (e.g., Romney and Batchelder 1999; Romney et al. 1996; Moore, Romney, and Hsia 2000).

Before describing this model in detail, a general note of caution is in order. The CCM does not prescribe which ideas should be studied, any more than statistical tests such as analysis of variance dictate which variables should be measured. It is not a theory of culture or of the cultural transmission of information. It is only a tool that can be used to evaluate such theories.

The CCM assumes that widely shared information is reflected by a high concordance among individuals. When there is a single cultural consensus, individuals may differ in their knowledge or "cultural competence." Estimation of individual competencies is derived from the pattern of interinformant agreement on the first factor of a principal-components analysis (essentially factor analysis). These competency scores should not be mistaken for scores of expertise. The cultural model provides a measure of culturally shared knowledge and hence the levels of competencies measure the extent to which an individual shares what everyone else agrees on.

The CCM has many important uses. For instance, it can establish that a consensus is indeed present. A statistically reliable difference across two groups may not be meaningful or may be misinterpreted unless one first demonstrates a within-group consensus. The CCM can also be extremely useful in the analyzing the basis of cross-group and even within-group differences. But we are getting ahead of ourselves again. First we will describe a few technical details and then we will try to make the ideas more intuitive.

There are three standard assumptions of the CCM: (1) each item has a (culturally) "correct" answer (items are dichotomous), (2) items are conditionally independent, and (3) each respondent has a fixed competence over all questions (i.e., the items are homogeneous). Batchelder and Romney have analyzed the effects of relaxing these axioms or assumptions in a number of subsequent publications (e.g., Batchelder and Romney 1989; Romney, Batchelder, and Weller 1986; Karabatsos and Batchelder 2003).

Although the CCM is a formal model designed for fixed-format or dichotomous responses, it can also be used as a "data model" for more open-ended responses such as sorting items into a hierarchical taxonomy. In this instance the data consist of a matrix of distances between all pairs of items. The participant-distance matrices are then correlated with each other and represent a measure of the degree to which each participant's taxonomy agrees with every other participant's taxonomy. The participant-by-participant correlation matrix is the input to the principal-components analysis. Assuming that the correlation between two informants' sorting patterns is entirely due to the connection of each of them to the consensus knowledge, the data-model approach creates a quantity in the first factor that is a proxy for consensus knowledge (Batchelder, personal communication, January 2004; see Romney 1998 for further discussion and an application). For interval data, the first factor loading in a principal-components analysis becomes an estimate of how much an individual knows. In other words the data model provides estimates of consensus as the correlation of the individual with the aggregate. This data model is similar to reliability theory with the role of individual and item reversed, and produces an insignificant reliability overestimation compared to the formal model. This is because an item in the formal model is supposedly correlated with the cultural "truth," whereas an individual in the data model is correlated with an aggregate including that individual (Romney, personal communication, 1995; see also Romney, Batchelder, and Weller 1986).[1]

A cultural consensus is found to the extent that the data overall conform to a single factor solution (the first latent root is large in relation to all other latent roots) and individual scores on the first factor are strongly positive. Of course, general agreement may be coupled with systematic disagreement and the CCM is an effective tool for uncovering both shared and unshared knowledge.

Basically, the CCM allows one to see if it is reasonable to assume that there is a single consensus or "cultural truth" among some sample of informants for some set of probes. The more people agree with each other, the more evidence one has for a single consensus. In the case of an existing consensus, the CCM justifies the aggregation of individual responses into a "cultural model." The CCM gives an estimate of the levels of agreement among the informants. Therefore, it is possible to use this model to explore agreement patterns both within and across different populations, the latter describing potential "metacultural" models. This promotes exploration of possible pathways of learning and information exchange within and between cultural groups, illuminating more general processes of cultural formation, transformation, and evolution.

Another desirable characteristic of the CCM is that degree of agreement can be used to determine the minimum sample size needed to estimate the cultural consensus within some range of tolerance. In some of our studies as few as ten informants are needed to reliably establish a consensus.

If there are subgroups within some sample that have different knowledge, values, or beliefs, the CCM typically can detect this fact, either through the absence of an overall consensus or by means of looking at "residual agreement." The analysis of residual agreement allows one to see if members of a subgroup agree with each other more than one would expect based on the overall consensus.

The CCM is also an effective tool for examining within- and across-group differences. For example, Boster (1986a) found that among the Aguaruna Jívaro (Ashuar) people there was a shared cultural model for the identification of various varieties of manioc and that deviations from this shared model were related to membership in kin and residential groups (that is, agreement within these groups is higher than what one would predict on the basis of the overall cultural model).[2]

Here is a brief summary of the technical details. After the consensus parameters are estimated for each individual, the expected agreement between each pair of subjects is generated (as the product of their respective consensus parameters). Next, the expected agreement matrix is subtracted from the raw agreement matrix to yield a matrix of deviations from expected agreement (see Hubert and Golledge 1981). If raw and residual agreement are significantly associated, then a significant portion of residual agreement consists of deviations from the consensus. One can then explore other factors (e.g., cultural subgroups, social network distance), which might predict or explain the residual agreement.

Another marker for reliable residual agreement is when an analysis over two or more groups reveals systematic differences in factors beyond the first. If two groups differ in their second factor scores, then within-group agreement extends beyond the overall consensus. For example, Medin et al. (1997) asked tree experts to sort local species of trees and found a clear overall consensus, coupled with second factor scores correlating strongly with occupation (e.g., parks maintenance, taxonomist, landscaper). Subsequent comparisons revealed systematic differences in the basis for sorting across groups.

Our method of modeling cultural consensus allows us to avoid synthetic interpretations of people's thoughts and actions (as part of this or that "culture") and to describe emergent cultural patterns derived statistically from measurements of individual cognitions and behaviors. Rather than merely assuming cultural consensus from statistical reliability, we impose additional conditions that allow us to identify and demonstrate patterns of consensus more precisely (e.g., aggregated folktaxonomies) so as to better make independent predictions about a population (e.g., use of taxonomy to generate biological inferences).

Once cultural differences are found, we can proceed to ask a series of more analytic questions about things like the following: (1) Are these ideas spread by means of abstract models and inference strategies or is the information conveyed in quite literal, concrete form? (2) Do factors like income or occupation or density of social networks or a variety of other input conditions moderate cultural differences (either within or between groups)? Within the present framework the goal in studying variation is to have a theory about the distribution of ideas and flow of information, not to isolate some (magical, reified) entity, "culture."

3.6   Summary

With these sampling and methodological issues as background, we are ready to turn to our research framework and the associated empirical studies. To preview, we argue that there are strong, universal constraints on how people organize their local knowledge of biological kinds. These evolutionary constraints form a "learning landscape" that shapes the way inferences are generalized from particular instances or experiences. In some cases it produces consensus even though specific inputs vary widely in richness and content. Thus, many different people, observing many different exemplars of dog under varying conditions of exposure to those exemplars, may nonetheless generate more or less the same concept of *dog*. In other cases, especially involving groups having little direct contact with the natural world, we find striking group differences. The patterning of universal and experience-dependent performances not only reveals the texture of the folkbiological module but also brings into relief the cognitive consequences of diminished contact with nature.

4 Devolution and Relative Expertise

Earlier we described several principles of folkbiology that are plausible as products of evolutionary processes. Before we turn to our experiments, some additional amplifications and clarifications are in order. We hypothesize a folkbiological system (FBS) of the human mind that discriminates and categorizes parts of the flux of human experience as "biological," and develops complex abilities to infer and interpret this core cognitive domain.

In a general sense, there is nothing different about FBS—in terms of innateness, evolution, or universality—from the visual system (VS) or any other evolved cognitive system (see Chomsky 2000). FBS is no more (or less) "autonomous" from the surrounding social environment, or from other mental systems, than VS is detachable from surrounding light and object patterning or from other physical systems (including linguistic and other cognitive systems of meaning; Marr 1982). In this chapter we develop and review criteria for modularity and apply them to folkbiology.

How FBS combines with local environmental conditions and cultural history to produce people's actions on the environment is the subject of chapters 7–9. How FBS interfaces with folkpsychological (Carey 1995) and folkmechanical (Au and Romo 1999) systems is a subject of current controversy in developmental and cognitive psychology. There is a substantial body of information on perceptual triggering conditions for attributions of animacy (e.g., Heider and Simmel 1944; Premack 1990; Bloom and Veres 1999; Csibra et al. 1999); however, there is only sparse and scattered work on how groups of animals and plants are assigned causal properties (by perceptual analyzers or otherwise) that distinguish them (e.g., as group essences) from inert objects on the basis of perceptual cues and mechanical indicators of boundary and movement. Therefore, we have little to say about the interface between folkbiology and folkmechanics. In contrast, ever since Carey's (1985) pioneering studies, the relation between folkbiology and folkpsychology has come under intense experimental scrutiny (Keil 1989; Gelman and Wellman 1991; Inagaki and Hatano 1993). We will take up this issue in chapter 5.

4.1 Evolutionary Context

Our present knowledge of evolutionary mechanisms and history is generally too poor to generate causal explanations of cognition. Often, evolutionary accounts are mere consistency arguments—"just-so stories"— that lack evidentiary standards for ruling out indefinitely many contrary evolutionary scenarios (Atran 2002). There have been more constrained evolutionary accounts of higher-order cognitive functions specific enough to motivate competing and informative research (e.g., Pinker and Bloom 1990; Cosmides and Tooby 1992). So far, however, these accounts may do little more than retrodict findings generated independently of any evolutionary considerations (e.g., Hauser, Chomsky, and Fitch 2002; Sperber, Cara, and Girotto 1995).[1] At the same time, we hope to illustrate how evolutionary argument can be useful—even if not necessary— to progress in the field. A factor motivating our experiments, and our interpretation of them, is evolutionary plausibility. We do not claim that evolutionary arguments have explanatory value here, but they may have important heuristic value.

Humans and their ancestors undoubtedly depended for their survival on intimate interaction with plants and animals, which likely required anticipatory knowledge of at least some plant and animal *species*. This makes it likely (but not necessary) that adaptations for special dealings with plants and animals evolved, and, further, that they evolved in a manner somewhat independent of adaptations for dealings with other people. For example, identification and categorization is different for humans, on the one hand, and for animals and plants, on the other. There are cognitive mechanisms primarily dedicated to tracking humans as individuals, such as facial recognition (e.g., Carey and Diamond 1977; Diamond and Carey 1986), syntactic and semantic structures of pronominalization and proper naming (Balogh, Swinney, and Tigue 1998; Arnold et al. 2000), social game strategies (Axelrod 1985; Nowak and Sigmund 1998), and so forth. For animals and plants, the default recognition strategies are focused at the collective, species level (individualization of pets involves anthropomorphic extensions of person-identification strategies). From an evolutionary vantage point, it hardly would matter *which* member of a plant or animal species a person could eat or be eaten by, but it would matter greatly *who* in particular a person could mate, fight, or cooperate with (Eldredge 1986). One implication of this analysis for folkbiological cognition is that results focused at the level of individuals do not necessarily carry over to studies at the level of species, and vice versa.

4.2 Biology as a Module of Mind

To say an evolved biological structure is "innate" is not to say that every important aspect of its phenotypic expression is "genetically determined." Biologically poised structures "canalize" development, but do not determine it—like mountains that channel scattered rain into the same mountain-valley river basin (Waddington 1959).

As outlined at the beginning of chapter 2, the human taxonomic system for organizing species appears to be found in all cultures (Berlin, Breedlove, and Raven 1973; Atran 1990).[2] It entails the conceptual realization that, say, apple trees and robins belong to the same fundamental level of (folk)biological reality, or *rank*, and that this level of reality differs from the subordinate level that includes winesap apple trees and mountain robin as well as from the superordinate level that includes trees and birds.

Different kinds of nonbiological categories may conform more or less well to a hierarchy (many social categories do not) and people may, at least in a weak sense, essentialize all categories (see Rips 1995). But a system of taxonomic ranks is not simply a hierarchy, and it is less clear that there is anything corresponding to a cross-culturally stable sense of teleological essences for nonbiological kinds (for an attempt to rank artifacts, see Brown et al. 1976; for opposing arguments, see Atran 1987; for findings contrary to attributions of essences to artifacts, see Sloman and Malt 2003).

We hypothesize that there is a naturally selected set of cognitive processes targeted on the biological world, which we call a "biological module" of the mind. This biological module is responsible for generating folkbiological taxonomy under appropriate experience. The empirical specificity and scope of taxonomic categories, and the inductive use to which taxonomic structures are put, vary with people's degree of exposure to the biological world and with their cultural background.

Modules
Different cognitive scientists have offered alternative and sometimes conflicting notions of modules, so we will take a few paragraphs to say what

we mean by modules. We consider that there are roughly two classes of evolved cognitive modules: perceptual modules and conceptual modules. A *perceptual module* has automatic and exclusive access to a specific range of sensory inputs, has its own proprietary database, and may not draw on information produced by other conceptual modules or processes. A perceptual module is usually associated with a constrained neural architecture, and fast processing that is not accessible to conscious awareness. Examples may be modules for facial recognition, color perception, identification of object boundaries, and morphosyntax (Fodor 1983).

A *conceptual module* works on a privileged, rather than strictly proprietary, database that is provided by other parts of the nervous system (e.g., sensory receptors or other modules), and that pertains to some specific cognitive domain (Atran 1990, 285). Examples include folkmechanics, folkbiology, and folkpsychology.[3] The argument for conceptual modules—as in the case of folkbiology—involves converging evidence from a number of venues. We list them here and discuss them after describing the associated empirical studies: functional design (Pinker 1997; Atran 1998), ethology (Cerella 1979; Herrnstein 1984; Brown and Boysen 2000), universality (Berlin, Breedlove, anad Raven 1974; Brown 1984; Atran 1990), precocity of acquisition (Stross 1973; Dougherty 1979; Hatano and Inagaki 1999), independence from perceptual experience (Gelman and Wellman 1991; Atran et al. 1997; Sousa, Atran, and Medin 2002), selective cerebral impairment (Sartori and Job 1988; Caramazza 2002), resistance to inhibition (hyperactivity), and cultural transmission. None of these criteria may be necessary, but presence of all or some is compelling, if not conclusive.

The sort of cultural information that is most susceptible to modular processing is the sort of information most readily acquired by children, most easily transmitted from individual to individual, most apt to survive within a culture over time (provided adequate input and cultural support), and most likely to recur independently in different cultures and at different times. Critically, it is also the most disposed to cultural variation and elaboration. It makes cultural variation comprehensible.

Our burden of proof is to show that the above analogy forms a meaningful pattern rather than a mishmash of vague ideas and speculations. As a guideline and overview, we provide a summary of our central theoretical and empirical claims, along with our assessment of the corresponding state of evidence, in table 4.1. We will return to this table at the chapter's end.

Table 4.1
Empirical and theoretical claims and the status of evidence bearing on them

Claim	Status of evidence
Essentialism is a universal bias.	Inductive generalization over several populations but needs further case studies.
Essence and inductively privileged species (e.g., robin), not life form (e.g., bird)	Appears to hold across a variety of levels; corresponds to generic populations but needs further case studies.
Basis for typicality ratings and typicality effects in reasoning knowledge-dependent and undergraduates are often the "odd group out."	Itza' Maya, bird experts, fish experts, and tree experts differ from undergraduates.
Standard populations (e.g., undergraduates) may use impoverished default categorization and reasoning strategies (e.g., abstract similarity judgments) relative to those used by most of humanity (e.g., content-rich strategies).	Substantial within the domain of folkbiology. An open issue for other domains.
Folkbiology represents an innate module, with coherent variation as a function of culture and expertise.	Framework useful; results only partially predicted in advance.

4.3   Folktaxonomies and Associated Reasoning Processes

Categorization tasks are of independent theoretical interest and self-contained, but they are also designed to provide the inferential framework for category-based reasoning. In this section we focus on models for use of categories in inductive reasoning in general, and biological inference in particular. The empirical phenomena of interest are referred to as typicality and diversity effects in reasoning. To set the stage for our discussion, we briefly review one of the most influential models of induction, the similarity-coverage model (SCM) of Osherson et al. 1990.

An important function of taxonomic classification is enabling generalizations between categories. Osherson et al. (1990), building on previous work by Rips (1975), identified a set of phenomena that characterize category-based inferences in undergraduates, and formalized a model that predicts the strength of those inferences. The model relies on the notion of similarity and similarity relations as a guide to induction.

   Rather than talk about inductive "inferences," Osherson et al. discuss inductive "arguments," in which facts used to generate the inference play the role of premises, and the inference itself plays the role of conclusion. Thus, inferring that all birds have ulnar arteries from the fact that jays and flamingos do, amounts to the argument: jays have ulnar arteries, and flamingos have ulnar arteries, therefore all birds have ulnar arteries. This argument is strong to the extent that belief in the premises leads to belief in the conclusion. For all SCM phenomena, the properties (e.g., have ulnar arteries) are said to be "blank." They are designed such that they do not favor one category over another at the same rank or level. For example, "has ulnar arteries" should be a priori equally likely to be true of jays and flamingos.

   The SCM predicts that the strength of an argument from a premise to a conclusion will vary with the similarity of the premise category to the conclusion category. For example, an inference from cows to horses should be stronger than an inference from squirrels to horses because cows are more similar to horses than squirrels are. The SCM also predicts that typical members of a category will have greater inductive strength than atypical examples for the conclusions about the entire category. For instance, an inference going from bears to all mammals should be stronger than an inference going from mice to all mammals because bears are more representative of the category than are mice. In the terms of the SCM, *bear* provides better "coverage" of the category than does *mice* because bears have greater average similarity to other category members than do mice.

   Diversity also relies on the notion of coverage. Consider the following argument: "Cows and horses get one disease, cows and squirrels get another disease; which disease is more likely to affect all mammals?" López et al. (1997) found that, for arguments like these, undergraduates strongly preferred the pair having the more diverse premises (in this case, cows and squirrels, rather than cows and horses). From the perspective of the SCM the argument with the more diverse premises is stronger because it provides better coverage. Cows and horses are each likely to have greater average similarity to members of the mammal category, but this coverage is redundant—the mammals to which cows are highly similar are the same ones to which horses are very similar. On the other hand, the mammals to which squirrels are similar are different from the ones to which cows are similar. The SCM relies on a measure of *maximal* average similarity and thus is sensitive to the presence of redundancy. Hence, the SCM predicts that diverse arguments will have greater inductive strength.

Of course to test the SCM model, one needs some measure of similarity. There are two problems with the idea of collecting pairwise similarity judgments by asking informants to rate the degree of similarity on some scale. The first is that, for many informants, rating scales may not be meaningful. The second is that the number of judgments required grows geometrically with the number of stimuli. For example, with 44 items, 946 judgments would be needed.

A convenient alternative strategy is to use a sorting technique to derive a metric of similarity. In the López et al. study, which we will take up shortly, participants were asked to sort local mammals into groups, to "put the animals that go together by nature into as many groups as you want." Subsequent sorting into sub- and superordinate categories created a hierarchical taxonomy for each participant, which were then combined to create a group taxonomic hierarchy. The rationale for eliciting such taxonomic hierarchies was to be able to indirectly, but "automatically," compute measures of similarity, typicality, and category coverage from a single cognitive structure. This method also directly links categorization (sorting) with reasoning. If the sorting reflects idiosyncratic or task-specific strategies, then the reasoning data should not be orderly. Thus, in a sense, the sorting and reasoning data are mutually reinforcing.

To justify combining individual sorts into an aggregate cultural taxonomy, López et al. first applied the Romney, Batchelder, and Weller 1986 cultural consensus model to the informant-by-informant agreement matrix for both the Itza' and undergraduate sample. Both groups showed a strong consensus. For undergraduates the similarity relationships were largely organized along the dimensions of size and ferocity, as other researchers have observed (e.g., Henley 1969). Indeed size alone accounted for more than 70 percent of the variance. A multidimensional scaling of Itza' sorting results is shown in figure 4.1. The two-dimensional solution is shown to be considerably less satisfactory and size accounted for only 16 percent of the variance. In addition to morphological similarity, ecological considerations come into play—both the otter, a water mammal, and the bat, an aerial mammal (considered to be a bird by the Itza') are isolated from the other mammals. In short, Itza' sortings were based on many factors and not just size.

With these results in hand, distance in the consensual group taxonomy provides a key measure of similarity. This measure was then used to study category-based inferencing.

Similarity predicts that the stronger inference should be the one where the premise is closest to the conclusion, with "closeness" measured as the

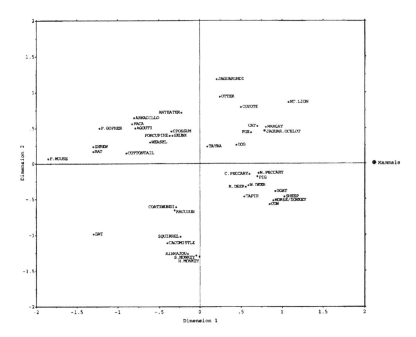

Figure 4.1
Multidimensional scaling of the Itza' taxonomy for local mammals. From López
et al. 1997.

number of nodes in the taxonomic tree (produced by cluster analyses)
that one has to go through to reach the conclusion category from the
premise category. Like similarity, the metric for typicality is also given
by the taxonomy itself, as the lowest average tree distance. Thus, the typicality of a taxonomic item (e.g., a generic species) is the average taxonomic distance of that item to all other items in the inclusive category
(e.g., life form). Finally, diversity is based on the average lowest tree distance between either of the premise categories and the members of the
conclusion category.

    López et al. (1997) used the similarity-coverage model to investigate in-
ductive reasoning about mammals among U.S. college students and Itza'
Maya speakers. Although we found reliable similarity and typicality
effects in both groups,[4] the groups differed markedly in the extent of their
use of diversity, as table 4.2 reveals. U.S. undergraduates demonstrated
powerful diversity effects, whereas the Itza' were reliably below chance
in the selection of arguments with more diverse premises both for mammals and palms.

Table 4.2
Mean number of responses in accord with phenomena, by condition

Phenomenon	(%)	M*	SD	t
American condition				
Similarity	(92)	3.67	0.65	8.86**
Typicality	(94)	3.75	0.45	13.40**
Diversity	(96)	3.83	0.39	16.32**
Itza' condition				
Similarity	(85)	3.42	0.79	6.19**
Typicality	(79)	3.17	1.03	3.93**
Diversity	(38)	1.50	0.91	−1.92

* Maximum score = 4.00; expected value = 2.00.
** $p < .01$.
Source: From Lopez et al. 1997.

Why do many experts and Itza' not show diversity? Consider, first, the Itza'. Their justifications revealed that diseases did not function as blank predicates for the diversity items but instead served as triggers for ecologically based explanations. In many cases, ecological considerations led participants to conclude that the argument with more diverse premises was actually weaker. For example, one Itza' woman favored the argument RAT, POCKET MOUSE / MAMMAL over TAPIR, SQUIRREL / MAMMAL. She argued that tapirs and squirrels are less likely to pass on the disease because they require an ecological agent (a bat biting them) to get the disease in the first place, whereas rats and pocket mice are close enough "companions" that they do not need an ecological agent (a bat biting them) to get the disease.

Ecological considerations also led to diversity-based inductions in a few cases. Thus, a different Itza' informant reasoned, to the contrary, that rats and pocket mice live only where there is corn, sleep above ground, and do not travel in parts of the forest where other animals may catch their disease.

We did a follow-up study with the Itza' using palms as stimuli. Again we did not observe diversity effects. For palms, although similar premises were chosen more frequently than diverse premises, the difference failed to reach significance. Nevertheless, Itza' preference for causally based ecological reasoning was evident here as well. For example, one person favored argument (v) over argument (vi), arguing that because the coconut and the royal palm are tall and treelike, their disease is more able to spread to other palms:

(v)   COCONUT (*kookoj*) & ROYAL PALM (*palmareaal*) / all PALMS (*tulakal uy-et'ok xa'an*)
(vi)   COCONUT (*kookoj*) & BASKET WHIST (*b'äyäl*) / all PALMS

In this case, as in many others, size is indicative of the broader ecological coverage of the forest's canopy. In other instances, ecological considerations again led to diversity-based inductions. For example, one informant accepted (vi) as being stronger than (v) by saying: "Don't you see that the coconut is a big tree and the basket whist clings to it worse than a vine, isn't that so? It can encounter the coconut, climb it and catch the same disease the other has [and give it to the other palms]." In other words, vinelike basket whists can help spread the disease of treelike coconuts to all other palms, whereas the treelike royal palm would presumably contribute little more to the spread of the disease than would the coconut alone. In this example, as in others, the focus seems to be on broader ecological coverage in terms of the vertical, or storied, relationships between forest species rather than in terms of horizontal relationships of broad spatial coverage.

In the absence of a theory—or at least presumption of a theory—of causal unity underlying disparate species, there is no compelling reason to consider a property discovered in two distant species as biologically intrinsic or essential to both. It may make as much or more sense to consider the counterintuitive presence of a property in dissimilar species as the likely result of an extrinsic or ecologically "accidental" cause. For Itza', taxonomic distance can provide one indication of the extent to which ecological agents are likely to be involved in predicting biological properties that do not conform to surface relationships. This may account for negative diversity on some tasks (López et al. 1997). This does not mean that Itza' fail to grasp or use a diversity principle. In justifications, Itza' clearly reject a context-free use of the diversity principle in favor of context-sensitive reasoning about likely causal connections. In tasks designed to assess risk-diversification strategies (e.g., sampling productivity from one forest plot or several), Itza' consistently showed an appreciation of the diversity principle in these other settings (Atran 1995; López et al. 1997).

More generally, what "counts" as a biological cause or property may be somewhat different for folk, like the Itza', who necessarily live in intimate awareness of their surroundings, and those, like American folk, whose awareness is less intimate and necessary. For Itza', awareness of biological causes and properties may directly relate to ecology, whereas for many American folk, the ecological ramifications of biological causes and properties may remain hidden. Historically, the West's development of a worldwide scientific systematics explicitly involved disregard of ecological relationships, and of the colors, smells, sounds, tastes, and textures that constitute the most intimate channels of Maya recognition and access to the surrounding living world. For example, the smell of animal excrement so crucial to Maya hunters, or the texture of bark, so important to their recognition of trees in the dark forest understory, simply have no place in a generalized and decontextualized scientific classification (Atran 1990).

Although the source of these findings on diversity initially was not at all clear (see Atran 1998 and Coley et al. 1999 for more discussion of possible explanations), two candidates are cultural influence and relative expertise. Perhaps diversity is a novice strategy used in situations where more specific knowledge is not available. Alternatively, perhaps it is a result of the emphasis on taxonomic classification in modern Western society.

Our work among U.S. biological experts suggests that neither answer alone will explain the findings. Proffitt, Coley, and Medin (2000) found that groups of U.S. tree experts differ in their use of diversity-based reasoning: taxonomists and landscapers show reliable diversity-based reasoning (albeit nowhere as high as López et al.'s undergraduates), whereas parks workers show below-chance diversity responding much like the Itza'. For example, for a probe where paper birch and river birch get one disease and white pine and weeping willow get another, thirteen of fourteen parks workers picked the disease of the birches as more likely to affect all trees. A typical justification is that birches are very susceptible to disease and are widely planted so there would be many opportunities for the disease to spread.

All three types of U.S. tree experts also frequently used content-based reasoning involving disease mechanisms and ecological diversity, which often led them to choose the less diverse premises (Proffitt, Coley, and Medin 2000). They did this both for predicates involving disease and for those involving enzymes. Apparently the experts thought that ecological factors influence the presence of enzymes (but see Shafto and Coley 2003 for evidence that experts distinguish between different types of predicates in their inferences). This suggests that neither relative expertise nor cultural influence alone determines whether diversity is seen as a viable inductive heuristic.

Interestingly, the tree experts did *not* show typicality effects. Their justifications for typicality probes often appealed to "family size," where family refers not to scientific families but to generic species. This result may indicate the psychological salience of the genus level.

To further test the generality of these findings on typicality and diversity, we tested Itza' on yet other kinds and properties (e.g., "has little things inside"), and we also tested other U.S. expert groups. Let's look at one of these lines of research in further detail.

Triangulating with Birds

Bailenson et al. (2002) studied three populations' categorizing and reasoning about birds. The populations were (1) Itza' Maya elders of Guatemala, (2) U.S. bird experts (bird watchers), and (3) U.S. novices recruited through ads placed on campus at Northwestern University.

The experts were ten men and ten women (mean age = 51 years) having either occupations or extensive experience related to birds. The average number of years spent watching and studying birds (termed "birding" hereafter) was 22 years. On a 7-point continuous scale with 1 indicating "very little knowledge about birds" and 7 indicating "total expertise," the mean self-reported rating for experts was 5.1. Most of them viewed birding as an extremely involving hobby, often dedicating their vacation time to traveling to places where they could find birds that they had never seen before. The novices were eight men and eight women (mean age = 21 years, range: 18–40) who were recruited through the university and paid for their participation. On the 7-point rating scale mentioned above, the mean self-reported rating for our novices was 2.33. The Itza' informants were eight men and two women (mean age = 66). All were bilingual in Itza' and Spanish, although experimental instructions and responses were in the Itza' language. It was assumed that all Maya elders would be experts given their continuous and extensive experience with forest plants and animals. All Itza' were well acquainted with the experimenters, and at relative ease in the session.

The stimulus materials were pictures of Chicago-area U.S. birds as well as pictures of birds of lowland Guatemala. The idea was to see if the experts responded differently to local versus exotic species. Itza' can be thought of as novices with respect to U.S. birds, but they have extensive experience with birds that they may bring to bear with novel bird species.

Each set consisted of full-color illustrations of 104 bird species laminated onto index cards. For the U.S. set, illustrations were taken from the Golden and National Geographic field guides, books designed to aid bird identification. The other set ("Tikal Birds") was taken from the book *The Birds of Tikal* (Smithe 1966). The specific selection of birds was based on the inventory list carried out by the University of San Carlos (Guatemala) for the UN-sponsored Maya Biosphere Reserve.

The structure of the scientific taxonomy representing the U.S. bird set was designed to correspond maximally with that representing the Tikal bird set. The Tikal bird set consisted of thirty families and seventeen orders, while the U.S. bird set consisted of thirty-three families and seventeen orders. One notable difference was in the number of passerines (songbirds) in the two sets. Although passerines are the numerically dominant group both in Chicagoland and Mayaland, they are somewhat more prevalent in Chicagoland. There were some birds and taxonomic groups that were common to both sets (eighteen shared orders, twelve shared families, twelve shared genera, and five shared species).

The first study used the López et al. sorting procedure. Again, we asked participants to sort pictures of local and exotic birds into groups that "go together by nature." The main goal of this study was to compare within- and across-group patterns of sorting. In that regard there are two important questions: (1) Do people within a group agree sufficiently in their sorting that it is sensible to claim that there is a consensual cultural or group model? (2) Are the patterns of sorting reliably different across groups? To address these questions we use the cultural consensus model (CCM), and looked at patterns of residual agreement. If the groups differ, then individuals within a group should agree with each other to a greater extent than is predicted by the overall consensus analysis.

What should we predict concerning agreement across groups and agreement with scientific taxonomy? Based on the work of Boster and his associates, we might expect that novice sortings would correlate highly with scientific taxonomy. Whether the two experts groups show a strong correlation with science should hinge on whether they have specialized goals. Given that the primary goal of birders is to identify birds, we see no reason for expecting that their goals violate the structure of bird taxonomy. Both bird-identification and traditional taxonomic systems are based on morphological similarities and differences. If this analysis is correct, then both U.S. experts and U.S. novices should base their categorization of both U.S. and Mesoamerican birds on the natural or default taxonomy and show good agreement with scientific taxonomy.

It was less clear what to predict the Itza' experts would do. On the one hand, they do have specialized goals with respect to some birds (e.g., hunting them for their meat) but, on the other, our prior work suggested

that they have rich ecological knowledge concerning relationships between particular kinds of birds and both plants and other animals. The
latter observation suggests a general-purpose (default) representation. If
the Itza' have both special-purpose and general-purpose representations,
then we would expect that the special-purpose representation should be
much more evident in their sorting of familiar Mesoamerican birds than
the unfamiliar U.S. birds.

All participants were tested individually. They were told that we were
interested in how they organized their knowledge about birds. First, we
showed them all 104 bird cards one at a time and asked them to name
them "as specifically as possible." Next, all 104 cards were placed in front
of the participant, for the sorting task. As in the López et al. studies, initial sorts were followed by lumping and splitting to produce a hierarchical
taxonomy for each informant.

Results: Naming Accuracy   The naming data are useful in providing an independent index of expertise and relative familiarity with the two picture
sets. We scored each naming response on a 3-point scale, with a 3 representing an exact species match, a 2 representing a correct genus match,
and a 1 representing a match at order or higher (i.e., a "bird" response
was scored a 1). For the Itza' this measure is somewhat conservative in
that, unlike novices, they rarely said "bird" and instead often used intermediate categories such as "flesh-eating bird." The three groups named
all the birds from both stimulus sets except the Itza', who only named
birds from the Tikal set. Experts were more accurate at naming U.S.
birds ($M = 2.55$) than Tikal birds ($M = 1.66$), but novices showed little
difference ($M = 1.25$ for U.S. birds versus 1.14 for Tikal birds). These
results established that the U.S. experts were more familiar with the U.S.
birds than the Tikal birds and that their naming skills were superior to
those of novices for both sets of birds. The Itza' averaged 1.92 for Tikal
birds and were less accurate at naming passerines ($M = 1.39$) than other
birds ($M = 2.11$). Notably, U.S. experts were equally good on passerines
and nonpasserines.

Sorting   Each informant's hierarchical sorting was used to derive a bird-
by-bird similarity (distance) matrix. The lowest level at which two given
birds go together in a folk taxonomy represents the distance between
them. In each condition, the bird-distance matrices produced by each
informant were correlated with each other, yielding a single pairwise

subject-by-subject correlation matrix representing the degree to which each subject's taxonomy agreed with every other subject's taxonomy.

Combined Consensus   We first applied the CCM to the full set of data to see if there was an overall consensus. There was: the ratio of the first factor to other factors was high and accounted for a large proportion of the variance. Although we observed robust overall agreement, this was coupled with reliable group differences. For the U.S. birds all three groups showed significant residual agreement. That is, in sorting U.S. birds, each group's sorts show internal consistency beyond that captured by the consensus across groups. For Tikal birds, there was significant residual agreement for novices and Itza' experts. These results point to differences in the taxonomies produced by each group, which we will take up in detail shortly.

Correspondence to Scientific Taxonomy   To compare performance from each group to science, we used the scientific taxonomy to derive a pairwise bird-by-bird folktaxonomic distance matrix, by calculating the distance between all possible pairs of birds in the taxonomy. We used classical evolutionary taxonomy because it represents a reasonable compromise between similarity-based "phenetic" or numerical taxonomy and theory-based cladistic or phylogenetic taxonomy (see López et al. 1997 for further discussion). We then compared the average matrix from each group to the science matrix.

The mean correlations for each of the groups on the U.S. birds were .38, .60, and .45 for novices, U.S. experts, and Itza' experts, respectively. Note that Itza' sorts agreed more with science than did novice sorts. The mean correlations for each of the groups on the Guatemalan birds were .34, .70, and .61 for novices, U.S. experts, and Itza', respectively. Again, Itza' sorts corresponded more closely with science than did novice sorts. This result is the opposite of the Boster and Johnson 1989 findings for commercial fishermen.

In summary, the data on correspondence with science reveal no evidence that expert sorts deviate more from science than novices. For U.S. experts this result is not surprising in that their primary goal is identifying birds and they often use guides that are organized in a manner concordant with scientific taxonomy. But what accounts for the relatively high Itza' correlation with science? There are two potential explanations that await further research. One is that Itza' interact with birds using multiple goals, which would tend to make a general-purpose representation fairly efficient. The other explanation focuses not on the Itza' but on the novices. Their correlations with science are reliable but quite low, in no case accounting for more than 16 percent of the variance. We take this as evidence that the structure of nature is not nearly so transparent as previous researchers have suggested (or perhaps that the structure of nature is not as transparent in pictures of birds as it is in pictures of fish). It may be that our novices have had so little by way of meaningful interactions with birds that they have failed to learn which aspects, features, or dimensions are most relevant to organizing and classifying birds.

Some evidence provides clear support for the second interpretation. Johnson and Mervis (1998) tested bird experts, fish experts, and novices on a triads task where participants were asked to pick out the two animals that were "most like the same kinds of thing." Some triads pitted overall morphological similarity against taxonomic membership. Not only were bird experts more likely to make the taxonomic choice for birds and fish experts to make the taxonomic choice for fish, but these two types of experts were also substantially more likely than novices to pick the taxonomic choice for the domain where they lacked expertise.

Johnson and Mervis suggested that experts had learned to weight modified parts as much as features more related to overall similarity, in contrast to novices, who apparently gave the latter type of feature more weight. In short, the Johnson and Mervis findings support the idea that some combination of perceptual learning and what they referred to as "intuitive theories" (e.g., understandings of the functional significance for the animal of different features) leads experts to organize biological kinds in a manner closer to scientific taxonomy. Our results are consistent with this general interpretation in that the two groups of experts were clearly using information not reflected in the novice sorts. In short, expertise appears to involve more than a passive reception of real-world structure—it includes learning to attend to the features and relationships that are most informative (see also Boster and D'Andrade 1989), which does not necessary correspond with overall similarity.

Cluster Analysis   One way to generate a visual summary of the similarity relationships among birds is to use what is known as cluster analysis. Cluster analysis is the conceptual equivalent of a group hierarchical taxonomy—similar birds are close to each other and dissimilar birds are far apart. A matrix representing mean pairwise distance between all birds was subjected to cluster analysis, using what is known as the average link method (Sneath and Sokal 1973). The results for nonexperts, experts, and Itza' for U.S. and Tikal birds are summarized in figures 4.2 to 4.7.

The cluster analysis produces a hierarchical taxonomy where examples within a cluster are more similar than examples across clusters. For instance, at the bottom of figure 4.2 one can see a tight cluster (wood duck, common loon, mallard, common merganser, green winged teal, and goldeneye), mostly members of the duck family. The corresponding cluster for the U.S. experts in figure 4.3 includes the black duck, wood duck, green winged teal, and mallard. Note that this cluster adds a duck that belongs to the same genus (*Anas*) and does not include the common loon, which actually belongs to a different order.

For both sets of birds, the three groups showed overall similarity, coupled with systematic group differences. As the figures indicate, for each of the taxonomies there were groups of predators, game birds, water birds, hummingbirds, and woodpeckers, to name a few of the groups. Some notable differences in the taxonomies are as follows. Whereas U.S. novices and U.S. experts generally kept passerines (small songbirds) in a large single group, the Itza' experts had them spread out across the taxonomy in several different clusters.

We also found a difference in subjects' sorting of "water birds." On the U.S. bird set, U.S. experts had a large "water birds" cluster, featuring ducks, grebes, geese, "shore birds," and herons/egrets. This cluster was fairly isolated from the rest of the taxonomy. Although novices also had a water-bird category, it was more spread out, was not as isolated from other birds, and was interrupted by non–water birds, such as gamebirds, nightjars (birds that eat insects while they are flying), the pigeon, and the turkey vulture. This also reduced the correspondence of novice sorts to scientific taxonomy.

Category-Based Induction   As in López et al., we used the data from the sorting study to develop typicality and diversity probes to see how participants used bird categories and salient examples of birds in reasoning. Again the focus was on typicality and diversity. Recall that in the category-based induction model of Oshcrson ct al. 1990, both of these phenomena hinge on coverage.

Given the results from López et al. 1997 as well as Proffitt, Coley, and Medin 2000, we expected that U.S. novices would exhibit more diversity responding than either of the other two groups. It would not be surprising if the U.S. bird experts showed some modest amount of diversity

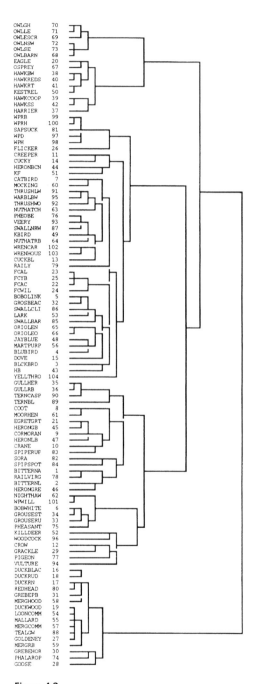

Figure 4.2
Cluster analysis of nonexperts sorting U.S. birds. The numbers next to the bird names correspond to an alphabetic sort of the names.

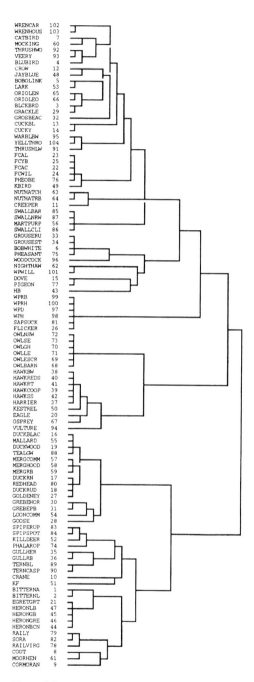

Figure 4.3
Cluster analysis of experts sorting U.S. birds.

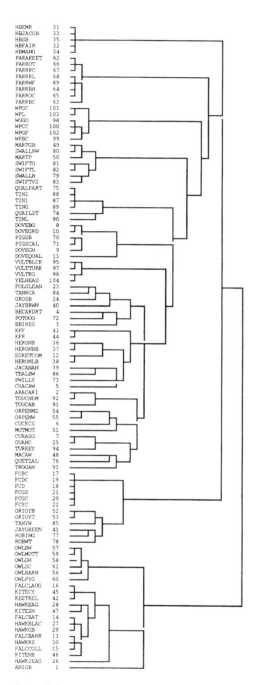

Figure 4.4
Cluster analysis of Itza' sorting U.S. birds.

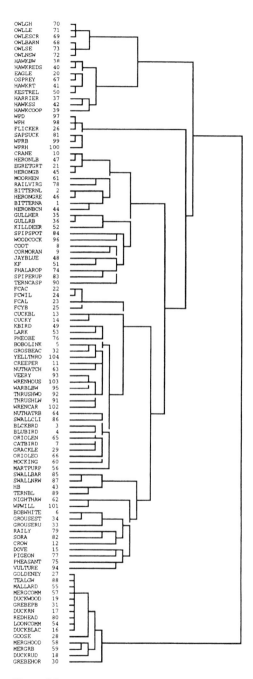

Figure 4.5
Cluster analysis of nonexperts sorting Tikal birds.

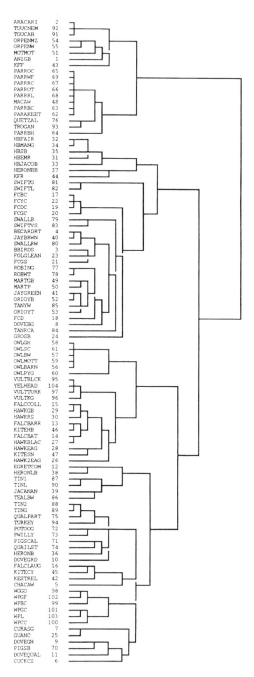

Figure 4.6
Cluster analysis of experts sorting Tikal birds.

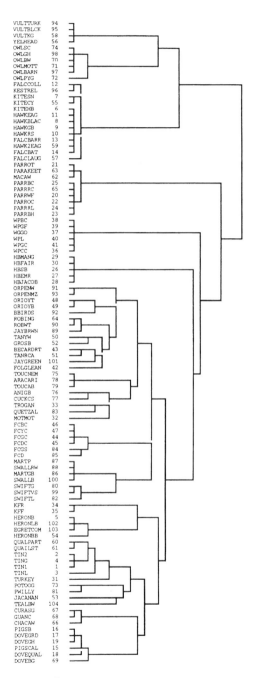

Figure 4.7
Cluster analysis of Izta' sorting Tikal birds.

responding given that they are quite familiar with the scientific taxonomy. Overall, however, our hypothesis was that domain knowledge makes it less likely that a person will employ abstract reasoning strategies. Instead we expected to observe more concrete justifications such as the ecological/causal reasoning.

Properties for Induction   Based on previous work we decided against using identical properties for the Itza' and U.S. induction probes. Half of the probes involved disease and this was constant across groups. For the other half we used "enzyme" for North American subjects and "little things inside" for Mesoamerican subjects. We piloted both terms with both groups. We found that North American adult participants are confused by "little things inside" but not "enzyme," "protein," or "disease X," whereas Maya subjects were confused by "enzyme" and "protein" but not by "little things inside" or "disease X." Earlier studies show that the patterns of results on different kinds of biological induction tasks for American undergraduates were statistically the same for "enzyme" and "disease," whereas the Itza' showed the same patterns of results for "little things inside" and "disease" (Atran et al. 1997; Coley et al. 1999). As in the sorting study we used probes involving both U.S. birds and birds of Tikal. There were no differences as a function of property so we collapsed across this variable.

For both kinds of probes we presented two pairs of birds and then asked about the property in question (disease, enzyme, or little things inside). For example, for the typicality trials, we displayed both birds in each pair and said: "Let's assume that we discovered two new diseases. All we know about these diseases is that Disease A is found in these types of birds and Disease B is found in these. Which disease do you think is more likely to be found in all birds?" Similarly, for the diversity trials, we placed one pair of birds on the left-hand side and one pair of birds on the right-hand side, and asked the same question.

Typicality Results   Only the undergraduates (novices) showed any indication of a typicality effect. A look at the justifications for choices confirms this pattern. The most striking difference is that novices use typicality as a reason for the choice more than half of the time, while experts and Itza' *never* indicate typicality. Both Itza' and U.S. experts tended to use range or ecological factors as justifications. These justifications are summarized in table 4.3.

Table 4.3
Expert, Itza', and nonexpert justifications on typicality trials by stimuli set in
Experiment 3

| Subject group | Justification type | | | | | |
	TYP	BEH	ECO	GEO	NUM	EVO
U.S. expert						
Tikal	0	0	18	39	2	21
U.S.	0	0	12	37	4	23
Itza'						
Tikal	0	12	60	18	1	0
U.S.	0	7	58	26	9	0
Nonexpert						
Tikal	47	2	7	4	18	2
U.S.	56	4	3	5	18	0

Note: TYP = Typicality, BEH = Behavior, MOR = Morphology, ECO = Ecology, GEO = Geographic range, NUM = Number, and EVO= Evolutionary age.

The Passerine Effect   We also analyzed the responses to the probes not simply in terms of typicality but also in terms of whether one of the birds in a pair was or was not a passerine. The U.S. experts and novices chose the passerine over the nonpasserine (66 and 86 percent, respectively) more than the Itza' (40 percent). In short, the Itza' experts tended to avoid passerines in their choices while the U.S. participants tended to choose them. As will be seen shortly, this difference probably derives from the salient role of nonpasserines in Itza' Maya folkbiology.

Diversity   Across conditions, U.S. experts chose the more diverse pair on 60 percent of the trials, the novices 58 percent, and the Itza' 45 percent. None of these percentages differed reliably from each other or from chance (50 percent). The diversity pattern for the experts was largely driven by two experts. The justifications are once again informative. The novices tended to use either typicality or diversity as a justification. Interestingly, they appeared to show something of a "learning effect" in that diversity justifications increased from 17 to 43 percent from the first to the second half of probes. It was as if once they hit on this strategy, they thought it was a good one and tended to continue using it. The two experts mentioned earlier gave almost exclusively diversity justifications, but the other U.S. experts and Itza' predominantly responded in terms of ecological/causal relations. (Experts and Itza' also showed no changes in patterns of justifications between the first and second half of probes.)

The Passerine Effect Again   The U.S. populations tended to choose probe pairs involving passerines while the Itza' tended to avoid them. This passerine effect suggests that the idealness of the birds may be driving our results more than coverage. To the Itza', passerines are not considered "true birds" to the same extent as other birds in the environment. Even though "passerine" was rarely cited as a justification, American subjects tended to pick small songbirds as generalizing to the population of all birds while the Itza' preferred larger, more perceptually striking birds.

Given the prominent role of the larger game birds in the behavioral ecology of Mayaland, and the more interactive goals of Itza' in monitoring their ecology, the information provided by their ideal birds would be more relevant to environmental understanding and management than information provided by songbirds. Itza' preferentially monitor those species in their ecosystem (e.g., gamebirds as opposed to passerines) that provide the most relevant information about the interaction of human needs with the needs of the forest. For example, Itza' tend to have the most detailed knowledge of, and to best protect, those species that are perceived to have the most interactions both with other species and with humans (Atran et al. 1999). For the Americans, whose interest in and interaction with the behavioral ecology is of a much reduced and altogether different order (gamebirds are not considered palpably crucial to survival of the human habitat), correlated perceptual information may be more relevant by default.

Summary of Bird Studies   Our triangulation strategy proved to be quite useful. For a number of important phenomena U.S. and Itza' experts clustered together and contrasted with U.S. novices. First of all, the expert groups sorted in closer correspondence with scientific taxonomy than did novices. This difference is particularly striking for the Itza' for U.S. birds because they were unfamiliar with Western science, scientific taxonomy, and the birds employed. U.S. novices had prior exposure to the birds and to Western science but their sorts corresponded less well with scientific taxonomy than those of the Itza'. This finding gives no comfort at all to relativists who see each culture as the single most important factor in conceptual organization. For that matter it also is inconsistent with the opposite extreme view that everyone naturally perceives the structure of nature unless goals and activities foster a special-purpose categorization scheme.

Instead, our data suggest that expertise confers benefits in abstracting important relationships in nature and, as a consequence, may lead to greater correspondence with scientific taxonomy. In that regard our results are well anticipated by the findings mentioned earlier by Johnson and Mervis (1998), who showed that bird and fish experts were better able to apprehend relational features tied to function and ecology than novices.

The category-based induction findings also reinforce the view that the novices were the "odd group out." Novices relied very heavily on familiarity or typicality as the basis of their choices on both the typicality and diversity trials. Neither the Itza' nor the U.S. experts *ever* gave typicality as a justification for either type of probe. Instead, they used knowledge about birds that the novices did not possess. For example, both the Itza' and U.S. experts frequently mentioned the geographic range of birds, an explanation that the novices rarely produced. This is a truly striking qualitative difference.

In our reasoning studies, typicality strategies are reliably used only by U.S. novices (undergraduates). Consequently, models invoking these principles may apply solely to situations where novices are reasoning about stimuli with which they have limited knowledge. Most work on the role of typicality judgments in natural categorization and reasoning stems from studies with college students. Those studies tend to support the view that similarity-based structures (e.g., central tendency, family resemblance) are the primary predictors for typicality in taxonomic categories, in general, and folkbiological categories, in particular (Rosch and Mervis 1975; Barsalou 1985). In this view, the mind's similarity assessments about typicality and the world's correlational structure are closely linked: typical members of categories capture the correlational structure of identifiable features in the world better than do atypical members. But for Itza' Maya, passerines are not very typical at all. One way to follow up these findings would be to study U.S. hunters who target gamebirds such as turkeys, grouse, partridges, ducks, and geese. With respect to the passerine effects, they might look more like the Itza' than other U.S. groups.

We do not doubt that similarity structures and similarity-based typicality and diversity are important determinants in natural categorization and reasoning. Our findings suggest that, at least for American undergraduates, these may be dominant factors. But for our relative experts (U.S.

experts and Itza'), who have substantial knowledge, goals, and activities involving the items they classify and reason with, information other than that derived from perceptual clustering and similarity judgment is relevant to understanding natural biodiversity. Behavior and ecology, for example, appear to be crucial to the deeper and broader understanding of nature that bird-watchers seek. Such concerns also may be critical to the way the Maya and perhaps other peoples in small-scale societies manage to live and survive with nature. If so, then it is practically impossible to isolate folkecological orientation from other aspects of cultural knowledge.

A Relevance Framework   We think that our pattern of results can best be understood with a theory that has not been applied previously to problems of category-based induction. One of our test sessions with a tree expert provided the impetus for this shift of view. The expert was being given typicality probes such as the following: "Suppose we know that river birches get disease X and that white oaks get disease Y, which disease do you think is more likely to affect all trees?" In this case, the expert said disease X, noting that river birches are very susceptible to disease, so "if one gets it they all get it." The very next probe involved the gingko tree and the expert chose the disease associated with it as more likely to affect all trees on the grounds that "gingkos are so resistant to disease that if they get it, it must be a very powerful disease." He then said that he felt as if he had just contradicted himself, but that nonetheless these seemed like the right answers.

   Normatively, this expert's answers do not represent a contradiction. Instead, he appeared to be using the information that was most salient and accessible to guide his reasoning (birches are notoriously susceptible to, and gingkos notoriously resistant to, diseases). Simply put, the expert was using the knowledge that he considered most relevant. We believe that Sperber and Wilson's (1986) relevance theory provides a good framework for understanding the patterns of responding in all our populations. Furthermore, it leads to a number of novel predictions that contrast with those of other models of induction.

   In relevance theory, relevance is seen as a property of inputs to cognitive processes:

An input is relevant to an individual at a certain time if processing this input yield *cognitive effects*. Examples of cognitive effects are the revision of previous beliefs, or the derivation of contextual conclusions, that is, conclusions that follow from the input taken together with previously available information. Such revisions or conclusions are particularly relevant when they answer questions that the individual had in mind (or in an experimental situation, was presented with). (Van der Henst, Politzer, and Sperber 2002)

In our experimental setting, background knowledge about properties of trees and diseases fosters just the sorts of contextual conclusions we see. Van der Henst and colleagues (2002) further elaborate:

Everything else being equal, the greater the cognitive effects achieved by processing an input, the greater its relevance. On the other hand, the greater the effort involved in processing an input, the lower the relevance.... One implication of the definition of relevance in terms of effect *and effort* is that salient information, everything else being equal, has greater relevance, given that accessing it requires less effort.

Consider again the Itza' pattern of sorting and reasoning about birds. Recall that their daily-life circumstances lead them to attend to the larger, more ecologically important forest birds. These are ecologically important both to perceivable effects on the forest and to Itza' needs. For example, raptors compete with the Itza' for large gamebirds (e.g., the wild turkey), and so Itza' hunters clearly must pay attention to both groups of birds. Consequently, their choices of nonpasserines on reasoning probes are driven by these omnipresent background concerns. Specifically, their extensive knowledge of large gamebirds and raptors has consequences for both effect and effort. All else equal, it is easier for them to retrieve knowledge about nonpasserines and when they do so, this retrieved knowledge has greater consequences.

Undergraduates, in contrast, have little background knowledge to bring to bear on the sorts of reasoning tasks we have used and consequently it is not surprising that they rely heavily on more abstract reasoning strategies. At the same time we do have evidence that their responses are sensitive to both effect and effort. This line of work was motivated by a follow-up study involving reasoning about mammals. Here we tested undergraduates individually and asked them to justify their responses. The one-on-one context implicitly asks for more effort, which should lead to more effect. Under these circumstances diversity effects were much reduced and we started to see justifications in terms of the range and population size of different mammals.

The above pilot study has led us to examine relevance effects in undergraduate populations more systematically (Medin et al. 2003). The probes rely on identifying accessible background knowledge to bring out the effect side of relevance and manipulating the premise and conclusion categories to show consequences on the effort side. As an example of the former, we find that the argument that bananas have enzyme X, therefore monkeys have enzyme X is rated to be stronger than the argument that mice have enzyme X, therefore monkeys have enzyme X. In this case relevant background knowledge that monkeys like bananas leads to a violation of similarity.

As an example of varying effort, undergraduates rate the inductive strength of the argument that grass has enzyme Y, therefore humans have enzyme Y to be less strong than the argument that grass has enzyme Y, therefore cows and humans have enzyme Y. (The arguments are not juxtaposed but rather are used in a between-subjects design.) In this case, we have what one could call a "conclusion conjunction fallacy" since, normatively, the former argument's conclusion cannot be less likely than the conclusion of the latter argument. From our perspective, we have made it easier for the participants to access a sensible causal pathway between grass and humans by providing the concept *cow*. We probably could have produced the same results by simply asking or not asking participants to recall the last time they had seen a cow before giving the grass-to-humans argument.

Summary and Conclusions   In some respects we have come full circle with respect to both theory and data on the use of categories in reasoning. We started by describing studies that reveal the standard undergraduate population as the odd group out, and then examined the basis for responding in "nonstandard" populations. But then we were able to use relevance theory to produce comparable phenomena with undergraduates (e.g., Medin et al. (2003), using categories and properties like those just described, were able to show nondiversity effects with students). Note, however, that in coming full circle we end up with a very different theory, one that holds promise for understanding inductive inferences in all of our populations. Equally important, it was the very use of nonstandard populations that allowed us to identify reasoning strategies that are salient among experts and Itza', but require careful attention to bring out in students. Had we restricted our focus to students, we might never have hit on the relevance of relevance theory to induction.

We now shift attention to direct ratings of goodness of example or typicality. Again undergraduates are the odd group out.

4.4   Ideals and Typicality

A key notion in the psychology of categorization is goodness of example or typicality effects. The idea is that some instances of a category may be better examples of a category than others. For example, a common intuition is that robins are better examples of birds than are chickens. Furthermore, the consensus has been that the basis of typicality effects is similarity relationships—robins are better birds because they are more similar to other birds than are chickens (for empirical and theoretical treatments of typicality, see Smith, Shoben, and Rips 1974; Rosch and Mervis 1975). Once again, however, these observations rest on a narrow empirical base with respect to study populations.

Work on typicality judgments among Itza' shows that inductively useful notions of typicality may be driven more by considerations of idealness than central tendency (Atran 1999a). In each case for which we have direct Itza' ratings, the "truest" or "most representative" living-kind categories are large, perceptually striking, culturally important, and ecologically prominent. For example, the three most highly rated mammals are the jaguar (also called "The Lord of the Forest"), the mountain lion (the jaguar's principal rival), and the tapir (also called "The Beast of All Seven Edible Kinds of Flesh"). The three most highly rated snakes are the large and deadly fer-de-lance (*Bothrops asper*, also called "The True Snake") and its companions, the large and venomous tropical rattlesnake (*Crotalus durissus*) and the smaller but deadly coral snake (*Micrurus* sp.). The three most representative birds are all large, morphologically striking, and highly edible galliformes (wild fowl): ocellated turkey, crested guan, and great curassow.

One might speculate that the instructions were not comparable or that typicality has a different meaning in the Itza' language. Further observations undermine this possibility. Lynch, Coley, and Medin (2000) found that U.S. tree experts based their typicality judgments on ideals (e.g., height, absence of undesirable characteristics) and that central tendency was uncorrelated with judgments. Lynch et al. used instructions that followed verbatim those by Rosch and Mervis (1975) in their original studies showing central-tendency-based typicality effects.[5] The best predictor of undergraduate typicality ratings was word frequency. This fits with the idea that many undergraduates do not know the referents of these terms and, therefore, rely on the only information they have.

Bailenson et al. 2002 also collected typicality ratings. Central tendency was correlated with judgments only for the novices. We did not try to measure ideals or other factors that might determine typicality ratings among bird experts, but in another domain of biology—freshwater fish—we did.

Culture, Ideals, and Typicality   To demonstrate the generality of these findings and to get a better understanding of ideals, we ran a study of culture and expertise in the domain involving fishing expertise and freshwater fish. In this experiment (Burnett et al. 2005) we collected an independent measure of desirability. (One limitation of the Bailenson et al. (2002) study is that there was no independent measure of ideals. Similarly, Lynch, Coley and Medin (2000) did not establish that height was an ideal, and height may have been correlated with other variables that influenced typicality.) Our participants were members of two different cultural groups who could be expected to have somewhat different ideals, so that if judgments are based on ideals, they should differ across groups.

Regular and avid fishermen in north-central Wisconsin were asked to give typicality ratings to a set of freshwater fish local to the area. They were also asked to sort these fish into class-inclusion hierarchies, from which we derive a measure of each fish's central tendency (see also chapter 9). This allows a test of the hypothesis that central tendency determines typicality.

We also considered centrality in the scientific taxonomy and four other possible predictors of a fish's typicality: desirability, familiarity to participants, size, and habitat. Other work, described in chapter 9, reveals differences in folkbiological thought between members of these two groups, and these differences give us some leverage for understanding the basis of goodness-of-example judgments. These differences include the following:

• Sturgeon are considered sacred by the Menominee (Beck 1995).
• Trout are relatively more salient and more valued by the Menominee than by majority-culture fishermen.
• Majority-culture fishermen tend to focus relatively more on gamefish, or sportfish, than do the Menominee.
• Majority-culture fishermen are more likely to classify fish as undesirable than are the Menominee, and their category of undesirable (so-called rough or garbage) fish is broader.
• Both groups have similar categories of (a) "panfish" that make "good eating" and (b) baitfish (minnows and shiners).
• Menominee fishermen are more likely to say that every fish has a role to play.

If typicality judgments are based on ideals, the following predictions should hold. First, typicality should be well predicted by desirability and not by centrality. Second, there should be a main effect of cultural group, with Menominee informants giving higher overall ratings. Third, this main effect should be accompanied by a significant interaction of cultural group and fish group. Specifically, Menominee fishermen should give higher ratings to trout, sturgeon, rough fish, and baitfish, whereas majority-culture fishermen should give higher ratings to gamefish (unless there is a ceiling effect). If goodness-of-example ratings conform to these predictions, this would constitute very strong evidence that typicality is driven by ideals among fish experts.

Participants were 66 male members of two communities—the Menominee reservation and a nearby county in north-central Wisconsin, where fishing is common. To get a rough measure of their knowledge, each participant was asked to say something ("anything that comes to mind") about each of the 44 fish used in this study (some of which are small and rarely seen) and to indicate whether he would be able to identify it by sight. By this measure, the average participant was familiar with 36 of the 44 fish (median = 37).

Procedure   Participants were interviewed individually and asked to complete three tasks, in this order: the familiarity task just described, a hierarchical sorting task, and a typicality rating task. The sorting task involved a set of cards printed with the names of 44 fish, selected to be broadly representative of the fish genera and families found in this part of Wisconsin. Cards corresponding to fish with which the participant was unfamiliar were removed from the deck. At each stage of the hierarchical sorting, the participant was asked to explain the group(s) he had created. Next, the participant was asked to provide typicality ratings for all the fish. If participants were unfamiliar with a fish, they did not give it a typicality rating. The instructions followed those of Rosch and Mervis 1975 verbatim. They introduce the idea that some examples are more representative of a category than others and that a good example is one that readily comes to mind when one thinks about the category. Printed on the rating form was the question "How good an example of the category fish?" Ratings were given on a 7-point scale with the following anchors: 1 = poor, 4 = fair, 7 = excellent.

Candidate Predictors of Typicality Ratings   Six variables were evaluated as possible predictors of typicality: folk central tendency (folk CT), scientific central tendency (scientific CT), desirability, characteristic adult size, familiarity, and habitat.

Folk CT was derived from participants' hierarchical sortings of the fish. Scientific CT is measured as a fish's average distance to the other 43 fish as they appear in the currently accepted evolutionary taxonomy,

Table 4.4
Typicality ratings and predictor variables

Fish	Typicality		Folk CT		Sci CT	Desirability		Fam	Size (cm)	Hab
	Me	MC	Me	MC		Me	MC			
American eel (lawyer)	2.4	1.6	−1.32	−0.89	−0.48	−.50	−.50	.64	152	1
Black bullhead	3.7	4.1	−0.08	0.20	0.02	−.17	.17	.92	62	0
Black crappie	5.3	5.3	0.42	0.43	0.52	.43	.33	.92	49	−1
Black sucker	4.1	3.1	−0.08	0.41	−0.23	−.17	−.58	.67	61	1
Blacktail chub	3.5	2.8	0.64	0.58	0.77	−.17	.00	.70	26	1
Bluegill	6.2	6.1	0.42	0.45	0.65	.43	.33	1.00	41	−1
Bluntnose minnow	4.0	2.6	0.86	0.14	0.77	−.17	.00	.50	11	1
Brook trout	6.8	6.3	−0.69	−0.88	−0.23	.14	.08	.98	70	1
Brown trout	6.8	5.9	−0.67	−0.87	−0.23	.14	.08	.97	103	1
Carp	2.8	3.2	−0.43	0.07	0.65	−.33	−.67	.94	122	0
Channel catfish	3.9	4.8	−0.43	−0.10	−0.10	.00	.08	.91	127	1
Dace	4.5	4.0	0.91	0.22	0.65	−.17	.00	.32	12	1
Darter	4.0	3.2	0.76	0.44	−0.10	−.17	.08	.30	10	1
Dogfish (bowfin)	2.3	1.9	−0.39	−0.15	−0.48	−1.00	−.83	.95	109	−1
Emerald shiner	3.5	3.5	0.69	0.71	0.90	−.17	.00	.59	13	1
Fathead minnow	4.0	3.2	0.61	0.27	0.77	−.17	.00	.88	10	0
Flathead catfish	4.5	4.8	−0.32	−0.18	−0.10	−.17	.00	.80	155	1
Gar (billfish)	2.5	1.9	−0.33	−0.33	−0.48	−1.00	−.83	.89	183	0
Golden shiner	3.9	3.8	0.52	0.25	0.65	−.17	.00	.94	30	0
Green sunfish	4.7	5.2	0.20	0.49	0.65	.57	.25	.85	31	−1

Lamprey eel	2.0	1.3	−1.34	−1.00	−5.73	−.67	−.42	.85	64	−1
Largemouth bass	6.7	5.9	0.31	0.21	0.52	.86	.50	1.00	97	−1
Mudminnow	3.7	2.9	0.91	0.23	−0.48	−.17	.00	.65	8	1
Musky	6.3	6.4	−0.26	−0.25	−0.23	.14	.67	1.00	183	0
Northern pike	6.0	6.5	0.09	−0.25	−0.23	.43	.67	.98	133	0
Pumpkinseed	5.3	5.8	0.42	0.49	0.65	.57	.33	.92	40	−1
Rainbow trout	6.9	5.9	−0.69	−0.84	−0.23	.14	.00	.92	114	1
Redhorse	3.6	2.5	−0.16	0.23	−0.23	−.17	−.58	.89	74	1
Redtail chub	3.7	3.3	0.56	0.54	0.77	−.17	.00	.71	23	1
River shiner	3.9	3.1	0.76	0.13	0.90	−.17	.00	.89	13	1
Rock bass	4.2	3.4	0.15	0.30	0.40	.40	.42	.98	43	0
Sauger	5.1	5.6	−0.16	−0.15	0.02	.14	.67	.67	76	0
Sheephead (drum)	2.7	2.4	−0.51	0.14	−0.48	−.33	−.67	.68	89	1
Smallmouth bass	6.1	5.9	0.24	0.22	0.52	.71	.50	1.00	69	0
Smelt	4.2	3.8	−0.42	−0.49	−0.48	.14	.00	.92	33	0
Spottail shiner	3.8	3.3	0.73	0.83	0.90	−.02	−.08	.61	15	1
Stickleback	3.4	1.9	0.30	0.19	−0.48	.00	.00	.38	7	1
Sturgeon	6.2	5.1	−0.75	−1.04	−0.48	.00	.08	1.00	274	1
Walleye	6.8	6.6	0.05	−0.02	0.02	.43	.75	1.00	91	0
White bass	4.9	4.4	−0.22	0.33	−0.48	.57	.50	.88	45	1
White crappie	5.3	5.3	0.33	0.46	0.52	.29	.33	.91	53	0
White sucker	3.9	3.3	0.00	0.38	−0.23	−.17	−.50	.82	64	−1
Yellow bullhead	3.7	4.0	−0.08	0.12	0.02	−.19	.25	.86	47	0
Yellow perch	6.0	6.1	0.12	0.05	−0.10	.43	.42	.97	40	−1

Note: CT = central tendency, Sci = scientific, Me = Menominee, MC = majority culture, Fam = familiarity, Hab = habitat.

standardized and multiplied by -1. Desirability was derived from justifications associated with the sorting task. Participants often formed categories of fish that they described as undesirable ("rough" or "garbage" fish) or desirable ("prestigious game fish" and fish that are "good eating"). Each fish's desirability was computed as the proportion of times it was assigned to desirable groups minus the proportion of times it was assigned to undesirable groups. This was done for the cultural groups separately and combined. Each fish's characteristic adult size was included as a possible predictor because it may be related to ideals and because size has been found relevant in related contexts (Hunn 1999; Lynch, Coley, and Medin 2000). Familiarity was computed as the proportion of participants who knew a fish during the initial familiarity task. Finally, a fish's habitat was coded as 1 if the fish is found mainly in rivers and streams, -1 if the fish is found mainly in lakes, and 0 if the fish is commonly found in both types of water.

Results   Typicality ratings and the values of the predictor variables are presented in table 4.4. The first thing to note is that high ratings were given to desirable game fish like musky, northern, walleye, and largemouth and smallmouth bass. High ratings were also given to other desirable fish like the bluegill, the trouts, and the yellow perch. Low ratings were given to rough (undesirable) fish like the gar and the dogfish. Minnows and other baitfish received intermediate ratings. To get a broad perspective, typicality, folk CT, and desirability were computed over all participants (rather than for each cultural group, as shown in table 4.4), and correlations among these and the other candidate predictors were computed. The correlations are shown in table 4.5. Typicality is very highly related to desirability ($r = .80$) and fairly well related to familiarity ($r = .50$). Both of these correlations are reliable ($ps < .01$), and no other predictor variable is reliably correlated with typicality.

Figure 4.8 collates much of the data in table 4.4 into subcategories corresponding to the predictions we described earlier. Gamefish comprise the musky, northern pike, sauger, largemouth bass, and smallmouth bass. Panfish include the black crappie, bluegill, green sunfish, pumpkinseed, rock pass, white crappie, and yellow perch and rough fish, the American eel, black sucker, dogfish, gar, lamprey eel, redhorse, sheephead, and white sucker. Baitfish comprise the minnows, shiners, and chubs.

As predicted, Menominee participants gave higher ratings overall,[6] and there was a significant interaction of cultural group and fish group.[7] This interaction took the form predicted in most respects. Menominee partici-

Table 4.5
Correlations among typicality and predictor variables

	Typi-cality	Folk CT	Sci CT	Desir-ability	Famil-iarity	Habitat	Size
Typicality		−.06	.28	.80**	.50**	−.24	.22
Folk CT			.64**	.24	−.38*	−.03	−.70**
Sci CT				.30*	−.05	.12	−.23
Desirability					.28	−.26	−.14
Familiarity						−.51**	.43**
Habitat							.02
Size							

Note: Because Menominee participants gave higher typicality ratings overall, ratings were standardized for each participant before being averaged and submitted to correlational analysis.
CT = central tendency, Sci = scientific.
* $p < .05$, ** $p < .01$.

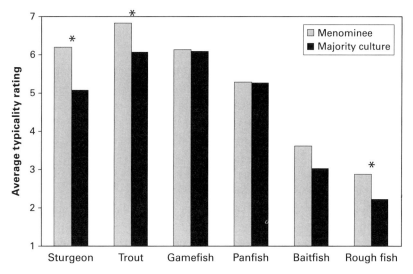

Figure 4.8
Average typicality ratings given to different types of fish by the two cultural groups.

pants gave higher ratings than majority-culture participants to the trout,[8] the sturgeon,[9] and the rough fish.[10] The difference for baitfish fell short of reliability. There were essentially no group differences for gamefish and panfish. The lack of a difference for gamefish might reflect a ceiling effect or the fact that many majority-culture fishermen focus not on gamefish generally, but on a single kind of gamefish (e.g., just smallmouth bass or just musky).

These findings, combined with our earlier results, constitute strong evidence that, for participants with significant experience of a category, typicality is driven more by ideals than by central tendency. Desirability accounted for 64 percent of the variance in typicality ratings, and the pattern of cultural differences reinforces the hypothesis that ideals are the key factor in determining fishermen's typicality ratings. This clarifies and complements the results of Lynch, Coley, and Medin 2000 and Bailenson et al. 2002.

In summary, we consistently find that among people knowledgeable about a domain, typicality judgments are based on ideals. Only undergraduates appear to rely on central tendency or word frequency. In the next section we take up what are known as basic-level effects. Here undergraduates show both devolution and evidence of resilience.

The traditional interpretation of typicality as central tendency arose from a general and well-established approach to concepts and categories, in which the formation, representation, and use of concepts are understood to be determined largely by a domain's intrinsic structure (similarities and dissimilarities among its members, clusters of correlated features, and so on). The present study provides support for an alternative approach that allows for strong influences of more extrinsic factors like ideals, goals, and habits of mind—even in domains that, like biology, have rich intrinsic structure.

Implications   We think that these results on typicality ratings, combined with our category-based induction findings, have strong implications for models of category learning and conceptual development. Specifically, we think it is very unlikely that category learning is a passive, bottom-up process that reflects intrinsic structure without bias. It is much more likely that the most relevant (and ideal) examples are learned first and that these initial representations guide further learning (see Love, Medin, and Gureckis 2004 for a network model based on this principle and Steyvers and Tenenbaum 2005 for an analysis of semantic networks that supports this general approach).

Although it is possible that category reorganization may take place in some cases, there is plenty of evidence for persistent influences of early learning. Atran (1999a) found that Itza' sorting of snakes was organized around the most poisonous snakes and that the correlation between folk distance and scientific taxonomic distance was extremely modest.

Converging evidence comes from linguistic anthropology and is nicely summarized in Berlin's 1992 book. He notes that often the name given to the best example of a category is also the term used for the entire category (as we noted on several cases for the Itza' in chapter 2). In addition, the best example is often referred to as the "true" example (see also Atran 1999a). Finally, it is sometimes the case that a kind that is similar to but not the same as a salient example is called "false" as in False Solomon's Seal. In short, new learning is guided and influenced by what is already known, and what is often learned first are the ideals associated with a category.

These observations render doubtful the usefulness of laboratory studies of category learning that throw in all of the to-be-learned examples right from the start and continue to present them with equal frequency in a random order. The learning that takes place is real but it is not realistic. Consequently it is unlikely to deliver useful generalizations or provide deep insights into how people learn about the world.

4.5 The Essence of the Basic Level

As noted at the beginning of chapter 2, the core of any folktaxonomy is the generic-species level (Berlin 1992). Generic species comprise the overwhelming majority of taxa in any folkbiological system (see Atran, Lois, and Ucan Ek' 2004). Generic species may also be the categories most easily recognized, most commonly named, and most easily learned by children in small-scale societies (Stross 1973). Indeed, ethnobiologists who otherwise differ in their views of folktaxonomy tend to agree that one level best captures discontinuities in nature and provides the fundamental constituents in all systems of folkbiological categorization, reasoning, and use (Bartlett 1940; Berlin, Breedlove, and Raven 1973; Bulmer 1974; Hunn 1982; Ellen 1993; Morris 1996; Descola 1996).

Given these observations, results of psychological studies of privilege or basicness are striking and puzzling. In a classic set of experiments, Rosch and her colleagues set out to test the validity of the notion of a psychologically privileged taxonomic level (Rosch et al. 1976). Using a broad array of converging measures they found support for the view that there is a "basic level" in category hierarchies of "naturally occurring objects," such as "taxonomies" of artifacts as well as living kinds (see Brown et al. 1976). For artifact and living-kind hierarchies, the basic level is the most abstract level where (1) many common features are listed for categories, (2) consistent motor programs are employed for the interaction with or manipulation of category exemplars, and (3) category members have similar enough shapes that it is possible to recognize an average shape for objects of the category. The basic level—the level first learned by children and the level at which entities can be categorized most rapidly—is also preferred in adult naming.

Thus, studies by Berlin and by Rosch both indicate a privileged level in category hierarchies. Moreover, both claim that this privileged take on naturally occurring objects is directly tied to objective discontinuities in the real world. But the basic level that Rosch et al. (1976) initially had hypothesized would accord with Berlin's folk-generic rank, did not prove to be privileged. For example, instead of maple and trout, Rosch et al. found that tree and fish operated as basic-level categories for American college students. Thus, Rosch's basic level for living kinds generally corresponds to Berlin's life-form level, which is superordinate to the generic-species level.

How can we reconcile the discrepancy between Berlin's observations and Rosch's data concerning privileged levels? In one attempt to do so, Dougherty (1978) argued that the basic level is a variable phenomenon that shifts as a function of general cultural significance and individual familiarity and expertise (see Tanaka and Taylor 1991; Johnson and Mervis 1997). Thus, most folk in industrial societies often have little distinctive familiarity with, knowledge of, and use for various species of trees, fish, birds, and so forth. As familiarity with the biological world decreases, there is a gradual attrition of folkbiological knowledge up the hierarchy, with the basic level devolving from the generic-species to the life-form levels. A related (but alternative) view of the Berlin/Rosch discrepancy is that it is sensitive to how privilege is measured. Specifically, some measures of privilege may be driven more by experience than others (see also Barsalou 1991).

In brief, discrepancies in findings for different populations suggest that the basic level is knowledge-dependent. There is evidence that biological experts have a more specific basic level than novices, but this describes results from a novice perspective. We offer a reframing. "Experts" and people from small-scale societies have "normal" basic-level categories, corresponding to a default inference/recognition strategy whose recognition component degenerates with lack of exposure, but whose inference component remains intact.

There is reason to prefer our framing. Our studies focus on inductive inference. One might expect novice, expert, and small-scale groups to privilege their respective basic levels for induction (e.g., TREE for U.S. students, OAK for experts and Maya); however, our studies indicate that both industrialized and small-scale populations prefer the same folktaxonomic rank for induction (Atran et al. 1997; Coley, Medin, and Atran 1997).

Inductive inference allows people to extend knowledge beyond their immediate experience and beyond the information they are given, and is a crucial part of category formation and use (Rips 1975; Smith and Medin 1981). Use of inductive inference as a tool is also motivated by the experiments in the last section suggesting that generic species are characterized by a presumption of essence that directs the search for underlying causal principles and theories (see Medin and Ortony 1989). Inductive inference must be a mainstay of any such search for underlying causal principles and its focus should be at the generic-species rank.

Examining inferences from a given rank to the adjacent higher-order rank among Midwestern U.S. college students as well as Itza' Maya adults, we found a sharp decline in strength of inferences to taxa ranked higher than generic species, whereas strength of inferences to taxa ranked lower than generic species were nearly equal and similarly strong (figure 4.9). While all ranks may not be relevant to all cultures—or not relevant in the same ways—some categorization processes may be relatively immune to cultural differences. Thus, people from traditional versus high-technology cultures may differ in terms of the level at which names readily come to mind, or the level at which taxa are most easily imaged, or the level at which their biological knowledge is most complete. Nevertheless, they may presume that the same rank is privileged for biological reasoning, namely, the rank of generic species.

A more comprehensive study of induction patterns among Midwestern college students in the United States and Itza' Maya confirmed these results but also provided evidence for secondary forms of inductive preference. Based on extensive fieldwork, we chose a set of Itza' folkbiological categories of the kingdom (K), life-form (L), generic-species (G), folkspecific (S), and folk-varietal (V) ranks. We selected three plant life forms (CHE' = tree, AK' = vine, $POK{\sim}CHE'$ = herb/bush) and three animal life forms ($B'A'AL{\sim}CHE'$ $KUXI'MAL$ = "walking animal," i.e., mammal; $CH'IICH'$ = birds, including bats; $K\ddot{A}Y$ = fish). Three generic-species taxa were chosen from each life form; each generic species had a subordinate

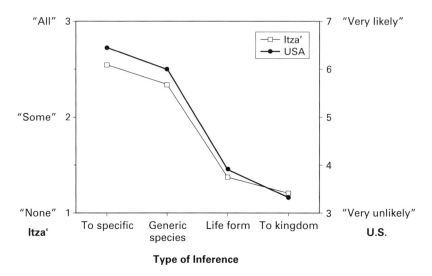

Type of Inference

Figure 4.9
Inductive inferences for Itza′ Maya and U.S. students compared (after Coley et al. 1997).

folkspecific, and each folkspecific had a salient varietal. The properties chosen for animals were diseases related to the "heart" (*pusik′al*), "blood" (*k′ik′el*), and "liver" (*tamen*). For plants, diseases related to the "roots" (*motz*), "sap" (*itz*), and "leaf" (*le′*) were selected. Properties were chosen according to Itza′ beliefs about the essential, underlying aspects of life's functioning. Properties used for inferences had the form "is suscep-tible to a disease of the ⟨root⟩ called ⟨X⟩." For each question, "X" was replaced with a phonologically appropriate nonsense name (e.g., "eta") to minimize the task's repetitiveness. All participants responded to a list of questions in which they were told that all members of a category had a property (the premise) and were asked whether "all," "few," or "no" members of a higher-level category (the conclusion category) also pos-sessed that property.

In one set of experiments, the premise category was at one of four levels: life-form (e.g., L = tree, mammal), generic-species (G = oak, dog), folkspecific (S = white oak, poodle), or varietal (V = swamp white oak, toy poodle). The conclusion category was drawn from a higher-level category. Thus, there were ten possible combinations of premise- and conclusion-category levels: L → K, G → K, G → L, S → K, S → L, S → G, V → K, V → L, V → G, and V → S. For example, a folkspecific-to-life-form (S → L) question might be: "If all white oaks are susceptible to the disease called eta, are all other trees susceptible?" If a participant answered no, then the follow-up question would be: "Are some or a few other trees susceptible, or no trees at all?"

We totaled the proportion of "all" responses for each kind of question (e.g., the proportion of times respondents agreed that if white oaks had a property, all oaks would have it). We counted a response of "all" as 3, "some or few" as 2, and "none" as 1. A higher score reflected more confidence in the strength of an inference. Examining inferences from a given rank to the adjacent higher-order rank (i.e., V → S, S → G, G → L, L → K), we found a sharp decline in strength of inferences to taxa ranked higher than generic species, whereas V → S and S → G inferences were nearly equal and similarly strong. For "all" responses, the overall Itza' and Michigan patterns were very similar (see figures 4.10a and 4.10b). For example, given a premise of folkspecific (white oak, poodle) and a conclusion category of generic-species rank (oak, dog), most respondents indicated that all members of the generic species would possess a property that the folkspecific has. A comparable number of respondents also indicated that a property possessed by a folk varietal (swamp white oak, toy poodle) would as likely be found with the generic species (oak, dog) as with the folkspecific (white oak, poodle). In contrast, few respondents believed that properties found in a folk varietal, folk-specific, or generic species would be found among all members of the superordinate life-form (tree, mammal) or folk-kingdom (plant, animal) categories, or that properties found in a life form would generalize to the folk kingdom.

Nevertheless, in the combined response scores ("all" + "few") there was evidence of increased inductive strength for higher-order taxa among Americans versus Itza'. In other words, both Americans and Itza' showed the largest break between inferences to generic species versus life forms; however, only American students also showed a consistent pattern of rating inferences to life-form taxa higher than to taxa at the level of the folk kingdom: G → K vs. G → L, S → K vs. S → L, and V → K vs. V → L. For the Americans, the preferred level of perceptual identification (life form) appeared to have a secondary effect on inference, whereas for Itza', the life-form level seems to carry no inductive privilege. Although the students cannot perceptually identify most bird or tree species, they can readily form (and draw) an abstract image of bird or tree. Itza' adults only consent to draw particular kinds of birds or trees.

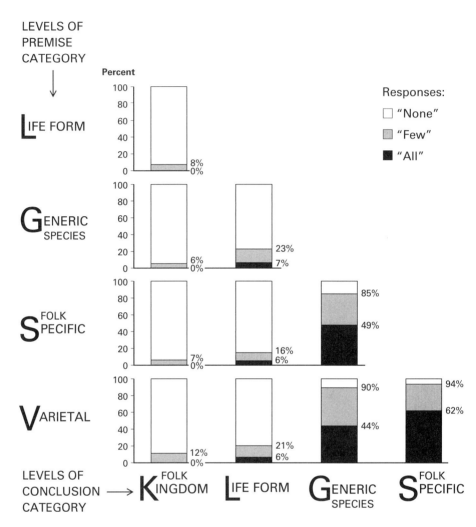

Figure 4.10a
Combined Itza′ results for all six life forms.

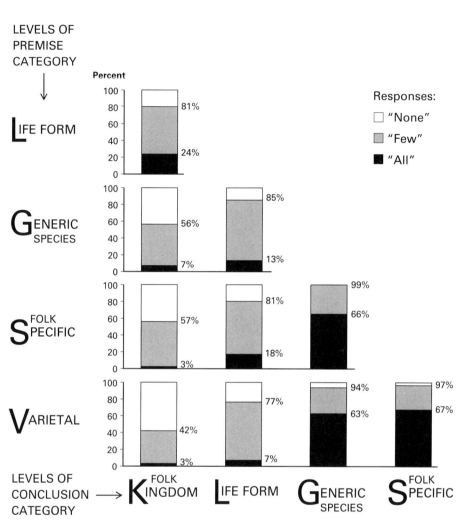

Figure 4.10b
Combined Michigan results for all six life forms.

Discussion of Results

These results indicate that both the inexperienced Americans and the Itza' elders prefer taxa of the generic-species rank in making biological inferences. If inferential potential were a simple function of perceptual similarity, then American nonexperts should prefer life forms for induction (as with Rosch et al. 1976). The findings suggest that root categorization and reasoning processes in folkbiology owe something to conceptual assumptions (about the causal locus of biologically essential attributes at the generic-species level) and not exclusively to general, similarity-based (e.g., perceptual) heuristics. To be sure, language may signal expectation that little or poorly known generic species are more biologically informative than better-known life forms for Americans (e.g., via common use of binomials, such as oak / red oak). But why presume that an appropriately tagged item is the locus of a "deep" causal nexus of biological properties and relationships? Why suppose at all that there is such a nexus that spontaneously justifies and motivates expectations, inferences, and explorations relating little-known or nonobvious aspects of a presumably fundamental biological reality? Indeed, our experiments still show reliable results in the absence of clear linguistic cues (e.g., oak / white oak / swamp white oak vs. dog / poodle / toy poodle).

In related work with U.S. botanical experts and undergraduates, Schwartz and Medin (2000) used a converging technique to get at inductive privilege. In their studies, premises and conclusions always involved the varietal level, but the two kinds varied as to whether they belonged to the same species, the same genus, the same family, or the same life form. For example, a premise involving fastigiata black alders and a conclusion involving heritage river birch trees would be a probe of the family level, since the most specific taxonomic rank including birches and alders is the family level. The dependent variable was rated inductive confidence on a 9-point scale. The advantage of this technique is that it allows one to probe for unnamed ranks.

The results are shown in figure 4.11. Both groups provide clear evidence of privilege at the generic-species level, again indicating that relative expertise does not affect where the inflection point in inductive confidence lies. On a finer level of detail there are expertise effects. The undergraduates show no difference between the life-form and family levels, where the experts do.[11] Shared genus (e.g., red oak, white oak) is marked in language whereas shared family usually is not. Apparently the undergraduates had no idea of taxonomic relationships other than those

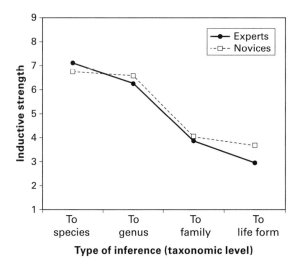

Figure 4.11
Interaction of level of expertise and taxonomic level for the kingdom "plants" (Experts, $n = 39$; Novices, $n = 24$).

marked in language. In contrast, the botanical experts did make this distinction with respect to secondary privilege.

More recently Coley et al. (2004) have both added a developmental component and provided evidence that the knowledge versus expectation may be specific to biological kinds. They tested U.S. 5-year-olds, 8-year-olds, and adults on feature-listing and induction tasks. For all age groups the greatest increase in features listed tended to occur at the life-form level, whereas the greatest increase in inductive confidence tended to occur at the generic-species level. Knowledge and induction were more concordant for artifact stimuli.

Undergraduates' lack of close contact with biological kinds may be precisely what allows us to tease apart the contributions of perceptual processes and abstract expectations to the privileged level in induction. There is now considerable evidence for perceptual learning (e.g., see Goldstone 1994; Schyns, Goldstone, and Thibaut 1998) in general as well as evidence that the basic level on perceptual tasks becomes more specific with expertise (e.g., Tanaka and Taylor 1991; Johnson and Mervis 1997).

Expertise is almost always a relative term and one equally could cast these results into a different frame: so-called expert performance on perceptual tests could be the default outcome of normal development, and undergraduate performance on perceptual tests (favoring the more abstract life-form level) could be the result of a failure to undergo "normal" perceptual development with respect to biological kinds. If this were true, then we would expect Itza′ to perform like experts on perceptual tests, and only for cases of impoverished input would we expect a discrepancy between abstract expectations and perceptual processes. Arguably, there is an evolutionary design to a cognitive division of labor between domain-general perceptual heuristics and (domain-specific) learning and inference mechanisms, the one enabling flexible adaptation to variable conditions of experience, and the other invariably steering us to those enduring aspects of biological reality that are both causally recurrent and relevant to the emergence of human life and cognition.

Summary We consistently found a decisive break in inductive strength just above the rank of generic species. Nevertheless, we also found secondary evidence that supports the downgrading of American folkbiological knowledge versus the upgrading of Maya knowledge, relative to the generic-species level. Specifically, we find Americans have more faith in inductions to superordinate life-form taxa than the Itza′, and Itza′ differentiate among subordinate taxa more than students. This observation, coupled with some suggestive data on the decreasing salience of biological kinds in Western societies, raises further issues concerning the relativity of expertise.

4.6 Implications for Categorization and Reasoning

This has been a long chapter and it is time to sum up. The results described in the chapter inform our understanding of folkbiology as a module and the cognitive consequences of diminished contact with nature. They also have important implications for the psychology of categorization and reasoning.

Categorization
Two of the most robust and significant findings in the psychology of concepts are basic-level and typicality effects. Our work suggests important modifications in each of these.

Typicality
The standard assumption has been that goodness of example, or typicality, is driven by similarity relations. A good example of a category is one

that looks like its fellow category members and unlike members of contrasting categories (e.g., Rosch and Mervis 1975; Smith, Shoben, and Rips 1974; Smith and Medin 1981). As we noted, the similarity-coverage model assumes that goodness-of-example effects extend to category-based induction.

Once again, however, results based on the standard undergraduate population proved atypical in the case of biological kinds. First, when the stimuli being judged are names of trees, undergraduates even fail to show similarity-based typicality. Instead, word frequency or familiarity is the best predictor (Lynch, Coley, and Medin 2000). Apparently, undergraduates know too little about trees to have a basis for computing similarities. More to the point, populations with domain familiarity, whether professional taxonomists or Itza' agroforesters, consistently organize categories in terms of ideals, such as the taxonomist's American elm or the Maya's wild turkey.

We believe that people who have serious commerce in a domain rarely approach it in a content-neutral manner, passively recording the regularities associated with the category. We saw that the Itza', for example, bias their observations of biological kinds toward those that are most perceptually and ecologically salient (e.g., large gamebirds, predators, and poisonous snakes). Parks workers worry about susceptibility to disease and other maintenance problems with local trees, and their typicality ratings reflect this concern. Majority-culture fishermen attend to gamefish and Menominee fishermen expand that focus to include sacred, culturally important fish. In brief, the ways people deal with the world affect the ways they cognize it.

Consequently, models of categorization need to be sensitive to the likelihood that the most relevant and best examples of a category will tend to be learned first, and that later learning will be affected by and build on earlier learning (again see Berlin 1992; Love, Medin, and Gureckis 2004; Steyvers and Tenenbaum 2005).

Basic Level and Essentialism

A serious conceptual problem is that both ethnobiology and cognitive psychology have argued for one, especially salient level of categorization but have disagreed about which specific level is privileged in biological taxonomies. The studies of Rosch et al. 1976, using measures of knowledge, naming preferences, and perceptual tests, found converging evidence for the life-form level as the most relevant. Ethnobiology favors the generic-species rank as privileged.

Our data are consistent with the idea that biological essentialism may be universal and linked to an evolutionarily adaptive appreciation of generic species. For contemporary peoples in small-scale societies who continue to live intimately with nature, the level of generic species is the most relevant, as it likely was for our hominid ancestors. When we used an induction task where performance can be based on knowledge or expectation or both, we found convergence across cultures and expertise on the generic-species level as privileged for biological inference. The fact that biological experts also privilege the generic-species level on perceptual tests suggests that the divergence in question has little to do with how psychologists versus ethnobiologists measure the basic level. Rather, the apparent salience of the life-form level for undergraduates on feature listing and perceptual tests appears to be a peculiarity of the devolved state of undergraduate biological knowledge in particular, and that of industrialized populations in general (for a example involving the German language, see Zubin and Köpcke 1986).

Why should the generic-species level be privileged for biological inference in the face of uncertainty? Because that is where the action was, and often still is, in human dealings with biological kinds. It would also be sensible for the perceptual system to be tuned to this same level of biological reality, and we suspect that this is the default condition for human beings who depend directly on nature for survival (i.e., without the intermediary of shops and supermarkets). Some perceptual learning may be necessary to achieve this consonance (e.g., Goldstone 1998; Schyns and Rodet 1997; Johnson and Mervis 1997), experience that undergraduates may lack. More generally, people may have a perceptual-familiarity heuristic that allows them to rapidly and economically navigate their everyday world. This heuristic may be importantly influenced by cultural support (Wolff, Medin, and Pankratz 1999). There is increasing evidence from studies with infants that words act as invitations to form basic-level concepts (Waxman and Markow 1995; Waxman 1999), which in our society tend to focus on the life-form level (except for familiar pets and domestic animals; hence, *bird*, *fish*, and *dog* are basic).

Category-Based Inference

Much the same story of abstract-reasoning strategies in novices and more content-laden strategies in more knowledgeable groups can be told for typicality effects in reasoning, where responses to probes may be better predicted from knowledge of ideals than from computed central tendency. It is important to emphasize that the use of ideals in reasoning is indirect, rather than direct. That is, idealness per se plays no role in the rationale for responses. Instead, it is the implicit organization of knowledge organized around goals that both creates category ideals and drives category-based inference. For example, the Itza' Maya find passerines less relevant than gamebirds and raptors for understanding the forest (the forest being the primary focus of their understanding of the biological world). Consequently, they have much more knowledge about the large birds, knowledge that is recruited on reasoning tasks.

Although previous induction models have implicitly assumed that diversity-based responding is universal, it clearly is not. When we probed Itza', bird-watchers, tree experts, and fishermen in areas where they had knowledge we hardly ever observed diversity responses (and sometimes found below-chance diversity). Obviously, observations such as these require a reformulation of inference theories, perhaps along the lines of relevance theory.

Itza' noncompliance with diversity-based reasoning apparently results neither from a failure to understand the principle of diversity nor from any problems of "computational load." As with the most evident divergences between American and Itza' performance on similarity and typicality tasks, divergence from diversity apparently results from real-world concerns. In the absence of a theory—or at least the presumption of a theory—of causal unity underlying disparate species, there is no compelling reason to consider a property discovered in two distant species as biologically intrinsic or essential to both (see also Proffitt, Coley, and Medin 2000). This does not mean that Itza' do not understand a diversity principle. In fact, in a series of tasks designed to assess risk-diversification strategies (e.g., sampling productivity from one forest plot or several) Itza' consistently showed an appreciation of the diversity principle in these other settings (López et al. 1997). This suggests that although diversity may be a universal reasoning heuristic, it is not a universally relevant aspect of folkbiological taxonomy, as we also found in U.S. populations having more direct interest in the natural world.

Autonomy and Universality

We have provided evidence for the structural and functional autonomy of folkbiology in human cognition. First, our induction studies on the basic level strongly suggest that folkbiological taxonomies are universally anchored on the generic-species level, where inductive potential is greatest. Second, our category-based induction experiments showed that people from diverse societies build topologically similar biological taxonomies that guide inferences about the distribution of biological and ecological properties. Just how the taxonomies are used may vary across groups. For undergraduates, the taxonomy is a stand-in for ideas about the likely distribution of biologically related properties (e.g., diseases). For the Itza' (and other knowledgeable groups), the taxonomy may constrain the likely operational range of ecological agents and causes.

These universal tendencies are most salient outside the center of industrialized societies but nonetheless discernible everywhere. Our observations provide a cautionary tale: at least in the case of folkbiology, standard populations may be nonstandard and vice versa. Trying to understand the structure of folkbiology by focusing exclusively on relatively unknowledgeable college students may be akin to an attempt to understand the structure of language by concentrating on feral children. That is, we may be able to understand a great deal (e.g., about which aspects of biological cognition are least dependent on input conditions and direct experience) but only if we recognize this population as being atypical in commerce with nature.

Overall, the pattern of results is quite strong and we think the summary in table 4.1 is a fair summary. We end this chapter by reviewing the criteria for a module in relation to the evidence we have presented.

4.7   Biology as a Module of Mind

As we noted at the start of this chapter, the argument for conceptual modules involves converging evidence from a number of venues: functional design (analogy), ethology (homology), universality, precocity of acquisition, independence from perceptual experience (poverty of stimulus), selective pathology (cerebral impairment), resistance to inhibition (hyperactivity), and ease of cultural transmission. None of these criteria may be necessary, but the presence of all or some is compelling.[12]

Functional Design

All organisms must function to procure energy to survive, and they also must procure (genetic) information for recombination and reproduction (Eldredge 1986). The first requirement is primarily satisfied by other species, and an indiscriminate use of any individual of the other species (e.g., energywise, it does not generally matter *which* individual lion eats you or *which* individual apple you eat). The second requirement is usually only satisfied by genetic information unique to individual conspecifics (e.g., genetically, it matters who is chosen as a mate and who is considered kin). On the one hand, humans recognize other humans by individuating them with the aid of species-specific triggering algorithms that "automatically" coordinate perceptual cues (e.g., facial-recognition schemata, gaze) with conceptual assumptions (e.g., intentions) (Baron-Cohen 1995). On the other hand, people do not spontaneously individuate members of other species, but as exemplars of the (generic) species that identifies them as causally belonging to only one essential kind.

Natural selection basically accounts only for the appearance of complexly well-structured biological traits that are designed to perform important functional tasks of adaptive benefit to organisms. In general, naturally selected adaptations are structures functionally "perfected for any given habit" (Darwin [1872] 1883, 140), having "very much the appearance of design by an intelligent designer... on which the wellbeing and very existence of the organism depends" (Wallace [1889] 1901, 138). Plausibly, the universal appreciation of generic species as the causal foundation for the taxonomic arrangement of biodiversity, and for taxonomic inference about the distribution of causally related properties that underlie biodiversity, is one such functional evolutionary adaptation. But a good story is not enough.[13]

Ethology

One hallmark of adaptation is a phylogenetic history that extends beyond the species in which the adaptation is perfected. For example, ducklings crouching in the presence of hawks, but not other kinds of birds, suggests dedicated mechanisms for something like species recognition. Some non-human species can clearly distinguish several different animal or plant species (Cerella 1979; Herrnstein 1984). Vervet monkeys even have distinct alarm calls for different predator species or groups of species: snake, leopard and cheetah, hawk, eagle, and so forth (Hauser 2000). Chimpanzees may have rudimentary hierarchical groupings of biological groups within groups (Brown and Boysen, 2000). To be sure, the world itself is neither in chaos nor flux: species are often locally self-structuring entities that are reproductively and ecologically isolated from other species through natural selection. But there is no a priori reason for the mind to always focus on categorizing and relating species qua species, unless doing so serves some adaptive function. Adaptive functions of organisms rarely, if ever, evolve or operate in nature as general-purpose mechanisms.

Universality

Ever since the pioneering work of Berlin and his colleagues, evidence from ethnobiology and experimental psychology has been accumulating that all human societies have similar folkbiological structures (Berlin, Breedlove, and Raven 1973; Berlin 1992; Hunn 1977; Hays 1983; Brown 1984; Atran 1990, 1999a). These striking cross-cultural similarities suggest that a small number of organizing principles universally define folkbiological systems. Basic aspects of folkbiological structure (e.g., taxonomic ranking, primacy of generic species) seem to vary little across cultures as a function of theories or belief systems.

Precocity of Acquisition

Acquisition studies indicate a precocious emergence of essentialist folkbiological principles in early childhood that are not applied to other domains (Keil 1995; Hatano and Inagaki 1999; Atran et al. 2001). We will provide further evidence on ease of acquisition in chapter 5.

Independence from Perceptual Experience

Experiments on inferential processing reported here show that humans do not make biological inductions primarily on the basis of perceptual experience or any general similarity-based metric, but on the basis of imperceptible causal expectations of a peculiar, essentialist nature.

Selective Pathology

Cerebral impairments (Williams syndrome, brain lesions caused by certain types of herpes virus, and so on) suggest selective retention or loss of folkbiological taxonomies or of particular taxonomic ranks. Neuropsychological studies have reported a pathological performance in recognition at the life-form and generic-species levels (e.g., recognizing an item as an animal but not as a bird or robin), and dissociation at the life-form level (e.g., not recognizing items as trees). Existing studies, however, do not say anything about the generic-species rank as the preferred level of representation for reasoning, perhaps because of methodology (linked to averaging over items and failure to include sets of generic species) (Warrington and Shallice 1984; Sartori and Job 1988; Job and Surian 1998; Caramazza 2002).

Resistance to Inhibition

One characteristic of an evolved cognitive disposition is evident difficulty in inhibiting its operation (Hauser 2000). Consider beliefs in biological essences. Such beliefs greatly help people explore the world by prodding them to look for regularities and to seek explanations of variation in terms of underlying patterns. This strategy may help bring order to ordinary circumstances, including those relevant to human survival. But in other circumstances, such as wanting to know what is correct or true for the cosmos at large, such intuitively ingrained concepts and beliefs may hinder more than help. For example, the essentialist bias to understand variation in terms of deviance is undoubtedly a hindrance to evolutionary thinking. In some everyday matters, the tendency to essentialize or explain variation in terms of deviation from some essential ideal or norm (e.g., people as mental or biological "deviants") can be an effortlessly "natural" but wrong way to think.

Because intuitive notions come to us so naturally they may be difficult to unlearn and transcend. Even students and philosophers of biology often find it difficult to abandon commonsense notions of species as classes, essences, or natural kinds in favor of the concept of species as a logical individual—a genealogical branch whose end points are somewhat arbitrarily defined in the phyletic tree and whose status does not differ in principle for that of other smaller (variety) and larger (genus) branches. Similarly, racism—the projection of biological essences onto social groups—seems to be a cognitively facile and culturally universal tendency (Hirschfeld 1996). Although science teaches that race is biologically incoherent, racial thinking is as notoriously difficult to suppress as it is easy to incite.

Ease of Cultural Transmission

Human cultures favor the rapid selection and stable distribution of ideas that (1) readily help to solve relevant and recurrent environmental problems, (2) are easily memorized and processed by the human brain, and (3) facilitate the retention and understanding of ideas that are more variable (e.g., religion) or difficult to learn (e.g., science) but contingently useful or important. Folkbiological taxonomies readily aid humans everywhere in orienting themselves and surviving in the natural world. The content of these taxonomies tends to be stable within cultures (high interinformant agreement, substantial historical continuity) and their structure isomorphic across cultures (see Boster 1991; López et al. 1997). Folkbiological taxonomy also serves as a principled basis for transmission and acquisition of more variable and extended forms of cultural knowledge.

Consider the spontaneous emergence of totemism—the correspondence of social groups with generic species—at different times and in different parts of the world. Why, as Lévi-Strauss (1963) aptly noted, are totems so "good to think"? In part, totemism uses representations of generic species to represent groups of people; however, this pervasive metarepresentational inclination arguably owes its recurrence to its ability to ride piggyback on folkbiological taxonomy. Generic species and groups of generic species are inherently well structured, attention-arresting, memorable, and readily transmissible across minds. As a result, they readily provide effective pegs on which to attach knowledge and behavior of less intrinsically well-determined social groups. Totemic groups thereby also become memorable, attention-arresting, and transmissible across minds.

These are the conditions for any idea to become culturally viable (see Sperber 1996 for a general view of culture along the lines of an "epidemiology of representations"). A significant feature of totemism that enhances both memorability and its capacity to grab attention is that it *violates* the general behavior of biological species: members of a totem, unlike members of a generic species, generally do not interbreed, but only mate with members of other totems so as to create a system of social exchange. Notice that this violation of core knowledge is far from arbitrary. In fact, it is such a pointed violation of human beings' intuitive ontology that it readily mobilizes most of the assumptions people ordinarily make about biology (Atran and Sperber 1991).

4.8   Conclusions

The sort of cultural information most susceptible to modular processing is the sort of information most easily transmitted from individual to individual, most apt to survive within a culture over time, and most likely to recur independently in different cultures and at different times. Critically, it is also the most disposed to cultural variation and elaboration. It makes cultural variation comprehensible. This evolutionarily constrained learning landscape can be viewed from two complementary perspectives. One the one hand, it is forgiving enough to allow strikingly different cognitions and behaviors among distinct cultural groups living in the same habitat. On the other hand, it also provides sufficient structure to allow us to understand these selfsame contrasts as variations on a panhuman theme of interactions between people and generic species.

In sum, folkbiology plays a special role in cultural evolution in general, and particularly in the development of totemic tribal religions and Western biological science. To say an evolved mental structure is "innate" is not to say that every important aspect of its phenotypic expression is "genetically determined." The particular organisms observed, actual exemplars targeted, and specific inferences made can vary significantly from person to person. This is because (1) inputs naturally cluster in causally redundant ways inasmuch as that is the way the world is (e.g., where there are wings there are beaks or bills, where there are predators there are prey, where there are fruit-eating birds there are fruit-bearing trees, and so on); and (2) dedicated mental modules selectively target these inputs for processing by domain-specific inferential structures (e.g., to produce natural taxonomies).

Within this evolutionary landscape of medium-sized objects that are snapshots in a single lifespan of geological time, biologically poised mental structures channel cognitive development but do not determine it. Cultural life, including religion and science, can selectively target and modify parts of this landscape but cannot simply ignore or completely replace it.

The full expression of the folkbiology module may require natural environmental triggering conditions (akin to those of ancestral environments) and cultural support perhaps lacking for certain groups in industrialized societies, including the usual subjects in most cognitive psychology experiments. These subjects, then, would be prime candidates for studies of knowledge devolution—at least in the domain of folkbiology.

In the next chapter studies of the development of folkbiology are described in a cross-cultural context. Again, we will see evidence both of devolution and of more robust processes that are likely universal.

5   Development of Folkbiological Cognition

In this chapter we review research on children's biology. As noted in the introduction, to assess both the generality of claims that have been made and to determine which aspects of the development of biological cognition are robust over culture and experience, it is important to go beyond the standard population of urban U.S. children living near major research universities. As will be seen, this work is also highly relevant to science learning in school settings. This work bears on both the existence of a folkbiological module and its ontological status. We begin with the latter.

5.1   Background: Relation of Folkbiology to Folkpsychology

In her influential 1985 book Susan Carey proposed that young children's understanding of living things is initially embedded in a folkpsychological, rather than folkbiological, explanatory framework and that human beings act as the prototype. Her data suggested that children did not develop an independent model of biology where humans were seen as one animal among many until they were 10 to 12 years old. In short, on this view, children have to undergo a fundamental conceptual change to achieve an autonomous biology.

A strong form of evidence for this theory comes from an inductive inference task where children are told that some novel property is true of one biological kind (e.g., "Humans have a little green thing inside them called an omentum"), then are asked whether that property is true of other biological kinds (e.g., "Do you think that dogs have an omentum?"). Three major findings bolster the claim that young children's conceptions of the biological world are anthropocentric. First, children more readily project properties from humans onto other living kinds than from other living kinds onto one another. The other two findings are consequences of this difference in induction potential. The second result concerns asymmetries in projection: inferences from human to mammals are stronger than from mammals to humans. Third, 4-year-old children violate projections according to similarity: inferences from humans to bugs are stronger than from bees to bugs. Together, these findings suggest that humans are the preferred base for young children's inferences about the biological world.

Carey's claims have not gone unchallenged and her book has served to stimulate a large body of research on children's biology. The current consensus appears to be that even young children do have distinct biological theories (for extensive reviews, see Carey 1999a; Inagaki and Hatano 2001; Gelman 2003), though these theories may differ systematically from the science that they must learn in school. Nonetheless Carey's induction task continues to be of interest. There is work indicating that the relative prominence of psychological versus biological construals of biological kinds is sensitive to contextual factors (Guntheil, Vera, and Keil 1998). Our work shows that there is an important cultural and experiential dimension that merits attention. Specifically, our evidence suggests that the anthropocentrism observed by Carey in young children does not reflect a failure to distinguish biology from psychology. Part of the story may be that humans are the only biological entity that young urban children knew very much about. But the picture is a bit more complicated—the ambiguous status of humans as animals versus contrastive with animals likely plays an important role as well.

Research on children's biology has been conducted almost exclusively with individuals from North American, urban, technologically advanced populations. In the few studies that go beyond this sample (e.g., Inagaki and Hatano in Japan), the focus is still on urban, majority-culture children from technologically advanced societies. Thus, it is not clear which aspects of children's naive biology are likely to be universal and which depend critically on cultural conceptions and conditions of learning.

5.2 Role of Culture and Experience in Induction

To evaluate the role of cultural milieu and conditions of learning in children's inductive reasoning, we initially studied four populations: urban Boston children, rural Wisconsin majority-culture children, Menominee children, and Yukatek Maya children of varying ages (4 to 11) and adults (Ross et al. 2003; Atran et al. 2001). All testing in the United States was in English; Yukatek Maya was used for the Maya children and adults.

Detailed color drawings of objects were used to represent base and target categories. Four bases were used in Mexico: human, dog, peccary, and bee. Targets were divided into two sets. Each set included a representative of the categories human (man, woman), mammal (deer, coatimundi), bird (eagle, chachalaca), reptile (boa, turtle), invertebrate (worm, fly), tree (kanan, gumbo limbo), stuff (stone, mud), artifact (bicycle, pencil), and sun (in both sets). The U.S. populations were given human, wolf, bee, goldenrod, and water as bases and a corresponding set of mammals, birds, reptiles, invertebrates, plants, stuff, and artifacts as targets.

As in Carey's studies, children were shown a picture of one of the bases and taught a new property about it. Thus, the experimenter might show the dog picture, and say, "Now, there's this stuff called andro. Andro is found inside some things. One thing that has andro inside is dogs. Now, I'm going to show you some pictures of other things, and I want you to tell me if you think they have andro inside like dogs do." Participants were then shown each of the targets and asked, "Does it have andro inside it, like the [base]?" Properties were unfamiliarly internal substances of the form "has X inside." A different property was used for each base.

Results   Although our methodology differed somewhat from the original Carey study, we can make a rough comparison to examine qualitative trends. The overall results are summarized in table 5.1. Our findings from studies of inductive projection among Yukatek Maya do not replicate Carey's results with urban American children (compare figures 5.1 and 5.2) and are not consistent with the claim that folkbiology is anthropocentric until late childhood. Here we present data from younger children (4- to 5-year-olds). First, for Yukatek Maya, (1) projections from humans are no stronger than projections from other living kinds, (2) there is no overall human-animal asymmetry, and (3) young children do not violate their own perceptions of similarity out of preference for humans as an inductive base.

There are, however, some asymmetry effects for the youngest Yukatek girls with respect to a wild- versus domestic-animal base (human → mammal > peccary → human) and for the youngest children overall, with respect to inferences involving invertebrates. The fact that such asymmetries are not generalized across the youngest age group suggests that they may be the result of familiarity rather than anthropocentric bias as such. Younger girls are less familiar with wild animals than younger boys, and younger children on the whole are less familiar with invertebrates than they are with humans or mammals. Less familiarity with

Table 5.1
Sousa et al. 2002: Means for Yukatek Maya induction task

	Young children (4–5)			Older children (6–7)			Adults		
	females	males	average	females	males	average	females	males	average
Human									
human	1.00	1.00	1.00	0.96	1.00	0.98	1.00	1.00	1.00
mammal	0.63	0.57	0.60	0.46	0.57	0.52	0.58	0.71	0.65
bird	0.63	0.43	0.53	0.50	0.48	0.49	0.25	0.58	0.42
reptile	0.75	0.36	0.55	0.38	0.19	0.29	0.17	0.46	0.31
invertebrate	0.67	0.43	0.55	0.62	0.33	0.47	0.13	0.25	0.19
tree	0.50	0.36	0.43	0.19	0.10	0.14	0.00	0.04	0.02
stuff	0.42	0.43	0.42	0.23	0.05	0.14	0.04	0.04	0.04
artifact	0.50	0.29	0.39	0.23	0.00	0.12	0.08	0.00	0.04
sun	0.58	0.50	0.54	0.42	0.38	0.40	0.13	0.08	0.10
Dog									
human	0.64	0.54	0.59	0.83	0.17	0.50	0.25	0.71	0.48
mammal	0.89	0.89	0.89	1.00	1.00	1.00	1.00	0.96	0.98
bird	0.46	0.68	0.57	0.33	0.58	0.46	0.17	0.42	0.29
reptile	0.64	0.46	0.55	0.17	0.25	0.21	0.04	0.38	0.21
invertebrate	0.32	0.39	0.36	0.17	0.25	0.21	0.21	0.17	0.19
tree	0.25	0.25	0.25	0.08	0.08	0.08	0.04	0.00	0.02
stuff	0.29	0.14	0.21	0.08	0.00	0.04	0.08	0.08	0.08
artifact	0.25	0.11	0.18	0.25	0.00	0.13	0.13	0.00	0.06
sun	0.36	0.32	0.34	0.17	0.25	0.21	0.08	0.08	0.08

Pec									
human	0.08	0.50	0.29	0.58	0.33	0.46	0.79	0.67	0.73
mammal	0.50	0.71	0.61	0.81	0.81	0.81	0.79	0.83	0.81
bird	0.42	0.36	0.39	0.58	0.62	0.60	0.25	0.54	0.40
reptile	0.50	0.50	0.50	0.46	0.33	0.40	0.17	0.46	0.31
invertebrate	0.42	0.29	0.35	0.58	0.33	0.46	0.17	0.42	0.29
tree	0.33	0.14	0.24	0.19	0.05	0.12	0.25	0.21	0.23
stuff	0.33	0.36	0.35	0.23	0.05	0.14	0.25	0.38	0.31
artifact	0.42	0.14	0.28	0.12	0.00	0.06	0.04	0.00	0.02
sun	0.33	0.50	0.42	0.31	0.19	0.25	0.13	0.08	0.10
Bee									
human	0.33	0.29	0.31	0.50	0.33	0.42	0.58	0.75	0.67
mammal	0.25	0.29	0.27	0.54	0.52	0.53	0.21	0.33	0.27
bird	0.46	0.29	0.37	0.38	0.52	0.45	0.08	0.29	0.19
reptile	0.50	0.29	0.39	0.42	0.43	0.43	0.00	0.29	0.15
invertebrate	0.92	0.39	0.65	0.85	0.76	0.80	0.75	0.63	0.69
tree	0.25	0.14	0.20	0.19	0.10	0.14	0.38	0.63	0.50
stuff	0.17	0.21	0.19	0.31	0.05	0.18	0.17	0.13	0.15
artifact	0.42	0.07	0.24	0.12	0.00	0.06	0.08	0.08	0.08
sun	0.58	0.36	0.47	0.27	0.19	0.23	0.13	0.13	0.13

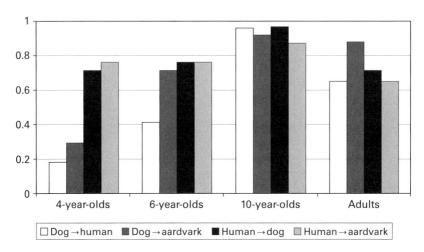

Figure 5.1
Urban U.S. subjects' willingness to project unknown biological properties (after Carey 1985).

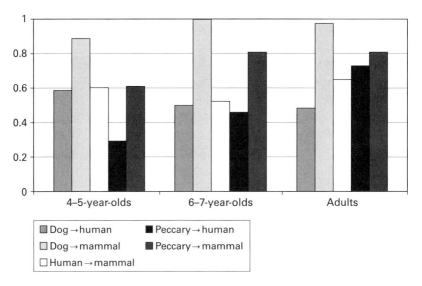

Figure 5.2
Yukatek Maya subjects' willingness to project unknown biological properties (after Atran et al. 2001).

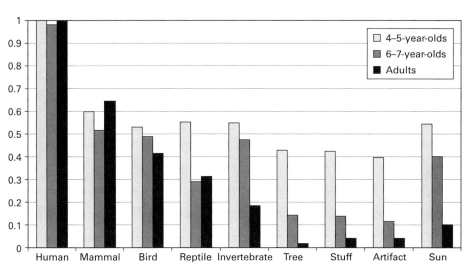

Figure 5.3
Yukatek Maya projections from human base.

wild animals and invertebrates may favor them less as sources of induction. The fact that dogs are a better base for induction than are peccaries is consistent with this observation. One candidate explanatory principle is that the more properties a child knows about some kind, the more likely they are to generalize some new property to other living kinds. We will evaluate this and other explanations later in this chapter.

Young children (especially the girls) generalized in a fairly undifferentiated way from humans (figure 5.3). It is not clear how to interpret this pattern of results. One possibility is that these children lack a clear grasp of how humans fit into the tree of life (the girls show the same pattern with the peccary, an animal with which they are unfamiliar). Another possibility is that humans, being the primary focus of ecological interactions, provide a plausible inductive base for thematic relationships that may have little correlation with taxonomic distance.

On the whole, Yukatek Maya children show some intriguing gender differentiation. These gender differences may reflect the strong sexual division of activity that is institutionalized early in the first year of life. In the *jeetz~meek'* ceremony, Maya girls are introduced by the women to household utensils, whereas Maya boys are introduced by the men to agricultural and hunting tools. Later in life, Maya women will spend their time almost wholly in the vicinity of the house and house garden, in close interaction with domestic animals. By contrast, Maya men spend days, weeks, and even months in the forest away from home. For Maya females, dogs are household animals, whereas men value dogs as hunting animals. Maya boys also venture out into the forest with their fathers at an early age, and so become familiar with wild animals, such as the peccary, before girls do. These findings suggest that induction patterns may be influenced by relative familiarity with animals and by the culturally specific character of the functional and ecological relationships between humans and other natural categories of elements.

Results with U.S. Populations   In this study (Ross et al. 2003) we compared urban majority culture, rural majority, and rural Menominee children's inductive generalizations. The pattern of responding varied substantially across groups. The young urban U.S. children (5–6-year-olds) generalized in a broad, almost completely undifferentiated manner. The only clear trend was greater generalization from a human base to a human target than to other targets. Older urban children (7–8 and 9–10-year-olds) generalized in terms of biological affinity but showed a strong asymmetry in reasoning between humans and other animals. Although these data do not replicate Carey's precise findings, they agree in the outcome that young urban children did not generalize based on biological affinity.

The young, rural majority-culture children revealed a different pattern; they showed the mature pattern of generalizing in terms of biological affinity. Interestingly, both they and older rural children showed asymmetries in reasoning between humans and animals and often justified a failure to extend a property from an animal to humans on the grounds that "people are not animals." This observation strongly suggests that the asymmetry does not derive from humans being conceptualized as the "prototypic" animal. Instead, seeing humans as animals may be something of a developmental achievement, as suggested by Johnson, Mervis, and Boster (1992; see also the sorting task in Carey 1985). Finally, older rural children gave some evidence of reasoning in terms of ecological relations, as when they justified generalizing from bees to bears because a bee might sting a bear or a bear might acquire the property by eating the bee's honey.

Menominee children demonstrated yet a third pattern. First, even the youngest Menominee often reasoned in terms of ecological relations. In addition, children of all ages generalized in terms of taxonomic relatedness and showed no reliable human-animal asymmetries. The Menominee origin myth has people coming from the bear, and even the youngest children are familiar with the animal-based clan system. In short, there is cultural support for a symmetrical relation between humans and other animals. As we will see, ecological relations play an important role in overcoming asymmetrics.

Overall, it appears that lack of intimate contact with plants and animals may be responsible for the anthropocentric bias observed with urban American children. Consistent with this view, Inagaki (1990) presented evidence that experience influences children's biological reasoning. She found that kindergartners actively involved in raising goldfish were more likely than their counterparts who did not raise goldfish to reason about a novel aquatic animal (a frog) by analogy to goldfish rather than by analogy to humans. This is also consistent with induction being based on degree of familiarity with a given base concept.

A Test of the Familiarity Hypothesis

Although the idea that willingness to generalize is driven by degree of familiarity is appealing, some further observations call this notion into question. To see this we need to look at the data in greater detail. In all of our observations generalization from a nonhuman mammal to another mammal is always greater than generalization from humans to another mammal. This tends to undermine the humans-as-the-prototypic-animal argument. One could suggest that humans are less similar to other animals and that this limits generalization. But this is not easy to reconcile with the basic notion of typicality. One could argue that humans are (according to humans) an ideal and that it is this notion of prototypicality that drives induction. Although this notion accounts for the asymmetries involving humans, it fails to address other asymmetries.

The familiarity account for asymmetries is less at risk. It does not seem so implausible to argue that there is a trade-off between projectability and similarity that produces both human-animal asymmetries and the nonhuman mammal being a better base than humans are for other mammal targets.

But the familiarity account is not, by itself, sufficient. If we look at a broader range of asymmetries a very different picture emerges (Medin and Waxman 2007). In particular, the Ross et al. data show that reasoning from plant to mammal is stronger than reasoning from mammal to plant (see table 5.2, where we have excluded the data from the youngest urban children since they generalized indiscriminately). This finding strongly undermines the idea that level of knowledge determines amount of generalization, because U.S. children surely know more about mammals than about plants.

Table 5.2
Ross et al. 2003 asymmetries

Population	Age							
	City		Rural			Menominee		
	7–9	9–11	5–7	7–9	9–11	5–7	7–9	9–11
Human-mammal	0.70	0.73	0.52	0.58	0.80	0.58	0.70	0.72
Mammal-human	0.33	0.35	0.24	0.16	0.47	0.42	0.47	0.52
Mammal-mammal	0.96	0.90	0.76	0.78	0.92	0.75	0.82	0.88
Human-insect	0.47	0.35	0.07	0.34	0.63	0.46	0.55	0.48
Insect-human	0.31	0.08	0.28	0.20	0.53	0.63	0.35	0.38
Human-plant	0.50	0.27	0.16	0.17	0.30	0.30	0.22	0.34
Plant-human	0.13	0.72	0.10	0.12	0.30	0.42	0.41	0.38
Mammal-insect	0.50	0.38	0.38	0.28	0.47	0.57	0.56	0.52
Insect-mammal	0.50	0.56	0.38	0.25	0.56	0.56	0.56	0.56
Mammal-plant	0.32	0.12	0.14	0.14	0.22	0.18	0.33	0.24
Plant-mammal	0.32	0.38	0.24	0.25	0.42	0.50	0.42	0.46
Insect-plant	0.40	0.44	0.26	0.30	0.58	0.46	0.40	0.42
Plant-insect	0.31	0.62	0.24	0.34	0.33	0.29	0.41	0.43

Distinctive Features and Categories   We think that different patterns of distinctive feature and category label activation play a major role in asymmetries. First consider category labels. In U.S. culture, humans are both considered to be animals (and not plants) and to be contrasted with animals (footnote: *animal* may also have a default meaning as "beast" or "mammal" or "quadruped"). Fleshing out this idea (no pun intended), one needs to add that distinctive features (categories) of the target diminish inductive confidence. The idea is that both "animal" and "humans as a contrast with animal" are associated with the category "people," but only "animal" is associated with the animals typically used. When some animal other than humans is a target, "animal" may be activated and tend to prime the sense of animal associated with humans. In contrast, when some nonhuman animal is the base and human the target, the category "human" may get activated in the target and the induction is called into question.

The argument would carry through in the same way for distinctive features. Mammal-to-human generalization is limited by the fact that humans have many distinctive features; the claim would be that other mammals have fewer distinctive features. (Note that this claim represents a means of incorporating familiarity effects, but in the form of limiting generalization to more familiar kinds, because greater familiarity implies greater knowledge of distinctive features.)

This view makes some clear predictions. First, the "people-aren't-animals" justification should occur more frequently when human is a target than when it is a base for induction. Our Wisconsin populations show this pattern. For example, older rural majority-culture children mention shared categories twenty out of twenty-six times when humans are the base and a mammal is the target versus six out of fourteen times when some other mammal is the base and humans are the target (Medin and Waxman 2007).

Second, we should expect the same pattern for mentioning common versus distinctive features (there should be more distinctive features when humans are the target rather than the base for induction).

Third, in cultures where the human-animal contrast is more salient (e.g., Indonesia), there may be diminished generalization between humans and animals and, as a consequence, diminished asymmetries. We have preliminary data from Indonesia supporting this prediction (Anggoro, Waxman, and Medin 2005).

Fourth, the justifications for failure to generalize should focus on distinctive features and/or categories of the target, not the base concept. This is what we observe more than 95 percent of the time in the Wisconsin data (again, see Medin and Waxman 2007).

The distinctive features/categories account implies that asymmetries are a natural finding even among populations with extensive biological knowledge. Of course, ecological reasoning may work to undermine and in some cases reverse asymmetries. A further look at justifications suggests that children are much more likely to reason ecologically when the active ecological agent (animals are more active than plants) is in the target position than in the base position. So the lack of human-animal asymmetries in younger Menominee children and Yukatek Maya may derive, in part, from people being seen as more active ecological agents. In support of this idea, we conducted a follow-up study in Wisconsin where we essentially eliminated ecological reasoning (more about this later). Under this circumstance we observed substantially higher human-animal asymmetries in both populations and for both age groups.

Asymmetrical use of ecological reasoning may account for the plant-animal asymmetries we noted before. In our rural majority-culture population we counted seventeen ecological justifications when the base was a (nonhuman) mammal and the target a plant and fifty-five ecological justifications for a plant as the base and a (nonhuman) mammal as the target.

The corresponding numbers when humans were the mammal in question are five and sixteen. This suggests that at least for majority-culture children (we do not have enough justifications from Menominee children to get a clear picture), other mammals are seen as more active ecological agents than are humans (a direct comparison of human to mammal versus mammal to human reveals thirteen cases of ecological reasoning versus eight, a trend consistent with this speculation).

Summary
These observations seriously complicate the interpretation of the induction task. Consequently, the induction task may have limited utility, unless it is supplemented by additional converging evidence, such as justifications. The justification data we do have imply that distinctive features and categories of the target category are crucial to asymmetries. In addition, ecological reasoning is more likely to be used when the ecologically active agent is in the target position. Despite these complications, our data indicate that anthropocentrism in reasoning is the exception, not the rule.

Before moving on, let's return to Carey and her procedure. It is the case that 4- and 6-year-olds were trained and tested on separate days, though this apparently was not done for older children and adults. The context was that children were being taught about "spleen" or "omentum" along with a review/probe of other, presumably more entrenched properties like "has a lung" or "has a heart." The teaching was fairly elaborate, including showing kids a diagram of just where the omentum is. The test probes asked if something was true of some kind without any explicit appeal to other kinds that might or might not have that property. The data analyses were restricted to children who did correctly attribute the practiced property to the practiced base. In any event, inferences invited by the experimenter (as in our studies) may show a different pattern than those that arise spontaneously where the task is not transparently about inference. We have some preliminary evidence that this is the case and that the pattern of task differences varies between urban and rural children. Even more intriguing, we have suggestive evidence that the anthropocentric pattern of reasoning in young urban children is an acquired cultural model. That is, 3-year-old urban children do not show the anthropocentrism that we observe in 4- to 5-year-old urban children. In short, we are not at the end of the story (Waxman and Medin 2007).

5.3   Childhood Conceptions of Species Essences

Given the framework outlined in chapters 1 and 2, we would expect that essentialism would be among the most robust features in children's (and adults') reasoning. Young of a species have the potential to develop certain adult characteristics before those characteristics appear. The origins of these characteristics can be explained in two broadly different ways: nature and nurture. Some characteristics seem likely to develop from birth because they are essential to the species to which the individual belongs, such as a squirrel's ability to jump from tree to tree and hide acorns. Other characteristics are determined by the environment in which the individual is reared, such as a squirrel's fear or lack of fear of human beings.

Gelman and Wellman (1991) argue that young children predict category-typical characteristics of individual animals based on the innate potential of the animal (i.e., the species of its birth parent) rather than the environment in which it was raised (i.e., the species of its adoptive parent). Using an adoption study, they showed that 4-year-old children judge that a baby cow raised by pigs will have the category-typical characteristics of cows (moos, straight tail) rather than pigs (oinks, curly tail). They interpret the results as showing that preschoolers believe that the innate potential or essence of species determines how an individual will develop, even in contrary environments.[1]

This study has been criticized as inconclusive with regard to children's assumptions about innate potential for two reasons. First, because the experimenters told the child that the baby and mother were of the same species, the study does not address the question of how the children identify to which species the baby belongs in the first place (Johnson and Solomon 1997). Given this explicit verbal identification, one cannot rule out that the children's performance reflects an essentialist bias that is a general property of language. That is, the children might expect that the animal would continue to have the properties of the labeled species, even in the absence of reasoning about the mechanism involved (Gelman and Hirschfeld 1999).[2]

Second, the study explored only known facts about species and their associated properties. It did not examine whether children use the concept of biological parentage as an inferential framework for interpreting and explaining hitherto unknown facts. It may be that a child has learned from experience, and as a matter of fact, that a calf is a cow because it was born to a cow. Still, the child may not know that having certain kinds of parents *causes* a cow to be a cow (Carey 1995).

We have been studying several culturally distinct populations to test the extent to which children's assumptions about innate species potential govern projection of both known and unknown properties. In one study (for details see Atran et al. 2001), Yukatek Maya children and adults were presented with a forced-choice task involving an adoption scenario. They were asked whether an adult animal adopted at birth would resemble its adoptive parent (e.g., cow) or birth parent (e.g., pig) on four different individual traits: known behaviors (e.g., moo / oink), known physical features (e.g., straight / curly tail), unknown behaviors (e.g., looks for chachalacas / looks for pigeons), and unknown physical features (e.g., heart gets flatter / rounder when it is sleeping). Known traits were context-free, category-typical features that the children readily associate with species, whereas unknown traits were chosen to minimize any possibility of factual or prelearned associations of traits with categories. Each unknown trait within a set was attributed to the birth parent for half the participants and to the adoptive parent for the other half. This ensured that projection patterns of the unknown traits were not based on prior associations.

Stories were accompanied by sketches of each parent. Sketches were designed to unambiguously represent a particular species of animal with minimum detail. In addition, sketches of known physical features (e.g., a sketch of a curly or straight tail), unknown physical features (e.g., flat versus round heart), and relevant aspects of unknown behavioral contexts (e.g., closed versus open eyes when afraid, stops in front of mahogany versus cedar trees) were shown to participants. These sketches in no way indicated the species to which the traits belonged.

The story was followed by two comprehension questions: (1) "Who gave birth to the baby?" and (2) "Who did the baby grow up with?" Children then were presented with the experimental probes. For example they might be told: "The cow mooed and the pig oinked. When the baby is all grown up will it moo like a cow or oink like a pig?" The probes were followed by a bias control in which the participant was asked, "When the baby was growing up did it eat with animals that looked like X or animals that looked like Y?" (Notice that this last probe involves an inference and is not simply a memory check.)

Overall, results showed systematic and robust preference for attributions from the birth parent (see table 5.3). This preference was observed for all Yukatek age groups and for known and unknown behavior and

Table 5.3
Percent birth-parent choice for each probe type for each group

Group	Known			Unknown			Kind	Blood	Bias control (Food)
	Behavior	Phys. feat.	Mean	Behavior	Phys. feat.	Mean			
4–5-year-olds	0.74**	0.68*	0.71	0.69**	0.68*	0.69	0.65	0.56	0.06***
6–7-year-olds	0.96***	0.97***	0.97	0.82***	0.83***	0.83	0.99***	0.79**	0.01***
Adults	1.0***	0.96***	0.98	0.90***	0.93***	0.92	0.97***	0.88***	0***
Mean	0.90	0.87	0.88	0.81	0.81	0.81	0.87	0.74	0.02

* $p < 0.05$, ** $p < 0.01$, *** $p < 0.001$.

Table 5.4
Percent birth-parent choice for Brazilian children (after Sousa et al. 2002)

	Known behavior	Known trait	Unknown behavior	Unknown trait	Blood	Control
4-year-olds	0.87***	0.87***	0.78**	0.83**	0.33	0.13***
5-year-olds	0.92***	0.96***	0.78**	0.87***	0.25*	0.00***
6-year-olds	0.71*	0.87***	0.71*	0.75*	0.26*	0.04***
7-year-olds	0.83**	0.83**	0.79**	0.83**	0.35	0.00***
Adults	1.00***	1.00***	0.83**	0.87***	0.96***	0.00***

$* p < .05, ** p < .01, *** p < .001$.

physical properties. The trend was somewhat stronger in older children and adults and slightly stronger for known than unknown properties. The low mean on the bias-control probe for all groups indicates that the method of the study did not bias participant responses toward the birth parent.

In work with U.S. urban and rural majority-culture children, with Menominee children, and with three groups of urban children in Brasilia (Brazil; see table 5.4), we also find that young children show a strong pattern of inferencing in terms of birth parents (e.g., Sousa, Atran, and Medin 2002). The developmental trajectory of this pattern varies across populations, sometimes weakening in older children and other times strengthening (table 5.3).

In addition, judgments about whether biological manipulations—such as, for example, a blood transfusion (where the baby's blood is replaced by blood from the adoptive parent)—change kindhood also vary across culture and development (Waxman, Medin, and Ross 2007). Overall the data are consistent with a universal initial assumption of an underlying essence for biological kinds that may be somewhat modified by the cultural landscape.[3] These findings, together with Gelman and Wellman's (1991) earlier results, raise the possibility that such an essentialist bias in children may be universal.

There are two types of objections to our claims that we will briefly consider. One is simply an empirical issue: Is this pattern of results truly universal? Bloch, Solomon, and Carey (2001) report that 7–13-year-old Zafimaniry children from a remote village in Madagascar reasoning about an adoption scenario show a bias toward adoptive parents, an apparent counterexample to our claims. We have three reservations about this study. First, the features attributed to adoptive and birth parents were not counterbalanced and tended to be much more negative for the adoptive parent. Informants may have the belief that negative properties are more powerful and dominate positive qualities (e.g., as in the historical "one-drop rule" in Southern states; see also Stoler 1995). Second, the children in the Bloch et al. study were older than they were in our studies. Thus, Hirschfeld (1996) shows that, for racial categories, fifth and sixth graders show strong social effects not apparent in second graders. We find greatest agreement (and a birth bias) in the youngest children in our various populations. The ideal test case for our hypothesis is a culture where the adults are not essentialists about ethnicity (see Astuti 1995, but also Gil-White 2001 for cautions concerning claims about adult conceptions). Here we would still expect that young children would be essentialists (certainly for animals and perhaps for humans as well) even if adults were not (though adults may be essentialists about animals other than humans).

Finally, there is reason to expect that reasoning about animal and plant species may be different from reasoning about people. Indeed, in follow-up studies with the Vezo of Madagascar, Astuti, Solomon, and Carey (2004) found a reliable birth bias for the youngest children they tested (6 years old) when animals rather than humans were used in the adoption scenario.

Another objection to our data is that we may be guilty of overinterpreting the results in the sense that projection on the basis of species membership should not be equated with projection on the basis of some essence (see Rips 2001 for an amplification of this criticism). An alternative view is that children are employing ideas about causal relations but that they may have no notion of "essence" whatsoever (Strevens 2000). Although this distinction may be subtle, we have discussed it at length elsewhere (see the Ahn et al. 2001 commentary) and will confine ourselves to a few remarks in the context of summarizing this section.

5.4 Summary

The combination of developmental and cross-cultural studies confirms universal aspects of children's folkbiological cognition, supports the claim that biology is a conceptual domain distinct from psychology, and indicates that anthropocentrism in young children is the exception, not the rule.

The attribution of essences to specieslike groupings has implications for the organization and structure of taxonomies and for the basic level. Our claim is that from a quite early age children have intuitions that the mechanisms underlying essential causes are biological. The essential causal relations are those involving, for example, birth, biological relatedness, and internal structure. Just how detailed these notions are and how they are modified by experience and cultural milieu await further comparative study.

These same sorts of comparative studies reveal components of biological cognition that vary systematically as a function of cultural milieu and input conditions (intimacy of contact with nature). The fact that young Native American children often reason in terms of ecological relations poses a challenge for interpreting patterns of projection on the induction task. On the other hand, the prominence of ecological reasoning points to a component of children's biology that has scarcely been studied, in part because this pattern is scarcely evident in developmental studies with "standard" populations.

5.5   Implications for Science Education

These studies may be of practical importance for understanding science learning in the classroom. Earlier we described results suggesting that Menominee children have a precocious understanding of biology. Indeed, on standardized tests, fourth-grade Menominee score above the national average in science and it is their best subject. Strikingly, however, by eighth grade, science is their very worst subject and they score below the national average. The fact that reading scores do not show a corresponding drop suggests that something peculiar to science instruction is the key. At a minimum these observations indicate that the educational systems are not taking advantage of the knowledge that Menominee children are bringing to the classroom.

What is responsible for science going from the best to the worst subject in just a few years? We have been conducting a range of interviews, observations, and follow-up studies but at this point we can only offer speculations. It seems to us that there is a mismatch between science as it is taught and Menominee culture on at least three levels: (1) specific facts, (2) knowledge organization, and (3) cultural values and practices.

On the level of facts, in Menominee culture (and in many cultures around the world) all of nature is alive, including not only plants and animals but also rocks and water. In the Ross et al. study, young Menominee children were twice as likely as their majority-culture counterparts to say that plants are alive, but also somewhat more likely to say that rocks and water are alive. Later on, we did another interview where we constructed more detailed probes where we asked whether things were alive, died, needed food, needed air, had babies, and so on. Under these conditions the percentage of Menominee children who said that plants are alive dropped dramatically (from about 75 percent to about 30 percent). We think that this reflects the conflict between cultural notions about what is alive and the formal notion of alive taught in science (the fact that young rural majority-culture children were somewhat *more* likely to say that plants are alive under this detailed probing suggests that it was not just that the task was confusing).

On a more abstract level, lack of transfer may result from a mismatch between cultural ways of organizing knowledge and the organization provided in science instruction. As we have seen and will see again later, Menominee children and adults often reason ecologically and if biology textbooks use ecology as an organizing principle, compatibility would be maximized. We examined some of the textbooks being used and found that when ecology was included it tended to be one of the last chapters in the book.

In our own research we have seen the consequences of this sort of mismatch. Specifically, in the follow-up study alluded to earlier we included both native or exotic species as bases (on separate days—one or the other on a given day) and the targets were always a mixture of native (squirrel, bee, pine tree) and exotic (lion, tarantula, cactus) species. Although our original objective was to compare reasoning with familiar and unfamiliar bases to familiar and unfamiliar targets (including the possibility that our exotic bases might be more familiar to urban than to rural children), the key result for our Wisconsin populations seems to have been that we dramatically reduced or eliminated ecological reasoning (e.g., an inference from bees to bears on grounds that bears eat honey or that bees sting bears). When we looked at the subset of data where the base and target matched a base and target used in the Ross et al. study, we found no difference for pairs where we had not seen ecological reasoning before and much reduced generalization for pairs where we had observed ecological reasoning before. This was true for all Menominee children and for the older rural majority-culture children. In short, the data suggest that we failed to access children's ecological knowledge because the mixed structure of our probes (both native and exotic) only made sense from a taxonomic sense (in other words, it was an ecological jumble). These results show that knowledge acquired outside the classroom will not necessarily find its way into the classroom.

The most abstract level of cultural models, values, and practices may turn out to be the most important. A number of educators have made the point that science (instruction) is not acultural or culturally neutral (e.g., Allen 1998). For her dissertation, Megan Bang (2005), a learning sciences graduate student at Northwestern University, systematically analyzed practices associated with science curricula and instruction and compared them with the practices of rural Menominee, rural European-American, and urban Indian parents and children. Her observations and interviews are consistent with the view that a major challenge to Indian children's learning science in school is the mismatch between school and community practices. Specifically, her interviews suggest that there is a better match between majority-culture parents' views of nature and science instruction than between Menominee parents' views and instruction. For example, both the texts and the majority-culture parents tend to imply that nature is an externality to be exploited, cared for, learned about, and so on (see Kellert 1993 for orientations toward the natural world). Menominee parents and urban Indian parents (only some of whom are Menominees) tend to emphasize that we are a part of nature and that nature is not an externality (Bang et al. 2005). This "a part" versus "apart" orientation may render some aspects of science education alien to Native Americans in the same way that an economic approach to a family (e.g., How many dollars is a daughter worth?) is repugnant to most people.

This brief description does not do justice to Bang's dissertation. She analyzed practices such as how diagrams presented in traditional science texts differed from diagrams in texts written by Native American educators. She also investigated differences in discourse style between European-American parents ("get to the point") and Indian parents ("provide the context first and the setting may be as important as the so-called topic or point of the story"). She measured the latter by asking parents to describe the last time they went fishing and counting the number of words before fish were mentioned (median of 27th versus median of 83rd word). Cultural compatibility between community and school practices was consistently higher for European Americans than for Native Americans (Bang, Medin, and Atran 2007).

The obvious way to test this analysis is to make science instruction more culturally consonant for Indian children and to see whether their learning improves. For example, one might structure biology units using ecosystems as the primary organizing principle and provide contextual grounding of new information. As a member of our research team, Bang will be examining these predictions both on the Menominee reservation and in an urban setting (Chicago). In short, what began as a theoretical question about the generality of Carey's results has evolved into a convergence of theory and application aimed at improving science education for Native American children.

Although we are nearer to a beginning point than to an end point in understanding how children's informal biology affects or is affected by science instruction, there is little doubt that understanding the relationship between formal and informal learning is a critically important task. And cultural knowledge, values, and models are an important part of the story. We will take a closer look at the interrelationships among these variables in chapters 7–10. First, however, we owe you an analysis of different theoretical approaches to understanding culture and cultural processes.

6 Culture as a Notional, Not Natural, Kind

In this chapter we review different approaches to the study of culture. Each view has strengths and limitations, but we will argue for a view of studying cultures as distributions of ideas. Intuitively, one might define culture as the shared knowledge, values, beliefs, and practices among a group of people living in geographic proximity who share a history, a language, and cultural identification (see Brumann 1999 and associated commentaries for examples of this approach in anthropology). From a psychological perspective, Campbell's (1958) proposed measures of social entitativity in terms of common fate, similarity, proximity, resistance to intrusions, and internal diffusion seem applicable to cultural groups.

But it is important to note that the question of how culture should be defined is separable from the question of how best to study it. Although we think a definition of a culture in terms of history, proximity, language, and identification is useful and (if not too rigidly applied) perhaps even necessary as a beginning point, it does not follow that the cultural content of interest must be shared ideas and beliefs.

It is not easy to escape from this intuitive notion of culture any more than it is easy for biology to escape from the notion of species as ahistorical, well-bounded entities sharing an underlying essence (e.g., Mayr 1989). In the same way that cultures are not natural kinds, biological kinds do not have the stable characteristics often attributed to them. Modern evolutionary biology is the study of change and not just stability. Continuing this parallel with evolutionary biology, we believe that modern cultural research must be able to overcome intuitive notions of culture in order to focus on causal processes associated with stability *and* change. Both biological and cultural research started with folk notions (of species and culture, respectively) and they have served each field well as starting points. Ultimately, though, such conceptions must be radically altered for further progress to be made.

At the end of the chapter we will return to the parallels between species in biology and intuitive notions of culture in cognitive science. Bearing in mind these issues concerning stability and change, we turn now to current stances on how culture and cultural processes should be studied. Each of them is useful for some purposes and all of them have limitations.

6.1 Culture as Norms and Rules

It appears natural to think that the cultural contents of interest must be shared in order to qualify as "cultural." Note, however, that this commitment undercuts the dynamic side of cultural processes: distinctive values, beliefs, and knowledge might or might not be consensual within a culture. For example, a culture may have a set of beliefs and practices known only to a privileged group of people (e.g., healers, elders, ruling elite) that nonetheless are powerful forces within a given culture (and distinguish one culture from another). In short, this view of culture as shared beliefs and practices not only prejudges the issue of what constitutes cultural content, but also, as a consequence, directs attention away from understanding the dynamic nature of social processes.

Some influential models of culture formation and evolution in biology and anthropology take a somewhat more liberal view of consensus. They are based on group-level traits that assume cultures are integrated systems consisting of widely shared social "norms" ("rules," "theories," "grammars," "codes," "systems," "models," "worldviews," and so on) that maintain heritable variation (Rappaport 1999; Laland, Olding-Smee, and Feldman 2000; Wilson 2002). Some political scientists also tend to view cultures as socially "inherited habits" (Fukuyama 1995)—that is, as socially transmitted bundles of normative traits (Huntington 1996; Axelrod 1997b).

The interest in heritable variation loosens the restrictions on consensus and raises questions about the basis for variation. But here cognitive scientists are likely to be disappointed by the implicit assumption that the gist of cultural learning is the (more or less automatic) absorption of norms and values from the surrounding culture (by processes no more complicated than imitation). We believe that there are two problems with such an approach. First, it is not clear how people would decide what exactly to imitate. Second, these assumptions do not pay sufficient attention to the sorts of inferential and developmental processes that allow human beings to build and participate in cultural life.

6.2   Cultural Psychology

The recent upsurge of interest in cultural psychology (for one review and critique, see Oyserman, Coon, and Kemmelmeier 2002 and associated commentaries) has produced a variety of intriguing findings and has done psychology a service by calling attention to cultural variation. Many of these studies show that knowledge systems previously thought to be universal actually vary widely across the world (for a review, see Cohen 2001). The lesson drawn is that "psychologists who choose not to do cross-cultural psychology may have chosen to be ethnographers instead" (Nisbett et al. 2001, 307). In brief, cultural psychology is succeeding in divesting academic psychology of implicit and ingrained ethnocentric biases.

What defines or constitutes cultural psychology? The area draws much of its inspiration from researchers such as Hofstede (1980) and Triandis (1995), who sought to characterize cultural differences in terms of a small number of relevant dimensions. The project is successful if multiple sources of evidence converge on the same small set of dimensions. Examples of such dimensions that have received a lot of attention are individualism versus collectivism and egalitarian versus hierarchical social structure. Other researchers such as Nisbett (2003) have used sociohistorical analysis to derive dimensions of cultural differences in worldviews or preferred modes of thought. Examples of these dimensions are analytic and logical (categorical, axiomatic, and noncontradictory) versus holistic and dialectical (thematic, no first principles or excluded middle). In short, Nisbett and his associates are suggesting that cultural studies must include not only contents per se, but also thinking processes that themselves may be differentially distributed across cultures.

Cultural psychologists import the rigor and controls of standard experimental procedure into anthropological concerns, providing clear identification of the participants, thoughts, and behaviors tested. Cultural psychologists are thus able to systematically exploit anthropological insights to demonstrate that mainstream psychology's long-held assumptions about cognitive processes can be quite mistaken. In our opinion, cultural psychology has several limitations. First of all, the leap from statistical regularity in some sample population to "the culture" may suffer from precisely the sort of reasoning criticized in mainstream psychology's leap from Americans or Europeans (or, more typically, psychology undergraduates) to the world at large. The same inchoate conception of culture once used by many anthropologists and still used by most ordinary folk remains customary in much cultural psychology. In this view, culture becomes a stable and shared set of beliefs, practices, or strategies to be studied as yet another population parameter / personal attribute.

This ahistorical, consensual view of culture limits the ability to explain and understand cultural differences once they are encountered. In other words, it is not clear how explanation or interpretation can be extended beyond simple description. In some cases researchers have been able to exert some experimental control by priming tendencies to act individualistically versus collectively (e.g., Gardner, Gabriel, and Lee 1999; Briley, Morris, and Simonson 2000). These sorts of studies reinforce the dimensional analysis and potentially extend its scope. There is always the risk, however, of circularity in analysis. If priming does not affect some candidate task measuring individualism versus collectivism, then maybe the prime was ineffective or the task does not entail individualism and collectivism.

Perhaps we are guilty of prejudging the initial phase of a two-stage project. In stage 1, cultural psychologists tend to characterize culture as an external, historically determined system that becomes internalized in the individual through "acculturation" (or some other causally opaque process), either diffusely or as some specialized part of the psyche responsible for cultural (or social) cognition. A stage 2 focus on within-culture variations in modes of thought might illuminate how different cultural institutions shape ways of thinking and vice versa.

For cultural psychologists trained as anthropologists, the focus is on the "extrasomatic" or "extragenetic" nature of culture as an integrated corpus of external control mechanisms that program individual minds and bodies, molding them in patterned ways recognizable across individuals (Geertz 1973). We agree that expressions of the human psyche are profoundly embedded and structured within social and historical contexts, but we dissent from the invited implication of a one-way influence, with individual minds being passive recipients of "culture."

So far we have followed current practice in using the term *cultural psychology* to describe the recent upsurge of cross-cultural comparisons by cognitive and social psychologists. This may be a bit misleading in that one of the pioneers of the use of the term, Richard Shweder (1990, 87), uses it to refer to a set of ideas that entail rejecting psychic unity as well as rejecting the idea of characterizing cultural differences as variation along a small number of dimensions:

Cultural psychology interprets statements about regularities observed in a lab or observed anywhere else, on the street or in a classroom, in Chicago or in Khartoum, not as propositions about inherent properties of a central processing mechanism for human psychological functioning, but rather as descriptions of local response patterns contingent on context, resources, instructional sets, authority relations, framing devices, and modes of construal.

To avoid confusion in nomenclature, we will categorize Shweder's approach to cultural psychology under the next framework, context and situated cognition.

6.3   Context and Situated Cognition

There are alternative views of "cultural psychology" that call into question the use of standard forms of experimental procedure ("methodological behaviorism") as fundamentally flawed on grounds that they are ethnocentrically biased in their focus on the individual mind/brain. Instead of considering cognitions to be embedded exclusively in individual minds—with "culture" as just one component of individual cognition— these theorists maintain that human cognitions should be properly situated in cultural-historical context and "practical activity" (Cole 1996; cf. Vygotsky 1978). A related concern is that cultural cognitions may be better understood as "distributed cognitions" that cannot be described exclusively in terms of individual thought processes, but only as "emergent structures" that arise from irreducible levels of interactional complexity involving differential linking of individual minds in a given population (Hutchins 1995).

Researchers such as Michael Cole believe that culture cannot be entirely conceptualized in terms of cognitions, belief systems, and the like, but must instead consider a culture's artifacts (construed broadly enough to include language). Cole (1996) argues that subjects and objects are not only directly connected but also indirectly connected through a medium constituted of artifacts. These artifacts are simultaneously material and conceptual. One consequence of this view is an emphasis on studying "cognition in context," where cognitive labor may be distributed across individuals as well as artifacts (such as plumb lines or computers). Since context includes people's conceptions of artifacts, it is inherently relational.

We share some of these concerns raised by the situated view, such as (1) difficulties with standard experimental procedures, including 2×2

designs with culture, in effect, treated as an independent variable (Medin and Atran 2004), and (2) lack of concern with differential distributions of cognitions among minds within populations. For example, with respect to shared knowledge and beliefs, Cole (1996, 124) says that "in order to say anything useful, it is necessary to specify sources of coherence and patterning as a part of the ongoing activities that the inquirer wants to analyze." We also agree that a focus on norms and rules is overly narrow, that cultural notions are intimately tied to the study of development, and that one good research avenue involves looking at how cognition plays out in particular contexts.

Other aspects of the situationist view seem vague. The idea that cognition is "stretched across mind, body, activity, and setting" is a useful framework notion that leads one to consider more than individual minds. At the same time, however, we believe that cultural situations and institutions cannot literally enter individual minds; rather, like other sorts of environmental stimuli they stimulate (in controlled and sequenced ways) mental processes that construct representations in accordance with a host of internal constraints, including evolved cognitive aptitudes like the folkbiology module (Medin and Atran 2004). Cole (1996, 198) agrees with this assessment of internal constraints: "According to the version of cultural historical psychology I am advocating, modularity and cultural context contribute jointly to the development of mind."

Perhaps a fair summary is that claims about cultural, historical analyses represent something of a promissory note (with respect to individual cognition) and research has tended to focus on situations and practices rather than the mediating mental representations associated with them. Strategically, this makes a certain amount of sense. In commenting on this section of this book Ed Hutchins (personal communication, November 2004) said:

If we situated guys have erred on the side of focusing on "situations and practices rather than the mediating mental representations associated with them" it is because the latter have received plenty of attention, and the former are so understudied that their role in constituting the human mind has not been appreciated or understood by the majority of cognitive scientists. Furthermore, I believe that a better understanding of the former will change what we think to be accomplished by the latter.

Our only disagreement with this is that although cognition has been extensively studied, cognition in context has not; hence we see a continuing need to attend to mental representations.

6.4   Culture as a Superorganism

One of the oldest, and most persistent, approaches to the "science of culture" is to consider culture an ontologically distinct "superorganism" whose "laws" are sui generis and do not arise from individual thoughts and behaviors, but that govern how individuals think and behave in social contexts (White 1949). Anthropologist A. L. Kroeber ([1923] 1963, 94) first formulated the doctrine in this way: "Culture is both superindividual and superorganic.... There are certain properties of culture—such as transmissibility, high variability, cumulativeness, value standards, influence on individuals—which are difficult to explain, or to see much significance in, strictly in terms of organic personalities and individuals." This "American" school of cultural anthropology, which viewed culture as a superorganism, soon merged with the "British" school of social anthropology known as "functionalism" (Evans-Pritchard 1940). Functionalism holds that the beliefs, behaviors, and institutions of a society function with the machinelike regularity of a well-adapted organism so as to promote the healthy functioning of social groups. According to A. R. Radcliffe-Brown (1950, 3), "In reference to any feature of a system we can ask how it contributes to the working of the system. That is what is meant by ... its *social function*. When we succeed in discovering the function of a particular custom, i.e., the part it plays in the working system to which it belongs, we reach an understanding and explanation of it." For the last half century, anthropology has mostly abandoned pretensions to a "science of culture" based in the law-abiding functional regularity of the adaptive superorganism.[1] But this view has recently made a comeback under the evolutionary guise of "group selection." According to philosopher Elliot Sober and anthropologist David Sloan Wilson (Sober and Wilson 1998, 150–176), "In most human social groups, cultural transmission is guided by a set of norms that identifies what counts as acceptable behavior," and that "function largely (although not entirely) to make human groups function as adaptive units." Norms are functioning parts of a "complex and sophisticated machine designed to forge groups into corporate units."

From this level of analysis, mental structures can be effectively ignored when trying to make scientific sense of culture. Although human cultures perhaps developed "to function as adaptive units via many proximate mechanisms" (Sober and Wilson 1998, 182), it is possible to study cultures as "phenotypes" without describing the proximate computational machinery that generates them:

As long as the proximate mechanisms result in heritable variation, adaptations will evolve by natural selection. There is a sense in which the proximate mechanism doesn't matter. If we select for long wings in fruit flies and get long wings, who cares about the specific developmental pathway?... If humans have evolved to coalesce into functionally organized groups, who cares how they think and feel? (Sober and Wilson 1998, 193; see also Dennett 1995, 358–359)[2]

We believe, however, that understanding cultural formation and evolution depends profoundly on understanding the "proximate" cognitive mechanisms involved. Perhaps we can best summarize with an analogy: macroeconomics is a legitimate field of study and generates important insights into economic activity on the basis of assumptions, for example, of an efficient market (and optimal individual behavior). But these insights do not in the least undermine microeconomics; and, more to the point, observations from microeconomics, such as loss aversion (e.g., Kahneman and Tversky 1979) and mental accounting (e.g., Thaler 1985), have had a significant impact on macroeconomics.

6.5 The Grammar of Culture

In anthropology, there is a long tradition of considering culture along the lines of language—that is, as being a rule-bound system with its own "grammar." This view of culture is most strongly associated with the "structuralist" school of Claude Lévi-Strauss (1963b) in France and Mary Douglas (1970) and Edmund Leach (1976) in Great Britain. On this account the bewildering variety of social phenomena and cultural productions are variations generated from a universal structure of the mind (a grammar of culture), which allows people to make sense of the world by superimposing a structure based on a few underlying principles. The structuralist's task is to gather as many variations as possible of some grammatical subsystem of culture (e.g., myth, kinship) in order to identify the most fundamentally meaningful components in the subsystem, and to discern the structure through the observation of patterning. Following the linguistic theory of Ferdinand de Saussure in which phonemes (the smallest unit of linguistic meaning) are understood in contrast to other phonemes, structural anthropologists argued that the fundamental patterns of human thought are also based on a system of "binary contrasts" to produce more elaborate systems of cultural meaning.[3]

Structural anthropology had little knowledge of the theories of cognitive architecture developed over the last few decades by cognitive and developmental psychologists, neuropsychologists, or generative linguists.

The fundamental properties attributed to the human mind, such as "binary contrast," were few and simple-minded (or so general and vague as to be applicable willy-nilly to any phenomena at all).[4] This is not to deny the insights that structural anthropologists garnered into the relationships between different aspects of cultural life within and across populations (e.g., linking myth, kinship, folkbiology, hunting, and cooking practices, residential architecture, and so on). Instead, it is only to deny that structuralist theories provide any principled causal explanation concerning how these relationships might have come about.

More current anthropological views of the grammar of culture are less committed to a specific theory of the cognitive architecture responsible for cultural productions than to the belief that culture consists of a bounded set of rule-bound systems, each with its own grammarlike structure. A more recent work in linguistic anthropology describes the "culture-as-grammar" view as follows:

To be part of a culture means to share the propositional knowledge and the rules of inference necessary to understand whether certain propositions are true (given certain premises). To the propositional knowledge, one might add the procedural knowledge to carry out tasks such as cooking, weaving, farming, fishing, giving a formal speech, answering the phone, asking for a favor, writing a letter for a job application. (Duranti 1997, 28–29)

Anthropology, then, is the discipline of "writing" the grammar of culture (Keesing 1972, 302). From this perspective, it seems that virtually any patterned activity that numbers of people share in can be considered "grammatical," from pottery making to storytelling. For example, "Religion belongs to the elementary grammar of culture" (Kannengeiser 1995; cf. Lawson and McCauley 1990). But there may be nothing interestingly "grammatical" (generated by few and finite rules) about how various cognitive systems link up together to make up "religion" (Atran 2002; Atran and Norenzayan 2004) or "science" (Atran 1990, 1998) or "culture."

6.6 I-Culture

A somewhat similar view—one that is more sophisticated but also problematic—has recently arisen among (some) evolutionary psychologists. It is modeled on Noam Chomsky's distinction between the internal, individual grammar that a given person possesses ("I-Language," such as someone's particular knowledge of American English) and the external language ("E-Language," such as the countless dialects, words, and stylistic differences of the English language as it has developed across the world over the last thousand years or so). Just as the English language was shaped—and is still being shaped—by broad historical events that did not take place inside a single head (including the Norman invasion of England and the global Internet), so too has Western European or Chinese or Navajo culture been shaped by complex processes (Pinker 2002).[5]

If the analogy holds, then psychology's contribution to understanding "culture" might best focus on how children "grow" an I-Culture through the combination of an innate, biologically specified "culture acquisition device" and the exposure to stimuli in the world (or, equivalently, how individuals are capable at all of participating in "E-Culture"). As Gary Marcus (2004, 27) proposes, "The very ability to acquire culture is, I would suggest, one of the mind's most powerful learning mechanisms." This suggests a line of inquiry for culture studies parallel to that taken by generative linguistics over the past fifty years, in which the fundamental guiding questions include: "What do people know when they know 'culture'?" and "How do people come to acquire 'culture'?"

Unlike the structuralist version of "culture as grammar," this version does not prejudge the complexity or variety of cognitive mechanisms that may be involved in cultural acquisition. Like more current anthropological versions, however, it seems to assume that I-Culture is a bounded system, or an integrated collection of systems, generated (under appropriate experience) by some articulated set of cognitive principles.

But we contend that there is no systematically bounded or integrated culture as such. There is nothing at all "grammatical" or generatively rule-bound about the relations that connect, say, language, religion, the nation-state, and science (or that connect the capacities to acquire knowledge of, and participate in, languages, religions, nation-states, and sciences). There are only family resemblances to what is commonsensically referred to as "culture" (or "religion" or "science"), but no overarching or integrated structure.

6.7   Generativist (Agent-Based) Models of Culture

Recent advocates of agent-based computational models of cultural phenomena also sometimes borrow self-consciously from the framework of generative linguistics, where few and finite rules generate rich and complex structures. For most current agent-based models, however, the focus is not on the generative power of mental mechanisms as such (as it is for advocates of cultural grammar or I-Culture) but on "connectionist" and "constructivist" modeling of how (micro)processes at the level of individual decisions and actions yield macrostructural cultural norms and other social regularities, such as spatial settlements (Dean et al. 1999), economic classes (Axtell, Epstein, and Young 1999), political alliances (Axelrod and Bennett 1993), voting patterns (Kollman, Miller, and Page 1992), ecological management networks of religious water temples (Lansing and Kremer 1993), and so on: "To the generativist, explaining the emergence of macroscopic societal regularities, such as norms or price equilibria, requires that one answer the following question: How could the decentralized local interactions of heterogeneous autonomous agents generate the given regularity?" (Epstein 1999, 41). In agent-based models of cultural phenomena there is no central, "top-down" control over individuals. Rather an initial population of autonomous heterogeneous agents, situated in a specified spatial environment, begins to interact according to rather simple local rules (e.g., if agent X manifests behavior A in the immediate, spatially proximate neighborhood of agent Y at time T, then X and Y will both manifest A at time T1; never attack an immediate neighbor; trade with a neighbor only if that neighbor is red; and so on). Over time, these concatenated individual interactions generate—or "grow"— macrostructural regularities from the "bottom up":

Of course, there will generally be feedback from macrostructures to microstructures, as where newborn agents are conditioned by social norms or institutions that have taken shape endogenously through earlier agent interactions. In this sense, micro and macro will typically co-evolve. But as a matter of specification, no central controllers or higher authorities are posited *ab initio*. (Epstein 1999, 42)

There is much in this approach that we find congenial, including (1) the interpretation of society (or culture) as a dynamic and distributed computational network created by and for its constituent interacting individuals, (2) the realization that individual agents have "bounded" computing capacity and incomplete knowledge with regard to their own intentions and actions as well as to the intentions and actions of others, (3) the understanding that information in society is transmitted, canalized, formed, and possessed through endogenous interaction pathways (e.g., social networks), and (4) the realization that "emergent" macrostructural patterns and processes are neither wholly external to nor wholly internalized in individuals.[6]

From a cognitivist standpoint, however, the requisite mental microprocesses in current agent-based models are relatively simple (e.g., imitation, following conventional rules, and so on). These models also frequently incorporate functionalist views of cultural macrostructures as adaptive systems (cf. Sober 1996)—a simplifying assumption that can lead to theoretical insights and provoke new empirical research (e.g., to the extent that cultural systems inevitably fall short of adaptive equilibrium), but that may not produce accurate descriptions or explanations of cultural stability. This same taste for simplicity is associated with a relative neglect of ecological context (save for spatial proximity of agents) and social processes (other than dyadic contacts). These limitations are matters of practice, not principle, and reflect the goal of seeing just how much complexity can derive from minimal assumptions.

The most straightforward way to integrate our approach with agent-based modeling is to substitute empirical observations on cultural processes for the sorts of simplifying assumptions described above. Our enterprise (as well as that of other distributional theorists, such as Boyd and Richerson 1985) is compatible with agent-based cultural modeling. Our eventual contribution to agent-based generations of cultural macrophenomena is to (1) enrich microspecifications of agent behaviors and decisions by specifying the cognitive mechanisms involved, and (2) furnish ethnographically plausible patterns and principles for agent behaviors and decisions. Sufficiently enriched, agent-based modeling could become a key scientific instrument for understanding the distribution and stabilization of cultural phenomena, and a potentially powerful tool for empirical research.

Summary There are no absolute standards for evaluating different notions about what constitutes relevant cultural contents or processes and how they should be studied. Framework theories are typically judged, not by whether they are right or wrong, but rather by whether they are useful. Utility, in turn, may vary as a function of goals. All of the above approaches have strong value relative to the default condition of much of experimental psychology that focuses solely on U.S. undergraduates at majority universities. The relative merits of one approach versus others can be understood in terms of their positions on underlying dimensions such as scope and specificity. The situated view and cultural psychology represent two end points on this continuum. Cultural psychology aims to identify a small set of cognitive processes that (are thought to) operate very widely. Viewing cultures in terms of shared norms and values also can reveal important cultural differences. In contrast, situationists are more impressed with the lack of transfer of cognitive skills across settings (e.g., Lave and Wenger 1991).

The framework theory that we endorse draws on insights from a number of the theories we have just reviewed. In particular our focus is on cultural processes, and consequently our approach is first cousins of both the situation and agent-based modeling approaches. We now turn to our approach and lay out its methodological and conceptual implications.

6.8   Cultural Epidemiology

In the norms-and-rules approach (including "memetics," Dawkins 1976; Dennett 1995; Blackmore 1999; cf. Atran 2001b) there is a basic assumption that memory and transmission mechanisms are reliable enough for standard Darwinian selection to operate over cultural traits (i.e., the rate of mutation is significantly lower than the selection bias). On this view, inheritable variants (of ideas, artifacts, behaviors) are copied (imitated, reproduced) with high enough fidelity so that they resemble one another more than they do unrelated forms. Only then can they be repeatedly chosen as favorable for cultural survival or eliminated as unfavorable by selection.

We believe that these assumptions are limited because they pay insufficient attention to psychology; in particular, they tend to neglect the sorts of inferential and developmental cognitive processes that allow human beings to build and participate in cultural life. For these reasons, we also believe that these various proposals for cultural "replication," which are intended as generalizations of Darwinian processes of replication in biology, either suffer from vagueness (e.g., memetics) or pertain to highly limited sets of phenomena (e.g., the coevolution of animal domestication and lactose tolerance in Eurasian societies, or learning by imitation). Instead, we propose to look at cultures in terms of mental representations (and attendant behaviors) that are reliably but diversely distributed across individuals in a population (the population itself being circumscribed by the intersection of these various distributions). This is what we mean by "cultural epidemiology."[7]

Boyd, Richerson, and their colleagues have modeled the distributions of beliefs and practices within and across populations, and also the stabilizing role of psychological biases in transmission (Boyd and Richerson 1985, 2001), such as conformity to preferences that already prevail in the population and emulation in deference to the beliefs and behaviors of prestigious people (Henrich and Boyd 1998; Henrich and Gil-White 2001). We focus on the stabilizing role of cognitive structures in the production and transmission of ideas (and attendant behaviors) that achieve

Table 6.1
Approaches to cultural research and their stance on five issues

Approach	Issues				
	What is culture?	Cultural change	Within-culture variability	Cognitive processes and their relevance	Role of domain-specific processes
1. Intuitive	Shared values, ideas, customs	Viewed as loss	Viewed as noise	Learning and memory	Not addressed
2. Cultural psychology	Shared values, ideas, customs, processing mechanisms	Not addressed	Not addressed	Inference, reasoning, perception (cognitive "toolbox")	Not addressed
3. Situated cognition	Cognitions, belief systems, and artifacts	Cultures are dynamic	Variability associated with different practices and artifacts	Distributed, often context-specific	Not addressed
4. Culture as superorganism	Emergent system affecting individuals	Adaptive	Acknowledged, but not relevant	Ignored as inappropriate unit of analysis	Depends on domain-specific functionality
5. Culture as grammar	Shared knowledge, procedures, rules	Not addressed	Not addressed	Mental structures revealed by cross-cultural comparisons	Not addressed
6. I-culture	Bounded rulelike system organized by cognitive processes	Not addressed	Driven by E-culture	Universal cultural acquisition device	Important

7. Agent-based modeling of culture	Beliefs, rules, and norms as products of simple micro-processes	May be emergent outcome from perturbation of steady state	Treated as signal, key to analyzing cultural transmission processes	Imitation, rule following	Not usually addressed
8. Cultural epidemiology	Distribution of ideas, beliefs, and behavior in ecological contexts	Cultures are dynamic	Treated as signal, key to analyzing cultural processes	Inference, reasoning, perception, and notions of relevance	Important

widespread cultural distribution. These may not be exclusively or even mainly shared as nearly identical mental representations across individual minds, nor transmitted more or less intact from mind to mind through any other sort of high-fidelity replication (Sperber 1996; Atran 2001b). Imitation has strong limits with respect to replication—not only is it just a single way of transmission, but also, given the many-to-one mappings between acts and mental representations of them (including their meaning), there is no guarantee of any sort of fidelity. (Indeed, *imitation* often seems to us a term of folkpsychology that needs explanation rather than explains.) We suggest that much of the cultural transmission and stabilization of ideas (artifacts and behaviors) involves the communication of poor, fragmentary, and elliptical bits of information that manage to trigger rich and prior inferential structures.

The idea that cultural content may be distributionally unstable and seldom reliably replicated is far from new (e.g., Linton 1936; Wallace 1961; Roberts 1964; see Gatewood 2001 for a review). For example, Wallace (1961, 28) suggests that "culture shifts in policy from generation to generation with kaleidoscopic variety, and is characterized internally not by uniformity, but by diversity of both individuals and groups, many of whom are in continuous and overt conflict in one sub-system and in active cooperation in another." What may be relatively novel in our approach is the focus on variability as the object of study. The degree to which cognitive content is actually shared or similarly inferred across individual minds may depend on many factors in addition to preexisting cognitive structures, such as the way the physical and social environments channel the transmission of information (e.g., mountains hinder the communication and spread of ideas, classrooms facilitate them). The various distributions of ideas across populations may also be determined to a significant extent by the history of economic, political, and military relations between and within groups. In later chapters, we provide examples of how these different sorts of "canalizing" factors— cognitive, environmental, historical—interact to produce culturally identifiable behaviors.

6.9 Summary

At the risk of some oversimplifying, we summarize the eight approaches to culture under discussion according to their stances on five key issues in table 6.1. As we suggested earlier, the cultural epidemiology view is most similar to the agent-based and situated cognition views. It differs from both these views in its focus on inference. Specifically, we suggest that these preexisting and acquired inferential structures account for the cultural recurrence and stabilization of many complexly integrated ideas and behaviors (see Boyer 1994; Atran 2002 for religion) and set the parameters on allowable cultural diversification (Sperber and Hirschfeld 2004). In the next two chapters we provide evidence bearing on this claim.

7 Folkecology and the Spirit of the Commons: Garden Experiments in Mesoamerica

There is little or no detail available in typical normative accounts of social structure in the anthropological literature that would allow evaluation of patterns of individual variation, agreement, and disagreement within and between groups (but see Aunger 2002 for a counterexample). Without such detail, normative claims are difficult to verify or falsify. The overarching reason is simple: anthropologists are typically instructed to go out into the field alone for some months or—in exceptional cases— some few years and bring back a description of the society studied. The popular image of the anthropologist with a pith helmet and notebook is not very far off the mark, only now the pith helmet is a baseball cap or canvas fedora, and the notebook is a PC. In this situation, there is little alternative to normative description (except the "narratives" of antipositivist postmodernism, which do little to foster dialogue with the larger scientific community).

Detailed analyses of the relations between ecology, technology, social networks, and so forth require large interdisciplinary efforts, over many field seasons, at a cost that usually exceeds typical ethnographic fieldwork by one or several orders of magnitude. The pertinent academic and government funding institutions are not set up for this kind of project, and so the effort is rarely made (for a notable exception, see Henrich et al. 2001). We have been fortunate to be involved in two such efforts: one in Mesoamerica and another in North America.

A critical case for the importance of cultural selection versus environmental determination comes from a variation on the "common garden experiment" in biology. When members of a species have different phenotypes in different environments, samples are taken from both environments and replanted in only one. If the differences still exist, they are probably genetic (two genotypes); if not, then they are probably environmental (one genotype producing two phenotypes). Here we use a variation on this experimental approach. Our aim is not to distinguish genetic nature from environmental nurture, but rather to isolate the effect of certain sociocultural factors (social networks, cognitive models) from other economic (sources and level of income), demographic (family and population size), and ecological factors (habitat and species) in environmental management and maintenance. Evidence for the impact of culturally transmitted factors on behavior would show that groups of people who have different cultural histories and cultural ideas behave differently in the same physical environment.

The Lowland Maya region faces environmental disaster, owing in part to a host of nonnative actors having access to the forest resources (Schwartz 1995). A central problem concerns differential use of common-pool resources, such as forest plants, by different cultural groups exploiting the same habitat. In this chapter, we will analyze what is known as the "tragedy of the commons."

7.1 Background

In earlier studies (chapter 4), we found that Itza' Maya informants consistently appealed to ecological relations on category-based induction tasks. That observation, coupled with the Itza' Maya record of sustainable agroforestry, suggested to us that there may be a connection between folkecological models and behavior. In preliminary studies we also found that Spanish-speaking Ladino and Q'eqchi' Maya immigrant populations in the area practice agroforestry in a much less sustainable manner (Atran and Medin 1997). This situation provided the opportunity to see if understandings of the forest are correlated with action on it. These conjectures led us to a series of systematic cross-cultural and within-cultural comparisons that are pertinent to a variety of conceptual issues in cognition, decision making, and culture theory (Atran 1999a, 2002; Atran, Medin, and Ross 2005; Ross 2002).

The Common Setting
Our studies concern three cultural groups in the same municipality in Guatemala's Department of El Petén: native Itza' Maya, Spanish-speaking immigrant Ladinos, and immigrant Q'eqchi' Maya. Each group founded, and predominates in, a distinct locality: Itza' in the town of San José, Ladinos in the nearby settlement of La Nueva San José, Q'eqchi' in the hamlet of Corozal. Interviews were in Itza', Spanish, and Q'eqchi' for each community respectively.

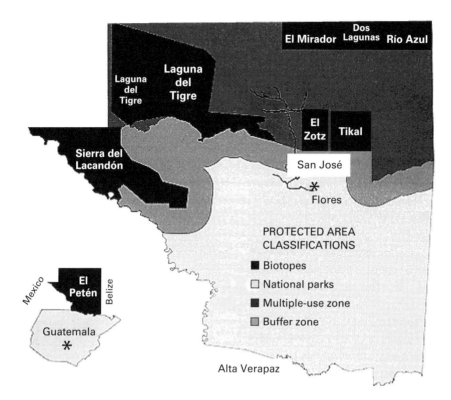

Figure 7.1
Map of the Maya Biosphere Reserve, El Petén, Guatemala (not drawn entirely to scale).

Our three groups lie within the Maya Biosphere Reserve's official "buffer zone" between 17°10' north latitude and Lake Petén Itza to the south (figure 7.1). Here, vegetation is quasi-rainforest; mean annual temperature is 25°C; mean annual precipitation is 1,600–1,800 mm. In the reserve and adjacent areas, Itza' comprise a majority of the population in only 1 settlement, Q'eqchi' are a majority in 25 settlements, Ladino immigrants are a majority in 134 settlements, and Ladino "Peténeros" (in the area for at least three generations) are a majority in six settlements (Grünberg and Ramos 1998).

In 1998, San José had 1,789 habitants. Most identified themselves as Itza', although only a minority spoke their native Mayan tongue. Itza' represent the last Lowland Maya with demonstrable ties of genealogy and practice to pre-Columbian civilization in Petén's northern forests (Atran 1993; Atran and Ucan Ek' 1999; Atran, Lois, and Ucan Ek'

2004), where the population once exceeded the region's current level by about an order of magnitude (Culbert and Rice 1990). Nearly all 625 people in neighboring La Nueva are Ladinos (mixed European and Amerindian descent).

As noted in chapter 3, Corozal was settled at the same time by Q'eqchi' speakers, a Highland Maya group. The Q'eqchi' now constitute the largest identifiable ethnic group in Petén, while maintaining the smallest number of dialects and largest percentage of monolinguals (Wilson 1995, 38; cf. Stewart 1980). This set of observations reflects the suddenness, magnitude, and relative isolation of the Q'eqchi' migration.[1]

For all groups, people pay rent to the municipality for a farm plot.[2] Itza' and Ladinos interact often, because their villages are 1 kilometer apart. All groups practice agriculture and horticulture, hunt game, fish, and extract timber and nontimber forest products for sale. Each household (about 5 persons) has usufruct rights on 30 manzanas (21.4 hectares) of *ejido* land (municipal commons). Farmers pay yearly rent of less than a dollar for each manzana cleared for swidden plots, known as *milpa,* whose primary crop is maize. Yearly crop patterns can vary widely, owing in part to microclimate and rainfall fluctuation. People can hold plots in scattered areas and can change plots. Plots from all groups may abut. Hunting is tolerated on neighbors' plots, but not access to another's crops or trees. Q'eqchi' live 18 kilometer from both groups; however, daily buses connect the Q'eqchi' to the other two groups (who also farm regularly around Corozal).

To ensure maximum social coverage from our sample, initial informants could not be immediate blood relatives (children, grandchildren, parents, grandparents, siblings, first cousins, nieces, nephews, uncles, aunts), immediate affines (spouses, in-laws), or godparents (*compadres*). The distribution view of culture that we adopt leads one to employ sampling techniques most likely to reveal cultural differences rather than focusing on estimating population parameters.

In the present study we assumed that younger Itza' Maya might have notions of biology that differed from those of Itza' elders and that these differences might reflect an assimilation to "Western culture." In addition, Itza' is a dying language and few younger Itza' speak it. Thus a random sample would tend to hide rather than emphasize the differences we were interested in. Instead of randomly sampling, we restricted our initial sample to Itza'-speaking Maya as the best representatives of Itza' Maya "culture." Cultural change is a constant and we assume that across time and outside influences (of varying nature), the knowledge base differs between individuals and across generations. Ultimately, our goal is to trace the distributions of ideas and beliefs both within and across generations. In chapter 8 we describe results from a younger, Spanish-speaking Itza' sample.

7.2   Historical Geography

In Petén, topographic and microclimatic variation allow for a dramatic range of vegetation over small areas, and sustaining both this diversity and people's livelihood over the past two millennia likely required correspondingly flexible agroforestry regimes (Puleston 1973; Harrison and Turner 1978).[3] Paleolimnological analyses of sediments in the central lakes region of Petén associates the demise of Classic Maya civilization toward the end of the first millennium with geometrically increasing rates of deforestation (Rice 1993). There is evidence of spiraling population growth (Culbert and Rice 1990), warfare (Chase and Chase 1989; Demarest 1993), and nutritional deficiency (Santley, Killion, and Lycett 1986). Economic infrastructure supporting perhaps 3 million people collapsed. Transport and communication links disintegrated between central Petén (e.g., Tikal) and other production centers (e.g., Caracol in Belize). While the central lakes region may have suffered less drastic population loss than neighboring Tikal, resettlement of Petén seems never to have surpassed the hundred thousand or so people estimated for the immediate pre-Conquest era.

Dense forest cover reappears during the Late Postclassic period, which precedes a brutal Spanish conquest in 1697 (Wiseman 1978). By and large, this cover endured through the mid-twentieth century. Since 1960, when the military government opened up Petén to "colonization and development," more than half of Petén's forest cover has been razed and coverted to agriculture (Schwartz 1995). The rate of deforestation, which averaged 287 km^2 yearly between 1962 and 1987, nearly doubled to 540 km^2 in 1988–1992, as the population rose from 21,000 to over 300,000. The lowest population estimates today exceed 1,000,000.

Most of southern Petén's rainforest has vanished. In a project engineered by the Agency for International Development (USAID) Guatemala's government set aside remaining forests north of 17°10' latitude as a Maya Biosphere Reserve. Yet, even within the Biosphere, forest continues to burn apace ("S.O.S.: se muere biosfera Maya," 1998).

Deforestation is especially prevalent along migration routes into northern Petén (Sader et al. 1997; Sader 1999). A new European-financed paved road now links Guatemala City to Flores, virtually ensuring the breakup of Mesoamerica's largest remaining contiguous tropical forest. The major cause of deforestation is population pressure from the overcrowded and tired lands of southern Guatemala (Schwartz 1995). There, over 11 million people live in an area roughly twice the size of Petén, and where nearly two-thirds of the land is controlled by about 2 percent of the people.

The present town of San José, is home to the last surviving concentration of Lowland Maya speakers in north-central Petén. Since pre-Columbian times, they have been called "Itza'."

The Itza'

The name Itza' itself is likely a compound of *itz* ("resin," "sap," "life essence," "vital substance," "hidden power") or the derivative *itz'in* ("brotherhood," "lineage," "kinship") and *(j)a'* ("water") (see Barrera Vásquez and Rendón 1963, 29). The Classic Maya *itz-am* (*am* = agentive marker, or "he who is") may denote a shaman who brings *itz* to the world (Freidel et al. 1995, 51). *Itz-am~na'*, then, would be the "Shaman's House" (*na'* or *naj* = "house") that enveloped the Classic Maya world.[4] By the time Classic Petén Maya civilization collapsed (Terminal Classic = 800–1,000 AD), the Itza', who may have originated as migratory Chontal lineages from western Petén, had replaced the Classic Chol-Yukatek lineages in parts of Petén (Seibal) and Yucatán (Chichén Itza') (Fox 1987; Tourtellot et al. 1992). Arguably, the *Itz~a'* thought of themselves as the "Water Wizards," ultimately extending the Classic Petén cult of *Itz-am~na'* into a Postclassic water cult centered at the Great Cenote of Chichen Itza in Yucatán (*chi'* = "mouth" + *ch'e'en* = "water hole") (see Barrera Vásquez and Rendón 1963, 25–29; Piña Chan 1980; Porter 1988).

During the Postclassic period, the Itza' vied with the Mexicanized Xiw Maya for control of Yucatán (*xiw* means "grasses," "herbs," or "reeds" in Yukatek and is a translation of the Nahuatl *totellin* or "Toltec" = "Reed People"). For a time, they kept the peace. In the league of Mayapan (*may* = calendrical cycle + *apan* = Nahuatl for "watering place"), the Itza' and Xiw agreed to disagree about who had the right calendar for understanding and controlling the course of events in the world. But the peace was periodically broken when important calendrical events conflicted. This happened, for example, when the ruler of Mayapan sacrificed the rain priest of Chichen, *Xib'~chaak* ("male [strong man] thunderstorm"), to demonstrate that the once all-powerful Maya rain god Chaak was now subordinate to the Mexicanized god *Kukul~kan* ("feathered serpent," a Maya translation of the name of the principal Toltec deity, Quetzalcoatl) (Tozzer 1941, 32–34; Barrera Vásquez and Rendón 1963, 147–149; Edmonson 1982, 15–20).

The Conquest

Ever since Villagutierre's (1701) *Historia de la Conquista de la Provincia de el Itza*, most scholarly opinion has it that the Itza' had resigned themselves to conquest because their religion fated that the time had come to self-destruct (see Puleston 1979).[5] For Villagutierre, "the true cause" (*la verdadera causa*) that motivated the "Itzaex ò Itzlanos" to give up Petén with hardly a fight was the same cause that had led to their earlier abandonment of Yucatán, namely, that "their idolatrous priests had prophecized the necessary occupation of these lands by the Spaniards" (Villagutierre 1701, bk. 1, chap. 6, 34).

The year of the conquest of Petén coincided with end of *waxak ajaw*, the last 20-year *ka'~tun* of the 256-year *may*, or calendrical cycle. That cycle began with the descent (or return) of the Itza' to Petén from *Chi'~ch'e'en* during the *May~apan* (Yucatán) civil wars between the Itza' and Xiw. Over the course of the seventeenth century, Franciscan friars negotiated with Itza' chieftains of the *Aj Kan~ek'* clan for conversion and submission on the basis of Maya prophetic cycles. This was a favorite tactic used by the Franciscans of Yucatán in an (ultimately unsuccessful) endeavor to outmaneuver both the secular clergy and the Dominicans of Guatemala in the competition for new converts (see Jones 1998). But the Itza' themselves evidently used their prophecies as a negotiating ploy to stall the Spanish and to obtain trade.

In interrogations a month after the conquest, the Conquistador Don Martín de Ursúa y Arismendi questioned his prisoner, the reigning chieftain *Ajaw Kan~ek'*, about his motives:

[Ursúa] asking what motive [did *Aj Kan~ek'* have] in sending amabassadors and requesting said fathers, if it was out of fear of the Spanish or some other reason.
[Canek] said that what had motivated him was the necessity of commerce and to have axes and machetes and to ask the fathers to baptize [the Itza']. (AGI Guatemala 343, *Declaración del reyezuelo Ahcanek en el Petén del Itza Nuestra Señora de los Remedios y San Pablo*, 16 April 1696, folios 329 verso–333 recto)

On March 22, 1697, nine days after the destruction at Lake Petén Itza' of the last independent Maya confederacy, Ursúa wrote to the King of

Spain of the finish to an abhorrent culture—a culture that nevertheless reflected the "ingenious abilities" of its native folk to create "exquisite" statues, temples, and glyphs "wherein much was found to be seen and admired," and that bode well for using corvée labor to build new Spanish cities:

And when the infidels heard our arms, and experienced the valor of those advancing, they began to flee in such a vile manner, men and women threw themselves into the water and filled it all the way to the mainland.

And I do not doubt that many would be imperiled by the advance, given what has been recognized.

And of the abandoned canoes, I have gathered up more than 125 and some Indian women and children.

And given the great multitude of infidels that garrisoned the lake and the island and those that crowned the land, it is considered a great miracle this victory whose happy end was already achieved by eight in the morning.

And the standard of Nuestra Señora de los Remedios with your royal arms was placed in the most prominent part of the stone sanctuaries.

All of us acclaiming the law of Jesus Christ to whom we gave infinite thanks for having obtained the impossible, played out without a single soldier being seriously put at risk.

... There were found twenty-one sanctuaries full of horrible and deformed idols.

And among these the shin bone of a horse which, according to an old Indian woman, was the horse of Don Fernando Cortes, who passed through these lands on the way to Honduras.

Homes were also found to be full of idols, with whose destruction [my] people were occupied from eight in the morning until five in the afternoon.

And I believe that these miserable waywards of the devil, deprived of the true light, must not have had any other activity than idolatry owing to their not having an economic form of settlement, but rather having all kin live together barbarously in one house.

The pleasantness and fertility of the land, the delightful beauty of this lake—the breadth and length of its waters on all sides, its inlets and streams, with its continuous waves giving it the appearance of the sea—is extraordinary, as is the highest quality of woven cotton fabrics in delicacy and dye.

The land yields two consecutive harvests of produce yearly; at present new maize is being gathered.

The ears and kernels are extremely thick, and everywhere very adequate.

There are gathered wild fruits, indigo, vanilla, cacao, anotta, cotton, wax, honey and every kind of vegetable and bean from [this] land and from Castile.

And although the males seem lazy, it is because they have small milpas that are expected to yield continual harvests.

Females to the contrary are known to work from sunup to sundown, without speaking a word. (AGI Guatemala 343, *Carta de Don Marttín de Ursúa y Arismendi al Real Acuerdo*, 22 Marzo 1697, folios 70 recto–71 verso)

In fact, the battle apparently was not the relatively bloodless coup that Ursúa suggests. It was a carefully planned campaign by a relatively well-trained European troop armed with galliot, cannons, muskets, and cross-bows against an Indian confederacy demoralized by civil war and armed only with stone and wood. Indeed, as the Mercedarian friar, Diego de Rivas, later testified, "Of the entry made by Don Martín Urzúa [I] state that so great was the number of those who opposed it, so innumerably many were those killed by the bullets we shot, it seemed like an island in the lake was formed by the bodies of the dead Indians" (AGI Guatemala 345, *Parecer de Fray Diego de Rivas*, 15 Noviembre 1698, folio 389 recto). Numbers of Itza' did flee into the forest, and some likely committed suicide by drowning themselves in the lake—not out of cowardice, barbarous stupidity, or fatalism, but more likely out of a desire not to be Spanish prisoners or slaves.

Cultural Survival

For both the Spanish and Itza', the immediate post-Conquest years were marked by a scorched-earth approach to dealing with the other side, virulent epidemics, and starvation. Deaths and desertions among the soldiers and settlers decimated and severly weakened the fledgling colony at Nuestra Señora de los Remedios y San Pablo, Laguna del Itza' (formerly *Noj~peten* and subsequently Flores). Nevertheless, the Spanish eventually managed to corral about 8,000 Itza' and Mopan into eighteen towns, or *reducciones*, under the control of the secular clergy (AGI México 3159, *Reporte de 1707 del Gobernador de El Petén*). Within a decade, nearly half of the surviving Indians fled or died from smallpox (*viruela*) and other European diseases (AGI México 702, *Informe de Luis Coello Gaytán al Rey leído en el Concejo de Indias*, 5 Febrero 1716; cf. Gerhard 1991, 60). This is far from the tens of thousands that *Ajaw Kan~ek'* was said to govern on the eve of the Conquest (Avendaño y Loyola [1696] 1987, 47–48; Villagutierre 1701, bk. 5, chap. 11, 332; Cano [1697] 1984, 8; Ximénez 1929–1931, vol. 2, bk. 4, chap. 68, 210–222).

The original mission of San Joseph, founded in 1702, was located between present-day Santa Elena and San Benito, opposite the former Itza' island capital. In the wake of the chaos and rebellion of the early post-Conquest years, a new *reducción* of San Joseph was established at the present site of San José sometime before 1750. The earliest marriage record from San José dates from that year (5 mayo 1750, Joseph Cante de San Joseph con María Tun de San Andrés, *Libro de Casamientos de la*

Parroquia de los Pueblos de San Andrés, San Joseph y San Gerónimo, año de 1751).

The extant (but partial) record of marriages and baptisms between 1751 and 1788 reveals the most frequently mentioned surnames to be those of Itza′ (and allied Kowoj and Mopan) patronyms present in the area before the Conquest. In descending order of frequency they are (in their original spelling): Tun (12), Chayax (11), Canek (9), Tz′in (7), Chabin (7), Kinyocte (7), Cuouh (6), Chata (6), Tut (6), Quixoban (5), Xiquen (5), Citcan (5), Cante (4), Chan (4), Puc (4), Kanchan (4), Tzuntecun (4), Tesucun (4) (see Ximénez 1971–1977, bk. 5, ch. 65; AGI Guatemala 345, *Razón Indibidual y General de los Pueblos Poblaciones y Rancherías de Esta Provincia del Zuiuha Peten Itza Por Declaración que han hecho El Rey Canek y El Kimcanek y El Capitán Don Martín Cham y El Capitán Kulut Coboh*, 9–10 Octubre 1698, 302 verso–311 recto).[6]

A social-network analysis of Itza′ speakers and their close intimates in present-day San José includes thirty-two surnames (for methodology, see Atran et al. 1999). Of these, eight are Spanish (Ramos, López, Díaz, Cortéz, Lines, García, Morente, Cinturon), eight are Yukatek families that came to San José between about 1750 and 1900 (Huex, Colli, Vitzil, Mex, Panti, Tz′ul, Mis, Yej), and sixteen are pre-Conquest names from Itza′-ruled territory (Chayax, Cohouj, Chan, Suntecun, Zacal, Tesucun, Zac, Cauich, Ek, Tut, Xiken, Batab, Cante, Chata, Quixchan, Chuc).

The three social tiers of Petén society lived within a somewhat less violent web of parasitic relationships than elsewhere in Guatemala (Schwartz 1990): *Criollo* (European origin), *Ladino* (Spanish speakers of mixed or Indian ancestry), and *Indio* (Mayan-speaking natives). Native Creoles and Ladinos continue to play an important, and sometimes dominant, role in Petén's social and economic life. By contrast, Lowland Maya communities now comprise an increasingly marginalized minority.

In the 1930s, Guatemala dictator General Jorge Ubico instituted a virulent anti-Maya language policy that led the Lacandón (Lakantun) Maya to flee Petén and resulted in loss of Itza′ as a first language in San José. Today in Petén, there are no Lowland Mayan–speaking groups between the Mopan-Q′eqchi′ town of San Luis in southeast Petén (a few thousand speakers) and the Itza′ settlement of San José on the northwest shore of Lake Petén Itza (a few dozen speakers). After some two millennia of recognizable continuity, Itza′ Maya language and forest culture verge on extinction.

The intense scholarly attention that pre-Conquest Itza′ continue to attract contrasts markedly with a lack of interest in the post-Conquest Itza′.

This is curious given that research and speculation about pre-Columbian Maya civilization often extrapolates from modern ethnographic sources. The reasons for this studious avoidance may have to do with the sorry state of Petén Maya society today compared to its illustrious past. This contrast in cultural fortunes—perhaps more glaring than elsewhere in Mesoamerica—has been wrongly interpreted as a complete culture gap.

For example, Colonel Modesto Méndez, on "discovering" Tikal, wrote in his diary (March 2, 1848) that the native Itza' who inhabited the region and guided him (e.g., Ambrosio Tut, Eulogio Chayax) to the site they called "the place of the wind [spirits]" (*ti-ik'al*) could not possibly be of the "race ... descended from those who wanted to immortalize their names" at Tikal (Soza 1970, vol. 1, 246).

Similar peremptory claims by influential historians (Means 1917) and archaeologists (Hellmuth 1977) that modern Itza' knowledge and culture bear no significant relation to that of pre-Columbian Petén Maya are supported by no empirical evidence or firsthand knowledge of modern Itza' language and culture.[7]

After the Conquest, many Itza' were moved around Petén to service cattle ranches. Spanish interest in native agriculture concerned only maize and beans. Because of this, and because until a generation ago Itza' were punished for speaking their language in public, reports on modern Itza' subsistence have been limited to farming (see Cowgill 1962; Reina 1967). Not that the colonizers were altogether unaware of a dazzling array of local crops, game, and uses of forest resources. But this merely underscored a conviction that absence of great fields and herds in the soil-poor tropical forest owed to savage sloth:

Meat, wheat and other things were not raised on the land; not because it wasn't fertile enough to produce them, but because of barbarity, poor upbringing, political and economic insufficiency.... These vast lands were quite suitable for Spanish towns ... among the richest, most productive and advantageous one could imagine.... The Indians had everything in their milpas, but little, because they did not cultivate them well. (Villagutierre [1701] 1985, bk. 10, chaps. 11–12)

Forest plants with nutritive value comparable to maize and wheat, like breadnut (ramón) and palmnut (corozo), were supposedly used more to sustain pack animals and other stock (Villagutierre [1701] 1985, bk. 7, chap. 7) than people (cf. Hellmuth 1977, 434). Itza' were forced to overextend maize cropping to sustain Spanish overreliance on cereal. Production often fell short of demand. Spaniards cried "famine," bewailing idle barbarian custom—such as relying on root crops, and seeking escape from hunger and exploitation in the fruits, game, and cover of the forest:

At times the Spanish and the rest of the population were "forced" (as the documents put it) to eat such foods as *ramón* ... *camote* (sweet potato), *yuca* (manioc), *ñame* and *macal* (yams), green plantains, and mamey and sapote fruit. Although this list may indicate that the Indians persisted in producing a diversity of crops other than grains despite the Spanish attempt to get them to concentrate on maize and beans ... the Spanish had culturally defined nutritional standards that hardly made these considerations good news. (Schwartz 1990, 55)

In fact, Itza' survived conquest and colonization with many pre-Columbian dietary and medicinal strategies, many of which arguably date to Classic times (Atran, Lois, and Ucan Ek' 2004).

7.3   Folkecology and the "Tragedy of the Commons"

The "tragedy of the commons" and other similar social and ecological dilemmas are basically variants of a deep problem in decision and game theories known as the "prisoner's dilemma" (Hardin 1968; Bromley 1992). Consider a group of n persons who share a common territory of fixed size on which they hunt (or graze) animals. Each hunter (or herdsman) has one of two choices: he can cooperate with the others by not overhunting (grazing) on the commons; or he can hunt (graze) in a way that is advantageous to him, but that ultimately results in the overuse and destruction of the common resource. The second option appears more rational in the short term: the short-term advantage to one who overhunts (grazes) (e.g., 1) always outweighs the short-term disadvantage to him when that disadvantage is equally distributed among the other hunters (herdsmen) ($1/n$). If all people cooperate, the common resource is preserved. But if the rationale of the prisoner's dilemma pervades the camp, no one will have an incentive to cooperate and all will defect.

Field and laboratory studies by anthropologists (Atran 1986; Berkes et al. 1989), psychologists (Thompson and Gonzalez 1997), and political scientists (Ostrom et al. 1994) indicate that individual calculations of rational self-interest collectively lead to a breakdown of a society's common resource base unless institutional or other normative mechanisms are established to restrict access to cooperators: it is irrational to continue to act to sustain a diminishing resource that others increasingly deplete. This so even when people's "basic needs" are satisfied (Boniecki 1977), no matter how small the group or how informed of the looming tragedy (White 1994). Earlier observations by our research team, however, suggested that exclusive concern with economic rationality and institutional norms might not sufficiently account for behavioral differences among groups in Lowland Mesoamerica (Atran and Medin 1997).

As noted earlier, Petén's forests comprise a common-pool resource that is rapidly being depleted. However, our data indicate that different groups engaging in the same activities have very different impacts on the environment, suggesting a more complex relation between population processes and ecological degradation.

Reported Agroforestry Practice

Although the three groups share a reliance on land and awareness of local species for survival, analyses of a 3-year period of milpa practice among twelve to sixteen informants in each group showed striking differences in the groups' utilization of land and knowledge of species. Data in this section are chiefly self-reports elicited from informants, but long-term spot checks and subsequent measurements (reported below) confirm a correspondence to actual behavior. Reports exhibit no evident bias (e.g., elicited maps of milpa plots depict land cleared in amounts systematically greater than municipal tax records show; elicited maps also tend to be more accurate and up to date).

ANOVAs were used to reveal group differences between Itza', Ladinos, and Q'eqchi', with the Scheffe statistic ($p < .05$) used for post hoc comparisons. The following abbreviations are used with the comparative statistics: I = Itza' Maya, L = Ladino, Q = Q'eqchi' Maya; M = milpa (swidden plot), G = guamil (fallow milpa), R = reserve (secondary forest). Analyses revealed no differences among groups in age, family size, land available to cultivate, or per capita income from all traceable sources.[8] Q'eqchi' produce one set of crops per year; Itza' and Ladinos usually produce two (table 7.1). Q'eqchi' cut and burn forest for new

Table 7.1
ANOVA of Petén swidden (milpa) practices

	N	Crops/ year	Years of land use	Hectares cleared	Years fallow	Species/ year cultivated
Itza' (R)	16	2	2.3	1.6	4.7	7.8
I (O)	10			2		9.7
Ladino (R)	16	2	1.8	2.6	3.6	3.3
L (O)	10			2.4		6.4
Q'eqchi' (R)	12	1	1	4.1	3.3	3.6
Q (O)	10			3.6		6.2
Other Q'eqchi'*			1.6	3.7	3.3	2.5

Note: (R) = reported practice, (O) = observed practices.

plots every year, compared with an average of 2.3 years for Itza' and 1.8 for Ladinos [I, L < Q].[9] Difference in burn frequency produces differences in destructiveness, independently of need for income.

Itza' differ from Ladinos and Q'eqchi' in reporting: amount of land cleared for cultivation [$F(2, 41) = 5.45$, $p < .01$, I < L, Q], fallow length [$F(2, 41) = 6.982$, $p < .002$; I > L, Q], and number of species cultivated [$F(2, 34) = 13.94$, $p < .001$; I > L, Q] (table 7.1). How can one map these different patterns of use onto an overall measure of destructiveness? For present purposes we make the strong simplifying assumption that destructiveness (D) is an increasing function of land used per cycle through a plot (L) and rate of cycling through a plot (R). That is, $D = L \times R$. To determine L and R we use A (amount of land a farmer clears), Yc (number of years a cleared plot is used continuously), and Yf (number of years the land is left fallow). From this it is straighforward to determine that $L = A \times (Yc + Yf)/Yc$ and that $R = 1/(Yc + Yf)$. Multiplying these two terms yields the result that $D = A/Yc$, which is simply land cleared per year. By this measure, Q'eqchi' destroy more than five times as much forest, but Ladinos less than twice as much, as Itza'.[10]

Q'eqchi' clear plots in a contiguous S-pattern that rolls through the forest leaving few trees within or between plots, including hill crowns. Ladinos intermittently leave trees between and within plots. Itza' regularly ring plots with trees, clear firebreaks around valuable trees inside plots, and change plots in a noncontiguous pattern. This is a strategy apparently shared with some groups of Lowland Lacandón and Yukatek Maya in Mexico, and there is evidence of a pre-Columbian origin (Gómez-Pompa et al. 1987; Remmers and De Koeijer 1992). Itza' explain it in terms of forest regeneration: birds, such as the chachalaca (*ix b'aach = Ortalis vetula*), roost in the milpa's outer ring (*t'ool che'*) but fly to inner stands (*watal che'*) to feed on crops and excrete undigested seeds of outlying trees. Left to fallow, areas around inner stands begin to emulate and bridge with the outer ring. Birds take undigested seeds of valuable inner-stand trees, such as the ramón (*'oox = Brosimum alicastrum*), to the outer ring, thereby increasing its value for people.

Remote sensing confirms extensive deforestation along Q'eqchi' migration routes into Petén (Grünberg and Ramos 1998; Sader 1999; Grünberg 2000). Reported patterns of crop diversity, coupled with awareness of greater ecological complexity and reciprocity between animals, plants, and people, also should favor regeneration of forest used by Itza' versus Ladinos. Despite mutual imagined similarities between Itza' and Q'eqchi', on nearly all reported measures, Ladinos are closer to Itza' than Q'eqchi' are to Itza'. This tendency is reliably confirmed by other measures, to which we turn.

7.4   Ground-Truthing: Biodiversity, Forest Cover, and Soil Conditions

Multiple converging measures of soils, biodiversity, and canopy cover indicate that Itza' promote forest replenishment, Q'eqchi' foster rapid forest depletion, and Ladinos fall somewhere in between (Atran et al. 1999, 2002).

To corroborate cultural behavior patterns, after a two-year lapse we measured for ten new informants from each group: plot sizes, species diversity, tree counts (minimum circumference > 0.3 m at 1–1.5 m from ground), coverage (m^2 foliage for each tree crown), and soil composition (10 cm and 20 cm depths). For every informant in each population we sampled 1 hectare (2.5 acres) plots from three locations: agricultural land (milpa), fallow land (guamil), and forest reserve. All locations were sampled after burning, planting, and weeding of a first-year milpa (when maize stalks reached 0.5–0.8 m before flowering). Reserve samples were 1 hectare and guamil was 3 years old on average.

Our initial study suggested that for all group measures relative to forest health and productivity, Itza' > Ladino > Q'eqchi'; hence, we report both two-tailed (Scheffe's $p < .05$) and one-tailed (Fisher PLSD $p < .05$) post hoc comparisons, the latter indicating marginal reliability in the predicted direction.[11]

Again, table 7.1 shows that Itza' plant more species (9.7) than Ladinos (6.4) or Q'eqchi' (6.2) and clear less land yearly (2.0 ha) than Ladinos (2.4 ha) or Q'eqchi' (3.6 ha); however, an ANOVA of crop species/ha as a function of group shows a reliable difference[12] only between Itza' and Q'eqchi'. For all groups, the most frequent crops are maize, then beans, then squash. Overall, Itza' cultivate forty-three different species in milpas, Ladinos twenty-six, and Q'eqchi' twenty-three, with a greater yearly species mix for Itza' (table 7.2). We predicted tree diversity to parallel crop diversity as a biodiversity indicator: Itza' average 9.0 species/ha, Ladinos 7.2, and Q'eqchi' 4.4.

Number of tree species were analyzed with an ANOVA using Group (I = Itza', L = Ladino, Q = Q'eqchi') and Location (M = Milpa, G = Guamil, R = Reserve). Results show effects of Group [$F(2, 81) = 10.48$, $p < .0001$; I, L > Q], Location [$F(2, 81) = 171.98$, $p < .0001$; R > M, G], Group × Location [$F(4, 81) = 4.45$, $p = .003$; M: I > L, Q; G, R: I, L(marginal) > Q]. As a relative measure of biomass, average

Table 7.2
Species counted in Petén milpa plots (year 3)*

Spanish name	Scientific name	Itza'	Ladino	Q'eqchi'	MEAN
achiote**	*Bixa orellana*	1	0	0	0.033
aguacate**	*Persea americana*	2	0	2	0.133
almendra**	*Terminalia catappa*	1	0	0	0.033
arroz	*Oryza sativa*	1	0	1	0.067
ayote	*Cucumis moschata*	8	6	8	0.733
banano (plátano)	*Musa acuminata*	1	0	0	0.033
cacahuate**	*Arachis hypogaea*	1	1	1	0.100
camote	*Ipomoea batatas*	4	0	0	0.133
cania	*Saccharum officinarum*	1	0	1	0.067
cebollín	*Allium cepa*	1	0	0	0.033
cedro**	*Cedrela mexicana*	1	0	1	0.067
chaya	*Cnidoscolus chaymansa*	1	0	2	0.100
chilacayote	*Sicana odorifera*	2	0	0	0.067
chile**	*Capsicum annum*	0	2	1	0.100
cilantro**	*Coriandum sativum*	1	0	1	0.067
ciricote**	*Cordia dodecandra*	2	0	0	0.067
coco**	*Cocos nucifera*	2	1	0	0.100
frijol abono	*Canavalia ensiformis*	2	6	3	0.367
frijol	*Phaseolus vulgaris*	6	8	6	0.667
guayaba**	*Psidium guava*	1	0	0	0.033
ib**	*Phaseolus lunatus*	0	4	0	0.133
ix pelon	*Vigna unguiculaa*	3	2	1	0.200
jícama	*Pachirrhyzus erosus*	3	2	2	0.233
jocote**	*Spondias purpurea*	2	1	1	0.133
limón**	*Citrus limonia*	3	1	1	0.167
maíz	*Zea mays*	10	10	10	1.000
makal	*Xanthosoma yucatense*	5	1	4	0.333
mandarina**	*Citrus reticulata*	2	0	0	0.067
mango**	*Mangifera indica*	2	0	0	0.067
nance agria**	*Byrsonia bucidaefolia*	2	0	1	0.100
nance dulce**	*Byrsonia crassifolia*	3	0	1	0.133
naranja agria**	*Citrus aurantium*	1	0	0	0.033
naranja dulce**	*Citrus sinensis*	1	1	0	0.067

Table 7.2
(continued)

Spanish name	Scientific name	Itza'	Ladino	Q'eqchi'	MEAN
ocoro	*Hibiscus esculentas*	1	3	3	0.233
papaya**	*Carica papaya*	0	1	0	0.033
payak	*Discorea alata*	4	0	1	0.167
pepitoria**	*Cucumis sativa*	1	0	0	0.033
pepino**	*Cucurbita mixta*	0	1	5	0.200
pimienta**	*Pimenta dioica*	1	1	1	0.100
plátanos (varios)	*Musa sp.*	5	6	4	0.500
sandia	*Citrullus anatus*	1	2	0	0.100
tecomate	*Lagenaria siceraria*	2	0	0	0.067
tuki**	*Annona purpurea*	1	0	0	0.033
tsol**	*Cucurbita pepo*	1	0	0	0.033
yuca	*Manihot esculenta*	1	1	2	0.133
yuquilla	*Maranta arundinaceae*	2	1	0	0.100
zapote mamey**	*Pouteria mammosa*	1	0	0	0.033
Mean		9.7	6.4	6.2	

*Does not include orchard or housegarden plants (e.g., tomatoes).
**Species usually cultivated in housegardens or tended in orchards.

tree cover shows the same pattern (figure 7.2), with effects of Group $[F(2, 81) = 6.17,$ $p = .003;$ $I > Q, L(marginal)]$, Location $[F(2, 81) = 75.08,$ $p < .0001;$ $R > M, G]$, Group × Location $[F(4, 81) = 3.43,$ $p = .01;$ M: I(marginal) $> Q;$ G: I $> Q$, L(marginal); R: I $> Q]$. For total land cleared (M + G), Itza' differ reliably from Q'eqchi' and Ladinos. Group differences cannot owe to base-rate differences in species frequency, given the adjacency of parcels across groups.

Soil analysis also suggests that Itza' agroforestry is least harmful and most productive. All soils are moderately alkaline with no significant group differences in pH or organic matter (Atran et al. 1999). Differences are most apparent for (normalized) measurements of phosphorus and nitrates. Neither is abundant in geological materials of limestone regions and their availability represents limiting factors on life-support systems (Rice 1993).

Each soil sample was rated on a scale of 1 to 22 as a joint function of texture (sandy clay loam < clay loam < silty clay loam < sandy clay < clay < silty clay) and structure (small grain < medium grain < large

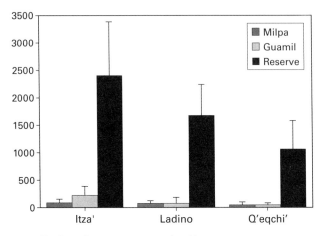

Biodiversity = no. tree species / ha.

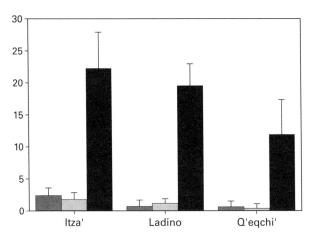

Tree cover = m²/ha.

Figure 7.2
Biodiversity (number of tree species) and tree cover (square meters per hectare) as a function of ethnic group and location type (error bars: 95 percent confidence interval).

grain < small block < medium block < large block). The best soil (= 1) is sandy clay loam composed of small granular structures that become neither too hard when dry nor too compact when wet to prevent water and root penetration. The worst soil (= 22) is silty clay structured in large blocks, which become rock hard when dry and extremely compact when wet. This scale reflects the fact that not all possible combinations of texture and structure were present. Physical character of soils was analyzed by ANOVA: Group (I, L, Q), Location (M, G, R) × Level (1 = 10 cm, 2 = 20 cm). Only Level proved significant [$F(1, 162) = 11.37$, $p = .001$; 1 < 2]. There were no reliable between-group differences for any location. Averages for each group across all locations fell within the range of clays with block structures (I = 14.1, L = 16.9, Q = 14.0). These are able to hold water and fix phosphorus, but become unworkable and impede root growth during very dry and wet spells (frequent in Petén). Erosion and lack of tree cover magnify the effect.

Phosphorus and nitrate levels were analyzed using Group × Location × Level ANOVAs. Phosphorus showed effects for Location [$F(2, 162) = 25.67$, $p < .0001$; M > G, R], Level [$F(1, 162) = 18.86$, $p < .0001$; 10 cm > 20 cm] and Group × Location [$F(4, 162) = 3.79$, $p = .006$; M: I, L > Q; R: L > I]. Itza' differ from Q'eqchi' in the upper milpa level ($p < .05$), where phosphorus is most abundant and useful to new plant growth. Nitrate levels show effects of Group [$F(2, 162) = 11.42$, $p < .0001$; I(marginally) > L, Q], Location [$F(2, 162) = 6.44$, $p = .002$; M > G) and Group × Location [$F(4, 162) = 2.87$, $p = .02$; M: I, L > Q; G: I > L, Q]. For total land cleared (M + G), Itza' differ marginally from Ladinos, significantly from Q'eqchi'.

Overall, Itza' have the highest milpa and lowest reserve scores for phosphorus, indicating greater phosphorus storage by plants in reserve with more available for release in milpa (figure 7.3).[13] High levels of phosphorus in milpa arise from burning; however, intense heat volatilizes nitrates essential to leaf formation. Thus, higher phosphorus levels should be correlated with lower nitrate levels (and perhaps less foliage cover in the long run). But for Itza', and to a lesser extent Ladinos, the reverse is true (figure 7.4). Interrelated factors allow Itza' to enjoy relatively high phosphorus and nitrate levels. Itza' cultivate more varieties of nitrogen-fixing pole beans that climb maize stalks than do Q'eqchi' or Ladinos. Q'eqchi' and Ladinos weed only once shortly after planting. Itza' weed a second time before maize has flowered and leave the weeds as mulch. Intense rainfall at this time favors bacterial decomposition of mulch, which releases nitrogen (also phosphorus, potassium, and magnesium). Finally,

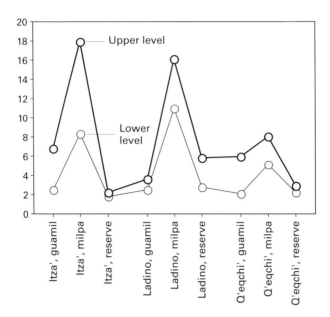

Figure 7.3
Phosphorus (micrograms per milliliter) as a function of cultural group (Itza', Ladino, Q'eqchi'), location type (guamil, milpa, reserve), and ground level (lower = 20 cm, upper = 10 cm).

Itza' tend to light smaller and more dispersed fires to clear land, and to protect valuable trees with firebreaks 2 m around in width. (A side effect is that the less intense heat causes less volatilization of nitrogen.)

In sum, physical measurements generally corroborate reported behaviors and track their consequences, indicating that Itza' practices encourage a better balance between human productivity and forest maintenance than do immigrant practices. However, significant differences in immigrant practices reveal that immigrant Ladinos are measurably closer in behavior to native Maya than are immigrant Maya. Studies of milpa practices among other immigrant Q'eqchi' communities in Petén confirm the patterns in our study (Fagan 2000). In this context, Itza' appear to behave "irrationally" insofar as their restraint subsidizes another group's profligacy: the more cooperators produce for free-riders, the more the free-riding population is able to expand and lay waste.[14] Interestingly, Itza' tend to believe that Ladinos are more destructive in their practices than Q'eqchi' (eleven of fourteen Itza' indicated this in an informal survey we conducted), perhaps because the Q'eqchi' have retained corporate rituals that the Itza' are now adopting.

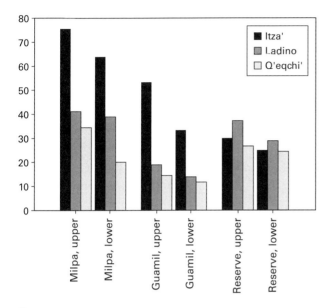

Figure 7.4
Nitrates (micrograms per milliliter) as a function of cultural group (Itza', Ladino, Q'eqchi'), location type (guamil, milpa, reserve), and ground level (lower = 20 cm, upper = 10 cm).

7.5   Mental Models of Folkecology

Because analyses revealed no between-population differences in age, family size, land available to cultivate, or per capita income from all traceable sources, we sought to determine if group differences in behavior are reflected in distinct cognitive patterns we elicited in folkecological models. In preliminary studies, we asked informants "which kinds of plants and animals are most necessary for the forest to live?" From these lists we compiled a set of twenty-eight plants and twenty-nine animals most frequently cited across informants (plant kinds were all generic species, except for two life forms, grass and bush).[15] The twenty-eight plant kinds in the study include twenty kinds of trees and 1 ligneous vine counted among the species in the preceding study. Although these twenty-one species represent only 17 percent of the total number of species enumerated, they account for 44 percent of all trees in Itza' parcels, 50 percent in Ladino parcels, and 54 percent in Q'eqchi' parcels. This confirms the salience of the species selected for the folkecology study (table 7.3).

Table 7.3
Petén forest plants and animals

Ref.	Plant name	Scientific name
	FRUIT TREES	
P1*	ramon	*Brosimum alicastrum*
P2*	chicozapote	*Manilkara achras*
P3*	ciricote	*Cordia dodecandra*
P4*	allspice	*Pimenta diocia*
P5*	strangler fig	*Ficus obtusifolia*
		F. aurea
	PALMS	
P6*	guano	*Sabal mauritiiforme*
P7*	broom palm	*Crysophilia stauracantha*
P8*	corozo	*Orbignya cohune*
		Scheelea lundellii
P9	xate	*Chamaedorea elegans*
		C. erumpens
		C. oblongata
P10	pacaya	*Chamaedorea tepejilote*
P11	chapay	*Astrocaryum mexicanum*
	GRASSES/HERBS	
P12	herb/underbrush	(various families)
P13	grasses	Cyperaceae/Poaceae
	OTHER PLANTS	
P14*	mahogany	*Swietenia macrophylla*
P15*	cedar	*Cedrela mexicana*
P16*	ceiba	*Ceiba pentandra*
P17*	madrial	*Gliricidia sepium*
P18*	chaltekok	*Caesalpinia velutina*
P19*	manchich	*Lonchocarpus castilloi*
P20*	jabin	*Piscidia piscipula*
P21*	santamaria	*Calophyllum brasilense*
P22*	amapola	*Pseudobombax ellipticum*
		Bernoullia flammea
P23*	yaxnik	*Vitex gaumeri*
P24*	kanlol	*Senna racemosa*
P25*	pukte	*Bucida buceras*
P26*	water vine	*Vitis tilaefolia*
P27	cordage vine	*Cnestidium rufescens*
P28	killer vines	(various epiphytes)

*Species counted in tree-frequency study.

Table 7.3
(continued)

Ref.	Animal name	Scientific name
	ARBOREAL ANIMALS	
A1	bat	Chiroptera
A2	spider monkey	*Ateles geoffroyi*
A3	howler monkey	*Allouatta pigra*
		A. palliata
A4	kinkajou	*Potus flavus*
A5	coatimundi	*Nasua narica*
A6	squirrel	*Sciurius deppei*
		S. aureogaster
	BIRDS	
A7	crested guan	*Penelope purpurascens*
A8	great curassow	*Crax rubra*
A9	ocellated turkey	*Meleagris ocellata*
A10	tinamou	*Tinamou major*
		Crypturellus sp.
A11	toucan	*Ramphastos sulfuratus*
A12	parrot	Psittacidae in part
A13	scarlet macaw	*Ara macao*
A14	chachalaca	*Ortalis vetula*
A15	pigeon/dove	Columbidae
	RUMMAGERS	
A16	collared peccary	*Tayassu tacaju*
A17	white-lipped peccary	*Tayassu pecari*
A18	paca	*Cuniculus paca*
A19	agouti	*Dasyprocta punctata*
A20	red-brocket deer	*Mazama americana*
A21	white-tailed deer	*Odocoileus virginianus*
A22	tapir	*Tapirus bairdii*
A23	armadillo	*Dasypus novemcintus*
	PREDATORS	
A24	jaguar	*Felis onca*
A25	margay	*Felis wiedii*
A26	mountain lion	*Felis concolor*
A27	boa	*Boa constrictor*
A28	fer-de-lance	*Bothrops asper*
A29	laughing falcon	*Herpetotheres cachinnans*

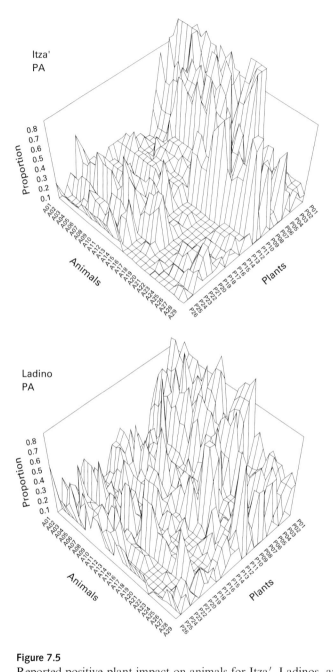

Figure 7.5
Reported positive plant impact on animals for Itza', Ladinos, and Q'eqchi'. Animal and plant numbers refer to the ordering of species in table 7.3. The height of each point refelects the proportion of informants reporting each interaction.

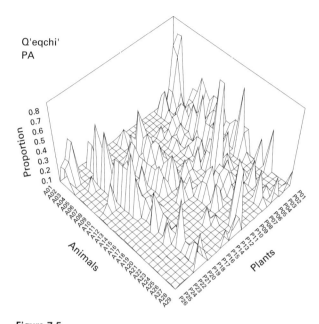

Figure 7.5
(continued)

How Plants Affect Animals

The plant and animal kinds are organized into categories used later in the analysis. Instructions and responses were given in Itza', Spanish, or Q'eqchi'. Equal numbers of informants were asked to explain how each plant helped or hurt each animal, and how each animal helped or hurt each plant.

The procedure had two parts. We asked participants how each plant affected each animal. The task consisted of twenty-eight probes, one for each plant. On each trial, all animal picture cards were laid out and the informant was asked if any of the animals "search for," "go with," or "are companions of" the target plant, and whether the plant helped or hurt the animal. Questions were pretested for simplicity and easy applicability across cultures. Unaffiliated animals were set aside. For each animal, informants were asked to explain how the plant helped or hurt the animal. Next, they were asked how each animal helped or hurt each plant. To explore interactions among people and plants, we asked each informant to explain whether people in their community actually help or hurt each item on the plant list, and vice versa.

For each task, we used the CCM to determine if a single underlying model of ecological relations held for all informants in a population. We collapsed over the different ways one kind might help or hurt another, and the dependent variable for each pair was whether the plant or animal in question helped, hurt, or had no effect on the other kind. Agreement across informants was determined by whether their answers match or mismatched for each pair. To establish consensus, all tasks involved a minimum of twelve participants from each group, with equal numbers of males and females. Data were adjusted for guessing (Romney et al. 1986). Finding consensus justifies further study of groupwide patterns. Analyses of residual agreement were used to reveal group differences.

Results on plants helping animals are summarized in figure 7.5. Each of the three groups produced a distinct model on the forest ecology task. Two results are apparent on how participants see plants affecting animals: (1) Itza' and Ladinos show a highly similar pattern of relations, and (2) Q'eqchi' perceive many fewer relations, which tend to be a subset of those seen for the other two groups. The overwhelming majority of interactions within each group involved plants helping animals by providing them food. Plants providing shelter to animals was also a common response. An ANOVA for plants helping animals showed Q'eqchi' reporting on average many fewer relations (46.8) than either Ladinos (163.2) or Itza' (187.5), who did not differ from each other.[16] Itza' and Ladinos showed a large overlap for which plants help which animals: r (I, L) = .82 versus r (I, Q) = .42 and r (L, Q) = .54.

A large cross-group consensus emerged. Often all Q'eqchi' reported no effect, making the modal answer "no effect." Thus, Q'eqchi' responses drive the overall consensus. Given this situation, residual analyses are more effective than simple measures of interinformant agreement in revealing cultural models. We analyzed a 3×36 residual agreement matrix. For each of thirty-six informants (twelve in each group) there were three measures: average residual agreement of that informant with members of the same group and that informant's average residual agreement with members of each of the other two groups. Within-group agreement proved reliably greater than across-group agreement.[17]

Itza' and Q'eqchi' have greater within- than between-group residual agreement. Ladinos show higher within- than between-group residual agreement vis-à-vis Q'eqchi', but do not share more residual agreement with one another than with Itza'. *This finding is consistent with the idea that the Ladino model for plant-animal relations is a subset of the Itza' model.* One distinction between Itza' and Ladinos was the latter's tendency to generalize the beneficial effect on animals of economically and culturally important plants, such as mahogany (the prime

wood export) and ceiba (Guatemala's national tree) without apparent justification (Atran et al. 2002). Relations noted by Q'eqchi' were basically
subsets of those reported by other groups. Overall, Ladino and Itza'
models converge on how plants help animals. The Q'eqchi' model is a
severely limited subset of the Itza' and Ladino models.

Animals Affecting Plants

Reports of how animals affect plants yielded even larger differences (figure 7.6). Q'eqchi' report too few interactions (only 10 out of 812 possible
relations) for consensus analysis. Itza' and Ladinos show strong cross-
group consensus, but also greater residual agreement within than between groups. Negative reports of animals hurting plants occur with
equal frequency (8.0 percent of cases by Itza', 8.2 percent by Ladinos).
Ladinos report few relations of animals helping plants. For example, Itza'
are 4 times more likely to report positive interactions and 3.4 times more
likely to report reciprocal relations (a plant and animal helping each
other).

   With respect to positive relations, Itza' report that classes of animals
differentially affected classes of plants, whereas Ladinos do not. To illustrate, plant kinds were collapsed into four categories (fruit, grass/herb,
palm, and other), as were animal categories (arboreal, bird, rummager,
and predator). An ANOVA reveals a plant-by-animal interaction for
Itza' but not for Ladinos,[18] (1) arboreals were much more likely to interact with fruit trees than with other plant groups, (2) birds were also most
likely to interact with fruit trees, but had moderate levels of interactions
with palms as well, (3) rummagers interacted primarily with grasses/
herbs, and to a lesser extent with fruit trees, and (4) predators showed
few if any interactions with plants.[19]

   On a qualitative level, although both groups acknowledge that animals
have a large impact on fruit trees, Itza' differ from Ladinos in understanding these relations. In their justifications of plant-animal relationships, Ladinos almost always see animals as harming plants by eating
fruit. Itza' justifications reveal a more nuanced appreciation of the relationship between seed properties and processing: if the seed is soft and
the animal cracks the fruit casing, the animal is likely to destroy the seed
and thus harm the plant; but if the seed is hard and passes through the
animal's body rapidly, the animal is apt to help the plant by dispersing
and fertilizing the seed (Atran and Medin 1997).

   A more detailed examination of positive and negative relations reinforces the view that Itza' and Ladinos are attending to the same relations

188 Chapter 7

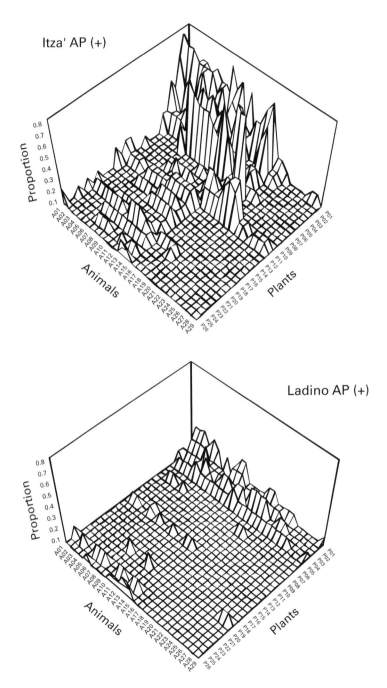

Figure 7.6
Reported positive and negative animal impact on plants for Itza' and Ladinos.
Animal and plant numbers refer to the ordering of species in table 7.3. The height
of each point reflects the proportion of informants reporting each interaction.

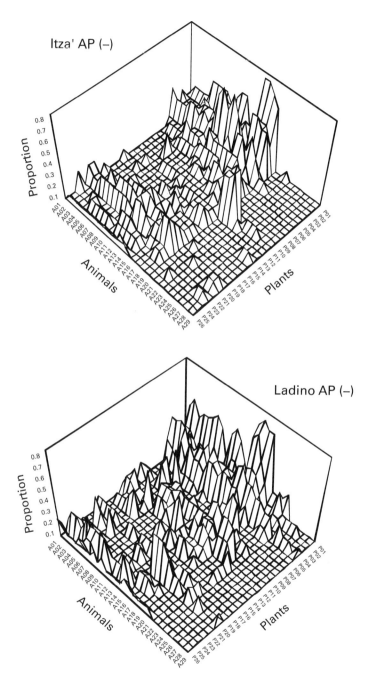

Figure 7.6
(continued)

but interpreting them differently. The two groups have essentially the same model of negative relations—for no pair was there greater than a .40 mean difference in endorsing a negative relation. For a given animal-plant pair both positive and negative relations could be reported. For both groups there was a reliable, positive correlation between reporting a positive relation for a pair and reporting a negative relation for that same pair.[20] The group difference is mediated by the fact that Itza' are much more likely to report a positive relation, even when a negative relation is also present. We will examine this difference in more detail when we consider mechanisms of cultural transmission.

These findings suggest a complex Itza' folkecological model of the forest, wherein different animals affect different plants, and relations among plants and animals are reciprocal. As Bartlett (1936) and Lundell (1937) noted when carrying out the first systematic ecological surveys of Petén, native Maya (Itza') awareness of local ecological associations served as remarkably detailed and accurate guides to subsequent scientific identification and analysis. On a qualitative level, the Ladinos appear to be operating under a different cultural model. In a preliminary interview where we asked Ladinos how animals help plants (thus presupposing that they do) the typical response was, "Animals don't help plants; plants help animals." Ladinos also possess a relatively elaborate model, but relations are more unidirectional and less specific. Q'eqchi' acknowledge a much reduced role for plants, and almost no role for animals in the folkecology of the forest.

Human-Animal Relations

To further distinguish the role of humans in Itza' and Ladino folkecology we did a follow-up study of interactions among animals and people (with twelve new informants for each group). Itza' and Ladinos share consensus on numbers and kinds of negative animal-human interactions,[21] based mainly on animal damage to milpa crops; however, Itza' report more positive animal-human interactions,[22] based on use of animals (e.g., in medicine) and their role in forest regeneration (e.g., optimizing seed distributions of valuable trees). This is the same pattern as in the animal-plant interaction study.

In sum, Itza' show awareness of ecological complexity and reciprocity between animals, plants, and people, and Itza' agroforestry favors forest regeneration. Q'eqchi' acknowledge few ecological dependencies, and Q'eqchi' agriculture is insensitive to forest survival. Ladino folkecology and practice are intermediate. Itza' agroforestry thought and practice encourage a potentially sustainable balance between human productivity and forest maintenance.

Human Impact

Explanations of responses regarding how plants help people focused on use. Response patterns for Itza' and Ladinos were similar; Q'eqchi' provided considerably fewer uses. Even so, at least two-thirds of the Q'eqchi' informants mentioned a use for the overwhelming majority of plants.[23] A look at the rank order of primary use categories for each population in table 7.4 reveals the priorities in each population's mental model of utility. The major difference between Itza' and Ladinos concerns the relative priorities of artisanry and firewood. Itza' are loathe to consider the use of ecologically or economically important trees for firewood if the wood can be used for other purposes. Although all populations consider nourishment among the top priorities, only the Q'eqchi' consider it primary. Even more significantly, whereas Q'eqchi' also consider cash value a high priority, Itza' and Ladinos assign cash value relatively low priority.

For each species we asked what its value was for people, and what people's effect was on the species. The species' value for people was coded for "use" or "cash," and human impact on species was assessed on a scale from negative (-1) through neutral (0) to positive ($+1$). Each population had sufficient statistical consensus among informants to warrant aggregating individual responses of the population into a cultural model of "impact signature"—that is, what people believe their impact is on forest species (table 7.5).

Table 7.4
Ranking of plant-use categories by percentages

Itza'	%	Ladino	%	Q'eqchi'	%
artisanry	27	housing	24	food	30
housing	25	food	22	housing	25
food	21	firewood	17	cash	17
medicine	7.5	artisanry	15	artisanry	15
firewood	5.7	medicine	8.5	firewood	10
cash	5.0	cash	5.0	medicine	2.6
ornament	1.6	ornament	0.9	ornament	0
other	7.3	other	8.2	other	0

Table 7.5
Rankings of human impact on plants and ecological centrality

Itza'			Ladino			Q'eqchi'		
impact	centrality	plant	impact	centrality	plant	impact	centrality	plant
1.00	0.64	ramon	0.75	0.20	guano	0.33	0.04	madrial
1.00	0.62	chicle	0.58	0.15	pacaya	0.25	0.09	broom palm
0.83	0.48	mahogany	0.58	0.10	xate	0.08	0.07	grasses
0.83	0.11	cedar	0.55	0.16	ceiba	0.00	0.21	ramon
0.83	0.11	ciricote	0.50	0.47	mahogany	0.00	0.17	amapola
0.75	0.20	xate	0.42	0.61	chicle	0.00	0.08	chapay
0.67	0.40	madrial	0.33	0.64	ramon	0.00	0.07	allspice
0.67	0.36	ceiba	0.33	0.12	allspice	0.00	0.05	herbs
0.67	0.09	allspice	0.17	0.36	madrial	0.00	0.04	mahogany
0.67	0.05	guano	0.17	0.25	grasses	0.00	0.02	pacaya
0.58	0.30	chapay	0.17	0.14	cedar	0.00	0.02	santamaria
0.58	0.25	amapola	0.08	0.30	ciricote	0.00	0.02	water vine
0.58	0.20	pacaya	0.00	0.29	amapola	0.00	0.01	jabin
0.58	0.13	corozo	0.00	0.22	broom palm	0.00	0.01	pukte
0.58	0.09	broom palm	0.00	0.17	cordage vine	0.00	0.01	yaxnik
0.50	0.34	grasses	0.00	0.00	yaxnik	0.00	0.00	ceiba
0.42	0.17	jabin	-0.13	0.14	pukte	0.00	0.00	corozo
0.42	0.07	chaltekok	-0.14	0.01	chaltekok	0.00	0.00	kanlol
0.42	0.06	manchich	-0.18	0.11	santamaria	-0.08	0.15	strangler fig
0.25	0.16	santamaria	-0.25	0.25	herbs	-0.08	0.03	cordage vine
0.17	0.37	herbs	-0.25	0.06	water vine	-0.08	0.01	killer vines

0.08	0.47	strangler fig	−0.33	0.09	chapay	−0.08	0.00	chaltekok
0.08	0.28	yaxnik	−0.44	0.13	jabin	−0.25	0.05	guano
−0.25	0.16	pukte	−0.50	0.20	corozo	−0.25	0.03	xate
−0.33	0.07	cordage vine	−0.60	0.00	manchich	−0.25	0.01	manchich
−0.33	0.01	water vine	−0.67	0.60	strangler fig	−0.58	0.13	chicle
−0.58	0.09	killer vines	−0.67	0.24	killer vines	−0.67	0.12	cedar
−0.58	0.03	kanlol	−0.75	0.06	kanlol	−0.75	0.09	ciricote

Impact signatures for Itza' and Ladinos were moderately correlated
($r = .65$, $p < .001$), suggesting somewhat similar views of how members
of their respective communities affect plants. Signatures for Q'eqchi'
were negatively correlated with those of Itza' ($r = -.28$) and Ladinos
($r = -.16$), suggesting a very different model of human effects on plants.
Itza' report beneficial impact on all ecologically and economically important plants, and absolute commitment to protecting ramón and chicle
(*Manilkara achras*). Itza' call ramón the "milpa of the animals" because
many bird and mammal species feed on its fruits and leaves (Atran 1993).
The chicle tree is also visited often by animals and, as with the ramón,
has a long history of local use. Extraction of chicle latex for chewing
gum was Petén's prime cash source in the twentieth century. Itza' report
variable impact on herbaceous undergrowth, strangler figs (*Ficus* sp.,
which nourish many animals but kill other trees), and yaxnik (*Vitex gau-
meri*), which Itza' qualify as a marginally useful "forest weed." Itza' report harmful impact on pukte (*Bucida buceras*), another "forest weed";
on kanlol (*Senna racemosa*), a "village weed"; and on vines cut for water
and cordage.

Ladinos also report highly positive impact for valuable plants (including *Ceiba pentandra*, Guatemala's national tree). For palms, they report
positive impact only for those used for thatch (corozo palm fruits are
also sold to a local NGO). For most plants they report variable impact.
Q'eqchi' report positive impact only for thatch palms, and negative
impact on Petén's most important cash sources: chicle, tropical cedar
(*Cedrela mexicana*), mahogany (*Swietania macrophylla*), and xate (deco-
rative *Chamaedorea* dwarf palms collected for export).

Interestingly, ramón and chicle, whose native uses the Spanish docu-
mented at the time of the Conquest (Landa [1566] 1985), are the two
most frequent species encountered in northern Petén forests (AHG–
APESA 1992). Moreover, only the Petén variety of ramón appears to
bear fruit any time of the year (Peters 1989). This suggests that cross-
generational care of ramón and chicle by Maya produced a highly
anthropogenic forest, which Itza' continue to foster and tend.

The fact that Itza' believe (on average) that they have a lot of beneficial
impact on important species does not logically entail or causally imply
that Itza' should choose costly conservation measures to protect certain
trees. But it is a matter of fact that they do (see below). Given that other
people (Ladinos, Q'eqchi') do not protect the trees that Itza' do, Itza'
conservation behavior does not seem to make sense from the individual's

standpoint. One might try to proffer a group-selection argument (sacrifice of individual advantage for the benefit of the group as a whole). But there is no evidence whatever that there are any such group-selection mechanisms operating. Later, we suggest that individual actions in accordance with spiritual values may be the part of the story, and that such values refine calculations of immediate self-interest in favor of long-term interest to individuals (on average).

7.6   Further Ground-Truthing

Itza' folkecological models also relate directly to observed behavior. Regression analysis revealed that for Itza', ratings of human impact (the extent to which people report their actions as helping or hurting particular species) and weed status (factoring out plants considered weeds) predicted frequencies of trees counted in informant parcels ($r^2 = .46$, $p = .004$, with both predictors reliable). No comparable relation emerged for Ladinos or Q'eqchi'. Regressions also revealed different predictors of human impact on plants for each group. For Itza', ecological centrality (number of associations in a group's consensual ecological model for a given plant) and combined utility (value of a plant for wood, shelter, and cash combined) predicted reported human impact ($r^2 = .44$, $p < .001$, with both predictors reliable). In short, ecological importance and overall utility predicted which plants the Itza' seek to protect, which in turn predicts the plants encountered in sample plots.[24]

For Ladinos, cash value was the only reliable predictor of impact, indicating that Ladinos protect plants having cash value. For Q'eqchi', none of these variables predicted impact signature and the (nonsignificant) correlations were consistently negative, indicating the Q'eqchi' tend to destroy valuable plants. In sum, the three groups have very different mental models of the forest, and correspondingly distinct patterns of use. Only Itza' seem to have a positive vision of the role of plants, animals, and humans in helping the forest survive that is based on species reciprocity. For neither of the other two groups is there a reliable association between mental models of the forest and patterns of use.

Our tentative line of reasoning is that Itza', and perhaps other native peoples with a long history of ecological maintenance,[25] might not treat resources as traditional decision and game theory suggests—that is, as objects of a payoff matrix (extensional items substitutable along some metric, such as one that assigns monetary value to every object). Instead, some people may treat resources, such as species, as intentional, relational entities, like friends or enemies.[26]

We asked people from each of the three Petén groups to rank-order each of twenty-one plant species in terms of their importance according to (1) members of their own community, (2) and (3) members of each of the other two communities, (4) God, and (5) the forest spirits. We looked for correlates of these rankings for each of the groups. Only Itza' see the forest spirits as actively protecting the forest: Itza' rankings from the point of view of the forest spirits are significantly related to Itza' reports of ecological centrality (number of associations in a group's consensual ecological model for a given plant) and human impact (the extent to which people report their actions as helping or hurting particular species). The most reliable combination of predictors for what (male Itza' believe) the spirits are thinking is ecological centrality and God ($r^2 = .65$, $p = 0.0001$). In turn, further multiple regressions show that male Itza' consensus on spirits (women seldom engage forest spirits) together with the overall Itza' consensus on combined use (value of the plant for wood, shelter, and cash) predicts reported human impact ($r^2 = .70$, $p = 0.0001$), with spirits and use equally reliable predictors. Ladinos and Q'eqchi' state belief in forest spirits, and Ladinos even provide normative and narrative accounts of spirit life similar to those of Itza'. Yet, in these two groups belief in spirits is not reliably linked to forestry practice. Itza' rankings of God's preferences (i.e., how Itza' believe God rates the importance of each species) are related to the measure of combined use but not ecological centrality.

Finally, we asked members of several local and international NGOs with over a decade of experience in the area to rank the same trees as did Itza' and Ladinos in terms of importance to forest life. The aim was to see if and how well NGO preferences correspond with ecological centrality, the values of the local groups, and/or metrics such as cash value. Cash value proved important and ecological centrality played no role at all. The most valued species for the NGOs were, in rank order: mahogany, tropical cedar, allspice, and chicle. These are the most important trees for the extractive economy and export market. The worst predictor of NGO rankings was male Itza' rankings of spirit preferences ($r^2 = .06$) and Itza' ratings of ecological centrality ($r = -.23$). NGO preferences partially predicted consensus on preferences expressed by Ladinos ($r^2 = .72$, $p < 0.01$) and Itza' ($r^2 = .44$, $p < 0.05$). (The Q'eqchi' did not reach a consensus on preferences.) In short, NGOs appear to focus more on economic development than on the welfare of the forest.

7.7 A Theory-of-Mind Experiment and Spiritual Games

To better undertstand how Itza' think about spirits and God we conducted an experiment on their "theory of mind." Cognitive and developmental psychologists use the notion of a "theory of mind" to refer to a
core aspect of folkpsychology, namely, the ability to correctly anticipate
the mental states of other intelligent agents. We showed seven female
and seven male Itza' Maya adults a tortilla container and told them,
"Usually tortillas are inside this box, but I ate them and put these shorts
inside." We asked each informant in random order what a person, God,
and the forest spirits (*arux*) would think was in the box. Each informant
(save one man) responded that God had a true belief because, as several
respondents stated, "He can see through the basket as if it were transparent." All (except the same man) thought a person coming upon the basket
would have a false belief about its contents. Six men and four women
thought the forest spirits (*arux*) would know the basket's true contents.
Overall (for men as well as women), mental states of humans also were
perceived as different from those of God[27] and forest spirits,[28] but God
and forest spirits were not significantly different from one another
(Atran and Norenzayan 2004).

To further explore the developmental trajectory of these sorts of beliefs,
we posed a similar but somewhat more comprehensive set of questions to
forty-eight Yukatek-speaking children (twenty-six boys, twenty-two girls)
(Knight et al. 2004). We asked each child in random order what a person,
God, the sun (*k'in*), principal forest spirits (*yumil k'ax'ob'*, "Masters of
the Forest"), and other minor spirits (*chiichi'*) would think was in the
box. As with American children (Barrett et al. 2001), the youngest Yukatek (4 years) overwhelmingly attribute true beliefs to both God and people in equal measure. After age 5, the children attribute mostly false
beliefs to people but attribute mostly true beliefs to God.[29] Thus, 33 percent of the 4-year-olds said that people would think tortillas were in the
container versus 77 percent of the 7-year-olds. In contrast, no significant
correlation was detected between answers for God and age [$r(46) = .06$].
Collapsing over ages, Yukatek children attribute true beliefs according to
a hierarchy of human and divine minds, one in which humans and minor
spirits are seen as easier to deceive (figure 7.7). Mental states of humans
were perceived as different from those of God ($Z = 3.357$, $p = .001$), and
from those of Masters of the Forest and the Sun Deity ($Z = 1.89$, $p = .06$
for both). God is seen as all-knowing, and local religious entities fall
somewhere in between (figure 7.7). In brief, from an early age Lowland

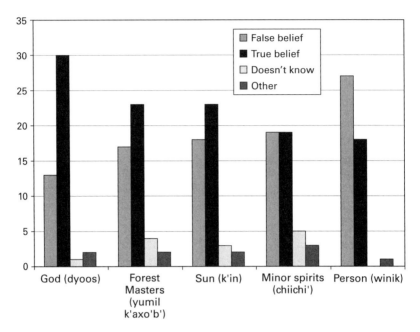

Figure 7.7
What's in the container? All Yukatek Maya children's responses.

Maya seem to reliably attribute to supernaturals cognitions that they believe are *different* and *truer* than those attributed to humans.

7.8   Implications for Conceptualizing the Commons

To date, rational-decision and game-theoretic accounts involving human
use of nonhuman resources generally have not considered nonhuman
resources (e.g., the forest) and humans both as "players" in the same
game, presumably because natural resources are assumed not to have
motives, desires, beliefs, or strategies for cooperation or deception that
would be sensitive, and systematically responsive to corresponding
aspects of human intention. Money, trees, fish, and other resources are
treated as inert objects in a game, not as interacting agents. Of course, it
is always possible to build game-theoretic models in which humans and
nonhumans interact (e.g., domestication) and, indeed, in which none of
the actors have intentions (e.g., bacteria and their hosts). Our point is
about practice, not possibility. People's conceptualization of resources
may make a difference in how they play the game. For example, people's

agroforestry behavior may differ as a function of whether they consider the forest to be an inert object or an actor that intentionally responds to their actions. Indeed, one claim for "animistic" and "anthropomorphic" interpretations of species in many small-scale societies is that the "intention gap" between humans and species is thus bridged (at least to human satisfaction) with outcomes mutually beneficial to the survival of species and of the human groups that live off those species (see Bird-David 1999).

In informal interviews and conversations Itza' men and women express the belief that they will be punished if they violate spirit preferences. It is important to note that this punishment is not carried out by humans and no human-based sanctioning system is in place to enforce compliance with the spirits' rules. Therefore, the Itza' forest spirits (*Arux*) cannot be understood as a social institution, even though the concept of *Arux* is socially constructed. Especially for men, the spirits are intermediaries or "spokesmen" for the forest species. This has intriguing implications for ecological decision theory and game theory in that individual Itza' may be basing their cognitive and behavioral strategies for sustaining the forest more by playing a game (i.e., negotiating costs and benefits of mutual cooperation) with spirits than by playing a game with other people (on the wider role of spirits in Itza' life and religion, see Atran 2001b).

From a long-term perspective, Itza' spirit preferences may represent the statistical summary of mutually beneficial outcomes over generations of human-species interactions. Note that, as pointed out by Hardin (1968), evolution itself provides mechanisms for interactive "games" that commensurate the apparently incommensurable (e.g., "strategies" of bacteria and their hosts), and so may human minds (semantically rather than biologically) in ways consistent with maintaining absolute or asymptotic respect for sacred or "taboo" values—moral beliefs—basic to long-term survival and quality of life (Fiske and Tetlock 1997; Medin et al. 1999; see also Tanner and Medin 2004; Atran and Norenzayan 2004).[30]

Theories of rational action predict that increases in the number of noncooperative players in the environment and their apparent disregard for the future should lead even native cooperators to abandon long-term interest for short-term gain, unless institutional restraints can compel individual action toward the common good. Yet native Itza' Maya, who have few cooperative institutions, show awareness of ecological complexity and reciprocity between animals, plants, and people, whereas immigrant Q'eqchi' Maya, who have highly cooperative institutions, acknowledge few ecological dependencies. No doubt economic rationality and institutional constraints are important factors in determining and describing actions on common-pool resources, but they may not suffice. There also appears to be an important cognitive dimension to behavioral research on how people learn to manage environmental resources. Valuation studies suggest that cognition of supernatural agents may serve not only to guarantee trust and foster cooperation between nonkin, as standard commitment theories assume (Frank 1988; Irons 1996), but also foster human interaction with nonhuman resources in relations of "indirect reciprocity" (Alexander 1987).

Summary It is no surprise that native Maya with centuries-old dependence on a particular habitat have a richer model of forest ecology than immigrants. But longevity in a given context does not guarantee sustainable agroforestry practices. Our observations suggest that Itza' have a complex of knowledge, practices, and beliefs associated with sustainability. One should be very cautious in moving from correlations to cause— we do not know whether any one component of the Itza' belief system is either necessary or sufficient to support Itza' practices. Given that important proviso, the extent to which knowledge, values, and beliefs about the forest spirits reinforce each other is remarkable.

It is also surprising that Ladino immigrants, who share no evident tradition with native Maya, come to measurably resemble them in thought and action. As we will see in the next chapter, network analyses reveal reliable but noninstitutionalized linkages that allow socially well-connected Ladinos access to Itza' forest expertise.

7.9   Further Observations from Mesoamerica

So far we have focused on a single case study—or "garden experiment"— in Petén. Several outstanding issues remain. For example, to what extent are our methods and theoretical approach generalizable to other populations and settings? To what extent are our findings about differences in populations that live off the same habitat the result of transgenerational differences in exposure and experience (e.g., recent immigrant versus long-standing settler populations) or the result of enduringly different historical knowledge bases?

To address these and related issues, we have used the same techniques to monitor ecological cognition and social networks for Highland Q'eqchi' Maya (Aldea Paapa, Alta Verapaz, Guatemala), Yukatek Maya (Xk'opchen) and Ladinos (Xkomha) in Quintana Roo (Mexico), and among Lacandon Maya (Chiapas, Mexico). We have done the same among Native American Menominee and majority-culture rural groups along the Wolf River in Wisconsin (Medin et al. 2002, 2005, 2006), and this work will be described in chapter 9.

Highland Q'eqchi'

One open issue is whether Q'eqchi' immigrants arrive in Petén with a cognitive model already impoverished with respect to knowledge of species relationships, or whether they are simply unable to use richer Highland models because these are inappropriate to Lowland ecology. For this reason, we sought to establish a cognitive baseline for Highland Q'eqchi' in their original home area of Alta Verapaz. We elicited mental models from Highland Q'eqchi' in Aldea Paapa near Cobán, employing the same techniques as in Petén. The kinds most frequently mentioned as important to the forest included twenty-seven animals and twenty plants. Nearly half the animals (thirteen) mentioned as important also counted among the most important Petén species. Plants mentioned as most important to the forest included only two of the most important Petén species (the pacaya palm and the allspice tree), and also included species primarily associated with orchard (e.g., peach tree, *Prunus persica*) and milpa (e.g., chili pepper, *Capsicum annum*). Although two animal kinds and half the plants must still be identified scientifically, patterns of interaction between plants, animals, and people can be reliably described (tables 7.6 and 7.7).

As we found for the Petén groups, Highland Q'eqchi' view plants as positively affecting animals, first by providing food and second by furnishing shelter. Consensus on positive plant-animal relations is marginal (eigenvalue 1:2 = 2.97, variance = 44 percent). Nearly 20 percent of all possible plant-animal relations are positive. This is about the same as for Itza' and Ladinos. Highland Q'eqchi' recognize more negative animal-plant relations (2.3 percent for all possible animal-plant relations) than immigrant Q'eqchi' (<1 percent), but less than Itza' (7.8 percent) or Ladinos (8.2 percent). Highland Q'eqchi' also recognize fewer positive relations of animal affecting plants (<1 percent) than Ladinos (2.1 percent), and far less than Itza' (8.2 percent). Q'eqchi' evince finer appreciation of local ecology in their Highland homeland than in their Lowland habitat. Still, such appreciation is significantly less rich than that of Itza' or even immigrant Ladinos. Highlanders also show good consensus on how humans negatively affect plants (eigenvalue 1:2 = 7.68, variance = 75 percent) but no consensus on how humans positively affect plants. This reinforces a picture of similar notions of how plants affect animals,

Table 7.6
Highland Q'eqchi' animals

Q'eqchi' name	Scientific name	Reference number
jeketzol	*Ortalis vetula*	A01
kiche' ak'ach	*Tyassu* sp.	A02
saqb'in	*Mustela frenata*	A03
kuk	*Sciurus* sp.	A04
kej	*Odocoileus virginianus*	A05
pich'	Picidae sp.	A06
jalaaw	*Agouti paca*	A07
kaqkoj	*Felis concolor*	A08
q'uq'	*Pharomachrus mocinno*	A09
uut'	Columbidae sp.	A10
pu'	*Penelope purpurascens*	A11
che'jej	Picidae sp.	A12
selepan	*Ramphastos sulfuratus*	A13
sosol	*Coragyps atratus*	A14
mukuuy	Columbidae sp.	A15
k'uch	*Buteo* sp.	A16
iq'b'olay	*Bothrops* sp.	A17
imul	*Lagomorpha* sp.	A18
kaqik'anti	*Micrurus* sp.	A19
ch'ojix	*Felis pardalis*	A20
sotz'	Chiroptera sp.	A21
xalaw	unidentified bird	A22
tz'unon	Trochilidae sp.	A23
rax k'aj	unidentified green snake	A24
aaqam	*Dasyprocta punctata*	A25
sis	*Nasua narica*	A26
yuq	*Mazama americana*	A27

but different cultural models of animals affecting plants, of positive animal-plant relations in particular, and of reciprocity between animals, plants, and humans generally (see figure 7.8).

Measures of human impact and use confirm this pattern in content-specific ways. For Highland Q'eqchi', regression analyses show that food value and ecological centrality predict human impact ($r^2 = .58$, both predictors $p = .06$). Food value and impact are positively correlated—that is, Highland Q'eqechi' tend to protect food plants. By contrast, ecological centrality and impact are negatively correlated (see table 7.7), as are ecological centrality and food value. Highland Q'eqchi' do not consider food

Table 7.7
Highland Q'eqchi' reports of impact and centrality*

Q'eqchi' plant	Scientific name	Reference number	Human impact	Ecological centrality
pach'aya	Poaceae/Cyperaceae	P13	0.92	0.1
turans	Prunus persica	P15	0.92	0.25
saqi tul	unidentified vine	P18	0.92	0.16
tzurmuy	Annona sp.	P16	0.83	0.2
ike	Capsicum annum	P14	0.75	0.12
peenz	Pimenta dioica	P10	0.58	0.19
sepres	Thuja orientalis	P05	0.5	0.41
ch'lin	Citrus sinensis	P07	0.5	0.24
tem che'	unidentified tree	P11	0.5	0.34
mes che'	unidentified tree	P12	0.5	0.36
k'iib'	Chamaedorea tepejilote	P20	0.5	0.29
chaj	Pinus sp.	P01	0.42	0.51
tza'aj	Venonia leicarpa	P06	0.42	0.33
sub'	unidentified tree	P19	0.42	0.36
oqob'	unidentified tree	P03	0.33	0.55
tz'inte'	unidentified tree	P08	0.33	0.3
j'k'l	unidentified epiphyte	P09	0.33	0.17
ch'ut	unidentified tree	P17	0.33	0.15
ji	Quercus sp.	P02	0.25	0.54
aam che'	unidentified tree	P04	0	0.44

*Correlation (impact, centrality) $= -0.623$.

plants ecologically important, and do not protect plants they consider ecologically important. The main predictor of ecological importance is use of the plant for firewood ($r^2 = .54$). Firewood and cash sale (as for Lowland Q'eqchi' immigrants) are arguably the least productive categories in terms of forest regeneration. Cash sale of important plants is not part of a local system of production. It is driven by an "extractive economy" that depends almost entirely on demand from outside markets and even outside the region.

It would take us too far afield to explore here the historical reasons for the relatively impoverished Q'eqchi' models. Nevertheless, a few summary observations are in order. There is scant evidence that the trauma of recent civil war is a key factor in immigrant Q'eqchi' attitudes toward Petén. Highland Q'eqchi' models of species relations were likely already impoverished, perhaps in part because of the relatively deforested Highland environment (compared to Petén), and earlier and ongoing Q'eqchi'

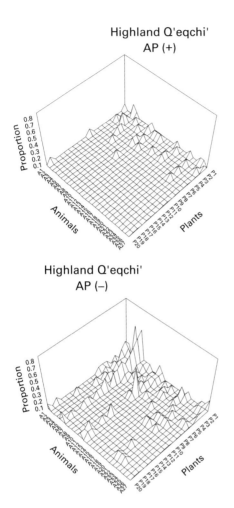

Figure 7.8
Reported positive plant impact on animals, and positive and negative animal impact on plants, for Highland Q′eqchi′. Plant and animal numbers refer to species listed in tables 7.6 and 7.7.

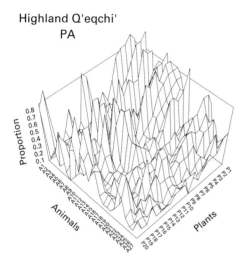

Figure 7.8
(continued)

migrations into the Lowlands show little concern with maintaining forest biodiversity. Under protection from Dominican clergy for centuries, Highland Q'eqchi' institutionally managed their own highly commensalist and intense forms of cultivation. When land was scarce, Q'eqchi' migrated into the Petén Lowlands, often for the short term.

Other Q'eqchi' communities that immigrated into Petén and adjacent areas of Belize both before and after the civil war behave similarly to our study group (Carter 1969; Fagan 2000). When environmentally related economic difficulties arise (e.g., banana blight, hurricanes, and so on), immigrant leaders may send delegations to sacred places in the Q'eqchi' Highlands to seek aid and redress from Highland spirits (see Schackt 1984). But our immigrant Q'eqchi' do not concern themselves with Lowland spirits or consult Itza'. When we asked why they fail to consult Itza' about the forest, the Q'eqchi' often remark that they do not feel the need to seek out or placate Lowland spirits as long as the Q'eqchi' remain true to their ancestral deities.[31]

One conclusion from these findings is that sacred values, per se, are not enough for sustainability. At the very least, a combination of rich ecological models and sacred values may be required. We do not know how this combination plays out under rising population densities, continuous environmental degradation, or even loss of traditional language and knowledge. We are currently exploring these issues in cross-generational studies with the Petén populations, as well as with Lacandón Maya—to which we now turn.

7.10 Lacandón Maya

Our studies with the Lacandón Maya were mainly concerned with inter-generational change among the men of the two adult generations living in the community of Mensäbäk. The rationale for this focus was twofold. First, given the distributional view of culture, we might explore within-culture differences that go beyond expertise effects. Second, within-culture differences among Lacandón Maya hold particular interest. Members of the second generation of married adults were born or grew up in village-like communities, whereas fathers and grandfathers originated from dispersed households and settlements.

To elicit mental models of folkecology, a freelisting task was used again to generate a list of species "most important for the forest to live." The CCM produced a single factor solution (ratio eigenvalue 1:2 = 16.4, variance 87 percent) indicating the existence of one underlying model shared by all informants. Nevertheless, members of the two adult generations separate on both their first and second factor loadings, further suggesting two submodels for the members of the two generations.

One difference is that members of the first generation report significantly more interactions than members of the second generation. The first generation's consensual model exhibits a clear structure that separates the animals and plants along lines of taxonomy and habitat (Ross 2002). This separation is based on specific plant-animal relations that involve certain physiological characteristics, such as having a hard shell (as we found with Itza').

We used the expert networks to explore possible links between relation to an expert and levels of agreement. Second-generation adults clearly regard first-generation adults as experts; however, we could find no evidence for a relation between proximity to an expert and ecological knowledge. In addition we failed to find reliable residual agreement between fathers and sons. As a whole, these data only describe expertise differences among the members of the Lacandón community. The differences appear to reflect a marked shift in recent history, namely, a dramatic change in settlement patterns that distanced the younger generation from forest life. The expertise differences observed cannot be easily explained as differences in amount of factual knowledge. Rather, differences in perceived goals (the need to tend the forest) and learning landscape (like Itza', Lacandón elders say that one learns by "walking alone" in the forest) lead individuals to draw different conclusions from the same observations.

Other research suggests that overall patterns of knowledge and behavior among native Lacandón Maya versus Tzeltal and Tzotzil Maya (born to immigrant families from the Highlands that had settled into the area) resemble that of Itza' versus Q'eqchi' immigrants (Nigh 2002). The fact that these descendants of immigrants have lived all their lives in the forest indicates that mere personal exposure to the local ecology is not a deciding factor in sustainability of practices.

7.11   Summary: Implications for Theories of Decision Making

The puzzle for decision theory is: How do people manage limited resources in a sustainable manner without apparent institutional or other obvious normative constraints to encourage and monitor cooperation? Multiple factors are involved in explaining the stability of representations within and across our study populations.

In the area of decision making and the commons, the prevailing view—at least in economics and political science—has been that human behavior in society is driven by self-interest, mitigated by institutional constraints. Like models of induction that rely on universal similarity, abstract decision models employ a homogeneous notion of utility, where content biases and protected values simply are annoying. For example, protected values are annoying because their "utility" may be hard to measure (Baron and Spranca 1997; Ritov and Kahneman 1997), and content biases only serve to distort rational calculations of utility (but see Tanner and Medin 2004 for a contrasting view).

Thus, analyses of the commons problem may appear to be trapped somewhere between isolated individual interests that lead inevitably to commons destruction and a focus on institutions that has little need for cognitive science. To be sure, there is a good body of social science research that identifies certain conditions for cooperation in artificial experimental situations (e.g., Messick and Brewer 1983; Ostrom 1998), but it is hard to see how to transfer these findings to complex, real-world situations such as we find in Petén and Wisconsin. Furthermore, this body of research provides no role for content or values other than in terms of fungible (transparently interchangeable) gains and losses. There is no place for absolute or sacred human values (Rappaport 1979), distinct kinds of concerns (see Tenbrunsel and Messick 2001 for a nice counterexample), or for calculating the "interests" of nature (Wilson 1992).

We find that content-structuring mental models are pertinent to environmental decision making. They not only predict behavioral tendencies and stated values, but also correlate reliably with the measurable consequences of those behaviors and values—even down to the level of soil composition and the number and variety of trees found on people's land (Atran et al. 1999). Perhaps most striking, Itza′ construal of the value of a forest species as relational and subjectively defined seems to recognize nature as a player with a stake in its own future. This is a different way people have of going about their business, and their environments may be the better for it. We think this sort of analysis opens the possibility of making models of decision processes more insightful for understanding human-environment interactions.

Our work casts a different light on the tragedy of the commons and associated game-theoretic analyses. First, individual cognitions or mental models of resources are not irrelevant to environmental decision making as assumed by content-free framing in terms of utilities.[32] Second, differing conceptions of a common resource may require different abstract analyses, as we saw in the case of the Itza′ belief in the forest spirits as guardians of the forest. In short, our unified approach to culture and cognition can inform—and indeed transform—models of cultural cognition, such as environmental decision making.

8 Cultural Epidemiology

In chapter 7 we observed large differences across the three groups of agro-foresters. Now we want to probe more deeply into cultural processes within and between groups. We begin by describing social and expert network data. The goal was to trace variations in knowledge and beliefs with variations in social distance from others, including experts. This is what we mean by *cultural epidemiology*.

8.1 Social and Expert Networks

Social network analysis bears out the close relationship in mental models and forest behaviors between Itza' and Ladinos. For each community we began with six men and six women not immediately related by kinship or marriage.[1] Each informant was asked to name, in order of priority, the seven people outside of the household "most important for your life." Informants were asked in what ways the people named in this *social network* were important for their lives. Some days later each informant was also asked to name, in order of priority, the seven people "to whom you would turn if there were something that you did not understand and wanted to find out about the forest/fishing/hunting." Informants were asked about the kind of information they would seek in these *expert networks*. After performing these tasks with our initial group of informants, we used a "snowball method" to extend these ego-centered networks to wider patterns of social relations in which they operate—that is, social networks and expert networks were then elicited from the first and last persons named in the social network. When either the first or last person named was not available, we interviewed either the second or sixth person named. The decision to establish network closure after a single iteration (one roll) was based on previous studies suggesting that in practice it is rarely necessary to seek direct ties involving more than one intermediary.

The three populations markedly differ in their social and expert network structures, with different consequences for the flow of information about the forest.[2] To fully appreciate the differences, one needs to consider the social and expert networks in conjunction. But first consider social networks, which are summarized in the graphs shown in figure 8.1.

As we will see, the circle graph of the Ladino network shows a clear gender division of the community. The Itza' social network is the most diffuse, and the two clusters correspond, not to gender but to the two major moieties (subgroups, often organized in terms of practices such as intermarriage rules). The MDS that accompanies each circle graph in figure 8.1 uses the pattern of connections as a similarity metric and scales the similarity relations—in this case—in a two-dimensional space (while preserving the connections shown in the circle graph): for the Itza', the first dimension differentiates the two major moieties and the second reflects the presence of clans and families that are connected in different ways to the major moieties but not each other. The Q'eqchi' form the most socially interconnected community. They show a dense, highly interconnected network, with no dominant individual or subgroup. The following analysis supports this impression.

To measure social connectedness we used the group λ-level. Lambda sets describe the line connectivity of nodes (Borgatti et al. 1990). The line connectivity for a pair of nodes is equal to the minimum number of lines that must be removed from the graph in order to leave no path between them. For our purposes, we use the group as the Lambda set and calculate the minimum connectivity (rather than the average) as an index of overall group cohesiveness. In the case of the Itza', for example, if one link is removed, then at least one member of the group becomes separated from the group. For Ladinos, two links must be removed to separate at least one member from the group. For Q'eqchi', four links must be removed to separate at least one member from the group. Level 5 ($\lambda = 5$) includes 90 percent of Q'eqchi', 21 percent of Ladinos, and only 10 percent of Itza'. In short, the Q'eqchi' are the most and the Itza' the least interconnected.

Representations of the Q'eqchi' show a dense, highly interconnected social network, with no dominant individual or subgroup. This redundant social structure favors communal and ceremonial institutions that organize accountability, and that are richer among Q'eqchi' than among Itza' or Ladinos. Only Q'eqchi' practice agroforestry in corporate groups: neighbors and kin clear and burn each household's plot, kin groups seed together, and the community sanctions unwarranted access to family

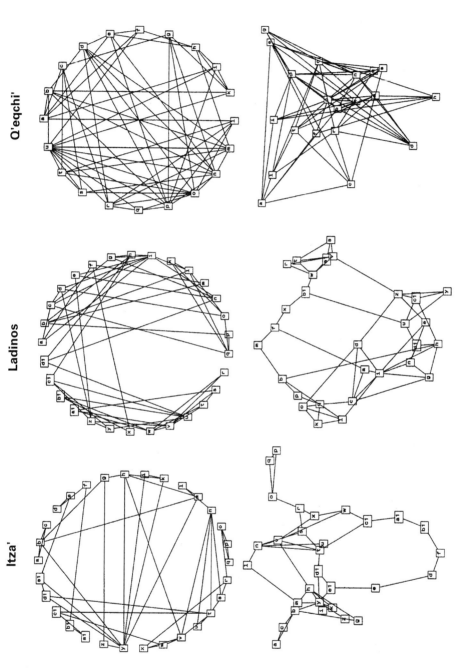

Figure 8.1
Social networks for Itza', Ladinos, and immigrant Q'eqchi'. Circle graphs (top) and multidimensional scaling (bottom) are alternative representations of the same data sets.

stands of copal trees (*Protium copal*), whose resin is ritually burned to ensure the harvest. This implies that institutional monitoring of access to resources, cooperating kin, commensal obligations, an indigenous language, and knowledge of the land (including recognition of important species) may not suffice to avoid ruin of common-pool resources. For the Q'eqchi' of Corozal, continued corporate and ceremonial ties to the sacred mountain valleys of the Q'eqchi' Highlands do not carry corresponding respect for Lowland ecology. A relatively closed corporate structure that channels information focused on internal needs and distant places may function to impede access to ecological information relevant to commons survival.

Q'eqchi' have the lowest agreement on who the forest experts are and Itza' the highest. The two "experts" cited most by Q'eqchi' (60 percent) are a Washington-based NGO and a Guatemalan government agency. While the social network of the Q'eqchi' might allow for speedy and repeated processing of new information, their expert network suggests two potential problems. First, Q'eqchi' seem not to have established links to reliable outside sources of information other than national and international NGOs, with whom they do not interact frequently. Second, within their community, they do not have established and trustworthy sources of important information about the forest ecology (clearly identified experts). As a result, the limited outside information there is seems unlikely to penetrate deeply into the Q'eqchi' community, because it is not conveyed by socially relevant actors.

For Itza', expert information about the forest appears integrally bound to intimate patterns of social life as well as to an experiential history traceable over many generations, if not millennia. For Ladinos, expert information is also likely to be assimilated into the community. Because Ladino experts (i.e., Ladinos most cited as experts by other Ladinos) are socially well connected, information that may come through Itza' experts (i.e., those Itza' most cited as experts by other Itza' as well as by Ladino experts) has access to multiple interaction pathways.

Representations of the Itza' network indicate that node Y is the best socially connected individual (figure 8.1). This person is also cited as the top Itza' forest expert. His expertise has been independently confirmed. For example, in the Bailenson et al. 2002 study of tropical-bird classification among American bird-watchers and Itza', Y scored highest among Itza' on measures of correspondence with scientific (classical evolutionary) taxonomy. Ethnographic interpretation of the MDS scaling reveals that the Itza′ community is currently divided into two social factions: one dominated by Y, the other by V–W and T–N. Person V is W's father and person T is N's father. V and T are also cited as two of the top three Itza′ forest experts. Y and V head two families that have continuous genealogical links to pre-Conquest Itza′ clans of the same name, Chayax and Tesucun.

8.2   Information Transmission

One possibility compatible with the Itza′ social structure is that ecological knowledge is directly transmitted from socially well-connected forest experts, such as Y, to other Itza′. To evaluate this possibility, we analyzed patterns of residual agreement in relation to social and expert network structure. We wanted to see how other individuals and subgroups compared to our most cited expert Itza′ informant, Y. We focused exclusively on the nonempty cells, because knowledge transmission should primarily take the form of noting an existing relation, not the absence of relations. Analyses within the Itza′ sample revealed little residual agreement and this agreement was inconsistent across different tasks. In no case could we discern relationships between residual agreement and social or expert network proximity. In other words, Itza′ social structure does not show evidence of specific pathways for learning about the forest, at least for our sample.

While this lack of evidence may be an effect of high repetition of information among all informants and the generally high level of expertise, there is an alternative scenario to learning about the forest that is more consistent with independent discovery than direct social transmission of ecological knowledge. When asked how they learn about the forest, Itza′ mostly claim to acquire knowledge elicited in our tasks by "walking alone" in the forest they call the "Maya House." For Itza′, diffusely interconnected social and expert networks suggest multiple social pathways for individuals to gain, and for the community to assimilate and store, information about the forest. Cultural stories, values, and the like may bias the interpretation of experience in different ways: for example, a bird or monkey eating fruit may be seen to be transparently harmful by Q′eqchi′ and Ladinos, but interpreted by Itza′ to be helpful.

Our analysis of cultural models and social transmission is frankly speculative, but it does have some testable consequences. The general idea is that a person's cultural upbringing primes that person to (1) pay attention to certain observable relationships at a given level of complexity, and (2) connect these observations through certain inferences (e.g., that animals and plants have reciprocal relations). In addition, each person may be culturally attuned to the relevant discoveries of other individuals whose knowledge forms part of the emergent cultural consensus. Such emergent belief structures resemble framework theories in their ability to integrate various background assumptions, and to take particular experiences and events and give them general relevance in terms of a much larger ensemble of complexly related cases (Wisniewski and Medin 1994).

Ladino folkecological beliefs may be at least partially parasitic on the Itza' network in the following sense: whereas Itza' observe the forest for what is important, Ladinos may observe, not only the forest, but also the Itza' for what is important. The circle graph of the Ladino network shows a clear gender division of the community: persons C1–R are women; persons A–Q are men. At the top center of the Ladino circle graph is person D1. This is the same person as W in the Itza' network (he is the mayor of the municipality and the only Itza' in the Ladino social network). The Ladino network points to person I as the best socially connected individual. He is also the most often cited Ladino forest expert and the founder of the community.[3]

More generally, the highest competence scores among the Ladinos in the combined Itza'-Ladino model of plant-animal relations belong to those Ladinos who most cite Itza' as their experts (Atran et al. 2002).[4] Furthermore, these Ladino experts are also the most socially well-connected members of the Ladino community, and the persons most cited as experts by the rest of the Ladino community. Putting these findings together not only suggests that Ladinos are learning from Itza', but also that the social and expert network structure strongly facilitates this learning between the Ladino and Itza' communities. This knowledge then appears to spread to Ladino women, who in their expert networks nearly always cite only Ladino men.

Over time, socially well-connected expert Ladinos converge toward the consensus of Itza' experts, at least with respect to plants helping animals. For example, we found that judgments of plant-animal associations for the mostly highly rated Ladino expert actually comprised a *proper subset* of the judgments made by the most highly rated Itza' expert (details in Atran et al. 2002). It is improbable that Ladinos, who approximate Itza' response patterns for hundreds of species relations, actually observe and copy what Itza' say and think about each of the species pairs in question. How, then, are Ladino experts learning specific contents?

8.3   The Learning Landscape

In line with evolutionary models of social learning, one may assume that, when in doubt or ignorance about a certain domain of activity vital to everyday life, people will look to those with knowledge in order to emulate them (Boyd and Richerson 1985; Henrich and Boyd 1998). One promising strategy would be to first look for knowledge from those to whom deference (respect) is shown by others (Henrich and Gil-White 2001). At least in many small-scale societies, knowledge bearers tend to be elders, political leaders, economically well off, and so on. In the Itza' case, forest experts are experts in a variety of relevant domains (e.g., soils, trees, hunting, collecting plants), elder males, and former political town leaders. Informally we have noted that Ladinos today continue to express doubt about their forest knowledge and express a desire to acquire knowledge from the Itza'. Apparently, the most respected and socially well-connected Ladinos attend to those Itza' to whom other Itza' defer; and these Ladinos, in turn, become subjects of emulation and sources of knowledge for other Ladinos.

But how do Ladinos go about obtaining the relevant knowledge without initially knowing how it is relevant? Observers do not have direct access to the deep knowledge they wish to emulate, only to surface "signs" or "markers" of that knowledge.

First of all, there may be some transmission of norms or rules—we have witnessed Itza' showing Ladinos how to control burns when clearing land for milpa and discussing where to plant different species of fruit trees. Other learning factors may be involved in transmitting knowledge, including normative prototypes and narratives, but in fairly indirect ways. Thus, Ladino prototypes and stories of Itza' experts as forest wizards may share little actual content with the normative pronouncements and narratives of the Itza' themselves. Moreover, Itza' disavow teaching the Ladinos anything about the forest. The line of reasoning that follows is frankly anecdotal, but one that should motivate further research.

For present purposes, of greatest relevance is evidence suggesting Ladinos may be acquiring knowledge through different isolated examples that trigger inferential structures to support generalizations. Our data suggest that two distinct forms of inference may affect mental models of the forest: (1) inferences from general knowledge of ecological relationships, such as whether relations are positive or negative and where in the forest they are likely to occur, and (2) category-based induction over ecological and taxonomic groups. Consider the first form of inference. A Ladino may observe or hear about a particular exemplar of ecological knowledge from a respected Itza' (perhaps embedded in a story), such as observing that Itza' elders look for fallen ramón fruits after spider monkeys have passed through the trees. Itza' do this because they know that spider monkeys like to play with and chew on ramón fruits, and then throw them onto the forest floor. From such a description of Itza' behavior, a Ladino observer may deduce that (1) ramón is desired and useful for people, and (2) spider monkeys can affect ramón seeds. They might also *incorrectly* infer that spider monkeys hurt the ramón tree (throwing the fruits to the ground), not knowing the fact (not reported in the story) that half-chewed fruits are even more likely than unchewed fruits to generate new ramón stands. In short, they tend to construe symmetrical relations asymmetrically.

Another form of inference is category relatedness. Although Ladino observers seem to lack the Itza' cultural bias of conceiving species relationships reciprocally, they are nevertheless able to spontaneously induce much more from a single instance of experience than simply (1) and (2).[5] For example, we should expect Ladinos to generalize their observations along much the same lines as Itza' do when Itza' and Ladino taxonomies coincide. In the above scenario, Ladinos should "automatically" infer that howler monkeys and kinkajous similarly affect ramón because Ladinos, like Itza', recognize both generic species as belonging to the same intermediate folktaxon as the spider monkey (see López et al. 1997). Further correspondences are predictable from the similarity between the two groups' appreciations of ecological associations. For both groups, the ramón and chicle trees have very similar ecological profiles. Thus, both groups should readily generalize relations from, say, spider monkeys and ramón trees to kinkajous and chicle trees. Analysis of response patterns indicates that this is consistently the case.

We also have tentative evidence for a form of inference based on plausible reasoning. For example, in the absence of direct observation of nocturnal, furtive felines, it is plausible to believe that they would hide out under the protective cover of leafy fruit trees to prey on other animals that feed on the fruit. Female Ladinos who seldom venture into the forest overwhelmingly (75 percent) infer that felines seek out fruit trees. Male Ladinos (17 percent) and Itza' (16 percent) know better, because they go into the forest. Because Itza' hunt at night, they are generally aware (63 percent) that felines stalk their prey in areas of grassland and underbrush, rather than deep forest, whereas few Ladinos (12 percent) show such awareness.[6]

A key constraint on inductive inference is the interpretation of the base event itself. In the above scenario, if the Ladino observer lacks a cultural propensity for conceiving of species relationships reciprocally, he will neither learn that spider monkeys help ramón trees nor infer that kinkajous help chicle trees. In one line of follow-up work we have been examining ecological models among younger (30- to 50-year-old), Spanish-speaking Itza'. Relative to older Itza' speakers, we find considerable overlap, but also what appear to be systematic under- and overgeneralizations for the case of animals affecting plants. In contrast to the Ladinos, the younger Itza' generalize along lines of reciprocal relations and report as many positive animal-plant relationships as the older Itza'. This suggests that the younger Itza' retain the cultural bias for construing species relationships reciprocally.

In some cases younger Itza' overgeneralizations reflect construing an asymmetrical relationship reciprocally, as is apparently the case for younger Itza' seeing the bat and several birds as helping palms by seed dispersal. Interestingly, the younger Itza' agree with each other on their overgeneralizations, suggesting that they are principled and linked to observations, even though according to their elders they are incorrect.[7]

In brief, individual Ladinos and younger Itza' seem to project fragmentary observations of older Itza' behavior onto a richly textured cognitive model of folkecology by *inference* in addition to any effects of direct instruction, imitation, or invocation of norms. (Even the notion of "reciprocity" that we invoke to interpret Itza' responses is only a gloss for a distributed network of ideas—that is, a reliable pattern of interinformant agreement showing recognition of plants positively affecting animals and of animals positively affecting plants.)

These data on learning and inference are far from definitive and, in some cases, they rely on accepting the null hypothesis—that is, on failure to find relations between social network distance and residual agreement. To support our speculative account and to develop and evaluate alternative hypotheses, we need the sort of data on social and experts networks and ecological models across multiple generations that we are currently collecting. At a minimum, however, we think we have shown that the acquisition of ecological models involves inferences and that cultural notions, such as reciprocity, can guide the interpretation of observations.

Other learning factors may be involved in transmitting knowledge, including normative prototypes and narratives, but not in exclusive or straightforward ways. Thus, Ladino prototypes and stories of Itza' experts as forest wizards may share little actual content with the normative pronouncements and narratives of the Itza′ themselves. How, then, might Ladinos eventually attain Itza′-like "spiritual" awareness?

Seeking to interview the two most cited Itza′ experts, we found that both had gone on that particular day to the Ladino town of La Nueva. When they returned we asked them in separate interviews if they ever teach anything about the forest to the Ladinos; both denied doing so. Then we asked why they had gone to La Nueva and what they did there. One said that he had gone because there were no lemons to be found in San José but he knew of some in La Nueva. He said that he had stayed so long in La Nueva after finding the lemons because he was trying to figure out with people there how it would be best to plant lemon trees. The other Itza′ said that he had gone from our field station to visit his daughter, who is married to the son of the most cited Ladino expert. There he stayed telling stories of the barn owl (aj xooch′ = Tyto alba), whose call augurs the death of strangers. People familiar with it cannot die from it. The Ladinos listened to every detail with obvious fascination.

A final anecdote concerns the sounds of the forest. This sensibility is not merely one of perception but of affective value. For example, Itza′ give the short-billed pigeon (Columba nigrirostris) the onomatopoeic name ix-ku′uk~tz′u′uy-een. Itza′ decompose this low, mournful sound into meaningful constituents, interpreted as follows: Pigeon was frightened of Jaguar's coming. Squirrel saw this and told Pigeon to leave her young with Squirrel for protection. Pigeon came back to find that Squirrel had eaten her young and that is why, as long as there is forest, one will hear Pigeon lament that "Squirrel (ku′uk) tricked (tz′u′uy = entangle) me (een)." But when we ask identifications from Ladinos, we are sometimes told that this bird's name, "Uaxactun-Uaxactun," signifies a lament for the ancient Maya spirits of Uaxactun and that is why "Itza′" named it like that. Unlike Tikal, these Classical Maya ruins were given the name Uaxactun (waxak~tun = "eight stone") in the early twentieth century by an American archaeologist, Sylvanus Morley. Thus, it is hardly likely that an Itza′ elder would ever describe the pigeon's sound as these Ladinos think the Itza′ do (although some non-Itza′-speaking descendants of Itza′ speakers describe it as do the Ladinos). Yet, this [mis]interpretation seems to reflect a sense of what a native Maya should attend to in the forest (see Atran 2001b on the role of stories).

In sum, we speculate that high degrees of overlap in knowledge across populations stem, not from "high-fidelity replication," but from inferences based on individual exposure to role models and their stories.

Summary We believe that social learning involves inferential processes that are mobilized according to several factors: (1) domain-specific cognitive devices (e.g., taxonomy for biological kinds), (2) prior cultural sensitivity to certain kinds of knowledge (e.g., species reciprocity in ecological relationships), (3) awareness of lack of knowledge and the motivation to acquire it, (4) selective attention (e.g., Itza' deference and attention to the forest itself, while Ladinos also focus on the behavior of Itza' elders), and (5) preexisting values (weighted preferences) with respect to a given cognitive domain (e.g., overvaluing economic utility relative to other determiners of interest, such as sacredness or role in the economy of nature).

Overall, then, Ladino knowledge is a subclass of Itza' knowledge that underrepresents the ecological complexity and spiritual integrity of Itza' knowledge. To be sure, the Ladinos use their own taxonomic and ecological knowledge of the forest to generalize their inferences from Itza' behavior. From studies of other Ladino communities in Petén, it seems that some "Peténero" Ladino communities have learned to think and act much as Itza' do after three or four generations of the kind of contact described between our Itza' and Ladino samples (Schwartz 1990). This may well involve assimilating "spiritual values," and associated forest narratives, of an Itza' kind.

8.4   Methodologies for Modeling Culture

We have presented a view of cultures as comprised of causally distributed networks of mental representations, their public expressions (e.g., artifacts, languages, dances, and so on), and resultant behaviors in given ecological contexts. Ideas and behaviors become "cultural" to the extent that they endure among a given population. Just as it was (and still is) difficult for biology to discard the essentialized notion of species in favor of species as a historical, logical individual (Ghiselin 1981), it is difficult to abandon the commonsense notion of culture as an essentialized body (of rules, norms, and practices). In biology, it makes no sense to talk about species as anything other than more or less regular patterns of variation among historically related individuals. Neither can one delimit species independently of other species. It also makes little sense to study cultures apart from patterns of variation.

Although we employed commonsense notions of culture in setting up comparisons of "Itza'," versus "Ladinos," versus "Q'eqchi'," our analyses indicate the extent to which these commonsense constructs represent statistically reliable distributions of cognitions and behaviors. Social network analyses further reveal that members of each of these communities almost never include people identified with other communities among their intimate social relations. These commonsense cultural constructs allowed us initially, if roughly, to distinguish populations that subsequently revealed themselves to consist of reliably distinct cognitive, behavioral, and social-relational patterns. In addition, we showed where patterns cross over populations.

Our use of the commonsense notion of culture to initially distinguish populations is not a case of circular reasoning, because patterns of similarities and differences within and between populations could not be predicted in advance. As with Darwin's use of the commonsense notion of species, which first focused his attention, subsequent discoveries revealed only rough correspondence between the commonsense construct (species) and historically contingent patterns of evolution (more or less geographically isolated and interbreeding populations). Darwin continued to use the commonsense idea of "species" (Wallace [1889] 1901, 1) only as a heuristic notion that could ground attention as diverse and often inconclusive scientific analyses advanced, while denying it any special ontological status or reality (Atran 1999b). Likewise, intuitions about what constitutes a "culture" may continue to help orient research, but should not be mistaken for a final or correct framework of explanation.

Thus, although our findings reinforce separating the Q'eqchi' from the other groups, our findings also strongly suggest that Itza' and Ladino populations are beginning to merge on a number of dimensions (male expertise, residential proximity, converging use of Spanish as the principal language, and so on). In fact, researchers in the area from several disciplines now refer to a more generalized "Peténero culture" that joins Itza' and Ladinos but still generally excludes the Q'eqchi' (Schwartz 1990). This merging of "cultures" probably owes in large measure to Ladinos assimilating certain Itza' values, or at least learning and adapting some of the important ways that Itza' imbue forest life with meaning, whereas perhaps Itza' are shedding some of the older—and in a commercial age, outworn—values that rendered the forest their sacred "Maya House."

The distributional view of culture implies a methodology that departs in distinct ways from traditional anthropology, where the intrepid explorer becomes immersed in culture X and returns to report how Xers think and behave: "We are not interested in what A or B may feel *qua* individuals ... we are interested only in what they feel and think *qua* members of a given community [where] their mental states receive a certain stamp, become stereotyped by the institutions in which they live" (Malinowski [1922] 1961, 23; cf. Murdock 1949). Rarely in ethnography does the explorer ever specify precisely which Xers think and behave this way (nor do they hint that all Xers might not think and behave this way). Social and political scientists treat culture as normative sets of rules and practices—an "inherited moral code" (Fukuyama 1995). Cultural and social psychologists who study culture explicitly acknowledge within-group differences, but seem content with showing statistically reliable differences.

Like modern biology, the distributional view of cultural phenomena does not take individual variation as deviation but as a core object of study. From this perspective, issues of cultural acquisition, cultural transmission, cultural formation, and cultural transformation are intricately interwoven and, together, constitute the object of study. We have also seen how the cultural consensus model (Romney, Batchelder, and Weller 1986) can be a valuable tool for analyzing patterns of relative agreement and disagreement within and across populations. In addition, social network analysis provided the means to examine likely pathways for learning and communicating information. Together, consensus modeling and network analysis enabled us to systematically explore the aforementioned issues in an integrated fashion.

To illustrate, consider again our Itza' and Ladino study populations. First, somewhat to our surprise, we could not reject the possibility that the consensual ecological model of the Itza'-speaking elders was based on a series of independent discoveries. We found no reliable residual agreement that could be traced through either social or expert networks. We know that this finding does not owe to the insensitivity of our measures because these same networks revealed evidence that Ladinos were learning from Itza'. Our analyses suggest that the relevant conceptual biases for acquiring reciprocal understanding of species relationships are diffused throughout Itza' networks (extending, as we also saw, to younger Itza'). In this sense, "reciprocity" pervades Itza' "culture."

The Ladino settlement of La Nueva did not begin as a "culture" in any sense: it was founded by nuclear families stemming from scattered towns and villages with no apparent historical connections among them. Today, at least with respect to models of nature, Ladinos are forming patterns of cultural consensus, by assimilating ecologically relevant information over expert and social networks, over- and undergeneralizing that information in conformity with their taxonomies, and interpreting information in accordance with their own conceptual biases (e.g., nonreciprocity). And so the Ladinos form their unique cultural understanding, transforming (with varying fidelity) Itza' cultural models into their own.

8.5   A New Approach to the Study of Culture and Cognition

We have argued that the study of culture is the study of variation within and across populations. From the theoretical perspective of decision theory, our work extends the tragedy of the commons to situations involving multiple groups transmitting knowledge and belief systems in distinct patterns that can be traced to historically conditioned conceptions of nature and social and expert network distance. This same perspective is also relevant to application: cultural cognitions affect environmental values, decision making, and prospects for human survival under conditions of global change (Atran, Lois, and Ucan Ek' 2004).

Our previous work on category-based induction enabled us to identify inferential patterns in acquisition and transfer of folkbiological knowledge. We saw that these patterns reflect both universal constraints on biological inductions and culturally specific biases in construal and organization of information. The view of culture as a patterned distribution of cognitions and behavior set the stage for addressing issues of learning, inference, and transmission of information, within and between cultural groups.

To explain cultural consensus and stabilization of folkecology we focused on the likely causal roles of (historically conditioned) mind-internal mental models for representing and processing cultural cognitions, and on mind-external ecological factors (including social arrangements) for transmitting cultural cognitions. We found that statistically consensual cultural cognitions and practices—or "cultures" for short—involve complex causal chains that go both inside and outside the mind. These chains irreducibly link individual minds and their internal representations with psychophysical interactions between individuals and their external environment (including interactions with other individuals).

By targeting the microprocesses (including evolved cognitive aptitudes like the folkbiology module) by which these cultural chains form, we have sought to account for regularities and recurrences in sociocultural macrophenomena. This contrasts with standard "explanations" in social psychology that seek to account for individual cognitions in terms of the "influences" of sociocultural macrophenomena—where the causal character of "influence" is left opaque. Our approach also runs counter to customary accounts in anthropology, sociology, economics, and political science that seek to explain sociocultural macrophenomena in terms of the "influences" of other sociocultural macrophenomena (see also Bloch and Sperber 2002 for a prior formulation of this point).

In sum, we have tried to illustrate a unified approach to culture and cognition that takes us from individuals' evolved cognitive aptitudes to historically contingent collective practices (such as managing a rainforest) in a systematic and reliable way. We have described the general character of the likely causal factors and linkages involved, although we have only set the stage for inquiry into the actual causal processes and occurrences at work. Nevertheless, we have found that the study of culture formations and cross-cultural relations requires careful attention to population dynamics as well as psychological processes.

We do not pretend to have presented a final, definitive picture of the commons in Petén. Indeed, we are currently collecting data on social and expert networks as well as ecological models that span three generations of Itza' and Ladino agroforesters. This will give us a much richer picture of cultural formation and transformation. There is one observation, however, that seems very sound: to understand cultural cognition and behavior, anthropology and psychology must become close companions.

In chapter 9 we head several thousand miles north to our field site in Wisconsin. To anticipate, there are striking similarities across settings in the role of mental models in organizing values and practices.

9 Mental Models and Intergroup Conflict in North America

One could think of our work in Petén as involving an elaborate case study. Although our research in Mesoamerica displays a great deal of internal coherence, we are also keen to demonstrate the generalizability and utility of our approach to environmental decision making. Our search for U.S. biological experts led us to Wisconsin, where our attention was quickly captured by a group that has practiced sustainable forestry for more than 150 years, the Menominee. Surprisingly, instead of being seen as natural resource paragons, Menominee and other Native American groups in Wisconsin are perceived by many majority-culture hunters and fishermen as depleting fish and game resources. In addition, there is a great deal of controversy over Native American hunting and fishing rights and practices. We decided to explore the possibility that differences in mental models of nature were a key factor in this intergroup conflict. Before describing our studies in detail we need to provide much more by way of background and setting. We begin with the Menominee.

9.1 A Brief History of the Menominee

The history of the Menominee people is relevant to understanding mental models and values, so we go into it in some detail. The Menominee have been in Wisconsin for a long, long time, maybe forever (Beck 2002, 1). Evidence from the tribe's oral tradition as well as archaeological records provides clear evidence that Menominee residence in the area dates back at least several thousand years. The word *Menominee* derives from the Algonquin word *manomin*, "wild rice," or *manomini*, "Wild Rice People" (Spindler and Spindler 1991, 220). The name relates to the Menominee's traditional dependence on wild rice (*Zizania aquatica*) as a major staple in their diet.

According to sacred legend, Menominee history began when the Great Bear emerged from the mouth of the Menominee River, soon to ᴜe followed by other spirit beings, including the eagle. These and other spirits (beaver, sturgeon, elk, crane, and wolf) became the Menominee. The Menominee have a clan system and these animals correspond to clans, the major ones initially being Bear and Eagle (or Thunder). The clan system continues to this day, and it marks the Menominee sense that people are not separate from the rest of nature ("Animals are our cousins; we're all related").

The Menominee are a woodland tribe. Prior to contact (that is, contact with white people), Menominee seemed to have followed a semisedentary seasonal village pattern that was organized around hunting, fishing, gathering, and horticulture. They occupied a considerable area of what is now Wisconsin (9 million acres by one estimate), concentrated in part in villages along the Menominee River. The glacial drift left this area with networks of streams, small lakes, and swampy areas linked to rivers flowing either east to the western shore of Green Bay or westward to the Mississippi (Keesing [1939] 1987). In the early days the area was covered with mixed hardwood and coniferous forest, and birch, basswood, oak, cedar, butternut, and hickory were particularly important.

Though hunting played an important role, at no time of the year did the tribe move far from rivers or lakes. The spearing of sturgeon, the largest freshwater fish in the area, carried special meaning. These fish were important both for the social and ceremonial life as well as for the Menominee's physical survival (Beck 2002, 11–12). In the spring, sturgeon migrate from Lake Winnebago (mainly) upstream on the Wolf River to look for spawning sites. It was here that Menominee fishermen waited for their arrival to spear the "first food of the year." Given the harsh winters in this part of the United States, the arrival of the sturgeon in the spring must have been an anxiously awaited and welcome event. According to mythology, sturgeon provided the first food to the bear, the first ancestor of the Menominee. Subsequently, sturgeon became the first offering to the powers that provided this food (Hoffman [1896] 1970, 39–44). The tribe continues to hold a sturgeon powwow and feast every spring.

At the time of contact, in the early 1600s (1637 is one "official" date), the Menominee tribe consisted of several villages inhabiting an area that roughly extended from Escanaba, Michigan, in the north to Oconto, Wisconsin. The survival of the Menominee as a people is something of a miracle, given the various assaults on it. In what follows we give a partial list.

1. *The fur trade era* Soon after their initial arrival, French traders established the fur trade. The French fur trade era was perhaps the most benign threat to the Menominee, at least at first. The area of the upper Great Lakes was extremely suitable for such an endeavor, given the existence of large tracts of forests intersected by rivers that would allow easy transportation and inhabited by an indigenous population that was very skilled in both hunting and trading (Beck 2002, 27). The trade in furs introduced sweeping changes to the local economy.

The French had no designs on Menominee lands, preferring to profit from trade. The French had congenial relations with Indians and intermarriage between French traders and Menominee women was not unusual. But the fur trade also changed the social structure of the Menominee. As the closest sources of beaver pelts began to run out, Menominee men had to travel longer distances in search of furs. As a consequence, the village structure gave way to smaller hunting groups or bands for significant portions of the year. It is difficult to estimate the impact of this shift on Menominee culture, but it no doubt disrupted the clan system to some extent. This may be one factor causing uncertainty about the precise structure of the Menominee clan system in the pre-contact period (e.g., Hoffman [1896] 1970). The French and Indian war marked the end of French influence in this area.

2. *Disease* Contact with whites meant contact with diseases for which native peoples had no natural immunities. The effects were devastating throughout the New World and the Menominee were not spared. A 1736 survey put the warrior strength of the Menominee at 160 (Keesing [1939] 1987). It is hard to get precise estimates, but it is probably safe to assume that at least half the Menominee population fell victim to disease.

3. *Religion* The Menominee were fairly receptive to early Catholic (French) missionaries, in part because Menominees did not conceive of religious beliefs as mutually exclusive. Later in the nineteenth century, under American influence, there were pressures to give up traditional beliefs. At the point that the Menominee people settled into permanent villages on the Menominee reservation, around midcentury, the Menominee who were Christians tended to settle in and near what is today Keshena and South Branch; the so-called pagans (following more traditional Indian religion) settled further away, north and west of Keshena. The present village of Zoar, established in 1881, continues to be a center for traditional spiritual practices.

Although most Menominees today are Catholics, many Menominees integrate this faith with beliefs and practices associated with their traditional religion. In addition, one can see that the church has, in some cases, incorporated Menominee symbolism. For example, the church in Keshena depicts corn on its exterior.

4. *Land and treaties* The French and the British came to Menominee country for trade. After the War of 1812, British influence all but disappeared, to be replaced by Americans who wanted more—the land itself. Settlers poured into the Midwest in general and Wisconsin in particular. The treaty era had begun.

The idea that land is something that one could own was alien to Indian sensibilities. Land was not an object or commodity, but a relational entity, like a grandmother. That is, you wouldn't, couldn't, and shouldn't sell land any more than you would sell your grandmother. Consequently, Indian conceptions, at least for initial treaties, were that they were receiving gifts for usufruct or use privileges, not giving up land ownership (again, because land is not the sort of thing that one owns).

As is commonly known, treaties meant displacement to less hospitable areas, often several thousand miles away from home. When the implications of treaties became clear to Indian tribes, they began to resist them, but it soon became clear that the U.S. government was going to take the land, treaty or no treaty. Although the treaties usually included payment for the land, the amounts were at best symbolic and usually only applied in order to provide a facade of legality. (In a treaty of 1831 Menominee received $285,000 for 3 million acres—about 8 cents per acre.)

Americans made their first appearance at Green Bay in 1815, and as they had done previously when the British replaced the French in 1761, the Menominee did their best to adapt to the new situation. In March 1817 at St. Louis, they signed their first treaty with the United States. A second treaty took place in 1831, and a third in 1836. In the latter Menominee surrendered another 4.2 million acres.

As Wisconsin statehood approached in 1848, Chief Oshkosh and the Menominee were pressured into ceding their remaining Wisconsin land in exchange for a 600,000-acre reservation on the Crow Wing River in Minnesota. Chief Oshkosh sent scouts to the Crow Wing area and they reported back that the land was desolate and inhospitable. This served to strengthen the Menominee resolve to resist displacement from their (remaining) land. Although the Menominee signed the treaty in 1848, they nevertheless refused to move to Minnesota. Instead they pled for a reservation in Wisconsin—their homeland. This was finally granted after many negotiations and interventions from outsiders, missionaries (includ-

ing Father Bonduel, for whom the town of Bonduel is named), and settlers (Beck 2002, 179).

The final settlement, the Wolf River treaty, was signed in May 1854
and established a reservation for the Menominee in northern Wisconsin. The terms of the treaty of 1854 assigned twelve townships to the
Menominee reservation. The agreement was changed in 1856, when the
Menominee (again, under pressure) ceded two townships for the purpose
of creating a separate reservation for the Stockbridge Indians (who had
been displaced from the East Coast). The newly established Menominee
reservation contained 235,000 acres of their original homeland, a tiny
fraction of the lands they had originally occupied. Figure 9.1 shows the
size and location of contemporary Menominee lands.

5. *Timber interests*   Before, during, and after the treaty era, businessmen
and settlers, aided by government officials, were eager to exploit Wisconsin's timber resources, including those on tribal lands. Today's
Menominee forest is not the result of a selection process that left the

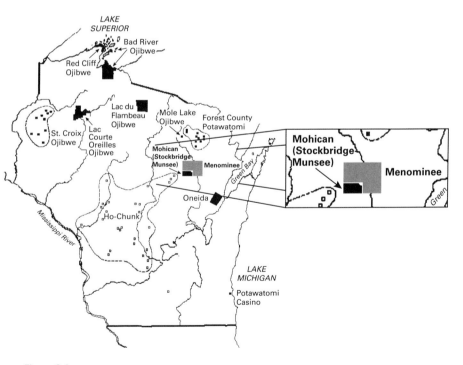

Figure 9.1
Map of Wisconsin showing current Menominee reservation lands.

Menominee with an advantageous area for forest. Quite the opposite. The logging frenzy by white settlers and the timber industry converted all but the Menominee reservation into pastureland with few and relatively small forest stands.

6. *The Dawes Act (the General Allotment Act of 1887)*   The idea of the Dawes Act was to "civilize" or assimilate Indians by forcing them to adopt the white model of ownership and individual industry. The General Allotment Act authorized the U.S. president to end tribal ownership of land by allotting 160-acre plots to individual tribal members. Any lands left over would be given to white settlers. In some states such as Oklahoma the lands "left over" were extensive and white settlers benefited from what can only be called a theft of land. Where allotment took place, most of the land assigned to individual Indians quickly ended up in the hands of whites.

Although the Menominee tribal council approved the Dawes Act, they and other Menominee leaders successfully stalled its implementation until the evil consequences of allotment were so transparent that talk of allotment of the Menominee reservation died out.

7. *Wardship and the BIA*   Although the tribe had some autonomy, many of its activities were under federal supervision. We will spare you the details of mismanagement and bad ideas (e.g., trying to convert the Menominees to farming on the reservation's sandy soils) and provide only the very briefest of summaries. Newman (1967) estimates that about one million board-feet of timber were stolen from Menominee lands between 1871 and 1890.

The Menominee efforts to develop (sustainable) logging as a source of employment and income were hardly aided by U.S. authorities. In 1871 the Secretary of the Interior agreed that Menominees could cut and sell logs to mills off the reservation, and in 1872 a tribal logging camp was organized (Grignon et al. 1998). But in 1878, in response to pressure from the Pine Ring, the Indian Department issued orders stop Menominee logging. In 1882 a congressional act gave permission to the tribe to cut dead and down timber, but six years later the U.S. Attorney General ruled that Menominees had the right of occupancy only and that the timber on the reservation was the property of the United States. This ruling was again reversed in 1890, when cutting of timber was allowed under the supervision of white supervisors. One index of just how inept this regulation and oversight were is that the Menominee tribe was awarded close to $8 million in 1951 for damages caused by the Department of Interior's logging superintendents between 1912 and 1926.

As we write this, the Bureau of Indian Affairs is being sued for literally billions of dollars for misuse and misappropriation of tribal trust funds. A major problem hampering the investigation is the BIA's inability to find relevant records in its offices.

8. *Boarding schools*   In the 1920s and 1930s there was an attempt to assimilate Indians to white culture by "taking the Indian out of them." Many Indian children were forced to attend boarding schools at considerable distances from their homes. Children from different tribes and language groups were thrown together, and students were punished for speaking their native language. Among other things, one product of this experience for many Native Americans was distrust of and disidentification with the educational system. Many parents avoided speaking the Menominee language in front of their children, so that their children would not be punished when they went to school. Menominee became a dying language. Over the past few decades, however, the tribe has made extensive efforts to keep the language alive.

9. *Termination*   The most recent threat to the Menominee as a people was the Termination Act of 1954. This ended federal recognition of Indian rights and privileges guaranteed by treaties. No new names were to be added to the Menominee tribal roll after 1954. The effort was, in effect, to legislate the Menominees out of existence. Concretely, when the plan went into effect in 1961, it meant that the Menominee were subject to a crushing financial burden. The tribal clinic and hospital soon closed. The tribal court system was ended, and the sawmill—the primary business on the reservation—had to focus on efficiency rather than maximizing Menominee employment. Menominee County became a pocket of poverty almost overnight and the tribe struggled to provide services.

Termination also led to a compromise on sovereignty. In 1959 a development group, Menominee Enterprises, was created by a general council meeting. About ten years later, in an attempt to raise funds and establish a tax base, Menominee Enterprises agreed to a project that involved creating a human-made lake, Legend Lake, and selling lakeshore lots to nontribal members.

But the Menominee people again proved resilient. The Legend Lake development triggered a storm of protest over the loss of land and the energy released by it fueled a broad, sustained effort to restore tribal recognition. One key development was a 1968 U.S. Court of Claims ruling that the Menominees did not relinquish their hunting and fishing rights when the tribe was terminated. This ruling set the stage for a Supreme Court ruling that Termination did not abrogate treaty rights. Land sales ended in 1972, though nontribal members continue to own land and live around Legend Lake.

The story of the restoration movement would make a book in itself (see Peroff 1982; Davis 2000; Beck 2002). After more than a decade of struggle, the tribe succeeded. The Menominee Restoration Act was signed by President Richard M. Nixon in 1973. Under the terms of the Restoration Act, the Menominee lands would be protected under the treaty trust relationship with the U.S. government. Furthermore, the Menominee achieved their greatest degree of autonomy since before the treaty era.

10. *Casinos and continuing threats to sovereignty* The relatively recent development of gaming compacts and tribally operated casinos has constituted an economic boon for many tribes, including the Menominee. It has allowed the tribe, among other things, to create and support the College of the Menominee Nation.

But there is also a strong downside to casinos. One is the misperception that Indians have all been made wealthy from casino profits. In the case of the Menominees, the highest per capita payment over the past five years has been $100 and for the past two years, when the tribe has had some budgetary problems, the per capita has been zero (per capita is the amount that each enrolled member receives). Compare this with the per capita of well over $1,000 that every Alaskan citizen receives each year (the figure was $1,540 in 2002) from the State of Alaska from oil and oil pipeline revenues.

A more significant downside is the pressure from members of the state legislature and the preceding governor (Tommy Thompson) to the effect that Wisconsin's tribe's should give up certain treaty rights in exchange for the renewal of gaming compacts. In the case of the Ojibwe or Chippewa, the aim has been to force them to relinquish their hunting and fishing rights in the ceded territories. (The Ojibwe did not give up their hunting and fishing rights when they ceded the land that makes up much of northern Wisconsin; consequently, they are entitled to hunt and fish on off-reservation lands.) Of most relevance to the Menominee tribe is the attempt to remove any legal standing Menominees may have for fighting off-reservation threats to the Wolf River, such as the proposed Crandon mine some 30–40 miles north of the reservation. Even without the mine, it is a reality that the absence of industrial production on the reservation provides no protection from acid rain and mercury contamination brought in from the outside.

Summary Anyone who knows Menominee history cannot fail to come away impressed with Menominee resiliency. Today about 4,000 Menominee live on the reservation and a slightly larger number live off the reservation (mainly in Milwaukee and Chicago but also in Green Bay and the town of Shawano, just south of the reservation). The large off-reservation population is, in part, a cumulative effect of efforts to assimilate Indians into the majority culture.

9.2 The Menominee Forest

Start with the rising sun and work toward the setting sun, but take only the mature trees, the sick trees, and the trees that have fallen. When you reach the end of the reservation, turn and cut from the setting sun to the rising sun, and the trees will last forever.
—Menominee leader, usually identified as Chief Osh Kosh

Looking at satellite images, one can readily locate the Menominee reservation because of the salience of the forest. This is true even on the northern border, where the reservation borders the Nicolet National Forest. The Menominee forest is richer in larger trees, has a richer mix of species, and is denser than the Nicolet forest. It also has a higher per acre production of timber and maintains a higher number of board-feet of commercial species (Davis 2000, 15).

The forest not only provides timber for the Menominee, but it is also a place for hunting deer, bear, and other game, as well as for gathering nontimber products such as berries, ginseng, and other medicinal plants. As in the past, hunting also provides the Menominee with an important food source. Menominee are avid hunters and both bow hunting and rifle hunting are practiced on the reservation. Bear are used for their meat, their fur, and also for medicinal purposes. The bear population appears to be healthy on the reservation. Given the isolation of the Menominee forest islands, no moose are found and the wolf population is small.

Hunting is regulated by the tribe. Individuals who want to hunt have to apply for a deer tag for each deer they want to kill. Limits are based on population numbers (actual and ideal), just as is the case off the reservation.

The reservation's other major natural resource is water. Over 300 miles of trout streams, over forty lakes, and several rivers provide plenty of opportunities for fishing, a major activity for Menominees. Menominee fish during all seasons and in all different kinds of waters and styles.

Trout are very important target fish, as are the different species of pan-fish. Just as for hunting, the tribe sets its own fishing regulations.

The average annual income on the reservation is about two-thirds of the income off the reservation (median family income in 2000 on the reservation was about $26,000, compared to $38,000 in Shawano County). Even these figures are somewhat misleading, because the average household size on the Menominee reservation is considerably larger than in Shawano County (3.74 versus 2.51). About 36 percent of the people on the reservation live below the poverty line compared with about 8 percent in Shawano County. The age distributions are also substantially different on and off the reservation. Slightly more than half of the Menominee are under 18 compared with a corresponding figure of about 25 percent for Shawano County.

Shortly after restoration, the Menominee developed their own constitution and a tribal government was established in 1977 (Ricciuti 1997, 30). Today this government consists of eight tribal legislators and a chairperson. Members are elected in three-year intervals. The tribe has its own court system and police department. Besides Menominee Tribal Enterprises, which manages the forestry business, the tribe receives revenues from its casino operation. Still, the revenues from gambling are barely enough to keep up with the costs of running an autonomous government.

In many respects Menominee today appear to adopt a rural majority-culture lifestyle. Quite a few Menominee seek employment outside the reservation, and some even send their children off the reservation to Wisconsin public schools in neighboring Shawano County. Similarities to majority-culture individuals can also be found with respect to outdoor activities such as fishing, hunting, snowmobiling, and so on. These activities are very popular in the general area and also attract many tourists each year. Still, these superficial similarities conceal large underlying differences reflecting history, values, and distinct perspectives on nature.

The visible results—the maintenance of the forest in light of large-scale deforestation in the surroundings as well as constant economic incentives to the contrary—are quite impressive and provide a literal ground-truthing of Menominee respect for nature. Perhaps the critical element is not values per se but rather what happens when one set of values come into conflict with another (Kempton, Boster, and Hartley 1995). The Menominee have demonstrated time after time that they are unwilling to trade their forest, lakes, and rivers for money or higher employment. Many Menominee believe that the Menominee would not be the

Menominee without the forest, in the same way that a farmer cannot be a farmer without land.

9.3 Majority Culture—Shawano County

There is less to be said about majority-culture history in Wisconsin in general and Shawano County in particular, in part because their history is shorter. For the first few hundred years postcontact, there was only a modest white presence in the form of explorers, traders, and soldiers. Then in the nineteenth century there was an explosion of white settlers and an associated removal of Indians from their lands via treaties.

According to Shawano County historical records, the first white person to explore this area was Samuel Farnsworth, who canoed up the Wolf River in 1843 to identify an area to set up logging operations. He and Charles Wescott set up a sawmill where the channel from Shawano Lake joins the Wolf River. Shawano County was established in 1853, at which time there were 254 registered inhabitants. In 1860 the first school was established in the county, and in 1898 there were 108 public schools in the county staffed with a total of 124 teachers. Shawano was incorporated as a village in 1871.

Business and industry in the early days were not dramatically different from those today. They consisted primary of logging, sawmills, cheese factories, and agriculture. The relative prominence of agriculture increased as the forests began to disappear. In the late nineteenth century a paper and fiber manufacturing company was established and the paper mill continues to this day to be a source of employment.

The 2000 census listed the population of Shawano County as 40,944. Agriculture and light industry (the county purchased an industrial park in 1958 and it has prospered) continue to be important. Perhaps the major economic change over the last half century is the emergence of outdoor recreation as a major industry. Hunting, fishing, snowmobiling, personal watercraft (jet skis), and boating not only keep the county's residents active, but also attract a large number of visitors. Shawano Lake is a particular attraction.

The recreational resources are one factor leading to a sense of stability. People may turn down job opportunities that would take them elsewhere. Stability also begets stability in that many people have their extended family living in Shawano County and are reluctant to leave. In this respect Shawano County resembles the Menominee reservation where family proximity and surrounding natural beauty make it difficult to leave.

People of Shawano and Menominee counties tend to think in terms of vocations, avocations, and jobs and not so much in terms of "careers." That is, "getting ahead" and "advancing oneself" are means to an end and not ends in themselves.

9.4 Intercommunity Relations

Intercommunity relations are multifaceted and almost all generalizations would be misleading. Here are just a few of these facets. First, there is some back-and-forth when it comes to employment. Menominee Tribal Enterprises awards logging contracts on a competitive basis that includes a point system rewarding contractors who either are themselves Menominee or hire Menominee loggers. Many majority-culture adults from the surrounding community attend the College of the Menominee Nation, which itself employs an ethnically diverse faculty. The Menominee casino has provided an economic stimulus not only to Menominee County but also Shawano County. In summary, there is a fair amount of interchange between the peoples of the two counties that is mutually beneficial.

Not everything is positive. As we noted earlier, there is resentment on the part of majority-culture sportsmen of tribes setting their own hunting and fishing regulations, especially when those regulations are more liberal than those of the state of Wisconsin. Typically these differences are seen as resource depleting. There is also a fair amount of real and perceived prejudice and stereotyping. Menominee complain about being followed about when they shop in certain stores, a form of "ethnic profiling." Some Menominee who fail to be recognized as Indians by majority-culture people tell stories about hearing more overt expressions of prejudice.

In short, there is a mixed picture of majority culture and Menominee relations. On the one hand, for issues like supporting U.S. troops in Iraq or fighting a proposed mining operation that threatens the Wolf River, the communities become one. On the other, there is always the potential for sharp divisiveness on issues where the interests of the communities are not perceived as shared. As we will see, even where the two groups have common superordinate goals, differing mental models and associated values and practices may lead to misperception and intergroup conflict.

9.5 Mental Models

The research in Wisconsin addresses the generalizability of our approach across different population settings, and the issue of the extent to which cultural differences depend on historically shallow (recent immigration) versus deep (transgenerational) exposure and experience in the area. As was noted earlier, both Wisconsin populations coexisted in this area for at least a century and a half. The Wisconsin studies concern fishing and hunting rather than agroforestry, but the theoretical question is the same: Are there distinct conceptualizations of nature that underlie the Menominee tradition of sustainable forestry (e.g., Hall and Pecore 1995), healthy rivers and lakes, and abundant fish and game? Our results to date are based mainly on fish and fishing and indicate that the answer is yes. Incomplete observations for hunting and forest ecology point to the same conclusion.

Native American fishing rights in the Midwest and elsewhere are a major source of conflict. Renewal of gaming compacts for tribal casinos is frequently the occasion for state governments to pressure tribes to give up their treaty-based hunting and fishing rights (Tracy, 1998). In the words of a Wisconsin state legislator, "The tribe should determine what is more important to them—fish or chips" ("Petition Seeks to Separate Spearfishing, Gaming," 1997). In the Midwest, particular attention and controversy has focused on Native American spearfishing rights (Nesper 2002). For example, in Wisconsin, sportsmen note that the allowable limit for walleyes—perhaps the most prized fish to eat—is substantially lower (typically three rather than the normal five) on lakes where Native Americans spear than where they do not ("Petition Seeks to Separate Spearfishing, Gaming," 1997; Wisconsin Department of Natural Resources 2003). These observations can lead to the conclusion that tribes are threatening fish populations (Graunke 2003). Native Americans, in contrast, may find it difficult to endorse fishing solely as entertainment. Exclusively practicing catch-and-release can be seen as disrespectful of fish in particular and nature in general.

Such observations suggest differences with respect to the value systems (fishing as a sport versus fishing for food) and the perceived impact each group's activity has on the environment. In this chapter we present data on cultural models of Menominee Indians and majority-culture (European-American) fishermen of central Wisconsin. In an initial step we studied cultural models of fish and fishing among expert Native American and majority-culture fishermen (Medin et al. 2002, 2005, 2007; Medin, Ross, and Cox 2006). Standard sorting techniques and other probes were used to explore each group's categorization of local fish species, and perceived ecological relationships (fish-fish interaction). A second set of studies targeted the values and goals of each population, as well as perceived group differences. To foreshadow the results, the data suggest that both groups of experts share a knowledge base concerning the environment of local freshwater fish, though that knowledge is organized differently across the groups. In addition, the two groups generally share values and goals with respect to fishing. The key, surprising finding is that *perceived* group differences swamp *actual* differences, especially in the case of majority-culture perceptions of Menominee. We begin with a summary of our findings on knowledge organization and then turn to values and practices.

9.6 Knowledge Organization

In a first step we studied cultural models of fish and fishing among expert Native American and majority-culture fishermen (Medin et al. 2002, 2005). We identified experts based on peer nominations and using a snowball method. We later confirmed expertise by probing for familiarity with forty-six species of local fish (see Medin et al. 2002). The two groups did not differ in age, amount of formal education, years of experience fishing, or expertise.

Category Organization

Standard sorting techniques and other probes were used to explore each group's categorization of local fish species. On a spontaneous sorting task involving forty-four local species of fish, fifteen Menominee and fifteen majority-culture experts showed overall consensus,[1] but also reliable group differences. An analysis of variance on residual agreement (Nakao and Romney 1984) revealed greater within- than between-group agreement and a significant population by within- versus between-group interaction. The form of this interaction is that only the Menominee informants displayed reliably greater within- than between-group residual agreement. In short, it appears that the Menominee and majority-culture informants share a common cultural model of fish but that the Menominee, in addition, share a somewhat distinct conceptual organization of fish.

Additional analyses indicate that the Menominee consensus contains an ecological component absent in the sorting of majority-culture experts. Multidimensional scaling (MDS) yielded a dimension for Menominee experts that correlates with fish habitat. In addition, Menominee experts were reliably more likely than majority-culture experts to mention habitat in their explanations for the sorts they created. This difference reflects preferences for organizing categories rather than knowledge differences per se. When we specifically asked Menominee and majority-culture fish experts to sort fish by habitat we observed a strong overall consensus and no group differences.

Ecological Relations

A subset of 21 fish species was selected to probe directly for ecological relations. We presented all possible pairs (210) to 15 majority-culture and 15 Menominee fish experts with a question, "Does fish A affect fish B and/or does B affect A?" If the answer was yes, the expert was asked elaborate on the relation. Again we find a cross-group consensus,[2] coupled with reliable between-group differences (Medin et al. 2005). For relations reported by 70 percent or more of informants from either group, we find 85 percent reported by both groups, 14 percent by Menominee but not majority-culture experts, and 1 percent by majority culture but not Menominee fishermen. Content analysis reveals Menominee experts answer in terms of the entire life cycle of fish (e.g., spawn, fry, fingerlings, adults); majority-culture experts generally answer in terms of adult fish. These results suggest that majority-culture experts organize their knowledge around goals that target adult fish.

We hypothesized that these were not differences in knowledge as such, but rather knowledge organization. In a follow-up study ($n = 14$ per group), we again asked about fish-fish interactions, but reduced the number of pairs from 210 to 34 and ran the task at a slower pace (30 seconds per pair rather than about 10 seconds per pair). For these 34 pairs the Menominee experts had reported 64 percent more relations (a mean of 28 versus 17). If majority-culture experts have the same knowledge base but not necessarily one organized around ecological relations, the group differences should disappear. They did. Using the relations reported for these 34 pairs on the longer task as a base, we found that majority-culture experts now report reliably more relations (means of 29.3 versus 17.3), including more relations involving spawn and more reciprocal relations. Menominee experts showed no reliable changes across tasks (their mean on the slower task was 32.4), and the 64 percent advantage noted for Menominee fishermen on the longer task was reduced to a nonsignificant 11 percent. This suggests that the cultural differences are in "habits of mind" or knowledge organization, rather than knowledge per se.

We have also begun to examine folkbiological models in less expert Menominee and majority-culture populations. Results from our initial sorting task reveal an interesting picture of explanations given for sorting. Like Menominee experts, Menominee nonexperts tended to give relatively more ecological justifications (40 percent), and fewer goal-related (29 percent) and taxonomic-morphological (31 percent) justifications. The majority-culture nonexperts, by contrast, gave fewer ecological justifications (16 percent) and more goal-related (43 percent) and taxonomic-morphological (41 percent) justifications. Whereas the pattern of Menominee justifications is robust across the two levels of expertise, the majority-culture pattern changes, such that, with expertise, majority-culture informants come to give more taxonomic-morphological and fewer ecological and goal-related justifications. Some majority-culture experts explicitly mentioned how their orientation toward fishing had changed over the years, moving away from the stereotypic sportsman's model that targets fishing contests or going for the "trophy fish."

Summary   Menominee fishermen tend to take an ecological orientation to conceptualizing fish. They also commonly express the attitude that every fish has a role to play and are less likely than majority-culture fishermen to think of fish in terms of positive (gamefish) or negative ("garbage fish") utility. Although both groups report wanting to save fish as a resource, the goal of conservation is supported by different strategies in the two groups. Menominees have a strong "do not waste" ethic and tribal regulations prohibit the wanton destruction of any fish, even the fish that Wisconsin DNR regulations (WDNR 2002) refer to as "rough fish." Majority-culture experts, in contrast, tend to focus on catch-and-release as a conservation strategy.

These group differences might be best described as different orientations, with majority-culture experts being more goal-oriented and Menominee more ecologically oriented. Although both groups presumably share the goal of preserving fish as a resource, we wondered how the differences in orientation might be reflected in values and attitudes toward different fishing practices.

9.7   Values and Practices

Ranking of Fish
In a first task we asked individuals to rank-order fifteen species according to the importance each fish has for the individual. Species involved in this task were sturgeon (*Acipenser fulvescens*), black sucker (*Catastomus commersonnii*), yellow bullhead (*Ameiurus natalis*), bluegill (*Lepomis macrochirus*), brook trout (*Salvelinus fontinalis*), brown trout (*Salmo trutta*),

gar (*Lepis osteus*), bluntnose minnow (*Pimephales notatus*), muskellunge (*Esox masquinongy*), largemouth bass (*Micropterus salmoides*), smallmouth bass (*Micropterus dolomieu*), northern pike (*Esox lucius*), river shiner (*Notropis blennius*), walleye (*Stizostedion vitreum*), and perch (*Perca flavescens*). Fish species were represented on name cards and individuals were asked to arrange these cards in order of descending importance.

In a second task we asked our experts to rank-order a set of six goals for fishing. The goals were extracted from previous interviews and the literature. They include: (1) fishing as a way of being close to nature, (2) fishing as a challenge to outsmart the fish, (3) fishing as a food source, (4) fishing to get a trophy-sized fish, (5) fishing for relaxation, and (6) fishing as an activity to pass on to future generations. If an expert indicated that he could not rank-order the goals, he was asked to rate them on a 7-point scale with 1 representing not a goal at all and 7 representing a very important goal. We later converted these ratings into rank orderings.

For the third and final task experts were asked to rate seventeen different fishing practices on a 7-point scale where 1 represents strong personal disapproval, 4 a neutral attitude, and 7 strong approval (see table 9.1). These practices emerged from previous interviews.

Table 9.1
Items for probing fishing attitudes toward various fishing practices

1. Doing catch-and-release only
2. Spearfishing suckers and/or carp
3. Spearfishing walleyes or northern pike
4. Having a trophy fish mounted by a taxidermist
5. Fishing for bluegill or sunfish for food
6. Fishing for northern pike or muskie for food
7. Fishing for largemouth or smallmouth bass for food
8. Using setpoles to catch trout
9. Selling a fish
10. Keeping undersized fish
11. Participating in fishing contests
12. Fishing on spawning beds
13. Pretending to fish for suckers hoping to get a sturgeon on the line
14. Culling out smaller fish to get the largest possible limit
15. Using fish finders
16. Someone taking more than their limit in order to feed their family
17. Someone giving away all of the fish they catch

Table 9.2
Average species rankings by Menominee and majority-culture fish experts
(Lower numbers indicate higher value)

Species	Menominee	Majority culture
Black sucker	12.0	12.1
Bluegill	5.4	4.8
Bluntnose minnow	13.0	12.0
Brook trout	2.2	6.8
Brown trout	2.6	7.9
Gar	14.5	13.7
Largemouth bass	4.4	6.4
Muskellunge	8.7	5.4
Northern pike	6.5	5.5
Perch	5.9	5.9
River shiner	11.9	11.0
Smallmouth bass	7.3	6.5
Sturgeon	9.1	8.6
Walleye	4.6	2.9
Yellow bullhead	11.1	10.0

Rank Ordering of Species

The consensus rankings of the fifteen species of fish are summarized in table 9.2. Lower numbers correspond to higher rankings. Somewhat to our surprise we found a strong cross-group consensus[3] between Menominee and majority-culture fishermen. Nonetheless the overall consensus was coupled with reliable group differences.[4] These differences indicate the existence of clear cultural submodels. Looking at the actual rank ordering, we find the biggest differences with respect to brook and brown trout (average ranking for Menominee: 2.1 and 2.6; average ranking for majority culture: 6.2 and 7.2; the differences for both fish are highly significant[5]) as well as with respect to the muskie and walleye (average ranking for majority culture: 5.3 and 3.0; average ranking for Menominee: 8.7 and 4.5; only the difference for muskie is significant[6]). Although both groups value all of these fish, Menominee assign a higher value to the two trout species, and majority-culture fishermen preferentially value muskie and walleye. These modest differences should not distract us from the wider consensus that exists between the two groups. For example, the six fish ranked lowest are not only the same for both groups but are even placed in exactly the same order. The overall cross-group correlation of rankings was +.81.

Table 9.3
Goal rankings

Goal rankings	Majority culture			Menominee		
	Self	Group	Ogroup	Self	Group	Ogroup
A. Being close to nature	2.4	3.2	4.6	3.0	3.0	3.2
B. For the challenge of outsmarting fish	3.4	3.7	3.3	4.4	4.6	3.7
C. As a source of food	4.6	3.9	3.7	2.7	1.7	2.5
D. To catch a "trophy fish"	4.6	3.9	1.9	5.0	5.4	4.5
E. As a way to relax	2.6	2.4	2.6	2.4	3.1	3.5
F. As an activity to pass on to future generations	2.9	2.9	4.2	3.2	3.3	3.5

Note: The column labeled "self" gives the average of the individual ratings in Experiment 1 broken down by group (first and fourth column). "Group" refers to predictions for one's own group and "Ogroup" to predictions by the other group in Experiment 2. Lower numbers correspond to greater importance.

Goal Rankings

The average rankings for the six goals are summarized in the first and fourth columns of table 9.3. Given that each goal has been endorsed by several experts in earlier interviews, we had no strong reason to expect consensus either within or across groups or even a clear ranking of goals. Indeed, we did not find consensus across groups or for either of the two groups individually. Despite the lack of consensus, we were nonetheless able to detect group differences on specific goals. Menominee experts give significantly higher importance to "fishing for food,"[7] while majority-culture experts tend to place higher value on "fishing as a challenge to outsmart the fish" (the latter difference was marginally significant[8]). These data are in line with the observation that majority-culture fishermen tend to see fishing as a contest or sport.

Ratings of Practices

We expected to observe a number of differences in ratings of practices related to both specific goals and historical practices. For example, for centuries the Menominee have speared fish in the spring when they are spawning as an efficient means of food gathering. Obviously, spearing is self-defeating with respect to catch-and-release. Consequently, it would have been surprising if there were no group differences in rating practices like spearfishing. The full set of ratings is summarized in columns 1 and 4

Table 9.4
Reported and anticipated rating of different practices

	Majority culture			Menominee		
	Self	Group	Ogroup	Self	Group	Ogroup
Catch-and-release only	4.5	3.1	4.3	4.7	3.3	3.1
Spearfish suckers/carp	5.9	5.9	3.4	5.1	5.0	6.2
Spear walleyes/northern	1.0	1.1	1.2	4.0	5.4	5.9
Trophy mounted	4.4	4.8	6.7	4.9	3.9	4.6
Bluegill/sunfish food	6.0	6.4	6.2	6.9	7.0	6.5
Northern/muskie food	2.9	3.2	5.6	6.1	6.8	5.7
LM/SM bass food	3.4	3.8	5.5	6.5	6.8	5.7
Setpoles for trout	2.5	2.6	1.1	3.3	3.3	6.1
Selling fish	2.0	1.7	1.7	1.3	1.5	4.4
Keep undersized fish	1.6	2.6	2.2	2.3	2.4	4.8
Fishing contests	4.9	4.9	6.7	4.3	5.0	4.4
Fishing spawning beds	3.0	4.2	4.0	2.8	4.3	5.9
Suckers for sturgeon	3.6	3.8	3.0	2.1	2.9	5.7
Cull for biggest limit	2.9	3.2	3.4	1.9	3.5	4.9
Using fish finders	5.9	5.9	6.5	3.6	4.8	6.1
Exceed limit for family	2.9	4.1	2.8	5.2	5.3	6.0
Giving all fish away	3.9	3.3	3.2	4.8	5.1	4.8

Note: "Self" is the average individual rating in Experiment 1. "Group" refers to predictions for one's own group and "Ogroup" refers to the other group's predictions for the group in question in Experiment 2. The practices are described in full in table 9.1 and abbreviated here. Lower numbers reflect disapproval and higher numbers indicate approval.

of table 9.4. We found modest overall consensus[9] and reliable group differences. The main group differences are as follows. Menominee experts gave higher ratings to catching bass, northerns, and muskie for food (strong approval versus neutral), higher ratings to someone taking more than the limit to feed their family (modest approval versus modest disapproval), and higher ratings to spearfishing walleyes (neutral versus strong disapproval). The Menominee fishermen were sharply divided on spearfishing walleyes and the average reflects an equal mixture of strongly positive and strongly negative ratings. Menominee opposed to it say that females are being speared and their spawn wasted. Menominee in favor of spearing say that they only spear the males. (Data to be reviewed later on Ojibwe spearfishing suggests that about ten males are speared for every female walleye speared.)

Majority-culture fishermen gave higher ratings to using fish finders (strong approval versus neutral) and to pretending to fish for suckers hoping to get a sturgeon (neutral versus strong disapproval). It is illegal to fish for sturgeon with hook and line; some fishermen engage in this practice in the spring when sturgeon come upriver to spawn. As we noted earlier, historically, sturgeon have been sacred for the Menominee (Beck 1995), so this difference in values is not surprising.

Summary   Before shifting to the follow-up study it is important to note the broad commonalities across groups. For example, the rank ordering of species was highly correlated across groups. (Menominee rank trout somewhat higher, perhaps reflecting the presence of many rivers and streams on the reservation and the fact that one does not need a boat to fish for trout.) Most important, however, are the similarities in attitudes toward various fishing practices. Both groups condemn selling fish, keeping undersize fish, fishing on spawning beds, using setpoles to catch trout, and culling smaller fish to get the largest possible limit. The key question is to what extent these groups are aware of their modest differences and their substantial shared values.

9.8   Intra- and Intergroup Perception

Our follow-up study addressed the question of the relationship between the actual similarities and differences noted in the first study and *perceived* within- and between-group similarities and differences. In this task we asked the same questions as before. However, rather than exploring each individual's goals and values (to be aggregated statistically into group models), we asked each informant to report what he thought would be the response of members of his own group as well as members of the other group. Specifically, we asked informants how they thought equally expert members of their community or the other community might answer the probes concerning values, goals, and attitudes.

There is good evidence that people perceive both other groups and their own reference group as more extreme than it objectively is. For example, Prentice and Miller (1993) found that college students systematically overestimated the amount and perceived desirability of alcohol consumption among other students and that, at least for male students, this misperception led to an increase in drinking. In other words, misperception of a group norm can cause a self-fulfilling prophecy that feeds back to make the perceived group norm even more extreme. This has obvious implications for negotiation and conflict resolution (for an analysis see Ross and Stillinger 1991; Thompson and Gonzalez 1997).

There is other evidence that people tend to believe that their behavior speaks for itself, that they see the world objectively, and that only other people are susceptible to bias and misconstrual of events (e.g., Ross 1990). This raises the possibility that members of one group will feel no need to try to take the perspective of members of the other group in understanding intentions, values, and behaviors. If you see the world objectively and someone does something transparently inappropriate (e.g., keeping a largemouth bass), then the conclusion that their motives are bad may be so automatic that it comes to you as a fact, not an inference. To the extent that this tendency is common it creates greater opportunities for intergroup misperception.

The rank-ordering and ranking tasks were exactly the same as before. The only difference was that each participant was asked to answer each of the probes twice. For the first iteration informants were asked to answer the questions the way they thought the typical fisherman from their community, equally expert, would answer them. We added that in many cases, the answers would probably be the same as they themselves would give, but that sometimes people recognize that their preferences and values might not agree with a typical expert's answers. After the species-ranking, goal-ranking, and practices-rating task was completed, informants were asked to repeat the task, this time answering from the perspective of an equally expert fisherman from the other community (for Menominee informants, how majority-culture experts from this area would answer the questions, and for majority-culture experts, how Menominee expert fishermen would answer). After these tasks were completed, we showed participants the mean ratings for each group from the earlier study.

Perception of Relative Importance of Fish
The results for rank ordering of the importance of fifteen species of fish for (1) members of one's own group and (2) members of the other group are summarized in table 9.5. Each number represents the average ranking, so smaller numbers correspond to more highly valued fish. For example, Menominee experts gave highest rankings to brook trout and brown trout. Note also that both Menominee and majority-culture informants correctly thought that trout were more important for Menominee than majority-culture fishermen. Both groups also predicted that majority-

Table 9.5
Projected fish value rankings for own and other group

Raters	Menominee		Majority	
Rated	Menominee	Majority	Menominee	Majority
Black sucker	11.9	11.7	11.5	11.9
Bluegill	4.7	6.7	6.1	4.0
Bluntnose minnow	13.4	13.4	12.2	13.2
Brook trout	1.6	5.5	2.4	5.1
Brown trout	2.3	5.6	3.1	7.1
Bullhead	10.9	10.3	10.6	10.0
Gar	14.4	13.9	13.9	14.1
Largemouth bass	4.2	2.8	6.8	4.3
Muskie	8.6	4.6	7.9	5.9
Northern pike	6.0	5.5	6.2	5.4
Perch	7.5	7.8	6.2	6.2
River shiner	12.4	12.9	12.6	12.5
Smallmouth bass	7.5	7.3	7.5	7.2
Sturgeon	9.6	8.7	5.4	10.9
Walleye	4.3	1.4	4.8	2.1

culture fishermen would rank walleye and muskie very highly (and more highly than the Menominee), and that also was the case.

Overall, each group very accurately anticipates the rankings that members of the other group would give. The two groups generally agree on their rankings (the cross-group correlation was $+.87$), but this accuracy extends well beyond general agreement. Menominee estimates of majority values correlate $+.95$ with majority values, and majority estimates of Menominee values correlate $+.93$ with Menominee values.

Goal Rankings

The predicted rankings for the two groups are summarized in table 9.3 (p. 243). Again, smaller numbers refer to higher priorities. Columns 2 and 5 give predictions for one's own group, and columns 3 and 6 give the predictions by the other group. Each group was fairly accurate at anticipating the goals of members of their own group. Menominee experts thought that majority-culture experts would be much more focused on catching a trophy-size fish than they actually are. Menominee fishermen also underestimated the importance for majority-culture experts of fishing as an activity to pass down to future generations and for being close to nature. The largest discrepancy for majority-culture predictions is the underestimation of the importance to Menominee experts of fishing as a way to relax.

Values and Attitudes Concerning Practices

The results on values and attitudes came as a shock to us. Predictions for own group and other group are summarized in table 9.4 (p. 244). Columns 2 and 5 give predictions for one's own group and columns 3 and 6 give the predictions by the other group for a given group. Table 9.4 indicates that Menominee experts think that majority-culture fishermen would be more approving of fishing contests and getting a trophy fish mounted than majority fishermen report. Table 9.4 also shows that majority-culture experts think Menominee experts would approve selling fish, keeping undersized fish, fishing on spawning beds, culling smaller fish to get the biggest-sized limit, and using setpoles to catch trout. As we noted before, such practices are disapproved of by both groups. Majority fishermen even believe that Menominee would approve fishing for suckers hoping to get a sturgeon on the line (sturgeon are sacred for the Menominee).

A cross-group consensus analysis was conducted to see how well the two groups agree in their perceptions. That is, do majority-culture and Menominee experts (1) have the same beliefs about majority-culture values and attitudes and (2) have the same beliefs about Menominee values and attitudes? This cross-group analysis reveals consensus for both majority-culture and Menominee experts only with respect to the majority-culture responses.[10] In light of the individual group consensus this suggests that the Menominee model of majority-culture experts is in basic agreement with majority-culture experts' perceptions of their own values and behaviors. This basic cross-group consensus is coupled with significant residual group differences, because members of both groups differ significantly on their second factor scores.

Corresponding cross-group analyses with respect to the Menominee response pattern fail to show consensus. This underscores an asymmetry with respect to cross-group perception. While Menominee and majority-culture experts concur on a model of majority-culture expert values and behavior, both groups differ widely in their perceptions of Menominee values. In short, majority-culture models of Menominee are strikingly different from Menominee individual responses and Menominee predictions for the group consensus. Overall, these data indicate that majority-culture fishermen hold strong, incorrect expectations concerning Menominee attitudes and values.

9.9   Sources of Misperception

Where do these misperceptions come from? We believe that these misperceptions come from differences in specific goals and knowledge organization, reinforced by patterns of media coverage. Differences in specific goals can lead to rejection of another group's values and practices.

In an exploratory analysis we have examined relationships between the fish-ranking task and stereotyping. There is one final discrepancy between perception and actuality that we have deferred talking about until now. The majority-culture fish experts thought that the Menominee experts would rank the sturgeon more highly than they actually do. The Shawano dams on the Wolf River prevent sturgeon from being able to reach the reservation itself. Many majority-culture fishermen may be aware of Menominee efforts to get ladders installed on these dams so that sturgeon could return to the reservation for spawning. Some may know that sturgeon are considered sacred. So it is not surprising that majority-culture experts thought that Menominee experts would value sturgeon highly. Indeed, we ourselves were initially surprised that our Menominee experts did not rank sturgeon more highly. The responses of the Menominee experts tend to be more pragmatic. A typical comment was "we don't have them on the reservation any more." One expert who is an elder did not rank sturgeon high because he thinks the meat is too rich.

The overall mean of 5.4 for the majority-culture expectations about Menominee ranking conceals a great deal of variability, and we decided to investigate further. Specifically, we looked how answers to the values probe "pretending to fish for suckers hoping to get a sturgeon on the line" correlated with beliefs about Menominee valuing sturgeon more than white fishermen. Recall that Menominee disapprove of this practice but that expert majority-culture fishermen as a group thought that Menominee would approve of it more than their own group does. For each majority-culture expert we computed two scores: (1) rating for Menominee approval of pretending to fish for suckers minus the same anticipated rating for majority-culture fishermen and (2) anticipated Menominee ranking of sturgeon versus expected ranking for majority-culture experts. We then correlated these two scores across our majority-culture fish experts.

One hypothesis is that experts who knew enough about Menominee culture to know that they value sturgeon would be less likely to think that Menominee would approve of trying to get sturgeon on their lines for entertainment. If that were the case then we should observe a negative correlation between the two scores. The observed correlation was +0.70, highly significant and in the opposite direction! Those that thought Menominee experts would value sturgeon also thought that they would approve of getting sturgeon on the line for entertainment.

Another way of describing the results is that the majority-culture experts who know enough about Menominee fishing values to anticipate that they would *not* rank sturgeon highly were also those experts who judge that Menominee would *not* approve of pretending to fish for suckers hoping to have a chance to wrestle with a sturgeon.

We also looked at the correlation between thinking that Menominee would rank sturgeon high and a combined measure of values and practices associated with stereotyping: (1) selling fish, (2) keeping undersized fish, (3) culling smaller fish to get the largest bag limit, (4) fishing on spawning beds, (5) using setpoles to catch trout, and (6) pretending to fish for suckers hoping to get a sturgeon on the line. Again for each majority-culture expert we took the difference between anticipated approval by Menominee versus majority experts as our index of stereotyping. The correlation between this index and thinking that Menominee experts would rank sturgeon comparatively higher was +0.65, which is statistically significant. So the correlation holds not only for the item concerning suckers and sturgeon but also for stereotyping as a whole.

Overall, these observations suggest that knowing a bit about Menominee values in the abstract was not enough to undermine stereotyping, but knowing Menominee fishermen's specific values was. Of course, it could be that the judgment that Menominee fishing experts would not value the sturgeon more highly than majority-culture fishermen was based on lack of knowledge rather than a specific belief. To address this question, we did a final correlation analysis.

Recall that majority-culture experts as a group knew that Menominee place greater relative value on trout. In another analysis we looked at the correlation between predicting that Menominee would value sturgeon relatively more and knowing that Menominee value trout relatively more. The correlation was significant and negative (−0.62). In other words, the majority-culture experts who correctly thought that Menominee value trout tended to think correctly that Menominee would not preferentially value sturgeon. Using the six items mentioned previously to get an overall measure of stereotyping, we find a reliable negative correlation (−0.49) between knowing that Menominee preferentially value trout and stereotyping. The better the majority experts knew Menominee rankings, the less stereotyping they displayed. We are currently gathering social network data as a converging source of evidence, and so far our data are consistent with the idea that knowing specific Menominee who fish is negatively correlated with stereotyping. Finally, we examined relationships between fish ranking and stereotyping. Specifically, we look at ranking of the "big five" sportsfish (walleye, northern, muskie, smallmouth bass, largemouth bass). The higher this ranking, the greater the stereotyping (+.50).

9.10   Real versus Perceived Cultural Differences

The most striking finding is that the very modest actual differences in goals, values, and attitudes are accompanied by massive perceived differences. Furthermore, the effect is strongly asymmetrical. Menominee fish-expert judgment modestly exaggerated the sportsman's model of fishing, but majority-culture judgments of Menominee values are wildly discrepant from stated Menominee values. One explanation that can readily be rejected is that the Menominee stated values do not correspond to actual behaviors. Recent surveys of fish populations in lakes and rivers on the Menominee reservation show that fish populations are healthy and abundant (Schmidt 1995). In short, the Menominee tribe has done a good job of managing fish as a reservation resource.

We suggest that these misperceptions are mediated by differences in specific goals and associated knowledge organization, reinforced by patterns of media coverage (for related analysis of effects of media coverage see Gilens 1996; Gilliam and Iyengar 2000). The sportsman's model of searching for trophy-sized fish is common in the media. It is easy to get the idea that getting a trophy fish is the be-all-and-end-all of fishing. Fishing contests on cable television only reinforce this impression. Sporting magazines are full of photographs of particularly large gamefish that anglers have caught. Rarely does an article mention someone catching two 16-inch walleyes and making a nice meal from them (and there certainly would be no photo). It is also important to note that although the Menominee as a whole tended to have stereotypes about majority-culture fishermen, there were a number of exceptions—these are group trends that do not hold for every individual.

If the gap between prediction and reality is large for Menominee predicting majority-culture values, then it is enormous for majority-culture fishermen predicting Menominee values. The fact that they thought that Menominee would be more approving of spearfishing walleyes than they are is not so surprising. But they also thought, contrary to fact, that Menominee fishermen would strongly approve of virtually every practice that both groups condemn.

9.11   Cultural Support

Differences in specific goals can lead to rejection of another group's values and practices. For example, Menominee fishermen uniformly endorse eating largemouth and smallmouth bass, a practice that many majority-culture fishermen reject because "they are such good fighters that one should only do catch-and-release." Fishing for sport is institutionally sanctioned and encouraged. For example, the ethic of catch-and-release (Hummel 1994) is reinforced by Wisconsin Department of Natural Resources (WDNR) policy. In parts of Wisconsin the WDNR fishing regulations include a "catch-and-release only" season for largemouth and smallmouth bass in the spring when bass are spawning (Wisconsin Department of Natural Resources 2002).

Media coverage of the controversy surrounding Native American spearfishing exacerbates the effects of these differing orientations, especially when these rights cover off-reservation waters. When we revealed the Menominee ratings to majority-culture fishermen, a common response to the mismatch between majority predictions and Menominee ratings was, "You know, I think I was answering the way that the Chippewa might answer." (Another common response was, "Well, I know Menominees really take care of their forest, so it makes sense that they also take care of their fish.")

The Chippewa (or Ojibwe) have received the greatest publicity as the only tribe with off-reservation fishing rights (in the territories they ceded in the nineteenth century, which cover much of northern Wisconsin). In these waters, the daily limit on walleyes is lower than in the rest of Wisconsin, and it is a natural inference that spearfishing of walleyes in the spring when they are spawning depletes the resource. A decade ago Ojibwe spearfishing of walleyes and the associated demonstrations and protests in the spring by organizations like Protect Americans' Rights and Resources (PARR) attracted almost nightly attention. This attention seemed to have the goal of creating heat, not light. Moderate voices were rarely quoted and the television coverage focused on the controversy, not on factual information that might be relevant to it.

These facts are as follows. Records over the past decade (WDNR 2000, 2002) indicate that sportsfishermen harvest more than twelve walleyes for every one taken by Ojibwe spearers. The Ojibwe also maintain fish hatcheries, strip the spawn from any females they spear, and restock in the same waters where they spear (e.g., in 1998 Ojibwe stocked ceded territory waters with over 26 million walleye fry and more than 700,000 walleye fingerlings; WDNR 2002). Despite these numbers, many sport-fishermen may balk at the image of spearers taking large female walleyes. But WDNR monitoring also undermines this image. Sexing of harvested fish during the 1985–1999 period shows a breakdown of 83 percent males, 10 percent females, and 7 percent of unknown sex. The average length of walleyes taken has been 15.5 inches. So the image that best fits is of a 15-inch male walleye, not a 25-inch female.

Overall, the most striking finding is the contrast between perception and reality: despite the strong overall consensus in knowledge, goals, and values, majority-culture fishermen see Menominee as vastly different. These results show that differences in how groups conceptualize nature are critical to understanding intergroup conflict over resources.

9.12   Conclusions

Our data show that expertise cannot be separated from cultural milieu, even when people engage in more or less the same activities. The parallels between the Itza' and the Menominee are striking, especially when one notes that both groups also have sustainable forestry practices. As with Itza' and Lacandón, some Menominee men express the belief that if a person treats nature in a greedy or wasteful manner then spirits will punish them, and offer tobacco as a prayer of thanks. Cultural paths (in the sense of reliable distributions of conceptual representations in a population of minds) appear to provide something of a framework theory for organizing experience. This is seen, for example, in the Itza' Maya tendency to see reciprocal relations (animals helping plants as well as being helped by them) and in Menominee fishermen's ecological orientation.

These studies reinforce the distributional view of culture. Residual analysis indicated that expert Menominee and majority-culture fishermen have a shared model, but that, in addition, Menominee fishermen have a distinct model based on salience of ecological relations. These differences, coupled with differences in underlying subordinate goals, can give rise to dramatic intergroup misperception, even when both groups share the same superordinate goal of resource conservation. The interaction of culture by expertise in the basis for sorting also suggests different developmental trajectories in the two groups. Indeed, our developmental data show parallel cultural differences in sensitivity to ecological relations in young Menominee and majority-culture children (Ross et al. 2003). These trajectories invite further analysis.

The most important results concern the cross-group misperceptions that appear to be a natural outgrowth of different perspectives on resources and resource management. Just as for the Itza', Q'eqchi', and Ladino differences, the Menominee and majority-culture differences reflect different framework theories that direct observations and dictate values and attitudes. It is these complexes or systems that must be understood in order to gain insight into cultural contributions to environmental decision making.

10 Conclusions and Projections

We have covered a lot of territory but our journey is far from complete. In this chapter we review our main findings in the context of discussing the implications of our results for theory, methodology, and application, including policy. This summary will be coupled with comments concerning current and future directions.

A Few Clarifications

Before turning to implications, we first try to avoid some possible misunderstandings by adding a few points of clarification.

Modules

One reviewer of an earlier draft of this book generally liked it, but took us to task for adopting "an extremist position on modularity." Although we made some changes here and there to reduce the likelihood that we would be misunderstood, we will say a bit more here. First, we do not claim that there is a distinct area of the brain dedicated to all and only biology. Second, we do not claim that the innate propensities for learning about the biological world necessarily have propositional content. All we claim is that there is enough there, so that with some minimal interaction with the world, a number of candidates for universal principles emerge, including the privilege of the generic-species rank and a presumption of underlying essence.

In chapter 4 we offered a set of converging criteria (operational guidelines if you will) for a biology module and reviewed a wide range of evidence bearing on these criteria. Others may disagree either with these standards or with the state of the evidence bearing on them. This is fine and conforms to our notions about how good science operates.

The Culture/Species Analogy

One of our most trusted colleagues advised us against employing the suggestion that cultures are like species. He offered two reasons: (1) the basis for an analogy should be grounded in stable, shared knowledge and readers might well have highly varied and incorrect notions about species, and (2) many invited implications of the analogy would also be incorrect. Perhaps our analogy would have been a bit more precise if we had instead suggested that people's misconceptions about culture are like people's misconceptions about species—for example, that they have universally shared essential properties. In any event, we will trust the reader to avoid the first problem and offer a few examples to address the second. First, cultures can blend and mix in ways that species almost always do not (sure, botanists will tell you that oak species are very promiscuous, but that is relative to other plant species where mixing is much rarer). Second, the ontogeny of an individual plant or animal is probably much more stable than the ontogeny of an individual member of some cultural group.

Units of Analysis

When we talk about a causally distributed set of mental representations and their public expression we are being deliberately vague about what the units of analysis are. Specifically, we do *not* take an atomistic view where "idea" is equated with a single, simple proposition. Similarly, we do not restrict "causally distributed" to situations where a mentally represented proposition is replicated in someone else's head (see again our critique of memes). In the limiting case, ideas may correspond to simple propositions, but they may also be as abstract and complex as ideational landscapes that orient inferences make some judgments more likely than others (for an example, see section 8.3).

We grant that our abstract definition does not explicitly mention a variety of factors that may be relevant to distribution processes and patterns, such as political processes and patterns of prejudice. For example, group identification may create borders, and some groups like the Amish deliberately adopt distinctive practices to reinforce these borders and a sense of being a distinct entity (entitativity). In other cases, various forms of prejudice and discrimination create borders that both limit and distort the flow of information across groups. These factors are often relevant and represent ways of elaborating our general framework in particular contexts.

Taking Sides

The reader could easily come away with the impression that we have failed to remain objective or neutral, instead transparently favoring the Itza' Maya and the Menominee. We reject both the framing of this accusation and its conclusion. First, being neutral is not the same as being objective. Generally our goal is to take the perspective (not the side) of whatever group we are working with and it is not clear what "neutral" means in this context. We think objectivity is more likely to emerge from taking multiple perspectives than from trying to take no perspective. In short, we would like to be accused of taking the perspective of all the groups we work with. Even in the case of interviewing candidate suicide bombers and their sponsors (which we do in our new work), we believe there is value in trying to understand the underpinnings for such an extreme action.

Second, we do not see cultural research as a one-way enterprise where we administer some interview or test and the participant gets paid with dollars (or some local currency). The research enterprise is more collaborative and some of our studies are based on suggestions made by participants. It is also not one-way in that the groups we work with may ask us to help in other ways. So we when are asked to speak at a Rotary Club, meet with a parents' group, teach a course at a tribal college, or help to establish a rainforest reserve, we generally try to be helpful. And when we need our horse or car serviced and one of our options is a stable or garage owned by one of our informants, guess where we take it.

Third, we think that there are some formal obligations when one is working with groups that historically have been underserved. For example, our work in Wisconsin has been based on an understanding of appropriate research methods for working with American Indian communities. There is a long history of research in American Indian communities that has often not been in their best interest (as they see it), a legacy that has made many native communities suspicious toward research. Over the years indigenous researchers themselves have worked to develop appropriate methods and criteria for conducting research (Hermes 1999; Smith 1999; Mihesuah 1998; Guyette 1983). There are some general lessons that have driven the approach to this work.

To begin, all of the literature generally agrees that the *participatory action research (PAR)* is the best framework of inquiry. PAR has generally been defined as an integrated approach that relies on the participation of community members to investigate the issues at hand, while building local skills for the purpose of increasing autonomy. PAR includes the following criteria: elder input; use of traditional language; community participation in research agenda, staff selection, and budget; community payoff; respect for cultural values; and informed consent (Hudson and Taylor-Henley 2001). Additionally, when conducting research with reservation communities, investigators must go through the tribal research approval process; a research board approval from a mainstream institution is not sufficient (Lomawaima 2000).

In Guatemala, there is less of a history of research exploitation, at least in Petén, but it has been no less important to work closely with community leaders in conducting research. Lois, Vapnarsky, and Atran also helped to organize a language program aimed at keeping Itza' Maya alive—for years government functionaries discouraged use of the language in public and banned children from speaking it in schools through fines and beatings. The language-program effort was based on community goals, and not an imposition of researcher values.

Finally, attention to and respect for cultural groups that have been neglected or oppressed may have some intrinsically beneficial aspects. To the extent that the research fosters cultural identification and dignity, it may support cultural survival and help people maintain their bearings even in the worst of circumstances. Count us in on this.

Shallow Ethnography

Although we have made protestations about the perils of parachute research—and solemnly sworn that we have conducted appropriate historical, linguistic, and ethnographic research—it would be misleading to claim that we have done everything that we could have. Ethnographic research is not like putting on a suit for a wedding where you have only one chance to get it right. We have recorded many Itza' stories and ceremonies (some already reported elsewhere, some to come), but it was not until we found qualitative differences in folkecological models that we started to think about looking for themes related to reciprocity. Similarly, it was only after discovering Menominee children's precociousness in ecological reasoning that it made sense to look for its roots in everyday Menominee cultural practices.

We are trying to make two related points here. One is that ethnography is never theoretically neutral and the other is that it is an iterative process. So our ethnographic research may be shallow with respect to some puzzles we would like to address but not with respect to others.

Theoretical Implications of Our Findings

Now we want to turn to the implications of the work described in this book for theory, methodology, and application. The distinction between these three categories is somewhat superficial but is convenient for purposes of exposition.

Folkbiological Universals

A handful of cultures does not a universe make. Nonetheless, our studies are consistent with a large body of work in ethnobiology (e.g., Berlin 1992) indicating that folk taxonomies follow structural principles that consistently yield a high correlation with scientific taxonomies. In addition, we found that, with respect to inductive confidence, the generic-species level is privileged, even in populations that have limited commerce with nature. This is also in agreement with Berlin's universal principles but our studies add a cognitive and developmental component to these analyses.

We described evidence indicating that young children have an understanding of biology that it distinct from psychology. In particular, children's reasoning appears to embody a presumption of essence (located at the generic-species level) that is responsible for generating basic morphological and behavioral properties (see Gelman 2003 for an extensive review of supporting evidence on children's essentializing). This pattern of results is remarkably robust, especially given the divergences seen in adult participants in these same cultures. For example, we found that rural Yukatek Maya adults retain a birth bias for all types of properties but urban Brazilian adults attribute behavioral properties to nurture.

All told, these results make a strong case for the idea that learning about biology is constrained. These constraints (biases or skeletal principles) make some things easy to learn and other things, like principles of evolution, much more challenging.

Devolution

One might claim that the primary value in studying folkbiology in college students at major research universities or among children in these same communities is for the purpose of examining the cognitive consequences of diminished contact with the natural world. These consequences are far from minor. The *Oxford English Dictionary* studies showed a striking quantitative loss of cultural support for learning about biological kinds in the twentieth century, and our studies with undergraduates yield little familiarity with kinds other than mammals.

It is likely the case that the list of folkbiological universals could be considerably lengthened and strengthened if one added a stipulation requiring some minimal experience (which would eliminate most college students at major research universities), just as language generalizations are amplified by excluding wholly artificial languages, such as Signed English (a language constructed by a committee that turned out to be unlearnable). The fact of devolution allows us to see which aspects of folkbiology are most resistant to loss.

But qualitative changes in folkbiological understanding may be even more important. One shift appears to be from an ecological orientation where people see themselves as an integral part of nature to a conception where nature is an externality and people are apart from it. In the Bang et al. interviews with majority culture and Menominee parents, one group difference was in what one might call "distancing discourse." For example, a Menominee parent might say "We use milkweed for soup" and a majority-culture person parent might say "Hard maple is used in flooring." The latter is more distancing than the former.

It is a challenge to identify factors that might lead to a qualitative shift in folkbiological orientation, but one can make some guesses. Just turn on the Discovery Channel to see programs devoted to wildlife. These programs almost always concern distant rather than local places. If you go to a bookstore that sells children's books, you will find lots of material devoted to animals. But you will struggle to find anything on local animals (a side bet: you'll find vastly more on dinosaurs), not to mention plants or ecosystems. In short, common sources of information about nature tend to focus on exotic species in distant places where ecological interactions typically do not go beyond predator-prey relations and flora are rarely more than stage props.

Finally, quantitative and qualitative changes almost surely interact. If all you know is oak, then you will not notice that some species of oaks grow near water and others do well on the edges of prairies. If you cannot distinguish the actors, then their interactions will not be meaningful to you.

Folkbiological Variability

One of our more striking results is the difference in folkecological models across cultural groups living in the same area and engaged in essentially

the same activities. These differences represent a challenge for future research. Should they be conceptualized in terms of how focusing on certain
kinds of goals leads to devolution? Are these differences mediated by differences in worldviews and mental models? What cognitive and cultural
processes are responsible for these large differences in mental models?
In rural Wisconsin we see cultural differences in ecological orientation in
the youngest children we have tested. So, whatever the source of the differences, it seems to be transmitted across generations at an early age. Although we have made some progress, we need to know much more about
the role of cultural and experiential factors in the development of folkbiological understandings.

Categorization and Reasoning

If the conceptions of biology held by undergraduates are impoverished,
then it should not be surprising to find that theories of categorization
and reasoning developed from research with undergraduates are limited
in scope and applicability. Consider categorization. The idea that all one
needs to know is the full set of similarity relations to describe both category structure and goodness of example or typicality just will not work.
We reviewed evidence from a number of populations indicating that typicality is driven by ideals and that later learning builds on earlier learning.
If category ideals tend to be learned first, then they will have an important role in the development of categories. The Steyvers and Tenenbaum
2005 paper is a welcome sign that modelers are beginning to shift to this
more active view of learning (see also Love, Medin, and Gureckis 2004).

Much the same holds for reasoning. Previous models of induction have
assumed that participants employ (abstract) similarity relations in reasoning. Our work suggests that this is more likely to be a strategy of last
resort, used only when more relevant information is unavailable ("last
resort" happens rarely for biologically informed people, like the Itza'
Maya, but almost all the time for undergraduates). We need models of
induction that describe not just this default condition, but also the range
of ecological and causal knowledge that is brought to bear from a richer
base of biological knowledge.

Meaning and Environmental Decision Making

Theory and data on decision making may be the biggest success story that
the cognitive sciences have to offer (Kahneman and Tversky 1983). Regardless of whether it derives from success or boredom, however, the field

appears to be experiencing dis-ease (for reviews see Fiske and Tetlock 1997; Goldstein and Weber 1995; Medin and Bazermann 1999; Markman and Medin 2004). This discontent takes two forms. One form worries about the generalizability of results based on bets involving varying probabilities and amounts. Although some researchers have suggested that such bets are the "fruitflies" of decision making, others (e.g., Goldstein and Weber 1995) worry that they may be the "nonsense syllables" of decision making (allowing precise experimental control but being too artificial to be enlightening).

The other response to this dis-ease is to become more ambitious with respect to the agenda for decision making research. Some researchers (e.g., Goldstein and Weber 1995; Tenbrunsel and Messick 1999; Rettinger and Hastie 2001) have suggested that there are distinct "kinds" of decisions. Others have suggested that decision making is relation-specific in that the principles involved depend on whether it involves a stranger, a friend, a family member, or a boss (Fiske and Tetlock 1997). Still other researchers have looked for more naturalistic contexts, such as firemen making decisions about how to fight a blaze (e.g., Klein 1999), where the decision makers may have no conscious experience of making a decision.

Our research on environmental decision making suggests that decisions are part of a system of knowledge and beliefs and that these mental models inform and direct decision making, often in ways that seem not to conform to calculations of self-interest (utility). We see these decisions as meaning making (Medin et al. 1999), as expressions of values, and in some cases as driven by moral imperatives. We believe that human decision making is infused with meaning. Decisions are meaningful to the person making them, and they often convey meaning to others who are affected by or observe them, sometimes intentionally so. This suggests that taking a semantic approach to human decision making can yield some insights into decision making operation that might not lie within the range of other approaches. The following quotation nicely summarizes this thesis:

The meanings elaborated in decision making have importance beyond the mundane realities of rendering decisions. Decision making and the activities surrounding it have considerable symbolic importance. In the course of making decisions, decision makers develop and communicate meaning not only about decisions but also more generally about truth, about what is happening in the world and why it is happening. They define what is morally important and what is proper behavior. They elaborate a language of understanding and describe how actions are properly explained and justified. (March 1994, 212)

Sacred or Protected Values and Decision Making

The twin facts that Itza' Maya devotionally value the ramón tree and see the forest spirits or *Arux* as protectors of the forest who will punish transgressors has led us to the view that morally motivated decision making plays a critical role in both environmental decision making and may also be important in intergroup conflict. Moreover, figuring strictly from a standpoint of maximizing current self-interest in a competitive environment, where other groups chop down ramón trees and otherwise degrade the forest, protecting ramón appears to make little rational sense. Preserving what others destroy seems to be a waste of time and energy and hence, in the long run, a waste of life. So why do Itza' continue to protect the forest much as they believe the forest spirits do? There is, of course, a body of work on morally motivated decision making, but we think our work provides a somewhat different perspective on it.

But first let's see what others say. Phil Tetlock and colleagues (2000) defines sacred values as "any value that a moral community implicitly or explicitly treats as possessing infinite or transcendental significance that precludes comparisons, tradeoffs, or indeed any other mingling with bounded or secular values." There has been more than a decade of research on sacred or protected values (PVs) and decision making, and some of their key properties have been identified. First of all, PVs are linked to moral outrage and other emotions (Baron and Spranca 1997), especially when a person holding a PV is offered a secular value in exchange for a PV (e.g., selling one's child, auctioning of body parts, or selling futures that bet on the likelihood of acts of terrorism; Medin et al. 1999; Tetlock 2002, 2003).

A second important generalization grows out of work by Jon Baron and collaborators. They have amassed considerable evidence that PVs are associated with a large omission bias (Baron and Greene 1996; Baron and Ritov 1994; Ritov and Baron 1992, 1995, 1999) and that this bias grows out of the use of deontological (e.g., "do no harm") rather than consequentialist decision rules. (A deontological decision rule is one based on "oughts and obligations or prohibitions" regardless of outcomes, in direct contrast to a consequentialist decision rule which mandates choice of the action that leads to the best overall outcome.) For example, in one scenario, people might be told about a threat to fifteen species of fish and then offered actions that will save those fifteen species but threaten a number of other species. In this sort of trade-off situation, some participants—typically those with PVs—say that they would not want to cause the loss of a single species.

The general finding is that participants with PVs are less willing to trade off than participants who do not express a PV, suggesting that these people are less sensitive to a trade-off's consequences than people without PVs. However, whether one appears to be focused on acts versus omissions also may to vary with (social) context. For example, when asked to imagine people in a position of responsibility, participants show an act rather than an omission bias (Haidt and Baron 1996), which may again represent the application of a deontological rule. In some contexts, people with PVs may feel a moral obligation to act, independent of the likelihood of success "because it is the right thing to do" (as Kant might have said, "Moral virtue is its own reward").

The characterization of devotional values as "biases" to be overcome has tended toward the pejorative, and researchers have bemoaned the fact that protected values get in the way of conflict resolution and trade-offs. For example, how can a court decide on monetary damages for cases like the oil spill associated with the Exxon-Valdez when Alaskans say that a pristine shoreline is of infinite value? As both Baron and Tetlock have noted, people with PVs seem to treat them as having infinite value (i.e., in refusing to consider trade-offs), but this premise entails a logical impossibility—if PVs have infinite value for people who endorse them, they should spend literally all their time protecting and promoting that value. For this reason, some have suggested that these values are only pseudo-sacred (Baron and Leshner 2000; Thompson and Gonzalez 1997). Others have noted that people with PVs may nonetheless engage in indirect trade-offs (McGraw and Tetlock 2005; Tetlock 2000b). One may be tempted to think of protected values as self-serving "posturing" but acts such as suicide bombings by well-educated and well-adjusted middle-class young adults (Atran 2003) or a monk's self-immolation (Gambetta 2005) undermine this stance (cf. Skitka and Mullen 2002).

Our work indicates that sacred or protected values cannot be dismissed as a form of posturing. Not only do Itza' say that the ramón tree is protected by spirits, but also when we do tree counts on their forest plots, we find a greater number of ramón trees than in adjacent plots managed by Q'eqchi' Maya and Ladinos.[1] These intriguing issues, coupled with world events where people with PVs engage in heroism in some cases and suicide terrorism in others (cf. Atran 2004), underline the importance of understanding morally motivated decisions, and suggest that there are significant empirical and theoretical challenges that demand further attention (Atran, Axelrod, and Davis 2007).

Tragedy of the Commons

Our environmental decision making research brings a new perspective to the tragedy of the commons. The thrust of previous research has been to suggest that common-pool resources will be exhausted by actors engaged in self-interested decision making (Hardin 1968) unless closed-access, institutional monitoring and punishment of cheaters is in place. Our work in Guatemala suggests that at least Itza' Maya operate sustainably in the absence of these institutional controls and that Ladinos are learning from the Itza' and moving toward sustainability. Furthermore, our studies of values indicate that the Itza' view the forest as an "active player" in the form of the forest spirits who punish improper behavior (harming ecologically central species). This observation suggests that different forms of game-theoretic analyses are needed when the resource is also a participant.

Our studies in Wisconsin also suggest that abstract game-theoretic analyses must be informed by an understanding of intergroup differences in mental models of resources, differences that may lead to misperception and misunderstanding of the behaviors of different players (cultural groups). A fishing practice that is coherent and well grounded in sustainability from a Menominee perspective may be transparently harmful when viewed through the lens of a European-American sportsman's model of sustainability.

Cultural Epidemiology

We do not need to dwell on the fact that, for our purposes, it is just a nonstarter to treat or define cultures and groups in terms of shared properties. In our initial studies with tree experts (Medin et al. 1997), we were prepared to find an overall consensus but our analysis suggested instead that there were three distinct subgroups that corresponded almost perfectly with type of occupation. In the same vein, ordinarily one would not expect a hodgepodge of immigrants coming from scattered areas to constitute a culture, but as we saw in chapters 7 and 8, the Ladinos are indeed forming a "culture" of sorts.

We are currently collecting data on folkecological models and social and expert networks for three generations of Itza' and Ladinos. This will allow us to trace knowledge change across generations and across groups. Almost any pattern of results will be interesting (Do the youngest Itza' retain the notion of reciprocity? Does the notion of reciprocity "jump" from Itza' to Ladinos? Do changes across generations show a different pattern as a function of gender?) It would be hardly conceivable to undertake this work without the cultural consensus model and a notion of cultural processes as dynamic. Finally, we note that the distributional view of cultural processes is compatible with agent-based modeling. The modeling, coupled with the network and mental models data, can be used to test ideas about information transmission as a function (for example) of compatibility of mental models.

Methodological Implications

It is impossible to do cultural research without taking methodological issues very seriously. We summarize a number of lessons learned here.

Beyond Standard Populations

Of crucial significance, we believe, are the implications of our research for standard operating procedure in cognitive psychology—that is, the almost exclusive focus on college students (mainly recruited from major research universities). In most of our studies, college students have been the odd group out and our confidence in the generalizability of results based on studies with undergraduates is badly shaken. We do not expect a major shift in practice but we hope to encourage at least a modest shift in concentration. In saying this we betray more confidence than does at least one internationally recognized cultural psychologist, Harry Triandis (2001, 6). Appealing to constraints of a different sort, he wrote:

Humans are universally lazy. This is clear from the universality of Zipf's (1949) law. Zipf determined that, in all languages he investigated (and he did look at a very large sample of languages), the shorter words are the most frequent and as a word becomes more frequent, it becomes shorter (e.g., Television becomes TV). The universality of this finding indicates that the principle of least effort is a cultural universal. For psychologists, least effort means to complete a study and then state: "What I found is an eternal verity, applicable universally." The principle of least effort, then leads psychologists to ignore culture because culture is a complication that makes their work more time consuming and difficult.... Thus, the major question of this field may be. Can cultural psychology develop if it is against human nature to develop it?

For those willing to swim upstream, the sights can be very rewarding. At the risk of belaboring the point, the generalizations concerning three of the most central phenomena in the cognitive science of categorization (typicality, basic level, and inductive reasoning) have been fundamentally changed by the sorts of cultural and expertise comparisons that this book illustrates. Similarly the characterization of children's biology based on studies with urban children (in particular, folkbiology's supposed dependence on folkpsychology and its lack of essential organizing principles) was a pale, if not distorted, reflection of the picture revealed by cultural comparisons.

Psychology and Anthropology Working Together

Cognitive and developmental psychology bring to cross-cultural comparisons some obvious strengths, such as concern for universal processes, statistical techniques for reliably sampling populations and distinguishing groupwide patterns (messages) in the midst of considerable (often noisy) individual variation, and controlled experiments that precisely delimit the object of study. But as we noted at the beginning of the book, these strengths can become weaknesses if not tempered by anthropological concerns, such as awareness of the need to avoid (1) essentializing cultural groups, (2) interpreting variation as deviation, or equating the use of artificial stimuli or stimuli in contrived contexts with natural referents and situations.

Anthropology's forte is the ability to extract cultural knowledge from groups of people and make it understandable to others, ideally without losing the information required to recontextualize it and make it relevant to those same peoples. Like a naturalist who would never imagine trying to understand pandas apart from the bamboo forest that sustains them, or water lilies without their ponds, so many anthropologists find it unacceptable to consider decontextualized categories, concepts, populations, and problems as representing the world, or what is psychologically most interesting about it. But anthropology's strengths, too, turn to weaknesses if not tempered by psychology's concerns, namely, wariness about counting the plural of anecdote as data or acknowledging that some informants' special knowledge bespeaks a unique or different sort of mind (however thickly embedded in narrative, history and the environment).

So, for us, the methodological union of psychology and anthropology is not merely one of practical convenience, but of intellectual necessity.

Cultural Consensus Modeling and Cultural Epidemiology

Perhaps the best illustration of the mutually reinforcing benefits that arise from this union of psychological and anthropological methods is the fit of cultural consensus modeling to cultural epidemiology, which we consider to be a major synthesis in our work. Rather than simply taking standard measures of statistical reliability in groupwide patterns as evidence for cultural consensus, we used cultural consensus modeling to impose additional constraints that enabled us to identify and demonstrate patterns of consensus more precisely (e.g., aggregated folktaxonomies, regularities in ecological reasoning), so as to better make independent predictions about a population (e.g., use of taxonomy to generate biological inferences, knowledge of differences in ecological reasoning to anticipate differences in environmental management). From the standpoint of cultural epidemiology, cultures are not bounded entities with component parts, but variable distributions of thoughts and behaviors through environments that are often fluid. In line with this stance, our use of cultural consensus modeling allowed us to avoid having to blend interpretations of people's thoughts and actions into component parts of a culture. Instead, we were able to describe emergent cultural patterns derived statistically from measurements of individual cognitions and behaviors, without losing any of the information and insight attending individual variation.

Again motivated by cultural epidemiology's view of cultures as intersecting distributions of thoughts, behaviors, and environments, we used cultural consensus modeling to examine the relations between agreement patterns both within and across different populations. This generated "metacultural" models that permitted us to trace possible pathways of learning and information exchange within and between cultural groups: for example, the likely transfer of Itza' ecological knowledge to socially well-connected Ladino male experts, and then on to Ladino women. The result illuminated more general processes of cultural formation, transformation, and evolution.

The merging of cultural consensus modeling with cultural epidemiology also sets the stage for potentially more informative agent-based and causal modeling. Thus far we have only revealed groupwide patterns of thoughts and behaviors, shown reliable correlations between different sorts of patterns, and identified likely interactive pathways between them, including key nodes (e.g., forest experts) in those pathways. But we have not yet demonstrated causal connections, much less how these connections are built up over time through exchanges between interacting agents. What we have done is to establish a general framework for informed agent-based and causal cultural modeling to take place.

Decision Making and Transcending Utility

There are two fairly novel aspects to our methods for dealing with decision making. First, we sought to "ground-truth" our own, and our informants', inferences about how their mental models of the environment translate into ecological behavior and how that behavior affects the environment, including measures of soil composition, canopy cover, crop diversity and species counts, as well as time-sensitive satellite imagery of deforestation patterns, and archival work on historical changes. Not only does such ground-truthing validate findings about the relationship between environmental thought and action, but without it we find that policymakers (and many scientists outside our main fields of interest) just will not take such findings seriously (nor should they).

Second, we extended our methods for eliciting mental models of ecological relationships among animals, plants and humans to the realm of spirits. In one of our most intriguing studies, we found that Itza' believed they would be punished if they violated spirit preferences, and that these fears translated into behavioral patterns whose consequences on the composition of the forest could be traced back more than a millennium. We also found that Menominee, like Itza', appear to conceive of relations between humans and animal species in reciprocal terms. The implication of these findings is that standard rendering of decision making in terms of utility maximization must be modified or rethought if these kinds of behavior are to make sense—as they do to members of the populations we study and to us.

This work has motivated us to branch out again, generalizing our concerns for resource conflicts to cultural (including political) conflicts more generally, and involving ourselves in new field sites in the Middle East, Southeast Asia, and elsewhere. These concerns, in turn, have compelled us to elaborate new methodological tools aimed at exploring the ways cognition and emotional judgments might interact in sacred values to affect decision making and risk among individuals and groups. These methods include tests of (1) psychological barriers to trade-offs (e.g., it is taboo to sell off cultural heirlooms or sell out one's country), (2) immunity from free-rider effects (e.g., conservationists make costly efforts not to deforest even if most people continue deforesting, and suicide bombers willingly die knowing their comrades will live), (3) disregard for material cost-benefit analysis (e.g., soldiers will rescue a buddy even if the rescue greatly endangers many additional lives), (4) action bias and resistance to certain framing effects (e.g., conservation efforts and risky military action for cherished goals may be just as likely under frames of loss and gain), (5) privileged ties with emotions (e.g., people respond with outrage to immoral offers, such as money or sex to become a traitor; and people morally outraged—e.g., humiliated—may pursue the agent of that outrage with a vengeance even if it kills them), and (6) homogenization and "entitavization" of group identity (essentialized beliefs prescribe dutiful behaviors for all individuals).

For example, our research team (Ginges et al. 2007) recently conducted studies indicating that instrumental approaches to resolving political disputes are suboptimal (and may even backfire) when protagonists transform the issues or resources under dispute into essential moral values, that is, values which a moral community treats as possessing transcendental significance that precludes comparisons or tradeoffs with instrumental values of *realpolitik* or the marketplace. Instrumental decision making involves strict cost-benefit calculations regarding goals, and entails abandoning or adjusting goals if costs for realizing them are too high. We found that emotional outrage and support for violent opposition to compromise over sacred values is (1) not mitigated by offering instrumental incentives to compromise but (2) is decreased when the adversary makes instrumentally irrelevant compromises over their own sacred values.

In a survey of Jewish Israelis living in the West Bank and Gaza (*settlers*, $N = 601$) conducted in August 2005, days before Israel's withdrawal from Gaza, we randomly presented participants with one of several hypothetical peace deals (see supporting online materials). All involved Israeli withdrawal from 99 percent of the West Bank and Gaza in exchange for peace. We identified a subset of participants (46 percent) who had transformed land into an essential value; they believed that it was never permissible for the Jewish people to "give up" part of the "Land of Israel" no matter how extreme the circumstance. For these participants, all deals thus involved a "taboo" trade-off. Some deals involved an added instrumental incentive, such as money or the promise of a life free of violence ("taboo+"), while in other deals Palestinians also made a "taboo" trade-off over one of their own sacred values in a manner that neither added instrumental value to Israel nor detracted from the taboo nature of the deal being considered ("tragic"). From a rational perspective, the taboo+ deal is improved relative to the taboo deal and thus violent opposition to the tragic deal should be weaker. However, we observed the following order of support for violence: taboo+ > taboo > tragic (see figure 10.1A); where those evaluating the tragic deal showed less support for violent opposition than the other two conditions. An analysis of intensity of emotional outrage again found that taboo+ > taboo > tragic (see figure 10.1C); those evaluating the tragic deal were least likely to report anger or disgust at the prospect of the deal being signed.

These results were replicated in a survey of Palestinian refugees ($N = 535$) in Gaza and the West Bank conducted in late December 2005,

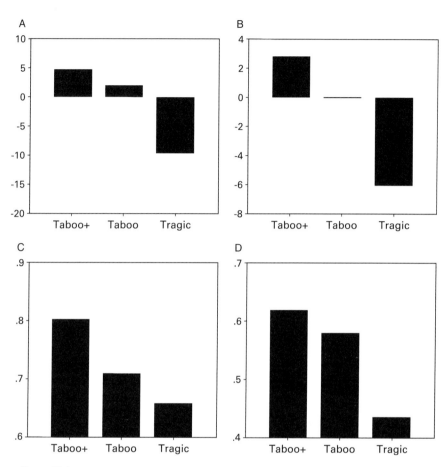

Figure 10.1

Predictions of the percentage of the population who would use violence to oppose: a peace deal perceived to violate a sacred value ("taboo" condition), the taboo deal plus an added instrumental incentive ("taboo+"), or the taboo deal plus a sacred value concession without instrumental value, from the adversary ("tragic") for (*A*) Israeli settlers (linear trend $F[1, 195] = 5.698$, $P = .018$), and (*B*) Palestinian refugees ($F[1, 384] = 7.201$, $P = .008$). Parallel results obtained for emotional reactions by: (*C*) settlers reporting "anger" or "disgust" at an Israeli leader who would agree to the trade-off being evaluated ($F[1, 260] = 4.436$, $P = .036$), and (*D*) refugees reporting "joy" at hearing of a suicide bombing according to the type of trade-off being evaluated ($F[1, 418] = 7.48$, $P = .007$). The trend of emotional intensity and support for violence in each case, taboo+ > taboo > tragic, could not be predicted by an instrumental rationality account of human behavior.

one month before Hamas was elected to power. In this experiment, hypo-thetical peace deals (see supporting online materials) all violated the Pal-estinian "right of return," a key issue in the conflict (Shamir and Shikaki 2005). For the 80 percent of participants who believed this was an essen-tial value, we once more observed that for violent opposition the order between conditions was taboo+ > taboo > tragic, where those evaluating a "tragic" deal showed lowest support for violent opposition (see figure 10.1B). Further, the same order was found for two measures ostensibly unrelated to the experiment: (1) the belief that Islam condones suicide attacks; and (2) reports of joy at hearing of a suicide attack (see de Quer-vain et al. 2004 for evidence of joy as a neurophysiological correlate of revenge). Compared to refugees evaluating a taboo or taboo+ deal, those evaluating a tragic deal believed less that Islam condoned suicide attacks, and were less likely to report feeling of joy at hearing of a suicide attack (see figure 10.1D). In neither the settler nor the refugee study did partici-pants responding to the "tragic" deals regard these deals as more imple-mentable than participants evaluating taboo or taboo+ deals.

These experiments, as well as recent follow-up studies with Palesti-nian and Israeli leaders (Atran, Axelrod, and Davis 2007), reveal that in political disputes where sources of conflict are cultural, such as the Israeli-Palestinian conflict or emerging clashes between the Muslim and Judeo-Christian world, violent opposition to compromise solutions may be exacerbated rather than decreased by insisting on instrumentally driven trade-offs, while noninstrumental symbolic compromises may reduce sup-port for violence.

Here we have only hinted at this new direction in our research (Tanner and Medin 2004) and its potentially important implications (Atran 2006), especially in regard to the complex and poorly understood relations between consequentialist (utility-oriented) and deontological (moral and sacred) reasoning. But it is worthwhile noting that this research would have never gotten off the ground if not for our rudimentary attempts at eliciting and exploring the behavioral effects of sacred values among the Itza' Maya and Menominee.

Applications and Policy Implications

We believe that theory, methodology and application go hand in hand. For each of the above issues we have raised so far in this summary chap-ter there are one or more implications. In this section we highlight a sub-set of these issues.

Conceptions of Culture

A fair amount of policy research treats ethnicity as categorical and equates ethnicity with culture. And much of this research is important for the allocation of health and educational resources. But the associated baggage of essentializing culture and treating culture as a categorical distinction is extremely costly and fosters misunderstanding. A key policy issue is how to navigate between folk concepts of culture and ethnicity on one side, and the sort of distributed view of culture that we have been advocating on the other side. A significant challenge is to combine an epidemiological view of culture that is sensitive to within and across group variability with the reality of how conceptions of culture and ethnicity affect people's everyday lives. For example, in the United States today, a child of a couple where one parent is black and one white is treated as black.

Education

Our research and the work of others such as Susan Gelman and Larry Hirschfeld show that some biological concepts, such as essentialism, are very easy to think and very hard to set aside. Quite apart from any religious conflicts associated with the concept of evolution, one must discard well-entrenched notions about the nature of species in order to understand evolutionary theory (Hull 1999). In contrast, young children appear to have rudimentary notions about inheritance that might provide an effective foundation for formal instruction on biological inheritance.

Our work has additional educational implications for Native American children in particular and perhaps children of color more generally. It is very easy for majority-culture parents, teachers, and children to think of culture as something that other people (those different from themselves) have. Consequently, they find it natural to think that instruction, including science instruction, is acultural, when in fact much of formal education in the United States (or Canada or France) is infused with practices that represent cultural barriers to minority children. An analogy may convey something of the flavor of what we think often takes place. Imagine tourists from a country where people drive on the right side of the road (e.g., United States) are transported to another culture where people drive on the left (e.g., England). Now let's look at the poor tourists in the role as pedestrians trying to cross the street—all of their attentional habits for looking before crossing will only get in the way. And, in fact, significant numbers of U.S. tourists get into car-pedestrian accidents when

walking in British cities. The analogy is straightforward: the set of practices that Native American children bring to the classroom are ones that
are natural outside of school, but create a clash in the classroom, because
the rules are different there.

As we noted earlier, we are currently analyzing in school and out of
school practices in Native American urban and Native American and
majority rural contexts. Our goal is to test the ideal that as cultural compatibility between in and out of school settings increases, classroom learning will increase.

The Environment and Environmental Decision Making

Policy implications for environmental decision making take various
forms. At the most obvious level, the finding that Q'eqchi' Maya in Petén
engage in quite destructive agro-forestry practices undermines what had
been the assumption of Guatemala's government, various Washington-
based NGOs and the World Bank that all Maya farmers will tend to treat
the environment alike. Our results also reinforce the current trend of
trying to bring all the relevant stakeholders to the table in developing
environmental policy. A few years ago we attended a conference on the
future of Peten, where, contrary to what we had been told would be the
case, local farmer-sylviculturalists (milperos) were not invited. Many of
the speakers represented the national government or NGOs. One of the
speakers argued that the key to the economic development of Petén was
to get the local milperos to plant the abono (or velvet) bean, because of
its rapid growth and nitrogen-fixing properties. Any local milpero could
have told the audience that plots where the abono bean are grown require
constant supervision, which interferes with other activities such as hunting and gathering chicle, and abono plots are also havens for snakes,
many of which are poisonous.

More broadly speaking a significant challenge is how to encourage
populations that no longer see themselves as a sufficiently integral part
of nature to care for it. Almost everyone is an environmentalist, but this
support tends to be a mile wide and an inch deep—when environmental
values are put in conflict with economic values, the latter often win
(Kempton, Boster, and Hartley 1995).

Sacred Values and Intergroup Conflict

There are no obvious solutions to resolving competing claims based on
protected values. Democratic decisions that are based on a voting majority or plurality,[2] or on economic criteria rooted in quantifiable costs

and benefits, will usually not get cultural minorities or ethnic groups to let others exploit territory, resources, symbols or names considered to be holy or integral to their identity. Although sacred values often block conflicting groups from reaching or even considering a negotiated settlement, such values may also provide *opportunities breakthrough and accommodation*. If one side can find unprotected values in the face of the other side's protected values, then even symbolic token concessions of trivial value for one side (the unprotected-values side) may yield huge benefits for both sides.[3] For example, a relatively low-cost gesture from majority-culture fishermen to the Menominee would be to support the installation of fish ladders on the three dams that currently block sturgeon (which the Menominee consider sacred) from migrating up to spawning grounds on the reservation in the spring. This might do wonders for improving inter-community relations.

Border Crossings

Studying how people think about and act on nature is intimately involved with a wide range of fundamental theory and policy concerns: from how minds, societies, and environments build each other, to bettering science education, environmental decision making, and the prospects for resolving resource conflicts. And the lessons may go beyond that to even more general issues of cultural conflict and survival. One consequence of globalization is that many aspects of life centrally involve cross-culture contact, communication, and negotiation. This is true not only across nations but also within them, as we have seen in Petén and in Wisconsin. For research in culture and cognition to be effective in addressing these issues requires a willingness and costly commitment to cross academia's cultural borders and perhaps to break some down.

Notes

Chapter Two

1. There are broadly three different kinds of competing scientific classification schemes for biological organisms: cladistics, phenetics, and classical evolutionary taxonomy. Cladists tend to focus only on those characters that reveal strict branching sequences in phylogeny (Hennig 1966). Pheneticists ideally attempt to base classifications on as many observable characters as possible without prior weighting in terms of their presumed relative importance in evolution (Sneath and Sokal 1973). Evolutionary taxonomists ideally use as many observable characters as possible, but weight them according to their likely evolutionary role in the process of natural selection (Mayr 1969). Because evolutionary taxonomy deals with the joint effects of phylogenetic descent and adaptive radiation, it uses *both* cladistic and phenetic perspectives to reconstruct limited patterns of evolutionary relationships among many morphological, behavioral, and ecological characteristics. For example, from a cladistic (phylogenetic) standpoint crocodiles are closely related to birds but not to turtles, whereas from a phenetic vantage point crocodiles are closer to turtles. From the perspective of evolutionary taxonomy, however, the novel and wide-ranging adaptation of birds to life in the air renders them a class apart (Aves) from both the crocodiles and turtles (Reptilia). Field naturalists, behavioral ecologists, and biogeographers tend to prefer evolutionary taxonomies for mapping natural diversity, whereas most recent comparative work in biogenesis, microbiology, and genetics uses cladistic analysis as a more reliable basis for making historical and causal inferences (but see the discussion below of Labandeira and Sepkoski 1993 for some surprising discoveries in paleobiology via evolutionary taxonomy). There are no absolute ranks in cladistic classifications, unlike in evolutionary taxonomies (e.g., species, genus, family, order, class, and so on), and one could argue that continued preference for ranking in evolutionary taxonomy owes to a lingering commonsense (folkbiological) bias that "artificially" boosts the correlation between evolutionary and folkbiological taxa.

2. Botanists and ethnobotanists see privileged folkbiological groups as more akin to scientific genera (Bartlett 1940; Berlin 1972; Greene 1983). Plant genera especially are often readily recognized morphologically without technical aids

(Linnaeus 1751). Zoologists and ethnozoologists tend to view them as more like scientific species, where reproductive and geographic isolation are more readily identified in terms of behavior (Simpson 1961; Diamond 1966; Bulmer 1970).

3. English speakers ambiguously use *animal* to refer to at least three distinct classes of living things: nonhuman animals, animals including humans, and mammals (prototypical animals). *Beast* seems to pick out nonhuman animals in English, but is seldom used today. *Plant* is ambiguously used to refer to the plant kingdom, or to members of that kingdom that are not trees.

4. Only animals and plants are always exclusively individuated in terms of their unique generic-species essence, whereas humans are variously individuated as both individual agents and as social actors in accordance with inferred intentions rather than expected clusters of body parts. Itza', like folk everywhere, always identify an individual animal or plant, first and foremost, as a member of the generic species that presumably causes that individual to be. But Itza', like most people in the world, individuate humans, or *winik*, without exclusive recourse to a single superordinate level of superordinate existence, such as the level of species. Depending on context, a person may be Itza' or Yukatek, Maya or Ladino, man or woman, mother or godmother, neighbor or stranger, hunter and/or farmer, or some combination that presumably determines that person's intentional self.

5. Life forms vary across culture. Ancient Hebrew or modern Rangi (Tanzania) include herpetofauna (reptiles and amphibians) with insects, worms, and other "creeping crawlers" (Kesby 1979), whereas Itza' Maya and (until recently) most Western cultures include herpetofauna with mammals as "quadrupeds." Itza' place phenomenally isolated mammals like the bat with birds, just as Rofaifo (New Guinea) place phenomenally isolated birds like cassowaries with mammals (Dwyer 1976). Whatever the content of life-form *taxa*, the life-form level, or *rank*, universally partitions the living world into broadly equivalent divisions.

6. According to Brown (1982, 102), Itza' see mammals as part of an unnamed "residual category" that includes invertebrates except for worms. For Mayan languages generally, he claims MAMMAL is a residual life form encompassing creatures left over after encoding BIRD, FISH, and SNAKE. The evidence for the former claim comes from Otto Schumann's (1971) superficial dictionary and the unpublished notes of Pierre Ventur (Brown 1979, 382). Evidence for the latter claim comes secondhand, via dictionaries. Overall, our experiments show that patterns of induction among mammals are the same as those for BIRD, FISH, TREE, or VINE (see chapter 4). In sorting tasks, mammals are always isolated from the other animals as an exclusive group, with two exceptions: the bat (*sotz'*) is always classified with the birds, and the otter (*pek'-il ja'*) is always classified with other mammals but occasionally cross-classified with some water-dwelling reptiles (crocodiles and turtles, but not water snakes). Brown also relies on linguistic evidence to claim that *kan* (snakes) is an Itza' life form. But sorting and inference tasks (Atran 1999a) clearly indicate that snakes and lizards (*uy-et'∼ok juj*) are taxonomically closer to one another than either of these intermediates is to other intermediates of the herpetofauna life form (*b'a'al∼che'+k-u-jil-t-ik-u-b'aj*), such as turtles (*aak*) or amphibians (*b'a'al∼che'+k-u-siit'*).

7. Mammals and herpetofauna also appear to be embedded under the mutually exclusive category QUADRUPED (i.e., *b'a'al~che'* sense 2), which can be explicitly rendered as *a'-b'a'al~che' yan uy-ok* ("animals having feet") or *kän-p'eel uy-ok* ("four-footed"). More often, *kän-p'eel uy-ok* refers exclusively to the herpetofauna, much as the old Yukatek terms *xaknal* or *xakatnal* might be translated as *quadrúpedo* but refer only to herps (Beltrán [1742] 1859, 228). Snakes are thought to have "hidden" feet that "only the dumb can see" (*chen ch'uch' k-u-cha'an-t-ik uy-ok kan*).

8. In the logical structure of folktaxonomy, outliers may be considered monotypic life forms with only one generic species (for a formalism, see the appendix in Atran 1995).

Chapter Three

1. There are a few simplifying assumptions associated with the use of the CCM as a data model. One is that the sorting method produces interval data and that the "answer key" consists of the simple mean (rather than a weighted mean based on competence scores). The other is that individual response characteristics (e.g., response bias) do not contribute to the correlation between two individuals (Batchelder, personal communication, January 2004; Romney 1998; see also Batchelder and Romney 1988). Using hierarchical sorting rather than simple sorting reduces the potential contribution of response bias, and in other applications we employ a correction for guessing (Atran et al. 1999; Medin et al. 2005).

2. Boster's (1986a) method of determining residual agreement motivated our initial interest in this method; however, this method is potentially flawed if the assumption of item homogeneity is violated. In that event overall agreement and residual agreement may be spuriously correlated. Accordingly, we use within-versus between-group residual agreement as our measure.

Chapter Four

1. This excludes—perhaps artificially—"lower-order" cognitions related to sex, kinship, and violence.

2. Phylogenetic comparisons of humans with other primates show some evidence for rudimentary biological conceptualization of species differences.

3. For Fodor (2000), the primary criterion for modularity is "encapsulation"—that is, exclusive access to a proprietary input. Encapsulation is supposedly true only of perceptual modules, such as language or facial recognition. In ordinary circumstances, internal principles of grammar, phonetic rules, and lexical structures provide a database for rapidly processing linguistic input with little or no influence from other cognitive systems. Similarly, folkbiological taxonomy may provide a privileged database for nearly "automatic" recognition of plant and animal exemplars in terms of the (folk) species to which they uniquely belong. Of course, almost by definition any conceptual system has some functional autonomy

and is therefore "encapsulated." Virtually any game (e.g., chess) or routine activity (e.g., car driving) relies on a restricted database that gives it privileged access to a certain range of input. This would seem to trivialize the notion of modularity and rob it of any descriptive or explanatory force.

Indeed, according to Fodor (2000, 23), the best case that can be made for the computational theory of mind (i.e., the view that all conceptual processes are Turing-like computations over syntactic-like representational structures) is in terms of conceptual modularity. However, because conceptual modularity "is pretty clearly mistaken," the claim is also likely to be mistaken that the computational theory of mind has very much to tell us about how the mind configures the world. For Sperber (2001), Fodor's pessimism is unwarranted because it ignores the fact that privileged access to an input set *depends on the competition for mental resources.* Evolutionary task demands generally favor certain naturally selected modular structures for processing certain types of naturally recurrent and statistically relevant input (all other things being equal). In principle, then, an explanatory account of modularity in terms of evolutionary task demands and related developmental considerations of modularity is preferable to a purely descriptive account in terms of "encapsulation," "mandatoriness," and the like.

4. At the time this study was conducted we thought that we were observing central-tendency-based typicality effects, but we realized later that typicality in this sense was confounded with typicality based on ideals. Subsequent studies (to be described shortly) suggest that idealness is the key factor.

5. Barsalou (1985) argued that idealness rather than central tendency predicts typicality in goal-derived categories (e.g., foods not to eat on a diet, things to take from one's home during a fire, camping equipment), although central tendency still supposedly predicts typicality in "taxonomic" categories (furniture, vehicles), including folkbiological categories (birds).

6. $F(1, 63) = 7.32$, $Mse = 3.5$, $p < .01$.

7. $F(5, 315) = 3.14$, $Mse = 0.88$, $p < .01$.

8. Means 6.8 and 6.1, $t(63) = 4.33$, $p < .01$.

9. Means 6.2 and 5.1, $t(64) = 3.06$, $p < .01$.

10. Means 2.9 and 2.2, $t(64) = 2.23$, $p < .05$.

11. The two-way interaction of level of expertise by taxonomic level was significant, $F(3, 183) = 2.78$, $Mse = 1.92$, $p < .05$.

12. Paul Griffiths (2002) argues that because the items on any such symptomatic list do not necessarily co-occur in any given case, and cannot unequivocally demonstrate innateness, then notions of innateness are inherently confused and should be discarded. The same could be said against modularity. But the list represents only an evidential claim, not a causal claim about innateness or modularity. It provides a family of heuristics rather than a causal diagnosis.

13. Although the adaptive relationship of structure to function is often manifest, as with the giraffe's neck or the rhinoceros's horns, often it is not. In such cases, evolutionary theorists adopt a strategy of "reverse engineering." Reverse engineering is what military analysts do when a weapon from an enemy or competitor

in the arms market falls into their hands and they try to figure out exactly how it was put together and what it can do. Reverse engineering is easiest, of course, if the structure contains some signature of its function, like trying to figure out what a toaster does given the telltale sign of toasted bread crumbs left inside. But in many cases recognizing the appropriate signs already requires some prior notion of what function the structure may have served. Thus, after a century and a half of debate, it is only now that scientists clearly favor the hypothesis that bipedality was primarily selected to enhance field of view. Comparative studies of humans with bipedal birds and dinosaurs, as well as experiments comparing energy expenditure and running speed in two-footed versus four-footed running and walking, appear to exclude the competing hypotheses that bipedality evolved for running or energy conservation. Paleontologists still do not know why triceratops had neck frills and stegosaurs had back plates (defense, thermal regulation, sexual or species signaling, and so on), except that lugging around all that cumbersome baggage for millions of years must have had some adaptive function(s). For most higher-order human cognitive faculties, however, there may be little useful comparative evidence from elsewhere in the animal kingdom. This is because of their apparent structural novelty, poor representation in the fossil record (e.g., stone tools tell little of language or theory of mind), and lack of surviving intermediate forms. The moral is that reverse engineering can be helpful, and occasionally successful, but success is by no means guaranteed even in the richest of evidentiary contexts.

Chapter Five

1. Still other characteristics may be explained in terms of individual, random variation; however, our use of paired category-typical characteristics minimizes this eventuality.

2. In another study, however, Gelman and Wellman (1991) asked children to reason about plants without identifying the species membership. For example, they described a seed that came from an apple and was planted in a field of corn, without identifying the seed as an "apple seed." The results were largely the same as with the animals and supported a nature-over-nurture bias (see Hickling and Gelman 1995; Gelman 2003).

3. For example, in Brazil, several of the 6- to 7-year-old children based their responding on an explicit analogy with the Disney movie, *Tarzan*, which was widely shown at the time of the study. They evinced a significant but weaker birth bias than 4- to 5-year-olds, consistent with *Tarzan*'s mixed human/ape behavioral characteristics.

Chapter Six

1. Functionalism, which is alive and well in biology, should not be confused with functionalism in anthropology, which has been in decline for at least half a century. Functionalism in anthropology, a dying metaphor, was initially derived

from nineteenth-century biological functionalism, which has since developed into an insightful and instrumental research strategy. One immediate drawback to functionalism in the study of human societies is that it takes no account of intention and other critical aspects of human cognition. In biology, disregard of intention led to a breakthrough in understanding. In anthropology, it led to an ossified form of naive realism that took (often ethnocentric) summary descriptions of exotic and colonized societies for the way things truly were (or were supposed to be). To a significant extent, the present-day focus of much of anthropology—in cultural studies and postmodernism—is a reaction to functionalism's procrustean view of society. Unfortunately, rather than seeking a new scientific approach that would renew dialogue with the other sciences, the dominant trend in contemporary anthropology has been to forsake all attempt at scientific generalization and to dwell on the incommensurability and irreducible diversity of different cultural representations and behaviors.

2. Sober and Wilson cite numerous examples from a worldwide ethnographic survey, *The Human Relations Area Files (HRAF)*, first compiled by anthropologist George Murdock (1949) over half a century ago, in order to "demonstrate" that human cultures are functionally built and maintained as superorganisms (see Wilson 2002). But analyses based on the HRAF that purportedly demonstrate the functionalism of "group-level traits," or "norms," and group selection face problems of circularity because the entries to the HRAF were chosen and structured so as to meet Murdock's selection criteria for being properly "scientific"—that is, functionally discrete parts of an "adaptive" social structure, existing independently of individuals but patterning their behaviors in lawful ways.

3. A countercurrent to structuralism developed in anthropology, known as "cultural materialism" and spearheaded by Marvin Harris. The emphasis is supposed to be on "objective, etic" units of behavior and material patternings of practices, artifacts, population settlements, and so forth, rather than on "subjective, emic" notions of meaning and thought (by analogy with phonetic versus phonemic analysis in linguistics). A mixture of Marxism and functionalism, cultural materialism relies on what is (at least to us) a wholly mysterious notion of "cause" that somehow produces ideas from behaviors. For example, according to Harris, the Aztec religious practice of large-scale human sacrifice stems from the fact that Mesoamerica has relatively few large mammals; hence, apart from the other humans they eat, people in the region have few substantial sources of protein (Harris 1974).

This sort of analysis resonates with many of the assumptions of sociobiology. According to biologist Edward O. Wilson (1978, 98), "Some of the most baffling of religious practices in history might have an ancestry passing in a straight line back to the ancient carnivorous practices of humankind." Such accounts often invoke ordinary material causes (genetic adaptations for carnivorous behavior) to explain ordinary material effects (cannibalism). Nevertheless, they fail to provide a hint of how the putative distal causes (genetic) enter into known material relationships with more proximate causes (mental and public representations) to actually produce the forms of behavior to be explained (religious beliefs, practices and artifacts causally connected within and between human minds and bodies). Such accounts hand-wave away the "superstructure" or "ideology" of cultural forms as "nonmaterial" or "epiphenomenal" "by-products" of underlying material causes (ecological, economic, or genetic) (see Atran 2002, chap. 8). We hold that ideas are just as material as behaviors and indispensably constitutive of the causal chains that produce cultural regularities.

4. In 1974, Atran interviewed Lévi-Strauss and asked him why he believed binary operators to be one of the fundamental structures of the human mind. He replied: "When I started there was still no science of mind. Saussure, Marx, Mauss, and music were my guides. Since then things have changed. Psychology now has something to say."

5. In all fairness, Pinker (2002, 65) explicitly calls for treating cultural phenomena in terms of an "epidemiology of mental representations" in the sense of Sperber (see below), and is well aware of the diverse and partial character of distributions of mental representations among individuals in a population. This makes his analogy of I-grammar with I-culture all the more puzzling.

6. There is much mystery and obfuscation surrounding the notion of "emergent" structures and processes. One thing emergence is *not* (at least from an agent-based modeling perspective) is an ontological trait over and above the constituent individual decisions and actions that give rise to it. The aim of agent-based modeling is, precisely, to identify the microprocesses that are necessary and sufficient to *deductively* generate the macrostructures (Axelrod 1997a). Nevertheless, actual modeling may (and often does) fall short of this goal because no explanation, in terms of microprocesses, may be fully *available at present*. In this sense (of not yet reducible in practice but expectedly reducible in principle), mental structures may be considered "emergent" from networks of neuronal activity (Hempel and Oppenheim 1948), or the laws of biology "emergent" from physics (cf. Nagel 1961). In addition, even where a reduction is in principle possible, it may be more efficient and effective to perform analyses at higher levels, just as it is more efficient and effective to analyze a computer program at an algorithmic level than at a machine level (or at the level of the physics that implements machine-level codes).

7. The notion of "cultural epidemiology" has two distinct traditions: one focused on the relatively high-fidelity "reproduction" and patterning of cultural (including psychological) traits within and across human populations, and one focused on the ways cognitive structures "generate" and chain together ideas, artifacts, and behaviors within and across human populations. Jacques Monod (1971), the Nobel-Prize-winning biologist, was the first to use the concept of "culture as contagion"—although more as metaphor than theory. Cavalli-Sforza and Feldman (1981) were pioneers in working out a theory in which culture is conceptualized as distributed through a population; however, no microscale cognitive processes or structures were modeled or considered, only macroscale social psychological traits.

Two more fully developed epidemiological approaches soon emerged. Boyd and Richerson (1985) were able to show how biases in transmission, such as prestige or conformism, could help to explain the spread and stabilization of macrosocial psychological traits among populations. Sperber (1985) provided the first theoretical blueprint for how individual-level microcognitive structures (as opposed to invocation of imitation or other cultural reproduction processes) could account for cultural transmission and stabilization. Until now, there has been little fruitful interaction between these two traditions (see Laland and Brown 2002; Mesoudi et al. 2007; but also Henrich and Boyd 2002). We think that these two "epidemiological" traditions are compatible, and our empirical example suggests that they can be mutually informative (see chapter 8).

Chapter Seven

1. There is evidence for Q'eqchi' migration in baptism and marriage registers beginning in 1718 for the Petén towns of Santo Toribio, Dolores, and San Luis (Archivo Apostólica, Flores, Petén).

2. Rent does not vary as a function of the productivity of the land and is not based on a share of the product.

3. At the height of the growing season, July rainfall in Flores (site of the pre-Columbian Itza' capital) went from 121 mm in 1993 to 335 mm in 1996, and in nearby Tikal from 58 to 137 mm; in May, when crops are planted, there was no rainfall in Tikal in 1993 for 23 days, then 130 mm in 3 days, and so on (Guatemala Government Institute of Meteorology, INSIVUMEH 1998).

4. At the Temple of Inscriptions at Palenque in Tabasco, Mexico, one of the four scenes on pillars clearly shows *Itz-am~na'* as a world frame. Note the possible association between *na'* = mother and *naj* = house.

5. F. Comparato comments in his notes to Avendaño y Loyola (p. 40, n. 134): "Ursúa's assault on Tayasal occurred on 13 March 1697, exactly 137 days before the final appearance of the fateful 12.4.0.0.0.8 Ahau. Apparently the prophecy had done its work after all: despite their strength in numbers, reckoned to be 50 to 1, the Itza's quickly fled or surrendered after a few hours of battle."

6. The earliest baptism records, dated 1709, come from the mixed Itza'-Mopan reduction of Santo Toribio, south of Lake Petén Itza' on the way to Mopan (present-day San Luis). For example, those baptized in the earliest years of the Santo Toribio reduction include Ah Ix Zac, Ah Lam Tesucun, Ah Ik Ch'akan, Yx Kan Cischan, Yx Chac Chan, Ah Kuk Kin, Ah Cauil Pana, Ah Coat Canek, Yx Chili' Covoh, Ah Muluc Chamay, Yx Chuen Chem, Yx Manic Camal, Ah Akbal Chicuy, Yx Lamat Saquan, (indecipherable) Tzuntecun, (indecipherable) Tut. The most common Mopan patronyms in the records are Musul and Yahcab. The Musul appear to have been drawn in from the area around Tipu'. The Yahcab were concentrated around Mopan.

7. Hofling (1996, 111–112) declares that "the small Mayan-speaking populations in the Petén have received scholarly attention all out of proportion to their numbers," reflecting in part "exaggerated claims about the uniqueness of Itza' knowledge of the forest environment." This opinion is based on no presentation of data or replicable analysis.

8. Median family income, however, was lower for Q'eqchi' (US$730) than for Ladinos (US$1330) or Itza' (US$1460). In part, this may reflect less dependence

on public works projects for supplementary wages and greater reliance on sales of surplus maize.

9. $F(2, 41) = 12.92, p < .001$.

10. $F(2, 41) = 25.04$, $p < .0001$, $D(I) = .753$, $D(L) = 1.39$, $D(Q) = 3.92$. Our equation oversimplifies the consequences of different patterns of use, which involve a trade-off between costs of farming a plot longer versus benefits of fallowing longer. In theory, the costs and benefits could be quantified to assess sustainability, but we have already seen that these groups farm differently. One potential limitation of our formula is that a shorter growing period for Q'eqchi' could leave the land in better shape for recovery. But soil tests (reported below) reveal that nitrogen, a limiting factor in these calcified soils, is much more abundant in Itza' fallow land (guamil) than Q'eqchi' fallow.

11. We normalized highly variable distributions of raw scores with a natural log transformation.

12. $F(2, 27) = 3.339, p < .05$.

13. An ANOVA was performed on a composite of standardized scores for basic nutrient elements: $P + (K + Mg - Ca)$. Calcium is antagonistic to fixing of potassium and magnesium, so the composite represents a balance of the available nutrient elements: phosphorus for root growth, potassium for stem strength, magnesium for photosynthesis, calcium for cell formation. Results paralleled those of phosphorus for Location ($F(2, 162) = 15.15$, $p < .0001$; $M > G, R$), Level ($F(1, 162) = 34.10$, $p < .0001$; $1 > 2$), and Group × Location ($F(4, 162) = 4.02$, $p = .004$; M: I(marginally) $> Q$; R: $L > I$).

14. As more immigrants have moved into the municipality of San José, milpa use has shifted toward privatization. New immigrants are no longer automatically granted use rights to 30 manzanas of land and all farmers retain their current rights. In principle, farmers could benefit from personal investments aimed at preserving sustainability in their own plot. But whether 30 manzanas suffices for sustainability is not independent of the status of the surrounding land and the forest practices of one's neighbors. The same plot that would be self-sustaining when surrounded by healthy forest would not survive if surrounded by depleted land (Schwartz 1995).

15. Plant vouchers were deposited at the University of Michigan Herbarium. Vouchers numbers and photographs of plants appear in Atran, Lois, and Ucan Ek' 2004.

16. $F(2, 33) = 23.10, p < .001$.

17. For each group, $F(2, 22) > 23, p < .001$.

18. $F(9, 99) = 26.04, p < .0001$.

19. Participants were given two scores for each pairing of animal and plant groups, reflecting the proportion of positive and negative interactions acknowledged. A score of .25 for negative arboreal-fruit interactions indicates that the participant identified negative interactions between one-quarter of all possible pairings of arboreal animals and fruiting plants. Scores were entered into 2 (type of interaction: positive, negative) × 4 (animal group: bird, rummage, arboreal,

predator) $\times 4$ (plant: fruit, grass/herb, palm, other) analyses of variance. Thus, tests of plants by animals had 9,99 degrees of freedom. Ladinos showed main effects of interaction type ($F[1,11] = 6.95$, $p < .05$), plant ($F[3,33] = 9.89$, $p < .0001$), and animal ($F[3,33] = 14.40$, $p < .0001$) but not plant-by-animal interaction.

20. For Itza′, $r = .62$, $p < .01$; for Ladinos, $r = .57$, $p < .01$.

21. Ratio eigenvalue 1:2 $= 3.3$, variance $= 45\%$.

22. $F(1,112) = 98.38$, $p < .001$.

23. Itza′ gave 577 positive and 14 negative responses, ranging from 41 to 57 reponses per informant (modal response of 2 uses per plant). Ladinos gave 562 positive and 2 negative responses, with 40 to 58 per informant (modal response of 2). Q′eqchi′ gave 307 positive and 2 negative responses), ranging from 21 to 35 per informant (modal response of 1). Plants not given uses by at least a third of the Q′eqchi′ were grasses, the pukte tree, and the strangler fig.

24. Because of the relatively small number of both items and participants, we were not able to detect a direct link between ecological centrality and plants encountered in sample plots. Still, this seems to be a logical consequence from our data.

25. Given the Itza′ history of sustainable agroforestry, one could suggest that researchers should focus on the historical success of the behavioral correlates of this apparently functional activity (and ignore the "proximate" cognitive mechanisms involved in the generation, interpretation, and transmission of these practices). We do not wish to rehearse the behaviorism-cognitivism debate here. We claim that insight into cognitive mechanisms is crucial for understanding the historical production, transmission, and stabilization of these practices and for generalizing these findings to other contexts and cultural settings.

26. There is nothing in principle to prevent rational-choice theory from assigning extensional values to relational entities (e.g., people may be willing to choose to save their pet over a favorite tree, their child over their pet, their nation over their children). Do sacred values form a special class of "protected values" that are internally negotiable but off limits to more mundane, monetary exchanges? It is not clear how current approaches could model such choices, except as ad hoc "externalized contingencies" or as "pseudo-sacred" values (posturing).

27. $Z = 3.207$, $p = .001$.

28. $Z = 3.000$, $p = .003$.

29. Only additional evidence could show whether children "continue" to think of God in the same way after they become aware of false beliefs (as Barrett et al. 2001 intimate), or (as seems more likely) come to have different reasons for thinking that God would not be deceived.

30. As researchers have noted (Baron and Spranca 1997; Tetlock 2003), although people with sacred values sometimes seem to treat them as having infinite utility (e.g., in refusing to consider trade-offs), this is something of a logical impossibility inasmuch as infinite value implies that people with such values should spend liter-

ally all their time and effort protecting and promoting that value. Moreover, infinite utility is incompatible with any sort of "preference schedule": expected utilities are weighted averages, which makes little sense when one of the terms is infinite. Thus, some have suggested these values are only pseudo-sacred (Baron and Leshner 2000; Thompson and Gonzalez 1997); others have noted that people with sacred values may nonetheless engage in indirect trade-offs (McGraw and Tetlock 2005; Tetlock 2000b). One may be tempted to think of sacred values as self-serving "posturing," but the reality of acts such as suicide bombings undermines this stance (Atran 2003a). Moreover, sacred values necessary to an individual's identity may take on truly absolute value only when value-related identity seems gravely threatened, just as food may take on absolute value only when sustenance for life is threatened. A deeper point is that notions of maximization of anticipated benefits perhaps cannot best account for such "spiritually driven" behaviors, and ad hoc moves to maintain standard (probabilities and utilities) rationality at all costs result in a concept of rationality doing little explanatory work.

31. In April 2001, we presented our findings on folkecology directly to the Q'eqchi', Ladino, and Itza' communities. The Itza' and Ladino experts in our studies acknowledged the plausibility of the analysis showing the latter's knowledge to be a proper subset of the former's. Q'eqchi' leaders also confirmed the general reliability of our results and analyses.

Q'eqchi' representatives asked for help from Itza' on two counts. First, in light of our findings that smaller fires allow Itza' to maximize natural fertilizers, including both phosphorus and nitrates in upper-level soils, the Q'eqchi' asked for instruction on Itza' burning techniques. Second, following presentations by Itza' women on the advantages of biodiversity for maintaining a living pharmacopoeia, Q'eqchi' women asked Itza' for instruction on which plants to preserve for medicinal uses. The meeting began and ended with Itza' and Q'eqchi' prayers.

Q'eqchi' did not express interest in conservation as such, but were eager to produce more crops with less land while maintaining a richer stock of medicinally useful plants. They asked that other meetings be organized on similar lines, that contacts between the communities be more regular, and that specimens or photographs and descriptions of Itza' medicinal plants be made available.

32. A further observation is that the Itza' consider the ecologically central ramón tree to be always worthy of protection and unlike the other two groups would never use ramón as firewood. Although research in the psychology of decision making sometimes views sacred or protected values as a hindrance to proper decision making and a source of cognitive biases (e.g., Baron and Spranca 1997), there is other evidence suggesting that protected values may be associated with the absence of framing effects and related biases (Fetherstonhaugh et al. 1997; Friedrich et al. 1999; Tanner and Medin 2004).

Chapter Eight

1. To ensure maximum social coverage from our sample, initial informants could not be immediate blood relatives (children, grandchildren, parents, grandparents,

siblings, first cousins, nieces, nephews, uncles, aunts), affines (spouse, in-law), or godparents (*compadres*).

2. The greatest overlap in the two networks occurs among Itza′ and the least among Q′eqchi′. For Itza′, fourteen of the most cited social partners are among the twenty-two most cited forest experts. Although the Itza′ social network is not highly centralized, the most cited social partner is also the second most cited forest expert, whereas the top forest expert is also the third most cited social partner. For Ladinos, eleven of the most cited social partners are among the twenty-five most cited forest experts. Of these eleven, all are Ladino men. Ladino women tend to mention Ladino men as experts; however, the top Ladino experts most often cite the same Itza′ experts as the Itza′ themselves do, suggesting diffusion of information from Itza′ experts to a select group of socially well-connected Ladino men. For Q′eqchi′, who have by far the most densely connected and centralized social networks, only six of the most cited social partners are among the eighteen most cited forest experts (these are cited much less often as experts than outside institutions are).

3. Note that I is not directly connected to D1 (who belongs to the Itza′ faction opposed to Itza′-Y and to which I is allied).

4. For Ladinos, three of the four most cited Itza′ experts are also the three named most by Itza′. We combined Itza′ and Ladino responses about plant-animal relations and found a metacultural consensus (first factor scores all positive, ratio eigenvalue 1:2 = 10.4, variance accounted for = 52%). Then we regressed gender and frequency of being cited as an expert against Ladino first factor scores in the combined consensus model. The r-square on Ladino scores was .63 ($F(2, 10) = 6.97$, $p = .02$) with gender ($p = .02$) and expertise ($p = .008$) reliable. One subgroup of men (with one woman) averaged 5.8 expert citations, 6.0 social network citations, and an average culture competence (i.e., mean of first factor scores) of .73 (versus .75 for Itza′). Averages for the other subgroup (with one man) were respectively 0, 1.3, and .59.

5. We have independent evidence that people in these communities form and use taxonomic hierarchies that correspond fairly well with classical scientific taxonomy (and especially so at the generic-species level). For example, using standard sorting experiments (see Medin and Atran 2004), we elicited highly consensual mammal taxonomies (see López et al. 1997). For each population there was a single factor solution (I = 7.2:1, 61%; L = 5.9:1, 50%; Q = 5.8:1, 48%). First factor loadings were uniformly positive, and mean first factor scores reflected highly shared competence for each population (I = 77, L = .71, Q = .68). The aggregated Ladino taxonomy correlated equally with Itza′ and Q′eqchi′ taxonomies ($r = .85$), indicating very similar structures and contents. All three populations grouped taxa according to general-purpose similarity rather than special-purpose concerns (e.g., wild peccary with domestic pig, house cat with margay, and so on). Special-purpose clusters, such as domestic versus wild, or edible versus nonedible, can also be elicited (Lois 1998). But they do not belong to the general consensus of "kinds that go together by nature" (see the idiosyncratic version of "Itza′ folk taxonomy" in Hofling and Tesucun 1997).

6. One possibility is that these data may simply indicate a social learning system in which women are influenced by women and men by men. To evaluate this idea we conducted a residual analysis of the Ladino plant-animal relationships to see if residual agreement was higher among men and among women than across genders. It was not. Instead, we found that women agreed with women reliably more than men agreed with men [$F(1, 10) = 9.64$, $Mse = 3.16$, $p = .01$]. We think this result reflects the stability of inference processes at the family and genus level on the part of women, relative to the diversity of concrete experience among Ladino men.

7. One might interpret this cultural bias toward reciprocity as a shared abstract expectation, but it requires additional supportive observations.

Chapter Nine

1. Ratio of first eigenvalue = 7.6 to 1, 57% of variance accounted for, average first factor score = .75.

2. Ratio of first to second eigenvalue = 4.2:1, 30% of variance accounted for, average first factor score = .52.

3. Ratio of first to second factor eigenvalue: 7.2; first factor explains 63% of the variance, all first factor scores positive and high, average: 0.76.

4. Expressed in significant differences with respect to the second factor loadings, $F = 22.9$; $Mse = 1.2$; $p = 0.000$.

5. $F = 21.6$; $Mse = 164$; $p = 0.000$.

6. $F = 8.2$; $Mse = 86$; $p = 0.007$.

7. $F = 11.8$; $Mse = 26$; $p = 0.002$.

8. $F = 3.6$; $Mse = 7.5$; $p = 0.06$.

9. Ratio of first to second eigenvalue = 2.6, first factor = 44% of variance, mean first factor = .63.

10. Eigenvalue = 9.3 to 1, 66% of variance accounted for by the first factor, and average first factor score = .80.

Chapter Ten

1. There is also more recent research suggesting that moral values may be associated with less rather than more bias. Connolly and Reb (2003) criticized the paradigm used to assess omission bias and under their improved procedure, omission bias all but disappeared. Earlier we mentioned the Tanner and Medin (2004) findings that protected values led to, if anything, an act bias. In addition, they found that protected values eliminated framing effects (i.e., the shift in choices when the same objective situation is described in terms of gains versus losses—negative framing leads to more risk seeking, i.e., "loss aversion"). Dan Bartels in our laboratory has also found that protected values are associated with the reduction

in another decision bias known as proportion dominance. (Bartels also tested Menominee tribal office workers on environmental decision-making scenarios like those used by Baron and Ritov (1994) and failed to find any relation between protected values and omission bias. Thus the generality of results from studies with undergraduates may again need to be called into question.) Finally, when we used the Connolly and Reb (2003) procedure, we found that protected values led to less omission bias (Bartels and Medin 2007).

More recent work by Bloomfield (2006) shows that standard framing effects for scenarios involving human lives are almost completely eliminated when pictures of the potential victims accompany the scenarios. Although technically this may not be an instance of sacred values, her study does make the point that laboratory studies with abstract scenarios may not generalize to vivid real-world contexts where much decision making takes place.

2. In discussing the issue of Indians used as mascots for sport teams, Billy Mills (a Cheyenne former Olympic star) offered the following analogy: if you gave a dinner party and had ten guests you probably would not consider the party a success if seven of the guests were pleased but the three others were deeply offended.

3. Here is one example that involves values that, though perhaps not quite sacred, played on nonutilitarian symbolic worth. In the 1970s, communist China and capitalist America were at a standoff. A group at the University of Michigan suggested that the U.S. State Department send Ping-Pong teams to China (Eckstein 1993). Ping-Pong was virtually China's national sport, but meant next to nothing to Americans (a basement game). So, when the Chinese repeatedly defeated the Americans in Ping-Pong it meant a great deal, symbolically, thus facilitating a strategic breakthrough in communication and mutual understanding. (Note that attempts at "cricket diplomacy" between Pakistan and India may have failed, in part, because cricket means too much to *both* sides.) Contrast this with the efforts of Japan to conciliate China in 2005, which were destroyed by the Japanese prime minister's symbolic attendance at a World War II shrine. Also, much of the back-and-forth between the American colonies and Britain in the lead-up to the revolutionary war concerned the validity of a tax that Britain deliberately set at a low level to make the symbolic point that it had the right to tax the colonies as it chose.

References

Adanson, M. 1763. *Familles des plantes*. 2 vols. Paris: Vincent.

AHG–APESA. 1992. *Plan de desarollo integrado de Péten: Inventario forestal del Departamento del Péten* (Convenio Gobiernos Alemania–Guatemala). Santa Elena, Péten: Agrar- und Hydrotechnik Gmbh. and Asesoría y Promoción Económica.

Ahn, W.-K., C. Kalish, S. Gelman, D. Medin, C. Luhmann, S. Atran, J. Coley, and P. Shafto. 2001. Why essences are essential in the psychology of concepts. *Cognition* 82:59–69.

Alexander, R. 1987. *The Biology of Moral Systems*. New York: Aldine de Gruyter.

Allen, N. J., and F. E. Crawley. 1998. Voices from the bridge: Worldview conflicts of Kickapoo students of science. *Journal of Research in Science Teaching* 35:111–132.

Anggoro, F., S. Waxman, and D. Medin. 2005. The effects of naming practices on children's understanding of living things. In B. Bara, L. Barsalou, and M. Bucciarelli, eds., *Proceedings of the Twenty-seventh Annual Meeting of the Cognitive Science Society*, 139–144. Mahwah, NJ: Lawrence Erlbaum Associates.

Arnold, J., J. Eisenband, S. Brown-Schmidt, and J. Trueswell. 2000. The rapid use of gender information: Evidence of the time course of pronoun resolution from eyetracking. *Cognition* 76:B13–B26.

Astuti, R. 1995. "The Vezo are not a kind of people": Identity, difference, and "ethnicity" among a fishing people of western Madagascar. *American Ethnologist* 22:464–482.

Astuti, R. 2002. A cognitive and anthropological study of animal and human categorization among the Vezo of Madagascar. Paper presented to the Department of Anthropology Colloquium Series, University of Toronto, February 14.

Astuti, R., G. Solomon, and S. Carey. 2005. Constraints on conceptual development. *Monographs of the Society for Research in Child Development* 69:vii–135.

Atran, S. 1983. Covert fragmenta and the origins of the botanical family. *Man* 18:51–71.

Atran, S. 1985. The nature of folk-botanical life forms. *American Anthropologist* 87:298–315.

Atran, S. 1986. *Hamula* [patrician] organisation and *masha'a* [commons] tenure in Palestine. *Man* 21:271–295.

Atran, S. 1987. Ordinary constraints on the semantics of living kinds. *Mind and Language* 2:27–63.

Atran, S. 1990. *Cognitive Foundations of Natural History*. Cambridge: Cambridge University Press.

Atran, S. 1993. Itza' Maya tropical agro-forestry. *Current Anthropology* 34:633–700.

Atran, S. 1994. Core domains versus scientific theories: Evidence from systematics and Itza'-Maya folkbiology. In L. Hirschfeld and S. Gelman, eds., *Mapping the Mind: Domain Specificity in Cognition and Culture*. New York: Cambridge University Press.

Atran, S. 1995. Classifying nature across cultures. In E. Smith and D. Osherson, eds., *An Invitation to Cognitive Science*, Vol. 3, *Thinking*. Cambridge, Mass.: MIT Press.

Atran, S. 1998. Folkbiology and the anthropology of science: Cognitive universals and cultural particulars. *Behavioral and Brain Sciences* 21:547–609.

Atran, S. 1999a. Itzaj Maya folk-biological taxonomy. In D. Medin and S. Atran, eds., *Folkbiology*. Cambridge, Mass.: MIT Press.

Atran, S. 1999b. The universal primacy of generic species in folkbiology: Implications for biological, cultural, and scientific evolution. In R. Wilson, ed., *Species: New Interdisciplinary Essays*. Cambridge, Mass.: MIT Press.

Atran, S. 2001a. The case for modularity: Sin or salvation? *Evolution and Cognition* 7:46–55.

Atran, S. 2001b. The trouble with memes: Inference versus imitation in cultural creation. *Human Nature* 12:351–381.

Atran, S. 2001c. The vanishing landscape of the Petén Maya Lowlands: People, plants, animals, places, words, and spirits. In L. Maffi, ed., *On Biocultural Diversity: Linking Language, Knowledge, and the Environment*. Washington, D.C.: Smithsonian Institution Press.

Atran, S. 2002. *In Gods We Trust: The Evolutionary Landscape of Religion*. New York: Oxford University Press.

Atran, S. 2003a. Genesis of suicide terrorism. *Science* 299:1534–1539.

Atran, S. 2003b. Théorie cognitive de la culture (une alternative évolutionniste à la sociobiologie et à la selection collective). *L'Homme* 166:107–144.

Atran, S. 2004. Combating Al Qaeda's splinters: Mishandling suicide terrorism. *Washington Quarterly* 27:67–90.

Atran, S. 2005. Adaptationism in human cognition: Strong, spurious, or weak? *Mind and Language* 20:39–67.

Atran, S. 2006. The moral logic and growth of suicide terrorism. *Washington Quarterly* 29:127–147.

Atran, S., R. Axelrod, and R. Davis. 2007. Sacred barriers to conflict resolution. *Science* 317:1039–1040.

Atran, S., P. Estin, J. Coley, and D. Medin. 1997. Generic species and basic levels: Essence and appearance in folk biology. *Journal of Ethnobiology* 17:22–45.

Atran, S., X. Lois, and E. Ucan Ek'. 2004. *Plants of the Petén Itza' Maya.* Museum of Anthropology, University of Michigan Memoirs, No. 37. Ann Arbor: Museum of Anthropology Publications.

Atran, S., and D. Medin. 1997. Knowledge and action: Cultural models of nature and resource management in Mesoamerica. In M. Bazerman, D. Messick, A. Tinbrusel, and K. Wayde-Benzoni, eds., *Environment, Ethics, and Behavior: The Psychology of Environmental Valuation and Degradation.* San Francisco: Jossey-Bass.

Atran, S., D. Medin, E. Lynch, V. Vapnarsky, E. Ucan Ek', and P. Sousa. 2001. Folkbiology doesn't come from folkpsychology: Evidence from Yukatek Maya in cross-cultural perspective. *Journal of Cognition and Culture* 1:3–42.

Atran, S., D. Medin, and N. Ross. 2005. The cultural mind: Ecological decision making and cultural modeling within and across populations. *Psychological Review* 112:744–776.

Atran, S., D. Medin, N. Ross, B. Lynch, J. Coley, E. Ucan Ek', and V. Vapnarsky. 1999. Folkecology and commons management in the Maya Lowlands. *Proceedings of the National Academy of Sciences USA* 96:7598–7603.

Atran, S., D. Medin, N. Ross, E. Lynch, V. Vapnarsky, E. Ucan Ek', J. Coley, C. Timura, and M. Baran. 2002. Folkecology, cultural epidemiology, and the spirit of the commons: A garden experiment in the Maya Lowlands. *Current Anthropology* 41:1–23.

Atran, S., and A. Norenzayan. 2004. Religion's evolutionary landscape: Counterintuition, commitment, compassion, communion. *Behavioral and Brain Sciences* 27:713–770.

Atran, S., and D. Sperber. 1991. Learning without teaching: Its place in culture. In L. Tolchinsky-Landsmann, ed., *Culture, Schooling and Psychological Development.* Norwood, N.J.: Ablex.

Atran, S., and J. Stern. 2005. Small groups find fatal purpose through the web. *Nature* 436:620.

Atran, S., and E. Ucan Ek'. 1999. Classification of useful plants among Northern Petén Maya. In C. White, ed., *Reconstructing Ancient Maya Diet.* Salt Lake City: University of Utah Press.

Au, T., and L. Romo. 1999. Mechanical causality in children's "folkbiology." In D. Medin and S. Atran, eds., *Folkbiology.* Cambridge, Mass.: MIT Press.

Aunger, R. 2002. Exposure versus susceptibility in the epidemiology of "everyday" beliefs. *Journal of Cognition and Culture* 2002:113–157.

Avendaño y Loyola, Fray Andrés de. 1987 [1696]. *Relation of Two Trips to Peten Made for the Conversion of the Heathen Ytzaex and Cehaches.* F. Comparato, ed., C. Bowditch, and G. Rivera, trans. Culver City, Calif.: Labyrinthos.

Axelrod, R., and D. Bennett. 1993. A landscape theory of aggregation. *British Journal of Political Science* 23:211–233.

Axelrod, R. 1985. *The Evolution of Cooperation.* New York: Basic Books.

Axelrod, R. 1997a. Advancing the art of simulation. *Complexity* 3:193–199.

Axelrod, R. 1997b. *The Complexity of Cooperation: Agent-Based Models of Competition and Collaboration.* Princeton, NJ: Princeton University Press.

Axtell, R., J. Epstein, and H. Young. 1999. The emergence of economic classes in an agent-based bargaining model. In S. Durlauf and H. Young, eds., *Social Dynamics.* Cambridge, Mass.: MIT Press.

Bailenson, J., M. Shum, S. Atran, D. Medin, and J. Coley. 2002. A bird's eye view: Biological categorization and reasoning within and across cultures. *Cognition* 84:1–53.

Balogh, J., D. Swinney, and Z. Tigue. 1998. Real-time processing of pronouns with contrastive stress. Poster presented at the 11th Annual CUNY Conference on Human Sentence Processing.

Bang, M. 2006. *Understanding Students' Epistemologies: Examining Practice and Meaning in Community Contexts.* PhD diss., Northwestern University.

Bang, M., D. Medin, S. Unsworth, and J. Townsend. 2005. Cultural models of nature and their relevance to science education. Paper presented at the annual meeting of the *American Education Research Association*, April 11–15, in Montréal, Quebec.

Bang, M., D. Medin, and S. Atran. 2007. Cultural mosaics and mental models of nature. *Proceedings of the National Academy of Sciences U.S.A.* 104:13868–13874.

Baron, J., and J. Greene. 1996. Determinants of insensitivity to quantity in valuation of public goods. *Journal of Experimental Psychology: Applied* 2:107–125.

Baron, J., and S. Leshner. 2000. How serious are expressions of protected values? *Journal of Experimental Psychology: Applied* 6:183–194.

Baron, J., and I. Ritov. 1994. Reference points and omission bias. *Organizational Behavior and Human Decision Processes* 59:475–498.

Baron, J., and M. Spranca. 1997. Protected values. *Organizational Behavior and Human Decision Processes* 70:1–16.

Baron-Cohen, S. 1995. *Mindblindness: An Essay on Autism and Theory of Mind.* Cambridge, Mass.: MIT Press.

Barrera Marín, A., A. Barrera Vásquez, and R. López Franco. 1976. *Nomenclatura etnobotánica Maya.* México, DF: INAH.

Barrera Vásquez, A., and S. Rendón. 1963. El libro de los libros de Chilam Balam, 2nd ed. México, DF: Fondo de Cultura Económica.

Barrett, J., R. Richert, and A. Driesenga. 2001. God's beliefs versus mother's: The development of nonhuman agent concepts. *Child Development* 72:50–65.

Barsalou, L. 1985. Ideals, central tendency, and frequency of instantiation as determinants of graded structure in categories. *Journal of Experimental Psychology: Learning, Memory, & Cognition* 11(1–4):629–654.

Barsalou, L. 1991. Deriving categories to achieve goals. In G. H. Bower, ed., *The Psychology of Learning and Motivation: Advances in Research and Theory*, vol. 27. San Diego, Calif.: Academic Press.

Bartels, D., and D. Medin. 2007. Are morally motivated decision makers insensitive to the consequences of their choices? *Psychological Science* 18:24–28.

Bartlett, H. 1936. A method of procedure for field work in tropical American phytogeography based on a botanical reconnaissance in parts of British Honduras and the Peten forest of Guatemala. *Botany of the Maya Area, Miscellaneous Papers I*. Washington, D.C.: Carnegie Institution of Washington Publication 461.

Bartlett, H. 1940. History of the generic concept in botany. *Bulletin of the Torrey Botanical Club* 47:319–362.

Batchelder, W., and A. K. Romney. 1988. Test theory without the answer key. *Psychometrika* 53:71–92.

Batchelder, W., and A. K. Romney. 1989. New results in test theory without the answer key. In E. E. Roskam, ed., *Mathematical Psychology in Progress*. Berlin: Springer-Verlag.

Beattie, J., and J. Baron. 1995. In-kind and out-of-kind penalties: Preferences and valuation. *Journal of Experimental Psychology: Applied* 1:136–151.

Beck, D. 1995. The importance of sturgeon in Menominee Indian history. *Wisconsin Magazine of History* 79:32–48.

Beck, D. R. M. 2002. Siege and survival: History of the Menominee Indians, 1634–1856. Lincoln: University of Nebraska Press.

Beltrán, Fray Pedro de. [1742] 1859. *Arte del idoma Maya*. 2nd ed. Mérida: J. D. Espinosa.

Berg, D. L. 1993. *A Guide to the Oxford English Dictionary*. New York: Oxford University Press.

Berkes, F., D. Feeny, B. McCay, and J. Acheson. 1989. The benefit of the commons. *Nature* 340:91–93.

Berlin, B. 1972. Speculations on the growth of ethnobotanical nomenclature. *Journal of Language and Society* 1:63–98.

Berlin, B. 1992. *Ethnobiological Classification: Principles of Categorization of Plants and Animals in Traditional Societies*. Princeton, N.J.: Princeton University Press.

Berlin, B. 1999. One Maya Indian's view of the plant world. In D. Medin and S. Atran, eds., *Folkbiology*. Cambridge, Mass.: MIT Press.

Berlin, B., D. Breedlove, and P. Raven. 1973. General principles of classification and nomenclature in folk biology. *American Anthropologist* 74:214–242.

Berlin, B., D. Breedlove, and P. Raven. 1974. *Principles of Tzeltal Plant Classification*. New York: Academic Press.

Bird-David, N. 1999. "Animism" revisited: Personhood, environment, and relational epistemology. *Current Anthropology* (supplement) 40:S67–S92.

Blackmore, S. 1999. *The Meme Machine*. London: Oxford University Press.

Bloch, M., G. Solomon, and S. Carey. 2001. Zafimaniry: An understanding of what is passed on from parents to children: A cross-cultural investigation. *Journal of Cognition and Culture* 1:43–68.

Bloch, M., and D. Sperber. 2002. Kinship and evolved dispositions. *Current Anthropology* 43:723–748.

Blok, S., G. Newman, J. Behr, and L. J. Rips. 2001. Inferences about personal identity. *Proceedings of the Twenty-Third Annual Conference of the Cognitive Science Society.*

Blok, S., G. Newman, and L. J. Rips. 2005. Individuals and their concepts. In W.-K. Ahn, R. L. Goldstone, B. C. Love, A. B. Markman, and P. Wolff, eds., *Categorization Inside and Outside the Lab.* Washington, D.C.: American Psychological Association.

Bloom, P., and C. Veres. 1999. The perceived intentionality of groups. *Cognition* 71:B1–B9.

Bloomfield, A., J. Sager, D. Bartels, and D. Medin. 2006. Caring about framing effects. *Mind & Society* 5:123–138.

Bock, W. 1973. Philosophical foundations of classical evolutionary taxonomy. *Systematic Zoology* 22:375–392.

Boniecki, G. 1977. Is man interested in the future? The psychological question of our times. *International Journal of Psychology* 12:59–64.

Borgatti, S., M. Everett, and P. Shirley. 1990. LS sets, lambda sets, and other cohesive subsets. *Social Networks* 12:337–358.

Boster, J. 1986a. Exchange of varieties and information between Aguaruna manioc cultivators. *American Anthropologist* 3:381–399.

Boster, J. 1986b. Requiem for the omniscient informer. In J. Dougherty, ed., *Directions in Cognitive Anthropology.* Urbana: University of Illinois Press.

Boster, J. 1987. Agreement among biological classification systems is not dependent on cultural transmission. *American Anthropologist* 89:914–920.

Boster, J. 1991. The information economy model applied to biological similarity judgment. In J. Levine, L. Resnick, and S. Teasley, eds., *Perspectives on Socially Shared Cognition.* American Psychological Association.

Boster, J., B. Berlin, and J. O'Neill. 1986. The correspondence of Jivoroan to scientific ornithology. *American Anthropologist* 88:569–583.

Boster, J., and R. D'Andrade. 1989. Natural and human sources of cross-cultural agreement in ornithological classification. *American Anthropologist* 91:132–142.

Boster, J., and J. Johnson. 1989. Form or function: A comparison of expert and novice judgments of similarity among fish. *American Anthropologist* 91:866–889.

Boyd, R., and P. Richerson. 1985. *Culture and Evolutionary Process.* Chicago: University of Chicago Press.

Boyd, R., and P. Richerson. 2001. Norms and bounded rationality. In G. Gigerenzer and R. Selten, eds., *The Adaptive Toolbox.* Cambridge, Mass.: MIT Press.

Boyer, P. 1994. *The Naturalness of Religious Ideas: A Cognitive Theory of Religion.* Berkeley, Calif.: University of California Press.

Braisby, M., B. Franks, and J. Hampton. 1996. Essentialism, word use, and concepts. *Cognition* 59:247–274.

Briley, D., M. Morris, and I. Simonson. 2000. Reasons as carriers of culture: Dynamic versus dispositional models of cultural influence on decision making. *Journal of Consumer Research* 27:157–178.

Bromley, D., ed. 1992. *Making the Commons Work.* San Francisco: Institute for Contemporary Studies Press.

Brown, C. 1979. Growth and development of folk botanical life-forms in the Mayan language family. *American Ethnologist* 6:366–385.

Brown, C. 1982. Growth and development of folk zoological life-forms in the Mayan language family. *American Ethnologist* 9:97–111.

Brown, C. 1984. *Language and Living Things: Uniformities in Folk Classification and Naming.* New Brunswick, N.J.: Rutgers University Press.

Brown, C. 1995. Lexical acculturation and ethnobiology: Utilitarianism and intellectualism. *Journal of Linguistic Anthropology* 5:51–64.

Brown, C., J. Kolar, B. Torrey, T. Truong-Quang, and P. Volkman. 1976. Some general principles of biological and non-biological classification. *American Ethnologist* 3:73–85.

Brown, D., and S. Boysen. 2000. Spontaneous discrimination of natural stimuli by chimpanzees (*Pan troglodytes*). *Journal of Comparative Psychology* 114:392–400.

Bruce, R. 1968. *Gramática Lacandóna.* México, DF: Instituto Nacional de Antropología e Historia.

Bruman, C. 1999. Why a successful concept should not be discarded. *Current Anthropology* (Special Issue) 40:S1–S14.

Buffon, G. 1774–1789. *Histoire générale et particulière. Suppl.* Paris: Imprimerie Royale.

Buffon, G.-L. 1749–1767. *Histoire Naturelle Générale et Particulière*, 15 vols. Paris: Impimerie Royale.

Bulmer, R. 1970. Which came first, the chicken or the egg-head? In J. Pouillon and P. Maranda, eds., *Echanges et communications: Mé langes offerts á Claude Lévi-Strauss.* The Hague: Mouton.

Bulmer, R. 1974. Folk biology in the New Guinea Highlands. *Social Science Information* 13:9–28.

Bulmer, R., and M. Tylor. 1968. Karam classification of frogs. *Journal of the Polynesian Society* 77:335–385.

Burnett, R., D. Medin, N. Ross, and S. Blok. 2005. Ideal is typical. *Canadian Journal of Psychology* 159:5–10.

Cain, A. 1956. The genus in evolutionary taxonomy. *Systematic Zoology* 5:97–109.

Campbell, D. 1958. Common fate, similarity, and other measures of the status of aggregates of persons as social entities. *Behavioral Science* 3:14–25.

Cano, Fray Augustín. [1695] 1984. *Manche and Peten: The Hazards of Itza Deceit and Barbarity*. F. Comparato, ed., C. Bowditch and G. Rivera, trans. Culver City, Calif.: Labyrinthos.

Caramazza, A. 2002. The organization of conceptual knowledge: The view from neuropsychology. Paper presented at the British Academy Symposium on "Conceptual Knowledge," June.

Carey, S. 1985. *Conceptual Change in Childhood.* Cambridge, Mass.: Bradford Books.

Carey, S. 1995. On the origin of causal understanding. In D. Sperber, D. Premack, and A. Premack, eds., *Causal Cognition*. Oxford: Clarendon Press.

Carey, S. 1999a. *The Origin of Concepts.* Cambridge, Mass.: MIT Press.

Carey, S. 1999b. Sources of conceptual change. In E. Scholnick, K. Nelson, S. Gelman, and P. Miller, eds., *Conceptual Development: Piaget's Legacy*. Mahwah, N.J.: Erlbaum.

Carey, S. 2003. The origin of concepts. Paper presented at the Joint Program Lecture Series in Culture and Cognition and Evolution and Human Adaptation, University of Michigan, Ann Arbor, February.

Carey, S., and R. Diamond. 1977. From piecemeal to configurational representation of faces. *Science* 195:312–313.

Carter, W. 1969. *New Lands and Old Traditions: Kekchi Cultivation in the Guatemalan Lowland*. Gainesville: University of Florida Press.

Cavalli-Sforza, L., and M. Feldman. 1981. *Cultural Transmission and Evolution*. Princeton, NJ: Princeton University Press.

Cerella, J. 1979. Visual classes and natural categories in the pigeon. *Journal of Experimental Psychology: Human Perception and Performance* 5:68–77.

Chase, A., and D. Chase. 1989. *The Investigation of Classic Period Maya Warfare at Caracol, Belize*. Mayab 5:5–18.

Chomsky, N. 2000. Minimalist inquiries: The framework. In R. Martin, D. Michaels, and J. Uriagereka, eds., *Step by Step*. Cambridge, Mass.: MIT Press.

Cohen, D. 2001. Cultural variation: Considerations and implications. *Psychological Bulletin* 127:451–471.

Cole, M. 1996. *Cultural Psychology*. Cambridge, Mass.: Harvard University Press.

Coley, J. 1995. Emerging differentiation of folkbiology and folkpsychology: Attributions of biological and psychological properties to living things. *Child Development* 66:1856–1874.

Coley, J., B. Hayes, C. Lawson, and M. Moloney. 2004. Knowledge, expectations, and inductive reasoning within conceptual hierarchies. *Cognition* 90:217–253.

Coley, J., D. Medin, and S. Atran. 1997. Does rank have its privilege? Inductive inferences in folkbiological taxonomies. *Cognition* 63:73–112.

Coley, J., D. Medin, J. Proffitt, E. Lynch, and S. Atran. 1999. Inductive reasoning in folkbiological thought. In D. Medin and S. Atran, eds., *Folkbiology*. Cambridge, Mass.: MIT Press.

Conklin, H. 1962. Lexicographical treatment of folk taxonomies. In F. Householder and S. Saporta, eds., *Problems in Lexicography*. Report of the Conference on Lexicography, November 11–12, 1960. Bloomington: Indiana University Press.

Connolly, T., and J. Reb. 2003. Omission bias in vaccination decision: Where's the "omission"? Where's the "bias"? *Organizational Behavior and Human Decision Processes* 91:186–202.

Cosmides, L., and J. Tooby. 1992. Cognitive adaptations for social exchange. In J. Barkow, L. Cosmides, and J. Tooby, eds., *The Adapted Mind: Evolutionary Psychology and the Generation of Culture*. New York: Oxford University Press.

Cowgill, U. 1962. An agricultural study of the southern Maya lowlands. *American Anthropologist* 64:273–286.

Csibra, G., G. Gergely, S. Bíró, O. Koós, and M. Brockbank. 1999. Goal attribution without agency cues: The perception of "pure reason" in infancy. *Cognition* 72:237–267.

Culbert, T., and D. Rice. 1990. *Precolumbian Population History in the Maya Lowlands*. Albuquerque: University of New Mexico Press.

D'Andrade, R. 1989. Cultural cognition. In M. Posner, ed., *Foundations of Cognitive Science*. Cambridge, Mass.: MIT Press.

D'Andrade, R., and C. Strauss. 1992. *Human Motives and Cultural Models*. Cambridge: Cambridge University Press.

Darwin, C. 1859. *On the Origins of Species by Means of Natural Selection*. London: Murray.

Darwin, C. [1872] 1883. *On the Origins of Species by Means of Natural Selection*. 6th ed. New York: Appleton.

Davis, T. 2000. *Sustaining the Forest, the People, and the Spirit*. New York: State University of New York Press.

Dawkins, R. 1976. *The Selfish Gene*. New York: Oxford University Press.

Dean, J., G. Gumerman, J. Epstein, R. Axtell, A. Swedlund, M. Parker, and S. McCarroll. 1999. Understanding Anasazi culture change through agent-based modeling. In G. Gumerman and T. Kohler, eds., *Modeling Small-Scale Societies*. New York: Oxford University Press.

Demarest, A. 1993. The violent saga of a Maya kingdom. *National Geographic* 183:95–111.

Dennett, D. 1995. *Darwin's Dangerous Idea*. New York: Simon & Schuster.

Descola, P. 1996. Constructing natures. In P. Descola and G. Pálson, eds., *Nature and Society*. London: Routledge.

de Quervain, D., U. Fischbacher, V. Treyer, M. Schellhammer, U. Schnyder, A. Buck, and E. Fehr. 2004. The neural basis of altruistic punishment. *Science* 305:1254–1258.

De Vos, J. 1980. *La paz de Dios y del Rey: La conquista de la Selva Lacandona por los Españoles.* Mexico City: Fondo de Culturas.

Diamond, J. 1966. Zoological classification of a primitive people. *Science* 151:1102–1104.

Diamond, J., and D. Bishop. 1999. Ethno-ornithology of the Ketengban people, Indonesian New Guinea. In D. Medin and S. Atran, eds., *Folkbiology*. Cambridge, Mass.: MIT Press.

Diamond, R., and S. Carey. 1986. Why faces are and are not special: An effect of expertise. *Journal of Experimental Psychology: General* 115:107–117.

Diver, C. 1940. The problem of closely related species living in the same area. In J. Huxley, ed., *The New Systematics*. Oxford: Clarendon Press.

Donnellan, K. 1971. Necessity and criteria. In J. Rosenberg and C. Travis, eds., *Readings in the Philosophy of Language*. Englewood-Cliffs, NJ: Prentice-Hall.

Donovan, M., J. Bransford, and J. Pellegrino. 1999. *How People Learn.* Washington, DC: National Academy.

Dougherty, J. 1978. Salience and relativity in classification. *American Ethnologist* 5:66–80.

Dougherty, J. 1979. Learning names for plants and plants for names. *Anthropological Linguistics* 21:298–315.

Douglas, M. 1970. *Natural Symbols*. Harmondsworth: Penguin.

Dupré, J. 1999. Are whales fish? In D. Medin and S. Atran, eds., *Folkbiology*. Cambridge, Mass.: MIT Press.

Duranti, A. 1997. *Linguistic Anthropology*. Cambridge: Cambridge University Press.

Dwyer, P. 1976. An analysis of Rofaifo mammal taxonomy. *American Ethnologist* 3:425–445.

Eckstein, R. 1993. Ping Pong Diplomacy: A view from behind the scenes. *The Journal of American-East Asian Relations* 2:327–343.

Edmonson, M. 1982. *The Ancient Future of the Itza*. Austin: University of Texas Press.

Eldredge, N. 1986. Information, economics, and evolution. *Annual Review of Ecology and Systematics* 17:351–369.

Ellen, R. 1993. *The Cultural Relations of Classification*. Cambridge: Cambridge University Press.

Ellen, R. 1999. Models of subsidence and ethnobiological knowledge. In D. Medin and S. Atran, eds., *Folkbiology*. Cambridge, Mass.: MIT Press.

Epstein, J. 1999. Agent-based computational models and generative social science. *Complexity* 4:41–60.

Evans-Pritchard, E. 1940. *The Nuer*. Oxford: Oxford University Press.

Fagan, C. 2000. *Cultural and Economic Constraints to Farming in a Core-Zone Community of the Maya Biosphere Reserve*. Durham, NC: Center for Tropical Conservation, Duke University.

Fetherstonhaugh, D., P. Slovic, S. Johnson, and J. Friedrich. 1997. Insensitivity to the value of human life: A study of psychophysical numbing. *Journal of Risk and Uncertainty* 14:283–300.

Fischhoff, B. 1997. Ranking risks. In M. Bazerman, D. Messick, A. Tenbrunsel, and K. Wade-Benzoni, eds., *Environment and Ethics: Psychological Contributions*, 342–371. San Francisco: Jossey-Bass.

Fiske, A., and P. Tetlock. 1997. Taboo trade-offs. *Political Psychology* 18:255–297.

Fodor, J. 1983. *Modularity of Mind*. Cambridge, Mass.: MIT Press.

Fodor, J. 2000. *The Mind Doesn't Work That Way: The Scope and Limits of Computational Psychology*. Cambridge, Mass.: MIT Press.

Fox, J. 1987. *Maya Postclassic State Formation: Segmentary Lineage Migration in Advancing Frontiers*. Cambridge: Cambridge University Press.

Frank, R. 1988. *Passions within Reason*. New York: Norton.

Freidel, D., L. Schele, and J. Parker. 1995. *Maya Cosmos: Three Thousand Years on the Shaman's Path*. New York: William Morrow.

Friedrich, J., P. Barnes, K. Chapin, I. Dawson, V. Garst, and D. Kerr. 1999. Psychophysical numbing: When lives are valued less as the lives at risk increase. *Journal of Consumer Psychology* 8:277–299.

Fukuyama, F. 1995. *Trust*. New York: Free Press.

Gambetta, D. 2005. *Making Sense of Suicide Missions*. New York: Oxford University Press.

Gardner, W. L., S. Gabriel, and A. Y. Lee. 1999. "I" value freedom, but "we" value relationships: Self-construal priming mirrors cultural differences in judgment. *Psychological Science* 10:321–326.

Garro, L. 2000. Remembering the past: A comparison of cultural consensus theory and cultural schema theory. *Ethnos* 28:275–319.

Gatewood, J. 2001. Reflections on the nature of cultural distributions and the units of culture problem. *Cross-Cultural Research* 35:227–241.

Geertz, C. 1973. *The Interpretation of Cultures*. New York: Basic Books.

Gelman, S. 2003. *The Essential Child: Origins of Essentialism in Everyday Thought*. New York: Oxford University Press.

Gelman, S., J. D. Coley, K. S. Rosengren, E. Hartman, and A. Pappas. 1998. Beyond labeling: The role of parental input in the acquisition of righly-structured categories. *Monographs of the Society for Research in Child Development*. Serial No. 253, 63(1).

Gelman, S., and L. Hirschfeld. 1999. How biological is essentialism? In D. Medin and S. Atran, eds., *Folkbiology*. Cambridge, Mass.: MIT Press.

Gelman, S., and H. Wellman. 1991. Insides and essences. *Cognition* 38:213–244.

Gerhard, P. 1991. *La Frontera Sureste de la Nueva España*. México. DF: UNAM.

Ghiselin, M. 1981. Categories, life, and thinking. *Behavioral and Brain Sciences* 4:269–313.

Ghiselin, M. 1999. Natural kinds and supraorganismal individuals. In D. Medin and S. Atran, eds., *Folkbiology*. Cambridge, Mass.: MIT Press.

Gilens, M. 1996. Race and poverty in America: Public misperceptions and the American news media. *Public Opinion Quarterly* 60:515–541.

Gilliam, F. D., Jr., and S. Iyenger. 2000. Prime suspects: The influence of local television news on the viewing public. *American Journal of Political Science* 44(3):560–573.

Gil-White, F. 2001. Are ethnic groups biological "species" to the brain? *Current Anthropology* 42:515–554.

Ginges, J., S. Atran, D. Medin, and K. Shikaki. 2007. Sacred bounds on rational resolution of violent political conflict. *Proceedings of the National Academy of Sciences* 104:7357–7360.

Goldstein, W., and E. Weber. 1995. Content and discontent: Indications and implications of domain specificity in preferential decision making. In J. R. Busemeyer, R. Hastie, and D. L. Medin, eds., *The Psychology of Learning and Motivation,* Vol. 32, *Decision Making from a Cognitive Perspective* 83–136. San Diego: Academic Press.

Goldstone, R. 1994. Influences of categorization on perceptual discrimination. *Journal of Experimental Psychology: General* 123:178–200.

Goldstone, R. 1998. Perceptual learning. *Annual Review of Psychology* 49:585–612.

Gómez-Pompa, A., J. Flores, and V. Sosa. 1987. The «pet kot»: A man-made tropical forest of the Maya. *Interciencia* 12:10–15.

Graunke, G. 2003. American rights guardian update. *Protecting American Rights and Resources Newsletter* 5, 7 (2003).

Greene, E. 1983. *Landmarks in Botany*. 2 vols. Stanford, Calif.: Stanford University Press.

Grice, H. 1975. Logic and conversation. In P. Cole and J. L. Morgan, eds., *Syntax and Semantics, Vol. 3: Speech Acts.* New York: Academic Press.

Griffiths, P. 2002. What is innateness? *The Monist* 85:70–85.

Grignon, D., R. Alegria, C. Dodge, G. Lyons, C. Waukechon, C. Warrington, C. Caldwell, C. La Chapelle, and K. Waupoose. 1998. *Menominee Tribal History Guide: Commemorating Wisconsin Sesquicentennial 1848–1998.* Keshena, Wis.: Menominee Indian Tribe of Wisconsin.

Grünberg, G., and V. Ramos. 1998. *Base de Datos sobre poblacion, tierras y medio ambiente en la Reserva de la Biosfera Maya*. Petén, Guatemala: CARE Guatemala and CONAP.

Grünberg, W. 2000. *Modeling Deforestation: Risks for the Maya Biosphere Reserve, Guatemala*. University of Arizona: School of Renewable Natural Resources.

Guntheil, G., A. Vera, and F. Keil. 1998. Do houseflies think? Patterns of induction and biological beliefs in development. *Cognition* 66:33–39.

Guyette, S. 1983. *Community-Based Research: A Handbook for Native Americans*. Los Angeles: University of California Press.

Haidt, J., and J. Baron. 1996. Social roles and the moral judgement of acts and omissions. *European Journal of Social Psychology* 26:201–218.

Hall, P., and M. Pecore. 1995. *Case Study: Menominee Tribal Enterprises*. Madison: Institute for Environmental Studies and the Land Tenure Center, University of Wisconsin at Madison.

Hardin, G. 1968. The tragedy of the commons. *Science* 162:1243–1248.

Harris, M. 1974. *Cows, Pigs, Wars, and Witches*. New York: Random House.

Harrison, P., and B. Turner. 1978. *Pre-Hispanic Maya Agriculture*. Albuquerque: University of New Mexico Press.

Hatano, G., and K. Inagaki. 1987. Everyday biology and school biology: How do they interact? *Quarterly Newsletter of the Laboratory of Comparative Human Cognition* 9:120–128.

Hatano, G., and K. Inagaki. 1994. Young children's naive theory of biology. *Cognition* 50:171–188.

Hatano, G., and K. Inagaki. 1996. Cultural contexts of schooling revisited: A review of the learning gap from a cultural psychology perspective. Paper presented at the Conference on Global Prospects for Education: Development, Culture and Schooling, University of Michigan.

Hatano, G., and K. Inagaki. 1999. A developmental perspective on informal biology. In D. L. Medin and S. Atran, eds., *Folkbiology*. Cambridge, Mass.: MIT Press.

Hatano, G., and K. Inagaki. 2003. When is conceptual change intended? A cognitive-sociocultural view. In G. Sinatra and P. Pintrich, eds., *Intentional Conceptual Change*. Mahwah: Erlbaum.

Hatano, G., and K. Inagaki. Forthcoming. The formation of culture in mind: A sociocultural approach to cognitive development. In J. Mehler, S. Carey, and L. Bonatti, eds., *Cognitive Development and Conceptual Change*. Cambridge, MA: MIT Press.

Hauser, M. 2000. *Wild Minds: What Animals Really Think*. New York: Henry Holt and Company.

Hauser, M., N. Chomsky, and W. T. Fitch. 2002. The faculty of language. *Science* 298:1569–1578.

Hays, T. 1983. Ndumba folkbiology and general principles of ethnobotanical classification and nomenclature. *American Anthropologist* 85:592–611.

Heider, F., and S. Simmel. 1944. An experimental study of apparent behavior. *American Journal of Psychology* 57:243–259.

Hellmuth, N. 1977. Cholti-Lacandon (Chiapas) and Petén-Ytzá agriculture, settlement pattern and population. In N. Hammond, ed., *Social Process in Maya Prehistory: Studies in Honor of Sir J. Eric S. Thompson.* London: Academic Press.

Hempel, C., and P. Oppenheim. 1948. Studies in the logic of explanation. *Philosophy of Science* 15:567–579.

Hennig, W. 1966. *Phylogenetic Systematics.* Urbana: University of Illinois Press.

Henley, N. M. 1969. A Psychological Study of the Semantics of Animal Terms. *Journal of Verbal Learning and Learning Behavior* 8:176–184.

Henrich, J., and R. Boyd. 1998. The evolution of conformist transmission and the emergence of between-group differences. *Evolution and Human Behavior* 19:215–241.

Henrich, J., and R. Boyd. 2002. On modeling cognition and culture. *Journal of Cognition and Culture* 2:87–112.

Henrich, J., R. Boyd, S. Bowles, C. Camerer, H. Gintis, R. McElreath, and E. Fehr. 2001. In search of *Homo economicus*: Experiments in 15 small-scale societies. *American Economic Review* 91:73–79.

Henrich, J., and F. J. Gil-White. 2001. The evolution of prestige. *Evolution and Human Behavior* 22:165–196.

Hermes, M. 1999. Research methods as a situated response: Toward a First Nations' methodology. In L. Parker, D. Deyhle, S. Villenas, eds., *Race Is ... Race Isn't: Critical Race Theory and Qualitative Studies in Education.* Boulder, Colo.: Westview Press.

Herrnstein, R. J. 1984. Objects, categories, and discriminative stimuli. In H. L. Roitblat, T. G. Bever, and H. S. Terrace, eds., *Animal Cognition.* Hillsdale, NJ: Lawrence Erlbaum Associates.

Hickling, A., and S. Gelman. 1995. How does your garden grow? Evidence of an early conception of plants as biological kinds. *Child Development* 66:856–876.

Hirschfeld, L. 1995. Do children have a theory of race? *Cognition* 54:209–252.

Hirschfeld, L. 1996. *Race in the Making.* Cambridge, Mass.: MIT Press.

Hirschfeld, L. 2002. Why don't anthropologists like children? *American Anthropologist* 104(2):611–627.

Hirschfeld, L., and S. Gelman, eds. 1994. *Mapping the Mind.* New York: Cambridge University.

Hoffman, W. J. [1896] 1970. The Menomini Indians. In *Fourteenth Annual Report of the US Bureau of Ethnology, 1892–93.* New York: Johnson Reprints.

Hofling, C. 1996. Indigenous linguistic revitalization and outsider interaction: The Itzaj Maya case. *Human Organization* 55:108–116.

Hofling, C., and F. Tesucun. 1997. *Itzaj-Maya-Spanish-English Dictionary.* Salt Lake City: University of Utah Press.

Hofstede, G. 1980. *Culture's Consequences: International Differences in Work-Related Values.* Beverley Hills, Calif.: Sage.

Hong, Y., M. Morris, C. Chiu, and V. Martinez. 2000. Multicultural minds. *American Psychologist* 55:709–720.

Hubert, L., and R. Golledge. 1981. A heuristic method for the comparison of related structures. *Journal of Mathematical Psychology* 23:214–226.

Hubert, L., and J. Schultz. 1976. Quadratic assignment as a general data analysis strategy. *British Journal of Mathematical and Statistical Psychology* 29:190–241.

Hudson, P., and S. Taylor-Henley. 2001. Beyond the rhetoric: Implementing culturally appropriate research projects in First Nations communities. *American Indian Culture and Research Journal* 25:93–105.

Hull, D. 1999. Interdisciplinary dissonance. In D. Medin and S. Atran, eds., *Folkbiology*. Cambridge, Mass.: MIT Press.

Hummel, R. 1994. *Hunting and Fishing for Sport: Commerce, Controversy, and Popular Culture*. Bowling Green, Ohio.: Bowling Green State University Press.

Hunn, E. 1975. A measure of the degree of correspondence of folk to scientific biological classification. *American Ethnologist* 2:309–327.

Hunn, E. 1977. *Tzeltal Folk Zoology*. New York: Academic Press.

Hunn, E. 1982. The utilitarian factor in folk biological classification. *American Anthropologist* 84:830–847.

Hunn, E. 1999. Size as limiting the recognition of biodiversity in folkbiological classifications: One of four factors governing the cultural recognition of biological taxa. In D. Medin and S. Atran, eds., *Folkbiology*. Cambridge, Mass.: MIT Press.

Huntington, S. 1996. *The Clash of Civilizations and the Remaking of the World Order*. New York: Simon & Schuster.

Hutchins, E. 1995. *Cognition in the Wild*. Cambridge, Mass.: MIT Press.

Inagaki, K. 1990. The effects of raising animals on children's biological knowledge. *British Journal of Developmental Psychology* 8:119–129.

Inagaki, K., and G. Hatano. 1993. Young children's understanding of the mind-body distinction. *Child Development* 64:1534–1549.

Inagaki, K., and G. Hatano. 1996. Young children's recognition of commonalities between animals and plants. *Child Development* 67:2823–2840.

Inagaki, K., and G. Hatano. 2001. Children's understanding of mind-body relationships. In M. Siegal and C. Peterson, eds., *Children's Understanding of Biology and Health*. Cambridge: Cambridge University Press.

Inagaki, K., and G. Hatano. 2002. *Young Children's Naïve Thinking about the Biological World*. New York: Psychology Press.

Inagaki, K., and K. Sugiyama. 1988. Attributing human characteristics: Developmental changes in over- and underattribution. *Cognitive Development* 3:55–70.

INSIVUMEH (National Institute for Seismology, Vulcanology, and Meteorology, Guatemala). 1998. *Meteorological Bulletins*. http://www.insivumeh.gob.gt/

Irons, W. 1996. Morality, religion, and human nature. In W. Richardson and W. Wildman, eds., *Religion and Science*. New York: Routledge.

Jeyifous, S. W. 1992. Developmental changes in the representation of word meaning: Cross-cultural findings. *British Journal of Developmental Psychology* 10:285–299.

Job, R., and L. Surian. 1998. A neurocognitive mechanism for folk biology? *Behavioral and Brain Sciences* 21:577–578.

Johnson, K., and C. Mervis. 1997. Effects of varying levels of expertise on the basic level of categorization. *Journal of Experimental Psychology: General* 126:248–277.

Johnson, K. E., and C. B. Mervis. 1998. Impact of intuitive theories on feature recruitment throughout the continuum of expertise. *Memory and Cognition* 26:382–401.

Johnson, K., C. Mervis, and J. Boster. 1992. Developmental changes within the structure of the mammal domain. *Developmental Psychology* 28:74–83.

Johnson, S., and G. Solomon. 1997. Why dogs have puppies and cats have kittens: The role of birth in young children's understanding of biological origins. *Child Development* 68:404–419.

Jones, G. 1998. *The conquest of the last Maya kingdom.* Stanford: Stanford University Press.

Jussieu, A. L. 1789. *Genera plantarum.* Paris: Herissant.

Kahneman, D., and A. Tversky. 1979. Prospect theory: An analysis of decision under risk. *Econometrika* 47:263–291.

Kahneman, D., and A. Tversky. 1983. Choices, values, and frames. *American Psychologist* 39, no. 4 (April): 341–350.

Kannengeiser, C. 1995. Enseigner les origins du Christianisme dans le cadre actuel des sciences religieuses au Québec. *Religiologiques* 11:111–119.

Karabatsos, G., and W. Batchelder. 2003. Markov chain estimation for test theory without the answer key. *Psychometrika* 68:373–389.

Keesing, F. M. [1939] 1987. *The Menomini Indians of Wisconsin: A study of Three Centuries of Contact.* Madison: University of Wisconsin Press.

Keesing, R. 1972. Paradigms lost: The new anthropology and the new linguistics. *Southwest Journal of Anthropology* 28:299–332.

Keil, F. 1979. *Semantic and Conceptual Development.* Cambridge, Mass.: Harvard University Press.

Keil, F. 1989. *Concepts, Kinds, and Cognitive Development.* Cambridge, Mass.: MIT Press.

Keil, F. 1995. The growth of causal understanding of natural kinds: Modes of construal and the emergence of biological thought. In A. Premack and D. Sperber, eds., *Causal Cognition.* Oxford: Oxford University Press.

Keil, F., D. Levin, B. Richman, and G. Gutheil. 1999. Mechanism and explanation in the development of biological thought. In D. L. Medin and S. Atran, eds., *Folkbiology.* Cambridge, Mass.: MIT Press.

Kellert, S. R. 1993. The Biological Basis for Human Values of Nature. In S. Kellert and E. Wilson, eds., *The Biophilia Hypothesis*. Washington, D.C.: Island Press.

Kempton, W., J. Boster, and J. Hartley. 1995. *Environmental Values in American Culture*. Cambridge, Mass.: MIT Press.

Kesby, J. 1979. The Rangi classification of animals and plants. In R. Reason and D. Ellen, eds., *Classifications in Their Social Contexts*. New York: Academic Press.

Klein, G. 1999. *Sources of Power: How People Make Decisions*. Cambridge, Mass.: MIT Press.

Knight, N., P. Sousa, J. Barrett, and S. Atran. 2004. Children's attributions of beliefs to humans and God: Cross-cultural evidence. *Cognitive Science* 28:117–126.

Kollman, K., J. Miller, and S. Page. 1992. Adaptive parties in spatial elections. *American Political Science Review* 86:929–937.

Kripke, S. 1972. Naming and necessity. In D. Davidson and G. Harman, eds., *Semantics of Natural Language*. Dordrecht: Reidel.

Kroeber, A. [1923] 1963. *Anthropology*. New York: Harcourt, Brace & World.

Labandeira, C., and J. Sepkoski. 1993. Insect diversity in the fossil record. *Science* 261:310–315.

Laland, K., and G. Brown. 2002. The golden meme: memes offer a way to analyse human culture with scientific rigour. Why are social scientists so averse to the idea. *New Scientist* 175:40–43.

Laland, K., and F. J. Olding-Smee. 2001. The evolution of memes. In Robert Aunger, ed., *Darwinizing Culture: The Status of Memetics as a Science*. Oxford: Oxford University Press.

Laland, K., F. J. Olding-Smee, and M. Feldman. 2000. Niche construction, biological evolution and cultural change. *Behavioral and Brain Sciences* 23:131–146.

Landa, Diego de. [1566] 1985. *Relación de la cosas de Yucatán*. Ed. M. Rivera Dorado. Crónicas de America, no. 7. Madrid: Historia 16.

Lansing, S., and J. Kremer. 1993. Emergent properties of Balinese water temple networks: Coadaptation on a rugged fitness landscape. *American Anthropologist* 95:97–114.

Lave, J., and E. Wenger. 1991. *Situated Learning*. New York: Cambridge University Press.

Lawson, E. T., and R. McCauley. 1990. *Rethinking Religion*. Cambridge: Cambridge University Press.

Leach, E. 1976. *Culture and Communication*. Cambridge: Cambridge University Press.

Lévi-Strauss, C. 1963a. The bear and the barber. *The Journal of the Royal Anthropological Institute* 93:1–11.

Lévi-Strauss, C. 1963b. *Structural Anthropology*. New York: Anchor Books.

Lévi-Strauss, C. 1966. *The Savage Mind*. Chicago: University of Chicago Press.

Linnaeus, C. 1735. *Systema naturae*. Leiden: Haak.

Linnaeus, C. 1751. *Philosophia botanica*. Stockholm: G. Kiesewetter.

Linton, R. 1936. *The Study of Man*. Norwalk, Conn.: Appleton-Century-Crofts.

Lois, X. 1998. Gender markers as "rigid determiners" of the Itzaj Maya world. *International Journal of American Linguistics* 64:224–282.

Lomawaima, K. T. 2000. Tribal sovereigns: Reframing research in American Indian education. *Harvard Educational Review* 70:1–21.

López, A., S. Atran, J. Coley, D. Medin, and E. Smith. 1997. The tree of life: Universals of folk-biological taxonomies and inductions. *Cognitive Psychology* 32:251–295.

Louv, R. 2006. *Last Child in the Woods–Saving our Children from Nature Deficit Disorder*. Chapel Hill, N.C.: Algonquin Books of Chapel Hill.

Love, B. C., D. L. Medin, and T. M. Gureckis. 2004. SUSTAIN: A network model of category learning. *Psychological Review* 111:309–332.

Lumsden, C., and E. O. Wilson. 1981. *Genes, Mind, and Culture: The Coevolutionary Process*. Cambridge, Mass.: Harvard University Press.

Lundell, C. 1937. *The Vegetation of Petén*. Carnegie Institution of Washington Publication 478. Washington, D.C.: Carnegie Institution of Washington.

Lynch, E., J. Coley, and D. Medin. 2000. Tall is typical: Central tendency, ideal dimensions and graded category structure among tree experts and novices. *Memory and Cognition* 28:41–50.

Mahalingam, R. 1998. Essentialism, power, and theories of caste: A developmental study. *Dissertation Abstracts International, 60* (2-B) (UMI No. AAM9919309).

Malinowski, B. [1922] 1961. *Argonauts of the Western Pacific*. New York: Dutton.

Malt, B. 1993. Concept structure and category boundaries. In G. Nakamura, R. Taraban, and D. Medin, eds., *The Psychology of Learning and Motivation*, Vol. 29: *Categorization by Humans and Machines*, 363–390. Orlando, Fla.: Academic Press.

Malt, B. 1995. Category coherence in cross-cultural perspective. *Cognitive Psychology* 29:85–148.

Mandler, J., P. Bauer, and L. McDonough. 1991. Separating the sheep from the goats: Differentiating global categories. *Cognitive Psychology* 23:263–298.

March, J. G. 1994. *A Primer on Decision Making*. New York: Free Press.

Marcus, G. 2004. *The Birth of the Mind*. New York: Basic Books.

Markman, A., and D. Medin. 2004. Decision making. In H. Pashler and D. Medin, eds., *Stevens' Handbook of Experimental Psychology, Vol. 2, Memory and Cognitive Processes*, 3rd Ed. New York: Wiley and Sons.

Marks, G., and M. Miller. 1987. 10 years of research on the false-consensus effect—an empirical and theoretical review. *Psychological Bulletin* 102:72–90.

Marr, D. 1982. *Vision*. New York: W. H. Freeman.

Maynard Smith, J. 1998. The origin of altruism. *Nature* 393:639–640.

Mayr, E. 1969. *Principles of Systematic Zoology*. New York: McGraw-Hill.

Mayr, E. 1982. *The Growth of Biological Thought*. Cambridge, Mass.: Harvard University Press.

Mayr, E. 1989. Species concepts and their application. In M. Ruse, ed., *Philosophy of biology*. New York: Macmillan.

McGraw, A. P., and P. E. Tetlock. 2005. Taboo trade-offs, relational framing, and the acceptability of exchanges. *Journal of Consumer Psychology* 15:2–16.

Means, P. 1917. History of the Spanish conquest of Yucatan and of the Itzas. *Papers of the Peabody Museum,* 7. Cambridge, Mass.: Peabody Museum.

Medin, D. 1989. Concepts and conceptual structures. *American Psychologist* 45:1469–1481.

Medin, D., and S. Atran. 1999. Introduction. In D. Medin and S. Atran, *Folkbiology*. Cambridge, Mass.: MIT Press.

Medin, D., and S. Atran. 2004. The native mind: Biological categorization and reasoning in development and across cultures. *Psychological Review* 111:960–983.

Medin, D. L., and M. H. Bazerman. 1999. Broadening behavioral decision research: Multiple levels of cognitive processing. *Psychonomic Bulletin and Review* 6(4):533–547.

Medin, D., J. Coley, G. Storms, and B. Hayes. 2003. A relevance theory of induction. *Psychonomic Bulletin and Review* 10:517–532.

Medin, D., R. Goldstone, and D. Gentner. 1993. Respects for similarity. *Psychological Review* 100:254–278.

Medin, D., E. Lynch, J. Coley, and S. Atran. 1997. Categorization and reasoning among tree experts: Do all roads lead to Rome? *Cognitive Psychology* 32:49–96.

Medin, D., and A. Ortony. 1989. Psychological essentialism. In S. Vosniadou and A. Ortony, eds., *Similarity and Analogical Reasoning*. New York: Cambridge University Press.

Medin, D., N. Ross, S. Atran, R. Burnett, and S. Blok. 2002. Categorization and reasoning in relation to culture and expertise. In B. Ross, ed., *The Psychology of Learning and Motivation: Advances in Research and Theory*, vol. 41. New York: Academic Press.

Medin, D., N. Ross, and D. Cox. 2006. *Culture and Resource Conflict: Why Meanings Matter*. New York: Russell Sage Foundation.

Medin, D., N. Ross, D. Cox, and S. Atran. 2007. Why folkbiology matters: Resource conflict despite shared goals and knowledge. *Human Ecology* 35:315–329.

Medin, D., N. Ross, S. Atran, D. Cox, J. Coley, J. Proffitt, and S. Blok. 2005. The role of culture in the folkbiology of freshwater fish. *Cognition* 92:1–37.

Medin, D., H. Schwartz, S. Blok, and L. Birnbaum. 1999. The semantic side of decision making. *Psychonomic Bulletin and Review* 6:562–569.

Medin, D., and S. Waxman. 2007. Interpreting asymmetries of projection in children's inductive reasoning. In A. Feeney and E. Heit, eds., *Inductive Reasoning*. New York: Cambridge University Press.

Mesoudi, A., A. Whiten, and K. Laland. 2007. Science, evolution and cultural anthropology. *Anthropology Today* 22:18.

Messick, D., and M. Brewer. 1983. Solving social dilemmas: A review. In L. Wheeler and P. Shaver, eds., *Review of Personality and Social Psychology*, vol. 4. Beverly Hills, Calif.: Sage.

Mihesuah, D. A. 1998. *Natives and Academics: Research and Writing About American Indians*. Lincoln, Neb.: University of Nebraska Press.

Monod, J. 1971. *Chance and Necessity*. A. Wainhouse, trans. London: Collins.

Moore, C., A. Romney, and T. Hsia. 2000. Shared cognitive representations of perceptual and semantic structures of basic colors in Chinese and English. *Proceedings of the National Academy of Sciences* 97:5007–5010.

Moore, C., A. Romney, T. Hsia, and C. Rush. 1999. The universality of the semantic structure of emotion terms: Methods for the study of inter- and intra-cultural variability. *American Anthropologist* 101:530–546.

Morris, B. 1996. *Forest Traders*. London: Athlone.

Murdock, G. 1949. *Social Structure*. New York: Macmillan.

Murray, J. 1989. O.E.D. preface and general explanations. In *The Oxford English Dictionary*, 2nd ed. New York: Oxford University Press.

Murray, K. 1977. *Caught in the Web of Words: James A. H. Murray and the Oxford English Dictionary*. New Haven, Conn.: Yale University Press.

Nabhan, G., and S. St. Antoine. 1993. The loss of floral and faunal story: The extinction of experience. In S. R. Kellert and E. O. Wilson, eds., *The Biophilia Hypothesis*. Washington, D.C.: Island Press.

Nagel, E. 1961. *The Structure of Science*. New York: Harcourt, Brace & World.

Nakao, K., and A. K. Romney. 1984. A method for testing alternative theories: An example from English kinship. *American Anthropologist* 86:668–673.

Nations, J. 1979. *Population Ecology of the Lacandón Maya*. University Microfilms International, No. GAX 79–20363. Ann Arbor, Mich.

Nesper, L. 2002. *The Walleye War: The Struggle for Ojibwe Spearfishing and Treaty Rights*. Lincoln: University of Nebraska Press.

Newman, J. G. 1967. *The Menominee Forest of Wisconsin*. Unpublished doctoral dissertation, Michigan State University.

Nigh, R. 2002. Maya medicine in the biological gaze. *Current Anthropology* 43:451–477.

Nisbett, R. 2003. *The Geography of Thought: How Asians and Westerners Think Differently . . . and Why*. New York: Free Press.

Nisbett, R., K. Peng, I. Choi, and A. Norenzayan. 2001. Culture and systems of thought: Holistic vs. analytic cognition. *Psychological Review* 108:291–310.

Nowak, M., and K. Sigmund. 1998. Evolution of indirect reciprocity by image scoring. *Nature* 395:573–577.

Osherson, D., E. Smith, O. Wilkie, A. López, and E. Shafir. 1990. Category-based induction. *Psychological Review* 97:85–100.

Ostrom, E. 1994. Neither the market nor state: Governance of common-pool resources in the twenty-first century. *IFPRI Lecture Series.* Washington, D.C.: International Food Policy Research Institute.

Ostrom, E. 1998. A behavioral approach to the rational choice theory of collective action. *American Political Science Review* 92:289–316.

Ostrom, E. 1999. Coping with tragedies of the commons. *Annual Review of Political Science* 2:493–535.

Oyserman, D., H. Coon, and M. Kemmelmeier. 2002. Rethinking individualism and collectivism: Evaluation of theoretical assumptions and meta-analyses. *Psychological Bulletin* 128:3–72.

Peroff, N. 1982. *Menominee Drums: Tribal Termination and Restoration 1954–1974.* Norman: University of Oklahoma Press.

Petition seeks to separate spearfishing, gaming. 1997. *Beloit Daily News*, October 23. Available at www.beloitdailynews.com/1097/4wis23.htm.

Peters, C. 1989. *Reproduction, growth, and the population dynamics of Brosimum alicastrum sw.* PhD diss., Yale University.

Piña Chan, R. 1980. *Chichen Itza: La ciudad de los brujos de agua.* México, DF: Fondo de Cultura Económica.

Pinker, S. 1997. *How the Mind Works.* New York: Norton.

Pinker, S. 2002. *The Blank Slate: The Modern Denial of Human Nature.* New York: Viking.

Pinker, S., and P. Bloom. 1990. Natural language and natural selection. *Behavioral and Brain Sciences* 13:707–727.

Porter, J. 1988. T168 as ITSA': Maya sorcerers and their succession. *Estudios de Cultura Maya* 17:65–86.

Posey, D. 1981. Wasps, warriors and fearless men: Ethnoentomology of the Kayapó Indians of Central Brazil. *Journal of Ethnobiology* 1:165–174.

Posey, D. 1983. Indigenous ecological knowledge and development of the Amazon. In E. Moran, ed., *The Dilemma of Amazonian Development.* Boulder, Colo.: Westview Press.

Premack, D. 1990. The infant's theory of self-propelled objects. *Cognition* 36:1–16.

Prentice, D., and D. Miller. 1993. Pluralistic ignorance and alcohol use on campus: Some consequences of misperceiving the social norm. *Journal of Personality and Social Psychology* 64:243–256.

Proffitt, J., J. Coley, and D. Medin. 2000. Expertise and category-based induction. *Journal of Experimental Psychology: Learning, Memory, and Cognition* 26:811–828.

Puleston, D. 1973. *Ancient Maya settlement and environment at Tikal, Guatemala: Implications for subsistence models.* PhD. diss., University of Pennsylvania. Ann Arbor: University Microfilms.

Puleston, D. 1979. An epistemological pathology and the collapse, or why the Maya kept the short count. In N. Hammond and G. Wiley, eds., *Maya Archaeology and Ethnohistory.* Austin: University of Texas Press.

Putnam, H. 1975. The meaning of "meaning." In K. Gunderson, ed., *Language, Mind, and Knowledge.* Minneapolis: University of Minnesota Press.

Radcliffe-Brown, A. R. 1950. Introduction. In A. R. Radcliff-Brown and D. Forde, eds., *African Systems of Kinship and Marriage.* London: Oxford University Press.

Radomski, P., and T. Goeman. 1995. The homogenizing of Minnesota lakefish assemblages. *Fisheries* 20:20–23.

Rappaport, R. 1979. *Ecology, Meaning, and Religion.* Berkeley: Atlantic Books.

Raven, P., B. Berlin, and D. Breedlove. 1971. Origins of taxonomy. *Science* 174:1210–1213.

Ray, J. 1703. *Methodus plantarum emendate et aucta.* London: Smith and Walford.

Reeve, H. 2000. Review of *Unto Others. Evolution and Human Behavior* 21:65–72.

Reina, R. 1967. Milpa and milperos: Implications for prehistoric times. *American Anthropologist* 69:1–20.

Remmers, G., and H. De Koeijer. 1992. The T'OLCHE', a Maya system of communally managed forest belts. *Agroforestry Systems* 18:149–177.

Rettinger, D. A., and R. Hastie. 2001. Content effects on decision making. *Organizational Behavior and Human Decision Processes* 85:336–359.

Rettinger, D. A., and R. Hastie. 2003. Comprehension and decision making. In S. L. Schneider and J. Shanteau, eds., *Emerging Perspectives on Judgment and Decision Research.* Cambridge: Cambridge University Press.

Ricciuti, E. R. 1997. *The Menominee (Native American People).* Vero Beach, Fla.: Rourke.

Rice, D. 1993. Eighth-century physical geography, environment, and natural resources in the Maya Lowlands. In J. Sabloff and J. Henderson, eds., *Lowland Maya Civilization in the Eighth Century, A.D.* Washington, D.C.: Dumbarton Oaks.

Rips, L. 1975. Inductive judgments about natural categories. *Journal of Verbal Learning and Verbal Behavior* 14:665–681.

Rips, L. 1995. The current status of research on concept combination. *Mind and Language* 10:2–104.

Rips, L. 2001. Necessity and natural categories. *Psychological Bulletin* 127:827–852.

Ritov, I., and J. Baron. 1990. Reluctance to vaccinate: Omission bias and ambiguity. *Journal of Behavioral Decision Making* 3:263–277.

Ritov, I., and J. Baron. 1992. Status-quo and omission bias. *Journal of Risk and Uncertainty* 5:49–61.

Ritov, I., and J. Baron. 1995. Outcome knowledge, regret, and omission bias. *Organizational Behavior and Human Decision Processes* 64:119–127.

Ritov, I., and J. Baron. 1999. Protected values and omission bias. *Organizational Behavior and Human Decision Processes* 79:79–94.

Ritov, I., and D. Kahneman. 1997. How people value information: Attitudes versus economic values. In M. Bazerman, D. Messick, A. Tenbrunsel, and K. Wade-Benzoni, eds., *Environment, Ethics, and Behavior: The Psychology of Environmental Valuation and Degradation.* San Francisco: New Lexington Press.

Roberts, J. 1964. The self-management of cultures. In W. Goodenough, ed., *Explorations in Cultural Anthropology: Essays in Honor of George Peter Murdock.* New York: McGraw-Hill.

Romney, A. K. 1998. Toward a theory of culture as shared cognitive structures. *Ethos* 26:314–337.

Romney, A. K., and W. Batchelder. 1999. Cultural consensus theory. In R. Wilson and F. Keil, eds., *The MIT Encyclopedia of the Cognitive Sciences.* Cambridge, Mass.: MIT Press.

Romney, A. K., W. Batchelder, and S. Weller. 1986. Culture as consensus: A theory of culture and informant accuracy. *American Anthropologist* 88:313–338.

Romney, A. K., J. Boyd, C. Moore, W. Batchelder, and T. J. Brazill. 1996. Culture as shared cognitive representations. *Proceedings of the National Academy of Sciences USA* 93:4699–4705.

Rosch, E. 1975. Universals and cultural specifics in categorization. In R. Brislin, S. Bochner, and W. Lonner, Eds., *Cross-Cultural Perspectives on Learning.* New York: Halstead.

Rosch, E., and C. Mervis. 1975. Family resemblances: Studies in the internal structure of categories. *Cognitive Psychology* 7:573–605.

Rosch, E., C. Mervis, W. Grey, D. Johnson, and P. Boyes-Braem. 1976. Basic objects in natural categories. *Cognitive Psychology* 8:382–439.

Ross, B. 1997. The use of categories affects classification. *Journal of Memory and Language* 37:240–267.

Ross, L. 1990. Recognizing the role of construal processes. In I. Rock, ed., *The Legacy of Solomon Asch: Essays in Cognition and Social Psychology*, 77–96. Hillsdale, N.J.: Erlbaum.

Ross, L., and C. Stillinger. 1991. Barriers to conflict resolution. *Negotiation Journal* 8:389–404.

Ross, N. 2000. Lacandon Maya intergenerational change and the erosion of folkbiological knowledge. *Proceedings of the 7th International Congress of Ethnobiology*, Athens, Georgia.

Ross, N. 2001. *Bilder vom Regenwald: Mentale Modelle, Kulturwandel und Umweltverhalten bei den Lakandonen in Mexiko.* Muenster: Lit Verlag.

Ross, N. 2002. Cognitive aspects of intergenerational change: Mental models, cultural change, and environmental behavior among the Lacandon Maya of southern Mexico. *Human Organization* 61:125–138.

Ross, N. 2004. *Culture and Cognition: Implications for Theory and Method.* Thousand Oaks, Calif.: Sage.

Ross, N., and D. Medin. 2005. Ethnography and experiments: Cultural Models and expertise effects elicited with experimental research techniques. *Field Methods* 17(2):131–149.

Ross, N., D. Medin, J. Coley, and S. Atran. 2003. Cultural and experiential differences in the development of folkbiological induction. *Cognitive Development* 107:1–23.

Russell, B. 1948. *Human Knowledge: Its Scope and Limits.* New York: Simon & Schuster.

Sabloff, J., and J. Henderson, eds. 1993. *Lowland Maya Civilization in the Eighth Century, A.D.* Washington, D.C.: Dumbarton Oaks.

Sader, S. 1997. *Forest Monitoring and Satellite Change Detection Analysis of the Maya Biosphere Reserve, Petén District, Guatemala.* Final Report submitted to Conservation International and USAID.

Sader, S. 1999. Deforestation trends in northern Guatemala: A view from space. In J. Nations, ed., *Thirteen Ways of Looking at a Tropical Forest: Guatemala's Maya Biosphere Reserve.* Washington, D.C.: Conservation International.

Santley, R., T. Killion, and M. Lycett. 1986. On the Maya collapse. *Journal of Anthropological Research* 42:123–159.

Sartori, G., and R. Job. 1988. The oyster with four legs: A neuropsychological study on the interaction of semantic and visual information. *Cognitive Neuropsychology* 5:105–132.

Satinoff, E. 1983. A reevaluation of the concept of the homeostatic organization of temperature regulation. *Handbook of Behavioral Neurobiology,* Vol. 6: *Motivation,* 443–474. New York: Plenum Publishing Corporation.

Schackt, J. 1984. The *Tzuultak'a*: Religious lore and cultural processes among the Kekchi. *Belizean Studies* 12:16–29.

Schlesinger, L. 1999. *The Ten Commandments: The Significance of God's Laws in Everyday Life.* New York: HarperCollins.

Schmidt, S. 1995. *A Survey of Lakes on the Menominee Reservation, Wisconsin.* Unpublished master's thesis, University of Wisconsin, Stevens Point.

Schumann, O. 1971. *Descripción estructural del Maya Itza del Petén.* Centro de Estudios Mayas, Cuaderno 6. México, DF: UNAM.

Schwanenflugel, P., and M. Rey. 1986. The relationship between category typicality and concept familiarity: Evidence from Spanish- and English-speaking monolinguals. *Memory & Cognition* 14:150–163.

Schwartz, H., and D. Medin. 2000. Expert and Novice Judgments of Inductive Inferences within Folk-Biological Taxonomies. Unpublished manuscript, Northwestern University.

Schwartz, N. 1990. *Forest Society: A Social History of Petén, Guatemala*. Philadelphia: University of Pennsylvania Press.

Schwartz, N. 1995. Colonization, development, and deforestation in Petén, Northern Guatemala. In M. Painter and W. Durham, eds., *The Social Causes of Environmental Destruction in Latin America*. Ann Arbor: University of Michigan Press.

Schyns, P., R. Goldstone, and J. Thibaut. 1998. Development of features in object concepts. *Behavioral and Brain Sciences* 21:1–54.

Schyns, P., and L. Rodet. 1997. Categorization creates functional features. *Journal of Experimental Psychology: Learning, Memory, and Cognition* 23:681–696.

Shafto, P., and J. D. Coley. 2003. Development of categorization and reasoning in the natural world: Novices to experts, naïve similarity to ecological knowledge. *Journal of Experimental Psychology: Learning, Memory, and Cognition* 29:641–649.

Shamir, J., and K. Shikaki. 2005. Public opinion in the Israeli-Palestinian two-level game. *Journal of Peace Research* 42:311–328.

Shweder, R. 1990. Cultural psychology: What is it? In J. Stigler, R. Shweder, and G. Herdt, eds., *Cultural Psychology: Essays on Comparative Human Development*. New York: Cambridge University Press.

Simons, D. J., and F. C. Keil. 1995. An abstract to concrete shift in the development of biological thought: The *insides* story. *Cognition* 56:129–163.

Simpson, G. 1961. *Principles of Animal Taxonomy*. New York: Columbia University.

Skitka, L., and D. Houston. 2001. The dark side of moral conviction. *Analyses of Social Issues and Public Policy* 2:35–241.

Sloman, S. 1993. Feature-based induction. *Cognitive Psychology* 25:231–280.

Sloman, S. 1994. When explanations compete: The role of explanatory coherence on judgments of likelihood. *Cognition* 52:1–21.

Sloman, S., and B. Malt. 2003. Artifacts are not ascribed essences, nor are they treated as belonging to kinds. *Language and Cognitive Processes* 18:563–582.

Smith, E., and D. Medin. 1981. *Categories and Concepts*. Cambridge, Mass.: Harvard University Press.

Smith, E., E. Shoben, and L. Rips. 1974. Structure and process in semantic memory. *Psychological Review* 81:214–241.

Smith, L. T. 1999. *Decolonizing Methodologies: Research and Indigenous Peoples*. NewYork: Zed Books.

Smithe, F. 1966. *The Birds of Tikal*. Cambridge: Harvard University Press.

Smyth, M., and D. Christopher. 1992. Large-site archaeological methods at Sayil, Yucatan, Mexico: Investigating community organization at a prehispanic Maya center. *Latin American Antiquity* 3:3–21.

Sneath, P., and R. Sokal. 1973. *Numerical Taxonomy*. San Francisco: Freeman.

Sober, E. 1996. Learning from functionalism: Prospects for strong artificial life. In M. Boden, ed., *The Philosophy of Artificial Life*. New York: Oxford University Press.

Sober, E., and D. S. Wilson. 1998. *Unto Others: The Evolution and Psychology of Unselfish Behavior*. Cambridge, Mass.: Harvard University Press.

Solomon, G., S. Johnson, D. Zaitchik, and S. Carey. 1996. Like father, like son: Young children's understanding of how and why offspring resemble their parents. *Child Development* 67:151–171.

S.O.S.: se muere biosfera Maya. 1998. *Prensa Libre*, Guatemala daily, April 22.

Sousa, P., S. Atran, and D. Medin. 2002. Essentialism and folkbiology: Further evidence from Brazil. *Journal of Cognition and Culture* 2:195–203.

Soza, J. M. 1970. *Monografía del Departamento de El Petén*, 2 vols. Guatemala: Editorial José de Pineda Ibarra.

Sperber, D. 1985. Anthropology and psychology: Towards an epidemiology of representations. *Man* 20:73–89.

Sperber, D. 1996. *Explaining Culture*. Oxford: Blackwell.

Sperber, D. 2001. In defense of massive modularity. Paper presented to the "Innateness and Structure of the Mind" Workshop, University of Sheffield, November.

Sperber, D., F. Cara, and V. Girotto. 1995. Relevance theory explains the selection task. *Cognition* 57:31–95.

Sperber, D., and L. Hirschfeld. 2004. The cognitive foundations of cultural stability and diversity. *Trends in Cognitive Sciences* 8:40–46.

Sperber, D., P. Premack, and A. Premack, eds. 1995. *Causal Cognition*. Oxford: Clarendon Press.

Sperber, D., and D. Wilson. 1986. *Relevance: Communication and Cognition*. Oxford: Blackwell.

Spindler, G., and L. S. Spindler. 1971. *Dreamers with Power: The Menomini Indians*. New York: Holt, Rinehart & Winston.

Spindler, G., and L. S. Spindler. 1991. Reactions and worries. *Anthropology & Education Quarterly* 22(3):274–278.

Stewart, S. 1980. *Grammatica Kekchi*. Guatemala: Editorial Academica Centro Americana.

Steyvers, M., and J. B. Tenenbaum. 2005. The large-scale structure of semantic networks: Statistical analyses and a model of semantic growth. *Cognitive Science* 29(1):41–78.

Stierle, A., G. Strobel, and D. Stierle. 1993. Taxol and taxane production by *Taxomyces andreanae*, an endophytic fungus of Pacific Yew. *Science* 260:214–216.

Stoler, A. 1995. *Race and the Education of Desire*. Durham, NC: Duke University Press.

Strauss, C., and N. Quinn. 1992. Preliminaries to a theory of culture acquisition. In H. L. Pick, P. Van Den Broek, and D. C. Knill, eds., *Cognition: Conceptual and Methodological Issues*, 267–294. Washington, D.C.: American Psychological Association.

Strevens, M. 2000. The naïve aspect of essentialist theories. *Cognition* 74:149–175.

Stross, B. 1973. Acquisition of botanical terminology by Tzeltal children. In M. Edmonson, ed., *Meaning in Mayan Languages*. The Hague: Mouton.

Sylvia, C., and W. Novak. 1997. *A Change of Heart*. Boston: Little, Brown.

Tanaka, J., and M. Taylor. 1991. Object categories and expertise: Is the basic level in the eye of beholder? *Cognitive Psychology* 23:457–482.

Tanner, C., and D. Medin. 2004. Protected values: No omission bias and no framing effects. *Psychonomic Bulletin and Review* 11:185–191.

Tenbrunsel, A., and D. Messick. 1999. Sanctioning systems, decision frames, and cooperation. *Administrative Science Quarterly* 44(4):684–707.

Tenbrunsel, A., and D. Messick. 2001. Power, asymmetries, and the ethical climate in negotiations. In J. Walsh and A. Brief, eds., *Social Influences on Ethical Behavior in Organizations*. New Jersey: Earlbaum Associates.

Tetlock, P. 2000a. Cognitive biases and organizational correctives: Do both the disease and cure depend on the politics of the beholder? *Administrative Science Quarterly* 45:293–326.

Tetlock, P. 2000b. Coping with trade-offs: Psychological constraints and political implications. In S. Lupia, M. McCubbins, and S. Popkin, eds., *Political Reasoning and Choice*. Berkeley: University of California Press.

Tetlock, P. 2002. Social functionalist frameworks for judgment and choice: Intuitive politicians, theologians, and prosecutors. *Psychological Review* 109:451–471.

Tetlock, P. 2003. Thinking the unthinkable: Sacred values and taboo cognitions. *Trends in Cognitive Sciences* 7:320–324.

Tetlock, P., V. Kristel, S. Elson, M. Green, and J. Lerner. 2000. The psychology of the unthinkable: Taboo trade-offs, forbidden base rates, and heretical counterfactuals. *Journal of Personality and Social Psychology* 78:853–870.

Thaler, R. 1985. Mental accounting and consumer choice. *Marketing Science* 4:199–219.

Thompson, L., and R. Gonzalez. 1997. Environmental disputes: Competition for scarce resources and clashing of values. In M. Bazerman and D. Messick, eds., *Environment, Ethics, and Behavior: The Psychology of Environmental Valuation and Degradation*. San Francisco: New Lexington Press.

Tomasello, M. 2001. *The Cultural Origins of Human Cognition*. Cambridge, Mass.: Harvard University Press.

Tournefort, J. 1694. *Elémens de botanique*. Paris: Imprimerie Royale.

Tourtellot, G., J. Sabloff, and K. Carmean. 1992. "Will the real elites please stand up?": An archaeological assessment of Maya elite behavior in the Terminal

Classic period. In D. Chase and A. Chase, eds., *Mesoamerican Elites: An Archae-ological Assessment*. Norman. Okla.: University of Oklahoma Press.

Tozzer, A., ed. 1941. Landa's relación de las cosas de Yucatán. *Papers of the Peabody Museum, 18*. Cambridge, Mass.: The Peabody Museum.

Tracy, L. 1998. State trends. *Council of State Governments Newsletter*, summer 1998.

Trager, G. 1939. "Cottonwood" = "tree": A Southwestern linguistic trait. *International Journal of American Linguistics* 9:117–118.

Triandis, H. 1995. *Individualism and Collectivism*. Boulder, Colo.: Westview Press.

Triandis, H. 2001. Individualism-collectivism and personality. *Journal of Personality* 69:907–924.

Tribal claims were too much. 1999. *Milwaukee Journal Sentinel*, April 25. Available at www.jsonline.com/news/editorials/apr99/0425tribal.asp.

Tversky, A., and D. Kahneman. 1981. The framing of decisions and the psychology of choice. *Science* 211:453–458.

Tversky, A., and D. Kahneman. 1986. Rational choice and framing decisions. *Journal of Business* 59: S251–278.

Van der Henst, J.-B., G. Politzer, and D. Sperber. 2002. When is a conclusion worth deriving? A relevance-based analysis of indeterminate relational problems. *Thinking & Reasoning* 8(1):1–20.

Villagutierre Soto-Mayor, Juan de. 1701. *Historia de la conquista de la provincia de el Itza, reduccion, y progressos de la de el Lacandon y otras naciones de indios barbaros, de la mediacion de el reyno de Guatimala, a las provincias de Yucatan, en la America septentrional*. Madrid: Lucas Antonio Bedmar, y Narvaez.

Villagutierre Soto-Mayor, Juan de. [1701] 1983. In F. Comparto, ed., R. Wood, trans *History of the Conquest of the Province of the Itza*. Culver City, Calif.: Labyrinthos.

Vygotsky, L. 1978. *Mind in Society*. Cambridge, Mass.: Harvard University Press.

Waddington, C. 1959. Canalisation of development and the inheritance of acquired characteristics. *Nature* 183:1654–1655.

Walker [Jeyifous], S. 1992. Supernatural beliefs, natural kinds, and conceptual structure. *Memory & Cognition* 20:655–662.

Walker, S. J. 1999. Culture, domain specificity and conceptual change: Natural kind and artifact concepts. *British Journal of Developmental Psychology* 17:203–219.

Wallace, A. F. 1961. Introduction. In A. F. Wallace, *Culture and Personality*. New York: Random House.

Wallace, A. R. [1889] 1901. *Darwinism*. New York: Macmillan.

Warburton, F. 1967. The purposes of classification. *Systematic Zoology* 16:241–245.

Warrington, E., and T. Shallice. 1984. Category specific semantic impairments. *Brain* 107:829–854.

Waxman, S. 1999. The dubbing ceremony revisited: Object naming and categorization in infancy and early childhood. In D. Medin and S. Atran, eds., *Folkbiology*. Cambridge, Mass.: MIT Press.

Waxman, S. 2004. Everything had a name, and each name gave birth to a new thought: Links between early word-learning and conceptual organization. In D. G. Hall and S. R. Waxman, eds., *From Many Strands: Weaving a Lexicon*. Cambridge, Mass.: MIT Press.

Waxman, S., and D. Markow. 1995. Words as invitations to form categories: Evidence from 12-month-old infants. *Cognitive Psychology* 29:257–302.

Waxman, S., and D. Medin. 2007. Experience and cultural models matter: Placing firm limits on anthropocentrism. *Human Development* 50:23–30.

Waxman, S. R., D. L. Medin, and N. Ross. 2007. Folkbiological reasoning from a cross-cultural developmental perspective: Early essentialist notions are shaped by cultural beliefs. *Developmental Psychology* 43:294–308.

Weller, S. 1987. Shared knowledge, intracultural variation, and knowledge aggregation. *American Behavioral Scientist* 31:178–193.

Wester, L., and S. Yongvanit. 1995. Biological diversity and community lore in Northwestern Thailand. *Journal of Ethnobiology* 15:71–87.

White, L. 1949. *The Science of Culture*. New York: Farrar, Straus.

White, S. 1994. Testing an economic approach to resource dilemmas. *Organization and Human Decision Processes* 58:428–456.

Williams, G. 1992. *Natural Selection*. New York: Oxford University Press.

Wilson, D. S. 2002. *Darwin's Cathedral*. Chicago: University of Chicago Press.

Wilson, E. O. 1978. *On Human Nature*. Cambridge, Mass.: Harvard University Press.

Wilson, E. O. 1992. *The Diversity of Life*. New York: Norton.

Wilson, R. 1995. *Maya Resurgence in Guatemala*. Norman: University of Oklahoma Press.

Wisconsin Department of Natural Resources. 2000. *Wisconsin's Lake Sturgeon Management Plan*. Milwaukee, Wis.: Bureau of Fisheries Management and Habitat Protection.

Wisconsin Department of Natural Resources. 2002. *Open Water Spearing and Netting in Northern Wisconsin by Chippewa Indians during 2001*. Great Lakes Indian Fish and Wildlife Commission Administrative Report, Wisc2002-01. Odanah, Wis.: Great Lakes Indian Fish and Wildlife Commission.

Wiseman, F. 1978. Agricultural and historical archaeology of the Maya Lowlands. In P. Harrison and B. Turner, eds., *Pre-Hispanic Maya Agriculture*. Albuquerque: University of New Mexico Press.

Wisniewski, E., and D. Medin. 1994. On the interaction of theory and data in concept learning. *Cognitive Science* 18:221–281.

Wolff, P., D. Medin, and C. Pankratz. 1999. Evolution and devolution of folkbiological knowledge. *Cognition* 73:177–204.

Ximénez, F. 1929–1931. Historia de la provincia de Chiapa y Guatemala, 3 vols. *Biblioteca "Goathemala" de la Sociedad de Geografía e Historia*, vols. 1–3. Guatemala: Tipografía Nacional.

Zipf, G. K. 1949. *Human Behavior and the Principle of Least Effort*. Boston: Addison-Wesley.

Zubin, D., and K.-M. Köpcke. 1986. Gender and folk taxonomy. In C. Craig, ed., *Noun Classes and Categorization*. Amsterdam: John Benjamins.

Index

Page references in *italics* indicate illustrative material.